THE BIG BOOK OF *TV GUIDE* CROSSWORDS

#2

Collins Reference
An Imprint of HarperCollinsPublishers

THE BIG BOOK OF TV GUIDE CROSSWORDS #2. Copyright © 1993 by News America Publications Inc. All rights reserved. Printed in the United States of America. No part of this book may be used or reproduced in any manner whatsoever without written permission except in the case of brief quotations embodied in critical articles and reviews. For information, address HarperCollins Publishers, 195 Broadway, New York, NY 10007.

HarperCollins books may be purchased for educational, business, or sales promotional use. For information, please e-mail the Special Markets Department at SPsales@harpercollins.com.

FIRST EDITION
ISBN 0-06096969-5

23 24 25 26 27 LBC 54 53 52 51 50

CROSSWORDS

Solutions begin on page 265.

June 9, 1956

55 Never (poet.)
56 Court cry
57 Sullivan, Murrow and
   Norton are ___

down

1 Squeals on *The Lineup*
2 TV censors do it
3 Flat-footed Disney star
4 A rating sometimes
   does it
5 It's human to ___
6 Oklahoma's nickname
7 The forefinger
8 The Big One's an
   Army film on TV
9 Poem
10 Over (poet.)
11 ___ Vegas
17 Land of liberty (abbr.)
19 Proceed
22 Vacation color
24 No sale (abbr.)
25 A prohibition (contr.)
26 Sole, single
27 An Annie Oakley
28 What bettors put up
29 Era
30 Umpire's thumb says it
32 Roy rides him
33 Owned
36 Ride '___, cowboy!
37 *Death ___ Days*
38 Newscaster
40 Tuesday night sergeant
41 Commercial
43 Auto antenna (abbr.)
44 Picnic crashers
45 Went, in Scotland
46 Barely exists
47 TV's ___ Murray
48 Anger
49 Fib
50 Add "G" for a
   cowpoke's first name

across

1 *Ozark Jubilee*'s
  Foley
4 He loves Lucy
8 Where stars swim
12 Pother
13 To press
14 Thought
15 Middle name of
   Lassie's rival
16 ___ *Showcase*
18 Lone males
20 Bud Collyer feathers
   yours
21 ___, the poor Indian!
22 Cowboy Ritter
23 To open
27 Augment
29 Mousketeers have big
   ones (sing.)
30 Star of TV's "20th
   Century"
31 Article
32 Sixteen of these
   made *Your Hit Parade*
33 Color
34 Baseball division (abbr.)
35 Bill's a sportscaster
37 Tub
38 Pigpen
39 Half
40 Not good
41 Reaction to a pun
42 "Annie Oakley"
44 Maxim
47 Dot's on *What's My
   Line?*
51 In *Zoo Parade*
52 Great Lake
53 It's *Superman!*
54 Last letter

5

June 16, 1956

down

1 Boat stop
2 Ocean occurrence
3 She's Maid Marian
4 Foot (Lat.)
5 Trickiest sergeant
6 Old barge canal
7 Allied Expeditionary Force (abbr.)
8 Mary Martin starred in TV's "___ Pan"
9 *Big Story* task
10 *Telephone* ___
11 Prophet
17 Red-coated cheese
19 Hotel
22 Snakelike fish
23 Forbid
24 Not he
25 Candy-loving *$64,000* quizzer
26 ___ jazz is real cool
27 Marge and Gower ___
28 One, own (Scot.)
29 Law degree
31 Wyatt Earp gives baddies their ___
32 Before (prefix)
34 Coffin
35 Jewel
36 They're portable on *Robin Hood* sets (pl.)
37 Star of *Make Room for Daddy*
38 Flies are easier to ___ than homers
39 Circle of light
40 Thing
41 Frog
43 Dry, as in *Death Valley Days*
44 Host John ___ on *What's My Line?*
46 Crazy
47 Live television audience (abbr.)

across

1 ___ *the Music*
5 Comedienne Lillie
8 Domestic animals
12 Bendix leads Riley's
13 Wrath
14 Ernie Kovacs' wife
15 Howard Duff is hers
16 *Chance of a* ___
18 Through
19 Capital telecaster
20 Hinder
21 Stars' unhitching post
23 Hangout of baddies
24 TV's Bishop ___
26 Bad actor
27 Hollywood is there
30 TV's ___ *of Fame*
31 Benny's announcer
32 ___ Silvers
33 45-inch measure
34 Yet, however
35 ___ *Ole Opry*
36 Garry Moore's is famous
37 Highbrow for think
38 Friar Tuck's term for county
41 Batterer in Robin Hood's day
42 Paper tablet
45 Willard plays Gildersleeve
47 Italian coin
48 On lee side
49 *Private Secretary* Sothern
50 Labor, drudgery
51 Male cats
52 *Queen for a* ___
53 *Wild Bill*'s Jingles

June 30, 1956

59 Codfish
60 Portico

down

1 Wrath
2 Dominion (abbr.)
3 One-spot playing card
4 Harmonicomic Herb
5 *This ___ Your Life*
6 Kind of coach in *Wyatt Earp*
7 Newsgal Bly
8 Mature twig
9 Banquet
10 Combining form of India
11 ___Hartford, Groucho's wife
13 It's hard to keep a dry one while watching *The Brighter Day*
20 ___ *the World Turns*
21 *Life Begins at 80's* stars
22 TV not on film
23 First-name initials of Godfrey, Caesar, Kovacs
24 Actor Leif Erickson (init.)
27 Caustic solution
29 *Your ___ Parade*
30 Present
31 Belonging to Linkletter
34 Fine shades of meaning
35 Old horse
38 ___ Raye
39 Hush!
40 Comedian Arnold ___
41 Exclamation
43 Unadvertised preview
45 *The Name's the ___*
46 Above
47 Every
48 The sun
52 An explosive
53 Self
54 Godfrey's favorite drink
57 The (Fr.)

across

1 Eddie Cantor's wife's
5 Is not (contr.)
9 For shame!
12 Jack Benny's right-hand man
14 Finish, termination
15 Grindstone corundum
16 It's quaffed in *Robin Hood*
17 Soft drink
18 That is (Lat. abbr.)
19 He's Ralph Kramden
21 ___ Bunce plays the happy hubby in *Ethel and Albert*
24 Hawaiian garland
25 Standard time (abbr.)
26 ___ MacKenzie
28 Huh?

30 Laugh
32 Each
33 ___ *Sanctum*
36 Rosemary ___ Camp
37 Ethel Merman (init.)
39 Mary ___ stars in *Search for Tomorrow*
40 Thus
42 Burnt part of Groucho's cigar
44 Jack Benny's always 39; he never ___
45 Ann stars in *Private Secretary*
48 Chemical symbol for tin
49 ___ Gardner
50 Feasted
51 Double quartet
55 Women like them
56 *The $64,000 ___*
58 Unit of energy

down

1. Made a mistake
2. Ann Sothern's TV job
3. Hardwood tree
4. You and me
5. Fairies
6. *Navy* ___ (pl.)
7. Short for Louise
8. Ghosts
9. She's in *I Married Joan*
11. Neighbor of *December Bride*
12. Ernie Ford's state
13. Eat
14. They're cheaper by the dozen
16. ___*side Theater*
20. He brings animals to *The Garry Moore Show*
23. Ancient
24. Gordon Mac___, singer
25. Products of giveaway shows
26. *My Little Margie*'s dad
27. Found in the morgue
28. Mr. Rogers of TV
30. Anything of value
31. A nobleman
33. Philbrick helps catch them
35. Famous TV cowboy
37. Southern plant
40. Head covering
41. Copy
43. TV Western marshal (init.)

across

1. Jacob's brother
5. Right-angle building additions
9. Attire
10. Airplane maneuver
11. Scorch
12. National TV publication (2 words)
15. "___ Since Eve"
16. What the sponsor pays
17. Prepare the stage
18. *Waterfront*'s tugboat gets high on this
19. News agency (init.)
20. What Patti Page can do
21. Leading emcee (init.)
22. Ripped
24. TV time costs
25. Mrs. Roy Rogers (2 words)
27. Count of Monte Cristo's weapon
29. Sow
30. News agency (init.)
32. Spring Byington's role
33. Socialist republic (abbr.)
34. Without hardship
36. ___ *Around the Town*
37. Uncovered
38. Trick
39. TV detective from Boston
41. Fall flower
42. Unusual
43. Boxing or wrestling
44. Health resorts
45. Declare untrue

48 *Studio* ____
49 Also
50 Legal claims
51 ____ (King) Cole

down

1 Not on
2 Kind of waves TV utilizes
3 Gleason plays Ralph ____
4 *Valiant Lady*'s ____ Emerson
5 Metal-bearing rocks
6 Merry
7 ____ *the World Turns*
8 John ____, storyteller-host on *Telephone Hour*
9 Language of Greece
10 Epoch
11 Organ of sight
16 What to do when TV sound is interrupted at source
18 Edible ice-cream holder
20 Actor Welles
21 Mad
22 Some call it fat
23 *I Married Joan*'s Miss ____
24 Arabian prince (var.)
25 ____ Hayworth (poss.)
27 Small Asiatic kingdom
30 Jeff ____, Gobel's TV wife
31 Jackie ____
33 Stevens, the diva
34 *Waterfront*'s boardwalk
36 Constellation
37 One of Maid Marian's locks
39 So be it
40 TV receiver
41 Not amateur
42 *Our Miss Brooks* star
43 Old play: "Three Men ____ Horse" (2 words)
44 Tennis necessity
47 How Caesar wrote "two"

across

1 Acorn tree in Sherwood Forest
4 Silvers' Sgt. Joan ____ (May 19 TV GUIDE cover girl)
9 You say this to a horse
12 Evergreen tree
13 Rub out
14 ____ Rogers
15 Fred Mertz in *I Love Lucy*
17 TV stagehands change it
19 ____ West (poss.), famed for her comeuppance
20 Double-reed woodwind
21 Sculptor's name
23 Imbiber
26 Aid, encourage
27 Tongue's silent function

28 Top stars have the do-re-
29 Sgt. Friday's man Alexander
30 Sod dug by golf duffer
31 TV contestants strive to ____ rich quick
32 *This ____ Your Life*
33 ____ *Hood*
34 Entreaty
35 Andy ____ plays Jingles in *Wild bill Hickok* (poss.)
37 Layers, stepped arrangement
38 Is not (contr.)
39 Region
40 Binge (rhymes with "see")
42 Faye ____
45 Unit of energy often used in crosswords
46 *I Led Three* ____

August 4, 1956

across

1 Dusting cloth
4 Jon Hall's TV role
9 ___ Gabor
12 Building wing
13 She's in Wonderland
14 Rin ___ Tin
15 Fourth letter
16 New England university
17 At what time?
18 Imitator
20 Honey maker
21 Church recess
23 *Maggi ___ Show*
28 Dinah ___
30 Group of cattle
31 Negative
32 Sunburn
33 Speak slowly
35 Damage
36 *This ___ Your Life*
37 Lyric poems
38 Run away to wed
40 Intervals of rest
43 Branches of learning
44 Golf gadget
45 *Toast of the ___*
47 King of beasts
49 Stalk
51 Harsh
54 Transgress
55 Intertwine

56 Born
57 River barrier
58 Consumed
59 Acquire

down

1 ___ Skelton
2 Malt drink
3 Jackie ___
4 Martha ___
5 Warning sound
6 Wire measure
7 Top card
8 Concerning
9 ___ *and Albert*
10 Contend
11 ___ Sothern
17 Unite metals
19 By means of
20 Milton ___

21 Moving
22 Aspect
24 Pursue
25 Not old
26 Not suitable
27 Tender spots
29 ___ Cantor
34 Soak, as flax
35 ___ *Show*
37 Not closed
39 Legal rule
41 *The Secret ___*
42 ___ Allen, emcee
46 Portent
47 *I ___ Three Lives*
48 Mr. Gershwin
49 Ocean
50 Make lace
52 Pinky ___
53 Allow
55 You and I

August 25, 1956

across

1 Where a scientist works (abbr.)
4 Dull
8 ___ the Press
12 Miss Lupino of TV
13 Mud
14 Earth goddess
15 Superlative of good
17 Bennett Cerf's job on *What's My Line?*
19 Express contempt
21 Ray Bloch's wand
22 Part of a necklace
24 ___ Wilson, Jack Benny's announcer
25 Comedian Bean's initials
27 Danny Thomas's former TV wife (2 words)
30 Tail-less monkey
31 Woes
32 And not
33 Sooty stain
34 Girl's nickname
35 *Masquerade Party* jurist (2 words)
37 Julius ___ Rosa
38 Miss Brooks
39 Sound a horn
40 Open
42 Lock of hair
45 ___ for Daddy (2 words)
48 *Name That* ___
49 Merit
50 *Lamp* ___ *My Feet*
52 Scotch for enclosure
53 Mardi ___
54 Burn
55 Japanese money

down

1 Ad-___ (pl.)
2 Arabian port
3 TV summer sport
4 Jerry Lewis's ex-partner (init.)
5 Lt. Masters of *Rin Tin Tin*
6 Nasser's league
7 Bea of *Burns and Allen*
8 A juicy fruit
9 Ireland
10 Norton, Sullivan, Murrow are ___
11 Make lace
16 "The impatient years"
18 English school
20 College cheer
23 Mr. Donlevy's show, ___ *Assignment*
25 Musical work
26 Louisa May Alcott character
27 TV songstress ___ Corey
28 Charles Lamb
29 An idol
30 Mr. Mack's interest
33 Loud nasal noise
35 "___ There," war song
36 Negative
38 Levels
40 Plant used in soups
41 Musical sound
43 Cut
44 Perceived
45 Princess Margaret's nickname
46 Swiss river
47 Metropolitan Transit Authority (abbr.)
51 Else

September 8, 1956

across

1 Line of joining
5 50 percent
9 For shame!
12 Operatic solo
13 Open surface
14 Peculiar
15 Hal —— of *$64,000 Question*
17 Roofing material
18 —— Sparks, actor
19 Dusting cloth
21 Jack Webb's TV role
23 Jackie ——
27 —— Gabor
28 *I —— Lucy*
29 He was "Mr. Television"
31 Negative reply
33 *Studio* ——
34 Stairway post
35 Ocean
36 You and I
37 Strong winds
38 Expense
39 Prohibit
40 Meals
42 *Stage Show* brothers
45 Golf gadget
46 Mr. Baba
47 Flap
49 Flower
53 Skelton or Buttons
54 Decorate

56 "And —— we go!"
57 Part of the foot
58 —— *of Night*
59 Repetition

down

1 —— Levenson
2 Historical period
3 Ventilate
4 Gordon ——
5 Laughter sound
6 —— Carney
7 Foliage item
8 Charlie ——
9 Henry ——
10 Thought
11 Whirlpool
16 Possesses
20 George ——
22 —— *Got a Secret*

23 Shine
24 *The —— Ranger*
25 —— Arden
26 More modern
30 Place again
31 *Feather Your* ——
32 Dobbin's dinner
34 —— Fabray
35 Distress signal
37 Cooking fuel
38 Sid ——
39 *December* ——
41 Pod vegetable
42 Arrow
43 Butter substitute
44 Three feet
48 —— *Town*
50 —— *for the Money*
51 Consume
52 Bread grain
55 Myself

September 22, 1956

across

1 *Strike It* ___
5 Bill of fare
9 Jalopy
12 Miss Fitzgerald
13 ___ *'n' Andy*
14 River (Sp.)
15 Brief comic sketch
16 ___ Clooney
18 Scotch cap
19 Perform on stage
20 Cry with the soap operas
21 *Meet Corliss* ___
24 Be obedient
27 Prizefighter
29 Knight's title
31 ___ Gabor
32 *Truth* ___ *Consequences*
33 Moisture on grass
35 Not bright
37 Overhead railway (colloq.)
38 Unhappy
40 Drink slowly
42 Frankie ___, singer
44 Spill over
46 ___ *Scouts*
48 Getaway (sl.)
50 ___ Bolger, comic
51 Third letter
54 Ed ___, emcee
57 Food fish
58 ___ Ray Hutton
59 Portion of a surface
60 Group of cattle
61 Paving substance
62 Observes
63 Catch sight of

down

1 Relax
2 ___ Chase of *Masquerade Party*
3 TV drama show
4 Fedora
5 Hal ___ of $64,000 quiz
6 Acts with feeling
7 Numbers (abbr.)
8 Utilizes
9 Buster ___
10 Atmosphere
11 ___ Rogers
17 Cow's sound
19 Land measures
22 ___ Buttons
23 Free of
25 Balanced
26 New England university
27 Foreman (colloq.)
28 ___ Roberts
30 *Life of* ___
34 Humor
36 ___ *Against Crime*
39 ___ *a Second*
41 *Zoo* ___
43 Feels like mosquito bites
45 Buddy
47 Highway divisions
49 *Our* ___ *Brooks*
52 *Wyatt* ___
53 Small whirlpool
54 Perch
55 Miss Merkel, actress
56 Contend
57 The lady

October 13, 1956

across

1 Ocean
4 First man
8 ___ 'n' Andy
12 ___ Linkletter
13 *What's My ___?*
14 Evergreen tree
15 Elvis ___
17 Sticking substance
18 *I ___ Three Lives*
19 Jeannie ___
20 ___ *Hood*
23 Dismounted
24 Dry, as land
25 Male deer
26 Plump
29 ___ *Scouts*
31 ___ *for Tomorrow*
33 Building wing
34 *Wyatt ___*
36 Uncovered
37 Challenge
38 What giveaways give away
39 Emcee of *Good Morning*
42 Papa
43 Dale ___, cowgirl
44 ___ Young
48 Snakelike fish
49 ___ Crosby
50 Armed conflict
51 Leg joint
52 ___ *of Night*
53 *Studio ___*

down

1 Tree fluid
2 Make errors
3 Had lunch
4 Burns and ___
5 Ceased living
6 One or another taken indifferently
7 Myself
8 Separate
9 *Our ___ Brooks*
10 Upon
11 Observed
16 Slip
17 Janis ___
19 Embrace
20 Fixed relation of quantity
21 Verbal
22 *Wild ___ Hickok*
23 In or near
25 *Playhouse of ___*
26 *Kukla, ___ and Ollie*
27 Land measure
28 Those people
30 Approaches
32 Dwelling place
35 Musical note
37 Thick
38 ___ and Gower Champion
39 Emit funes
40 Baking place
41 ___ Storm
42 *Ding ___ School*
44 Pot cover
45 ___ *for the Money*
46 Light brown
47 *You ___ There*
49 *It Could ___ You*

October 20, 1956

across

1. ___ for the Money
4. Knocks
8. Departs
12. Crone
13. ___ Roberts, TV evangelist
14. Wait in ambush
15. Not well
16. Cowboy TV star (2 words)
18. ___ Allen
20. ___ of Night
21. Gentlemen
23. ___ Bergen
27. ___ Sullivan
29. Fall flowers
32. Cry of triumph
33. ___ Rogers
35. Actress Gardner
36. Be obedient
37. Before
38. Wet thoroughly
40. Myself
41. Rock
43. Profit
45. Utilizes
48. House divisions
51. Canine TV star (3 words)
55. Line
56. Cutters ___ film
57. Accomplished
58. Three (prefix)
59. John ___, newscaster
60. Swing
61. Skirt edge

down

1. ___ Is Your Life
2. ___ Disney
3. Makes eyes at
4. Roy ___, cowboy
5. You ___ There
6. Window glass
7. Snow vehicle
8. Fastened with sticky stuff
9. Not in
10. Be mistaken
11. Cloud region
17. Grows old
19. Medicine bottle
22. Four ___ Playhouse
24. Chatter (colloq.)
25. Exclamation for attention
26. Martha ___
27. Lambs' mothers
28. Soil
30. ___ Arden
31. Sounded a bell
34. ___ G. Carroll
36. Midwestern state
38. ___ Arnaz
39. Art ___
42. Crazy (sl.)
44. Mr. and Mrs. ___
46. Concludes
47. Pack
49. Greater amount
50. Sink or ___
51. ___ Skelton
52. Mrs. Eddie Cantor
53. Nothing
54. ___ Ray Hutton

down

1 Native of Arabia
2 Martha ___
3 Jack Barr's TV quiz show
4 ___ *Holliday*
5 Object of worship
6 Obtain
7 Laughter sound
8 Make wavy
9 Pot cover
10 High card
11 Which person
17 Clamping devices
19 Cooking fuel
20 Eve ___
22 Low couch
23 Gale Storm's TV show (2 words)
24 Drinking vessels
25 Liberace pounds them
26 ___ Garroway
27 First man
28 Fodder towers
31 Endures
35 *Queen ___ a Day*
37 *Life of ___*
38 Mark ___
40 Game on horseback
41 ___ *Phoebe* (ex-TV show)
42 ___ *of Night*
43 Nightbird
44 By way of
45 Sum up
46 Not good
49 ___ *You Trust Your Wife?*

across

1 ___ Linkletter
4 ___ *Finance*
8 Cat's weapon
12 Uncooked
13 *The Big ___*
14 *Strike It ___*
15 Affirmative vote
16 Decay
17 This is TV
18 *Tales of the 77th ___ Lancers*
20 Point a gun
21 Scottish cap
22 TV's child-care expert
26 *Death Valley ___*
28 Portion of an object
29 Color
30 Commotion
31 *I Led Three ___*

32 Raymond Massey's *I ___*
33 Large truck
34 Mr. Ladd, actor
35 Be fidgety
36 Faye ___
38 Distress signal
39 The thing's
40 *Your Hit ___*
43 Egg-shaped figures
46 ___ Crosby
47 Newsman ___ Calmer
48 ___ *Wide World*
49 ___ Evans, TV cowgirl
50 Old horse
51 *Valiant ___*
52 Scent
53 *People ___ Funny*

November 24, 1956

down

1 Arrowhead
2 Pain
3 Buck
4 Quiet!
5 Mr. Godfrey's drink
6 He sings on *Your Hit Parade*
7 Annie Oakley (2 words)
8 Angry
9 Moving trucks
10 Nautical yes
11 Recent
16 Ralph Kramden's wife
20 Greek letter
22 ___ *Miss Brooks*
24 *Private*
26 ___ *Phoebe*
27 Rip
28 TV oldie, *Who ___ That?*
29 *Masquerade Party*'s ___ Chase
30 River in Scotland
31 Transgress
32 Short for Florence
35 Next
37 Vast age
38 Long fish
40 In front
42 Mr. Rogers
43 Wild plum
45 ___ *Wide World*
46 *Big* ___
47 Transmitted
48 Shady tree
49 Fish eggs
51 Mauna ___, largest volcano
55 ___ *and Mrs. North*

across

1 Evil
4 May be found in Sherwood Forest
8 TV's Mr. Sanderson
12 Expert pilot
13 Goddess of marriage
14 TV comedienne
15 Daughter of Uranus
17 French friend
18 Again
19 TV's Uncle Miltie
21 Narrow openings
23 ___ *Howdy Doody* time
25 Owing
26 ___ *Christian*
28 He plays Bob Victor (2 words)
32 Paid to an agent
33 Sheltered side
34 Roman numeral for 104
35 *Ethel and Albert*'s ___ Bunce
36 Republican President
37 TV's man from Tennessee (2 words)
39 Mr. ___, David Brian
40 *You ___ There*
41 TV receiver
42 ___ *My Line?*
44 Martin and ___
48 U.S. canal
50 ___ *Star Revue*
52 Autry and Rogers do this well
53 Girl's name
54 *Make ___ for Daddy*
56 Lair
57 Pinochle term
58 365 days
59 Dine

December 1, 1956

down

1. "___ and Peace"
2. Long period of time
3. Wreath of flowers
4. *Captain* ___
5. Eager
6. Cause of Chicago fire
7. *Person* ___ *Person*
8. Thick piece of stone, wood, meat
9. Revolve
10. Sea mollusk
11. Land set apart for public (abbr.)
14. Low grade
16. Seize with the teeth
19. *Your* ___ *Parade*
20. Talk in a grand manner
21. Type of music (sl.)
22. Southern state (abbr.)
23. Place for cars (abbr.)
24. Large-scale geologic period
25. Shade tree
29. To be or ___ to be
30. Coloring agent
32. ___ Francis
34. *Big* ___
35. Be ill
37. Dining
38. Postscript (abbr.)
40. Behold
42. Commercial
43. God or goddess
44. Go in
46. One of a pair
47. Part of a plant
48. A saint has one
49. Gov't. agency (abbr.)
52. ___ Sullivan
53. She's a star (init.)
54. Three-toed sloth of South America
55. ___ *You Want to Lead a Band*

across

1. Lawrence ___
5. Play a part
8. ___ *the Music*
12. Region
13. Goodbye and ___ (2 words)
15. "Over the ___"
17. ___ Baker
18. A light carriage
19. Associate closely
22. *It's a* ___ *Life*
25. Atmosphere
26. River in Italy
27. Worship
28. ___ *and Be Counted* (2 words)
31. Negative
32. "___ Wilderness"
33. Santa brings them
34. Staccato trumpet sound
36. Above (contr.)
38. ___ Porter of *December Bride*
39. "Liquid gold"
41. Cry of sorrow
43. Prefix meaning down
45. Conspired
47. Bishop ___
50. What some contestants do on quiz shows
51. Silent
52. Stritch and Malbin
56. Make joyful
57. Coming to an end
58. Exclamation
59. Harry Truman's birthplace (abbr.)
60. 365 days (abbr.)

December 29, 1956

down

1. *Kukla, ___ and Ollie*
2. *The ___ Ranger*
3. *___ the World Turns*
4. Slang for 18-Across
5. Groucho ___
6. ___ Francis
7. Coloring substance
8. Emcee of *You Asked for It*
9. Ireland
10. Wrongdoings
11. *Let's ___ a Trip*
13. Staple food at King Arthur's Court
19. *You Are ___*
21. Facts
23. ___ Ray Hutton
25. Everyone
26. Gorilla
27. ___ Wynn of *Noah's Ark*
28. Wagers
29. Jack ___
30. ___ Linkletter
31. Cooking fuel
33. Judge
35. *Hall of Fame's "___ and Superman"*
38. ___ *Boy*
40. ___ Thomas
41. Sound for attention
42. Program for the housewife
43. Burl ___, balladeer
44. Harvest
46. Knights need them
48. ___ *of Night*
49. Fling
51. Top card
52. ___ Caesar
56. Negative reply

across

1. Defect
5. Furious
8. *Father Knows ___*
12. ___ Clooney
14. Heard on *Voice of Firestone*
15. Article
16. Milton ___
17. Tight loop
18. Short for group of stations
20. Chopping tool
21. Adjective for Sherwood Forest
22. *Your ___ Parade*
24. Close by
26. Prayer ending
28. ___ *the Clock*
29. Sack
32. *Zoo ___*
34. ___ *Three*
36. ___ *on New York*
37. Engrave with acid
39. Picnic pests
40. ___ Arnaz
41. ___ Sothern
42. ___ *Holliday*
45. Cheering shout
47. Still
50. Stove compartment
51. Land measures
53. *___ You Trust Your Wife?*
54. Unkind
55. Bob ___
57. Catch sight of
58. Curved letter
59. Accomplishes

January 5, 1957

across

1 Sky ___
5 ___ Is Your Life
9 Cushion
12 Great Lake
13 Cry of pain
14 Studio ___
15 Hollywood sisters
17 Ever (poet.)
18 Roadhouse
19 Male sheep
21 Walt ___
23 Jack Webb's show
27 Insect egg
28 Comfort
29 Potato
31 Ma's spouse
33 Drink slowly
34 Frank Parker
35 ___ Power
36 Into
37 Tossed
38 ___ Guinness
39 Baked dessert
40 Phil ___
42 Danny ___
45 ___ on New York
46 ___ March
47 Part of the foot
49 ___ Kovacs
53 Noah's ___
54 ___ of Night
56 Canned fish

57 Beverage
58 Tatters
59 Head of cast

down

1 Beer barrel
2 Mr. Gershwin
3 Pen point
4 ___ Gobel
5 Person ___ Person
6 Color
7 Chilled
8 Herb ___
9 West ___
10 ___ Jeffreys
11 Contradict
16 Sprinted
20 Measured rhythm
22 ___ Lancelot
23 ___ Arnaz

24 Shower
25 Poisonous snake
26 Top ___ and New Talent
30 Adventures of Jim ___
31 Wharf
32 Curved lines
34 Matinee ___
35 Malt drink
37 ___ Considine
38 Prevents
39 It's ___ Time
41 Caustic solution
42 Name ___ Tune
43 Rabbit
44 Carbonated water
48 Breakfast food
50 Belongs with bolt
51 Miss Claire, actress
52 Hearing organ
55 Plural ending

across

1. Bridge
5. Solemn promise
8. ___ Garroway
12. Buddy Hayes plays it for Lawrence Welk
13. Fuss
14. *Playhouse 90*'s first show: "Forbidden ___"
15. Prayer's finale
16. *Garry Moore Show*'s Denise ___
17. Nearest
18. One of *The Brothers*
21. Thick black liquid
22. ___ *Earp*
26. ___ *My Line?*
29. ___ *Do*
31. Sticky substance (sl.)
32. Irish Republic
33. Conjunction
34. One of TV's horsy set
35. Glide on snow
36. *You ___ Your Life*
37. Forest plants
38. Tantalize
40. Pod vegetable
41. Miss Carson's TV show
47. Great Lake
50. Cereal plant
51. Puppeteers Bil and ___ Baird
52. *I ___ Lucy*
53. Miss Merkel, actress
54. Newscaster ___ Sevareid
55. Sharp
56. Relative (abbr.)
57. Window frame

down

1. Male deer
2. Mountain lion
3. Son of Adam
4. ___ Fabray
5. Ennobling quality
6. Scent
7. Unit of expression
8. ___ Thomas
9. *People ___ Funny*
10. Irritate
11. Have a TV snack
19. Source of energy
20. *You're on Your ___*
23. Chills and fever
24. Ripped
25. Playthings
26. ___ *Point*
27. Long walk
28. Solo operatic selection
29. Slice
30. Nearby
33. *It Could ___ You*
34. Miss ___, former TV schoolmarm
36. Hive tenant
37. Afternoon party
39. Bishop ___
40. Flower part
42. *Do You Trust ___ Wife?*
43. ___ Wyman
44. Girl's name
45. Spring flower
46. Apiece
47. Large deer
48. Fish eggs
49. ___ *Got a Secret*

February 23, 1957

across

1 Youngster
4 *Wyatt* ___
8 Long knife
12 ___ *Got a Secret*
13 Disturbance
14 Oil country
15 Sports show audience
16 One out of many
17 Lower classman at *West Point*
18 Mr. Ford's first name
20 *Noah's* ___
21 Before
22 Rosemary ___
26 High plateau
28 Become rough
29 "Much ___ About Nothing"
30 Yards (abbr.)
31 Sudden fancies
32 ___ *Tin Tin*
33 Negative (Scot.)
34 Well-known town in Nevada
35 Lucy's landlord
36 Bess Myerson, former Miss ___
38 By way of
39 Writing fluid
40 Corliss Archer's beau
43 Actor Arnold ___
46 Denise ___
47 Anger
48 Fine sand
49 Marries
50 Ignitable liquid
51 Neat
52 ___ *Wide World*
53 Actor Richard ___

down

1 *Howdy Doody* ___
2 Above
3 18-Across's state
4 Remove
5 Isn't (sl.)
6 ___ Rogers
7 Small Navy craft
8 Silvers' role
9 Mineral rock
10 Laboratory (colloq.)
11 *Twenty-*___
17 Theatrical necessities
19 Period of time
20 Davy Crockett's last stand
22 Charlie Chan's homeland
23 Most documentaries have this
24 ___ Adams
25 Thither
26 Species of talking bird
27 Cheese from Holland
28 Quiz-show winners get this
31 Squeeze
35 Repair
37 Hero dog
38 Poetry
40 Mouseketeer Jimmie ___
41 One of the Great Lakes
42 Depend
43 ___ *Preston of the Yukon*
44 Three
45 Help
46 Flowered wreath
49 Columnist and former TV emcee (init.)

March 9, 1957

61 *The Big ___*
62 Part of Fury
63 Thing in law
64 Salamander

down

1 Manner of doing
2 Mineral-bearing rock
3 The man called X
4 Butter substitute
5 Florenz Ames' role on *Blondie*
6 Opposed to aweather
7 Consecrate
8 Otherwise
9 Weekly musical show
10 *Our Miss Brooks*
11 TV receiver
19 Loud call
20 2000 lbs.
21 David Brian's TV role
22 *___ Hour*
26 Jack Larson on *Superman*
27 550 (Roman)
30 *Lineup* setting, ___ Francisco
32 Kit Carson's pal, ___ Toro
34 *___ Tell the Truth*
36 *Tales of the 77th Bengal ___*
38 Hush!
39 Relative
41 Small child
43 Indefinite article
46 Weapon used on Ramar
50 *___ That Tune*
51 Pennsylvania city
52 Norse god of wisdom and war
53 Medieval forced-entry technique
54 Cantor's wife
57 *Top Tunes and ___ Talent*
58 Consume

across

1 Characterization done by Coca
5 Small quantity
8 Orbs
12 Verbal
13 Unfavorable
14 *___ of Life*
15 Past tense of be
16 Wooden peg
17 Tallow
18 Famous valet on TV
21 *The Brighter ___*
23 Concerning
24 *Disneyland's "___ Dear to My Heart"*
25 Trough
28 Man's name (pl.)
29 Time periods (abbr.)
31 Lois Lane on *Superman*

33 Abridge
35 TV actor ___ Mineo
37 Ben Guthrie's rank (poss.)
38 Como often sings 'em
40 King of TV's singers
42 Ernie Ford's ___ Pickers
44 He asks the $64,000 question
45 *The Price ___ Right*
47 Express dissent
48 Schultzie on *The Bob Cummings Show*
49 Tom Tully's rank in *The Lineup*
53 TV actress Maria ___
55 Before
56 Star of *Wire Service*
59 First man
60 *___ Power*

23

down

1. *Tic* ___ *Dough*
2. Building wing
3. ___ Cooke of *Omnibus*
4. Ginger cookie
5. Uncle Sam's annual claim on income
6. Part of "to be"
7. Happen again
8. Pinky ___
9. Near, Middle or Far ___
10. Cowboy road
11. Gay frolic
16. Cow sound
18. ___ Godfrey
20. Cereal plant
22. What Jack Barry and Hal March do
23. Meadow
24. Golfers try to break it
25. Yelp
28. *I've Got a* ___
30. TV pianist
32. Cry
33. Illuminated
34. Nancy Kelly played one on *Studio One*
35. Strange
37. Picnic pest
39. *What's My Line?* props
40. Dismay (var.)
42. Painter's stand
43. Sailor
45. Carry (colloq.)
47. ___ Wyman
49. ___ Skelton
50. Write (sl.)
51. *Queen for a* ___
52. Female sheep
55. ___ *You Trust Your Wife?*

across

1. Afternoon party
4. *Four* ___ *Playhouse*
8. ___ *Take a Trip*
12. Wholly
13. ___ *That Tune*
14. *Wyatt* ___
15. TV drama show
17. Sid ___
19. Soak up
20. ___ *Miss Brooks*
21. Even score
22. Julie London's voice
24. *House* ___
26. French article
27. *Navy Log* locale
28. Perched
29. ___ March, emcee
31. ___*Aluminum Hour*
33. Ida ___ of *Mr. Adams and Eve*
36. Legendary bird
37. ___ *Power*
38. ___ Collyer of *Beat the Clock*
39. Pa's spouse
41. George ___ of *Wire Service*
43. Minister to
44. Liable
46. Have a snack
47. Jam container
48. Baseball, football, etc.
50. *Your Hit* ___
53. ___ Smith
54. Paradise
56. Crow talk
57. Sgt. Preston needs this
58. *The* ___ *Ranger*
59. ___ *on New York*

May 11, 1957

57 Office of Public
   Administration (abbr.)
58 Enough (dialect)

down

1 Next year may find a
   Sad one on TV
2 Songstress O'Brien
3 *Firestone* visitor ——
   Stevens
4 Buddy Hackett specialty
5 Art Baker likes you to
   do this
6 Sid Caesar's "Haircuts"
7 TV trigamist
8 Charles Farrell's role
9 Canine star
10 He has the lead role
13 First-rate, as a
   performance (sl.)
15 Designer —— Cassini
19 Measure in Dominican
   Republic
21 Famous ex-barber
23 Ordinance (abbr.)
24 Ex-*Today* weather-girl
   —— Meriwether
25 *Crunch and* ——
27 Miss Fabray
28 *Tic* —— *Dough*
29 —— *Anthony Show*
30 Years (abbr.)
32 Producer Walt ——
36 Muggs' species
37 If a performer has this,
   he's lively (sl.)
41 Spike Jones was
   noted for this
42 Pertaining to the
   constellation Whale
43 Aroma
44 Baseball team
45 *Let's Take a* ——
47 Soon
48 Symbol of goodness
49 Filming device:
   ——-motion
52 *Mr. Adams'* Eve

across

1 Stock medieval character
5 Prepositions
8 Victoria Crosses (abbr.)
11 Piece for *Voice of
   Firestone*
12 Hindu title
13 What Ralph Kramden
   threatens Alice with
14 Role for Duncan Renaldo
16 *Playhouse 90* opener:
   "Forbidden ——"
17 Act immediately before
   knighting
18 Dancer recently on
   The Ed Sullivan Show
20 Month (abbr.)
22 Angle (abbr.)
23 Adjective for movies
   like "King Kong"

26 Hero of many horse
   operas
31 TV director Roland ——
33 He's a prince in
   Abyssinia
34 TV comic Jack ——
35 Talented TV bongo
   player (2 words)
38 Boys' names
39 *I* ——
40 —— *Tin Tin*
42 Unite
46 —— *Ark*
50 Singer Adams
51 —— *Amateur Hour*
53 Arthur Godfrey's
   Mr. Marvin
54 Near the center
55 Perry Como sings
   this
56 Anger

July 20, 1957

across

1. Worthless bits
5. Likely
8. Loaned
12. Trading center
13. Meadow
14. Margarine
15. Type of malaria
16. Family name on *Father Knows Best*
18. Superman
20. Tom ___, TV actor
21. *I ___ Three Lives*
22. Lon and Dale
24. French friend
26. Blondie's surname
30. To lift
32. Knock
33. Likewise
34. Family on *Valiant Lady*
36. President's nickname
37. Assistant
38. Vanessa's sister in *Love of Life*
40. Inadequate
43. *Modern Romances* is one
46. Singer in *The Lawrence Welk Show* (2 words)
49. Adjective for Sgt. Friday
50. Shape of Garroway's *World*
51. From beau to spouse in 2 words
52. Tchaikovsky's "Marche ___"
53. Health resorts
54. Actor Ayres
55. Hitchcock atmosphere

down

1. Gen. Bradley
2. Frenzy
3. Disney's ___ *Adventures* (2 words)
4. Cesar Romero in *Passport to Danger*
5. Exclamation of sorrow
6. It's mightier than the sword
7. TV writer Mosel
8. One of TV's Youngs
9. Otherwise
10. Gas
11. Pitch
17. Supplements scantily
19. Art Carney in "The Honeymooners"
22. What Sgt. Bilko calls Pvt. Doberman
23. Referees at a ball game
24. Fruit drink
25. Marjorie Reynolds' role in *Life of Riley*
26. Actor Crawford, for short

27. Desirable
28. What viewers do on Art Baker's show
29. Actress Avedon
31. Miss ___ was head of *Ding Dong School*
35. Place
38. Myself
39. Obliterate
40. Tools
41. Portion of movie often shown on TV
42. You may see this on *Opera Theater*
43. White specks on a TV screen
44. Winged
45. Director of *The Jack Benny Show*
47. ___ Abner
48. Poem

August 3, 1957

64 Sweet potato
65 Cut (used with snick)

down

1 Harpo's instrument
2 To sheltered side
3 Barry Sullivan's TV role (3 words)
4 Pry into others' affairs
5 Macaw
6 Italian coin
7 *West* ___
8 *Meet* ___ *Press*
9 "Westward ___"
10 Wyatt Earp quality
11 East Indian tree
17 Command on *Highway Patrol*
20 *Victory at* ___
22 James Arness plays him (2 words)
24 Lt. ___ Masters
26 Motor fuel
27 Donkey
28 Much (sl.)
30 ___ Bolger
32 Golf's starting point
33 ___ *a Great Life*
35 One of the Gabors
37 Poetic contraction
40 ___ Cinders of the comics
42 Rin Tin Tin's foot
45 Morning shows, e.g.
47 Retains
48 ___ *Three*
49 Mineral rocks
51 Portico
53 Branch of work
54 Satisfy
56 Prefix denoting priority
57 Sound of good taste
60 ___ *the World Turns*

across

1 Very bad actors
5 Swiss mountain
8 *Name* ___ *Tune*
12 ___ Hale, Jr.,
13 River (Sp.)
14 "Freddie the Freeloader"
15 Nevada city
16 Get out of bed
18 The poor Indian
19 ___ Bill, cartoon cowboy
21 Cartoon character
22 ___ *of Annapolis*
23 Imitator
25 Roman garment
27 ___-*Star Theater*
29 ___ *Power*
31 Songstress Page

34 Shoe part
36 ___ Carroll, late of Caesar's camp
38 Let it stand
39 Sullivan's rival
41 *Lassie* sound
43 *Crunch and* ___
44 TV cowgirl Evans
46 Pen name of Munro
48 Hiram Holiday
50 ___ Vegas
52 *Tales of* ___ *Fargo*
55 *Truth* ___ *Consequences*
56 *Arthur Murray* ___
58 Charles Lamb's pseudonym
59 ___ *Phoebe*
61 Comic Costello
62 *Du* ___ *Theater*
63 Existence

September 7, 1957

across

1 Throws sideways
6 Songstress Teresa ——
12 Sunday *Challenge* man
13 Who goes there? (Fr.)
14 Veteran dragon
15 Set free
16 Per ——, by heads
18 TV Family man
21 Turkish hat
22 Grains
26 Jack ——
28 A religious painting (2 words)
31 Horses here have their ups and downs (3 words)
33 Marconi's invention
34 Regretted
35 *The Name's the ——*, old TV show
36 Kind of dancer
38 Period of time
39 Actress —— Farrell
42 Blank screen (2 words)
46 Decree of a Mohammedan ruler
50 Most TV movies (2 words)
51 Jan Peerce, e.g.
52 Ball team flirting with pay-TV
53 Helen ——

down

1 —— *Playhouse*, film series
2 Colleague of 12-Across

3 Indisposed
4 A kind of narrative poetry
5 Bundle of grain
6 Baseball strategy
7 Actor Montalban
8 —— Marie Saint
9 Yul Brynner doesn't use one
10 Ida Lupino role
11 Sportscaster Barber
13 Roles of 12-Across and 2-Down
17 What Wyatt Earp keeps
18 Anything from 5 to 90 minutes
19 Vocalist Arden and others
20 The U in UHF
23 *You Bet —— Life*
24 To follow

25 Villainous look
27 Leave —— laughing
29 Crime theme on TV
30 Robert ——, TV guest and film star
32 Describes Adolphe Menjou
37 Marilyn's impersonator
40 Told on *To Tell the Truth*
41 "Forbidden ——," *Playhouse 90* classic
42 A show that flops
43 —— Mintz, on *The Goldbergs*
44 Girl's name
45 *Mr. Wizard*, —— Herbert
47 "——one for tennis?"
48 —— Avedon
49 Sounds from a nervous speaker

October 19, 1957

across

1 One of the Angels
4 ___ Garroway
8 ___ Kennedy of *The Californians*
12 Greek letter
13 Type of set for *Captain Gallant*
14 Manufactured
15 Actor ___ Hunter
16 Born
17 Large fruit
18 The queen of the jungle
20 Window glass
21 ___ Milland
22 Gillis of *Life of Riley*
25 Matt Dillon is a good one
27 TV comedian is one (sl.)
28 Peculiar
29 Mortimer Snerd, for instance
30 House ___
31 Place to sleep
32 Wholly
33 Vases
34 Playing cards
35 ___ *Choice*
37 Affair of 1812
38 Inquisitive
39 *Frontier* ___
42 ___ Fisher
44 For each
45 Glide on snow
46 Actor Robert ___
47 ___ Roberts
48 Gold (Sp.)
49 Curved
50 Affectionate
51 ___ King Cole

down

1 What Sgt. Preston does to his man
2 Mormon State
3 Donald Gray's TV show (3 words)
4 ___ Thomas
5 Region
6 Contestants do this
7 Steve's rival
8 Correct
9 Star of *Wells Fargo* (2 words)
10 Fuss
11 ___ of Annapolis
17 Sock's wife on 35-Across
19 Dine
20 Actors' roles
22 Mends
23 Paradise
24 Sums up
25 Type of TV "opera"
26 Barbara ___ of *Perry Mason*
27 Star of *Dr. Christian*
30 TV rating service
34 *Tic* ___ *Dough*
36 *West* ___
37 *Wide Wide* ___
39 *Jimmy* ___
40 Vegetable
41 Uproar
42 Recede, as tides
43 ___ Avedon
44 Type of sport on theater-TV
47 *Edge* ___ *Night*

29

across

1 Mrs. Riley
4 Perry ___
8 Ernie ___
12 Commotion
13 Actor ___ Ladd
14 Martha ___
   comedienne
15 Pen point
16 Sportscaster Allen
17 Emcee of *You Asked
   for It*
18 Sunday night TV host
   (2 words)
21 Denise ___
22 *Annie* ___
26 Cry of surprise
28 ___ *Scouts*
31 ___ Lupino
32 Noted Italian family
34 Unit of work
35 *The* ___ *McCoys*
36 Had a TV snack
37 TV canine star
39 Myself
40 *The Lone* ___
42 Mountain pass in TV
   Westerns
44 Star of *O.S.S.* (2 words)
49 *Wagon* ___
52 Friend (Fr.)
53 Part of the foot
54 *Wyatt* ___
55 Brawl
56 Miss Gabor

57 Muggs and Kokomo
58 Otherwise
59 Skelton

down

1 Criticizes
2 Redact
3 George ___
4 ___ *Three*
5 Genus of trees
6 Shaded walk
7 ___ *Trial*
8 ___ Sinatra
9 Hardwood
10 Cereal plant
11 German article
17 ___ *the Clock*
19 Cast a ballot
20 Yearns
23 Recline

24 Dutch cheese
25 Ivy League school
26 Listen to
27 *The Thin Man*'s dog
29 Find out about
30 Stammering sounds
33 The Top ___
35 Peruse
37 Man's name
38 Set on fire
41 Suitcases
43 ___ Lawford of *The
   Thin Man*
45 Train track
46 ___ *'n' Andy*
47 *I* ___ *Lucy*
48 Starring role
49 Beverage
50 Knock
51 *People* ___ *Funny*
55 Concerning

December 7, 1957

across

1 English network (abbr.)
4 TV's Mr. Linkletter
7 Marion on *Robin Hood*
11 Verbal
12 Lt. Frank Ballinger on *M Squad*
13 "___ upon a Time"
14 Phyllis's *Thin Man* role
15 Meadow
16 Poems
17 Rusty Lee on *Steve Donovan, Western Marshal* (2 words)
20 Light metal
21 Hilda Crocker on *December Bride*
25 ___ *Train*
28 Adversary
30 Aural appendage
31 Equable
32 ___ *Miss Brooks*
33 *Tic Tac Dough*, e.g.
34 Bud to Jim on *Father Knows Best*
35 Schultzy on *The Bob Cummings Show*
36 TV announcer Dennis ___
37 Scotch cloth
39 Singer with Garry Moore
40 Gillis on *The Life of Riley* (2 words)
46 Route
49 Atmosphere
50 Seines
51 Buffalo's lake
52 Sailor
53 Yankee outfielder Slaughter
54 Pare
55 Foxy
56 Nickname for TV's youngest Burns

down

1 *Highway Patrol* star
2 Poet
3 TV's Lone Ranger
4 Cpl. Henshaw on *The Phil Silvers Show*
5 Irish dance
6 River duck
7 Last name of 3-Down
8 *Dick ___ the Duchess*
9 Diamonds (sl.)
10 Sandy Kenyon's TV role
11 *Twenty-___*
18 Contestant's goal
19 TV's Liza Hammond
22 Paper measure
23 ___ *That Tune*
24 Greek god of war
25 Cheyenne's region
26 Declare
27 Announcer on *The Steve Allen Show*
28 Sport
29 *Truth ___ Consequences*
32 Atop
33 *Perry Mason* creator
35 Commotion
36 *Ramar of the Jungle*
38 Lucy's neighbor
39 Harry Morton on *The Burns and Allen Show*
41 Rugs
42 Telephone part
43 *State Trooper* setting
44 English school
45 Beast of burden
46 Energy
47 *You ___ There*
48 On *Twenty-One*, this means another game

52 Sound a horn
53 Ernie Ford's state (abbr.)
54 Young insect
55 Schultzy on *The Bob Cummings Show*

down

1 Miss Horne, singer
2 Narrator of *Death Valley Days* (2 words)
3 Philbrick's job
4 Donate
5 Mrs. Groucho Marx
6 Afternoon TV theater
7 Mr. Wallace of TV
8 Salutation
9 *The Thin* ___
10 Termite
11 Overacting actor
18 *Brighter* ___
19 Distress call
21 Door opener
23 Peter Graves' role on *Fury* (2 words)
24 Tart
25 Rodents
26 Stop!
27 Pennsylvania place
28 Star on *Ramar of the Jungle*
29 Cleansing agent
31 Richard Diamond
34 Actress West
35 Utter
39 Comedian recently saluted on TV
40 TV actress Darvis
41 To revise
43 Soon
44 Tiger or lion
45 Small floor covering
46 Malt beverage
47 Sped
49 Greek letter

across

1 ___ Angeles, *Dragnet* locale
4 Precious stone
7 Peggy Wood to viewers
11 *Strike It Rich* to the needy
12 She plays Eve Drake
13 Regular visitor on *The Garry Moore Show*
14 Jingles on *Wild Bill Hickok*
15 An old soldier (sl.)
16 George Reeves' role on *Superman*
17 Disfigure
18 TV singer Lor
20 Alias (abbr.)
22 Negative
23 Container
26 Comedian Youngman
28 Hollywood and TV actress Tandy
30 Jason's ship
31 TV's Sgt. Friday
32 Leave out
33 TV producer, Max ___
35 Tommy ___
36 Region (abbr.)
37 Article
38 Sheena's companion
39 Junior on *The Life of Riley*
42 Col. Hall's secretary on *The Phil Silvers Show*
45 Hostess on *Climax!*
48 Emmy-winning comedian
49 Volcano
50 *Wyatt Earp*'s Bat Masterson, ___ Dinehart
51 Actor Wallach

February 8, 1958

44 Mother of Castor and Pollux
45 Single act

down

1 TV's Lone Ranger
2 Anderson children's reference to Robert Young (2 words)
3 Dined
4 New England state (abbr.)
5 *You Are* ___
6 Peel of a fruit
7 Vase
8 Captain Kangaroo
9 Edgar Bergen's dummy
11 Wound mark
12 TV sportscaster (2 words)
13 *The* ___ *Man*
14 Prop from *Circus Boy*
16 Island of Indonesia
20 PT of *Whirlybirds* (2 words)
23 "To ___ is human"
24 Alcoholic beverage
25 TV station
26 Arthur Godfrey's announcer
27 Sour
28 Scati
30 *The* ___ *Bergen Show*
31 Fills with fear
33 ___ Lynn
35 Dick Wesson's role on *The People's Choice*
37 Eager
40 Mineral deposit
41 Chinese Communist leader
43 Transportation on *Oh! Susanna* (abbr.)

across

1 Lament
5 Pacific Island base during World War II
9 Not north
10 Engage
11 Sound in the night
12 Panelist on *What's My Line?*
15 Last name of 12-Across
16 Sky King's plane, Song ___
17 The woman in question
18 Region
19 Malt beverage
20 Face part
21 Thoroughfare (abbr.)
22 *To* ___ *the Truth*
24 Sky King: Kirby ___
25 TV role played by Macdonald Carey
27 Inspector on *The Lineup*
29 Dagmar on TV's *Mama* show
30 One of the Kettles
32 Cleaning woman in England
33 Lion's home
34 Kid stars do it
36 Electrified particle
37 Breezy
38 Pit
39 Douglas Kennedy's TV role
41 British actor often seen on "Late Shows"
42 TV singer O'Brien
43 Joan Caulfield's TV role

February 15, 1958

60 Place of Napoleon's first exile
61 Pedal digits
62 *I ___ Three Lives*
63 Close by

down

1 Greek god of war
2 Ditch around a castle
3 Trade name of gasoline
4 Perceived
5 19th letter
6 Actor Erickson
7 Raymond Burr's TV role
8 Music director on Gisele MacKenzie's show
9 *___ Gun, Will Travel*
10 Malt beverages
11 Slight depression
19 TV actor Wallach
21 A Mouseketeer
23 Perform on TV
25 Beanie's mother on *Love of Life*
26 ___-Star Golf
27 *Movietime ___*
28 ___ *Gun*
29 Aural appendage
31 Meadow
32 Light brown
33 Total
36 TV's Friday or Smith
39 Utter
41 Woman on *The Phil Silvers Show*
43 Orchestra leader on Rosemary Clooney's show
45 ___ *Kangaroo* (abbr.)
46 Butter substitute
47 ___ Ranger
48 How they went thataway
50 ___ *Hearing*
51 Shoppers' special
52 Brass instrument
53 Winged
56 TV actor Glass

across

1 Family on *The Secret Storm*
5 Shady tree
8 Fish of the herring family
12 Red Skelton's orchestra leader
13 *Victory at ___*
14 Episode of *Wells Fargo*
15 Free from strain
16 Member of the family
17 Kiln
18 Ezra, ___ actor
20 Crunch on *Crunch and Des*
22 Musical note
24 Silent assent
25 Pvt. Doberman on *The Phil Silvers Show*
30 World War 2 Big Three meeting place
34 Otherwise
35 *Tic ___ Dough*
37 Pate
38 Window pane
40 Amy on *The Secret Storm*
42 TV writer Mosel
44 Amos McCoy is a grand one
45 Host of *To Tell The Truth*
49 Hostess on *Climax!*
54 Drug-yielding plant
55 TV's Harry ___ Zell
57 Jeff Kittridge on *Adventure at Scott Island*
58 Animal enclosures
59 Lyric poem

March 8, 1958

down

1 Chemist's workroom
2 *People ___ Funny*
3 Patrice Munsel sang here
4 *Highway ___*
5 Hello!
6 *___ of Night*
7 TV horses often do this
8 Richard ___ of *Tombstone Territory*
9 TV show's first performance
10 ___ Roberts
11 Marshal of Dodge City
16 *It Could Be ___*
20 Annoying children
21 Food fish
22 Apothecaries' weight
23 Like a horror movie
24 Make lace
28 Garden tool
29 *___ Flynn Theater*
30 *The Jack ___ Show*
31 Singer Williams
33 *Boots and ___*
34 *26 ___*
36 Small role
37 ___ Lor
38 Ralph ___, emcee
40 "At the ___," Nick Todd's record
41 Peggy Wood's old TV role
42 ___ Kennedy of *The Californians*
43 A jot
44 Needed on a quiz show
48 ___ Andrews of *The Gray Ghost*
49 Youngster
50 Capt. Frank Hawthorn, for example
53 The man

across

1 *___ unto My Feet*
5 *Look ___ !*
9 Actress Avedon
12 Region
13 *The Big ___* , TV oldie
14 Historical period
15 *The ___ White Show*
17 Cooking fuel
18 Prop for a Western
19 Star of *Trackdown* (2 words)
22 Roundabout way
25 Adjective for any of the Top 10
26 *The ___ McCoys*
27 Where shows try to be in the ratings
30 He "knows best" (sl.)
32 ___ Linkletter

33 Gale ___
34 *The Thin ___*
35 *___ Friend Flicka*
36 Meaner
37 Loser in a Western showdown
38 Comedian recently returned to TV
39 *The ___ Playhouse* (2 words)
41 *Gunsmoke*'s hero (2 words)
45 Fuss
46 ___ Costello
47 ZaSu ___
51 Deface
52 Engrave with acid
54 Type of TV "opera"
55 Girl's name
56 Purpose
57 Nelson ___, singer

May 10, 1958

across

1 Mineral spring
4 ___ Beach, Fla.
8 Section of a TV play
11 TV's Bob Keeshan
13 Phyllis Kirk's TV role
15 Borodin's prince
16 Overhead railways
17 Rynning of *26 Men*
18 About punishment
20 Meadow
22 Kind of lettuce
23 Beverly Garland's TV role
25 Violinist with Lawrence Welk
27 One of TV's Youngs
31 Actress Sophia ___
34 Female sheep
35 Help
37 Farewell
38 ___ *Rangers*
41 Afternoon TV theater
44 Andy's pal
46 Correlative of neither
47 ___-*Star Golf*
49 What a quiz contestant can't afford to do
51 A TV Chevy star
55 Island east of Java
57 Mr. Glass on *The Phil Silvers Show*
59 Unspecified amount
60 Tie on *Twenty-One*
61 Gail Stone on *The Eve Arden Show*
63 She's Schultzy
64 Flavoring for gin
65 ___ *of the Rainbow*

down

1 Mr. Homeier
2 *Big Record* hostess
3 Soon
4 Robert Young's role
5 *People* ___ *Funny*
6 To droop
7 TV writer Tad ___
8 Emmet (arch.)
9 Kelly of *Bachelor Father*
10 The McGuire Sisters
12 Princess of Monaco
14 The donkey
19 TV film studio and adjoining territory
21 Be ill
24 Home-school group (abbr.)
26 ___ *You Trust Your Wife?*
27 Permit
28 Be indebted to
29 Star of *Frontier Doctor* (2 words)
30 A Western hero must have a good one
32 TV's Liza Hammond
33 Born
36 Brad Crawford's role
39 Before noon (abbr.)
40 Rusty to Danny
42 TV's *Gray Ghost*
43 Sheena
45 Paparelli on *The Phil Silvers Show*
47 TV humorist Burrows
48 Volcanic substance
50 Resound
52 Short letter
53 So be it
54 Westerns group
56 *Robin Hood*'s The Blue Boar ___
58 Jeffreys and Sterling
62 ___ *Theater*

May 24, 1958

across

1 Mr. Mineo
4 *Zane ___ Theater*
8 Addition to a house
11 Oolong
12 Roof edge
13 Miss Lane of *Superman*
15 Branch
16 *Studio ___*
17 *___ and Allen*
18 Producer of *Omnibus* (2 words)
21 Droop
22 *___ Maverick*
23 Exist
25 Host of *G.E. Theater*
28 Sailor (colloq.)
31 Pile
33 Acquire
34 *A Turn of ___*
35 ___ Sothern
36 *___ Three*
38 ___ Sullivan
39 Tidy
41 Period of history
43 Costar of *Whirlybirds* (2 words)
48 *The ___ White Show*
49 Regret
50 Macaw
51 Nerve network
52 *Love That ___*
53 ___ *Lancelot*
54 Through
55 Milky-hued stone
56 A limit

down

1 *The ___ and the Story*, TV oldie
2 Air (comb. form)
3 Young sheep
4 Eddie's alternate
5 Talk noisily
6 Many Miss Ardens
7 Early pronoun
8 Avoid
9 ___ Young
10 A connection
14 "Against the Wind" actress (init.)
17 Scorch
19 *Wyatt ___*
20 Diminish
23 Cry of triumph
24 "___ of America"
26 A marble
27 Precious stone
29 Had a snack
30 ___ Skelton
32 ___ Funicello of *Mickey Mouse Club*
34 Card game
36 Canelike
37 Narrate again
40 To record
42 Degrade
43 *___ It in the Family*
44 *Let's Take a ___*
45 Hawaiian dance
46 Miss O'Brien, singer
47 *Scotland ___*
48 British (abbr.)
52 Miss Stafford

June 14, 1958

across

1 Woman on *The Phil Silvers Show*
4 Eve's husband
8 ___ *Point*
12 Building extension
13 A Daly term for "occupation"
14 Source of Samson's strength
15 Blanche on *The Burns and Allen Show*
16 Studio's territory
17 *House* ___
18 Ventriloquist Edgar
20 Small role
21 Singer on *The Garry Moore Show*
22 Richard Simmons' TV role
26 Track left by a ship
28 Worm on a hook
29 Liza Hammond
30 *You* ___ *There*
31 Jessica ___
32 Frank Ballinger on *M Squad*
33 ___ *Tin Tin*
34 Ritual
35 Western "group"
36 Young hero of *Leave It to Beaver*
38 Jim Brown of 33 Across
39 *Boots* ___ *Saddles*
40 He knows best
43 One of the Nelsons
46 Scottish cap
47 Short poem
48 Orchestra leader on Gisele MacKenzie's old show
49 Mrs. "Thin Man"
50 Born
51 Greek letter
52 Fragrance
53 Climax

down

1 TV's Sgt. Friday
2 One Mr. Cobb (2 words)
3 Superman (2 words)
4 The Frontier Doctor
5 Matt Wayne replaced him
6 Gregarious insect
7 Myself
8 ___ *My Line*
9 Hearing organ
10 Pose for a picture
11 Attempt
17 Devoutness
19 Lone Ranger's command to Silver
20 Spring Byington plays a winter one
22 British drawers
23 ___ *Time*
24 State of Polly's "Party"
25 Want
26 Not cool
27 *Voice of Firestone* specialty
28 Bil and Cora ___
31 Tendency
35 Strike
37 Miss Stoddard of *The Secret Storm*
38 Jon Hall's TV role
40 A game for Maverick
41 Groucho's wife
42 *Lineup*'s Fred Asher
43 Gentle blow
44 Chopping tool
45 Cleo's doc
46 *Gray Ghost*'s star
49 You wouldn't say this to M. Anthony

June 21, 1958

across

1 Marshall's *Lineup* role
5 *Tales of* ___ *Fargo*
10 Western show
12 Miss Davies of movie fame
13 Toward the inside
14 *This* ___ *Your Life*
15 Bil Baird's wife
16 Margaret Anderson, e.g.
17 Schultzy
19 Weapon for *Sir Lancelot*
21 ___ *Tunes and New Talent*
22 Tumult
24 Ed Norton in *The Honeymooners*
25 *The Thin* ___
26 TV's Mr. Murrow
28 Seth Adams
29 ___ *Got a Secret*
30 Margaret Irving on *The People's Choice*
31 A suit for Perry Mason
33 Mrs. James Mason
36 TV play section
37 The late Mr. Ziegfeld
38 *What's My* ___?
40 *Riley's* Honey ___
41 Aquatic mammals
43 Time zone (abbr.)
44 ___ *the World Turns*
45 Singer Copeland of *Your Hit Parade*
46 *Adventure* ___ *Scott Island*
48 Exclamation
49 Host of *Death Valley Days*, the Old ___
51 TV's Lone Ranger
53 Progeny
54 TV's Mr. Roberts

down

1 Mr. Tuck of *Robin Hood*
2 TV's youngest Burns
3 Steve Allen's rival
4 "Agnus ___"
5 Hugh Beaumont on *Leave It to Beaver*
6 Emergency Relief Administration (init.)
7 Chinese measure
8 Capt. Monastario on *Zorro*
9 TV singers' finger work
11 Ron Randell's series
12 Music director on Pat Boone's show
15 Small rope
18 A sign of assent
20 Article of merchandise
21 Summer hue
23 Wrench
25 TV writer Tad ___
27 Hail!
28 Skelton's "Freddie the Freeloader"
30 British jail
31 Coca's partner
32 Maverick's favorite card
33 Mr. Paar's show has a loose one
34 Two do it on *To Tell the Truth*
35 Cochise
37 Quiz contestants may feel this
39 Lucy's neighbor
40 Short-billed pigeon
41 Transportation for Sgt. Preston
42 Singer-dancer Davis
45 Past
47 Likewise
50 Not any
52 *Truth* ___ *Consequences*

```
 1 | 2 | 3 | 4 |   |   |   |   | 5 | 6 | 7 |   |
 8 |   |   |   |   | 9 |   | 10|   |   |   | 11|
12 |   |   | 13|   | 18|   | 14|   |   |   | 15|
16 |   | 17|   | 18|   |   |   |   | 19|   |   |
20 |   |   | 21|   | 22|   |   | 23|   |   |   |
   |   | 24|   | 25|   |   | 26|   |   |   |   |
   | 27|   |   |   | 28|   |   |   |   |   |   |
   | 29|   |   |   |   | 30|   |   |   | 31|   |
32 |   |   | 33|   |   | 34|   |   | 35|   |   |
36 |   |   | 37|   |   | 38|   | 39|   |   |   |
40 |   | 41|   |   |   |   | 42|   | 43|   |   |
   | 44|   |   |   | 45|   |   | 46|   |   |   |
   | 47|   |   |   |   | 48|   |   |   |   |   |
```

across

1 Species
5 Wally on *Leave It to Beaver*
8 TV show set in San Francisco
10 Subject of *The Verdict Is Yours*
12 Toro, Kit's Pal
13 Matt of *December Bride* (2 words)
16 Whole
18 Nap
19 Godfrey's drink
20 Smoke
22 ___ *Behind the Badge*
23 Rusty Lee of *Steve Donovan*
24 Furnish
26 Capt. Rynning of *26 Men*
27 Toothed wheel
28 2000 lbs., many times
29 Unemotional
30 Mr. Adams' Eve
32 Pace for Fury
33 Scotch cap
34 Describing TV's *Inner Sanctum*
36 Drowse
37 You'll find one on Welk's show
39 Affirmative
40 Gillis on *The Life of Riley* (2 words)
43 ___ *Theater*
44 Nugey paints these on *Oh! Susanna*
45 Actor on *Navy Log*

47 Born
48 Scheme

down

1 Culprit of many Westerns
2 Not beyond limits
3 Sgt. Pendleton
4 Membership fees
5 Shed drops
6 Petroleum
7 Creator of *Mickey Mouse Club*
8 Shakespearean king
9 TV actress and panelist, Betsy ___
10 Federal men (hyph.)
11 City in England
14 Intimate
15 ___ Charles Singers

17 Announcer on *Bold Journey* (2 words)
21 Sir Lancelot's position for knighthood
23 Kovacs or Ford
25 Robert Young on *Father Knows Best*
26 Favored 10
28 Abnormal swellings
29 Sing like Crosby
30 Bring a plane down
31 Western location
32 Explosive
33 Decades
35 River in France and Belgium
37 Story
38 Harvest
41 Expire
42 Be ill
46 Julius ___ Rosa

August 23, 1958

across

1. Contestant's aim
4. Apportion
8. Narrow opening
12. Summer drink
13. Eager
14. *U.S. Steel* ——
15. Darn
16. Scott Forbes' role
17. Sherry Jackson's role
18. Type of boat on *Harbor Command*
20. Epoch
21. —— *Power*
22. Host of *Person to Person*
26. Phil Silvers' hairdo
28. Actor Williams' TV role
29. Poem
30. Anger
31. Host of *You Asked for It*
33. TV's Captain Kangaroo
34. Five dollars (sl.)
35. TV writer Mosel
36. TV role Carlson made famous
37. Hugh Beaumont on *Leave It to Beaver*
39. That woman
40. *Halls of* ——
41. Host on *Telephone Time*
44. Kitty ——
47. Phil Silvers' WAC
48. Sign of a hit
49. Copied
50. Accumulate
51. Petroleum
52. Book by Zola
53. *To* —— *the Truth*
54. Born

down

1. *Navy Log* carrier
2. Concept
3. *Top Tunes and* —— (2 words)
4. Ward Bond's "rank"
5. Wicked
6. Master of *Lassie*
7. Art Carney's *Honeymooners* role
8. Clip wool
9. TV singer Denise
10. —— *Miss Brooks*
11. Attempt
17. —— *or Consequences*
19. Abolish
20. Emanate
23. *Wells Fargo* star
24. Effluvium
25. Star of *Dragnet*
26. Joe Sawyer's *Rin Tin Tin* role
27. Specialty on *Voice of Firestone*
28. *The Cisco* ——
31. TV's Mr. Donovan
32. Jack Benny's wife
36. Bewitch
38. Verna Felton's *December Bride* role
39. Miss Court, actress
41. First name of 28-Across
42. Lake between U.S. and Canada
43. Actor's part
44. Star follower
45. Wartime agency (init.)
46. Longing
47. Prevaricate
50. Craig Hill's *Whirlybirds* role

September 6, 1958

across

1 TV program
5 Breslin and Boone
9 Trinitrotoluene
12 Des Moines is the capital
13 African lily
14 Border
15 Perry Mason's secretary
17 Blanche Morton of *Burns and Allen*
18 Before
19 ___ *Tac Dough*
21 A Mouseketeer
23 Studio equipment
26 Employ
27 Repeatedly
28 Announcer on *The Jack Paar Show*
31 Exert
33 Clangor
34 Doctrine
35 ___ 10
36 Wynn or Sullivan
37 Inn
38 Military assistant
39 "Relatives," á la oaters
40 Lawrence Welk's "Sisters"
42 Pete Porter's phantom wife
45 Sink
46 Margin
47 Comedian Knotts
49 Jim Roberts' voice
53 Ida Lupino's role
54 Repute
56 Violinist with Welk
57 Legislator (abbr.)
58 Warren ___, producer
59 Toward the sheltered side

down

1 Mr. Caesar
2 Garden tool
3 Bird of prey
4 Grandpa McCoy
5 Robert Young's role
6 Long white linen vestment
7 Digits of the foot
8 Lloyd Bridges' show (2 words)
9 Thither
10 Fiddle-playing emperor
11 Government agents (hyph.)
16 ___ *Power*
20 *West Point* role
22 A dolt
23 ___ *Three*
24 Eager
25 ___ *of Annapolis*
29 The *Studio* in Hollywood
30 ___ *Fargo*
31 Extinct bird
32 Frank
34 Wally of *Leave It to Beaver* (2 words)
35 Soft metal
37 Concealed
38 Linda on *The Danny Thomas Show*
39 Charader on *Pantomime Quiz*
41 Consume
42 Stoneware (Fr.)
43 "In the flesh" TV
44 Soft drink
48 Error
50 Nothing
51 Suffix denoting like
52 Fish eggs
55 *Dough* ___ *Mi*

November 1, 1958

down

1 Witness TV
2 To append
3 State of many fall TV shows
4 Glossy paint
5 Youth
6 Contestant's fear
7 Chewing or bubble
8 Comedian Kaye
9 Steve Canyon, e.g.
10 Press
14 Solemn wonder
16 Ed Sullivan's orchestra leader
17 Fabulous bird
20 A digest
21 Dry
22 Grievous
23 He plays *Robin Hood*'s sheriff
25 A blow
26 Trouble
27 A fountain
28 Toy on a string
31 ___ Abner
33 Cochise on *Broken Arrow*
34 *Zorro*'s Monastario
35 Residue
36 College cheer
37 Had a special "50th Anniversary Show" in '57 (init.)
38 Teller of false tales
39 Land measure
42 Geological time
43 Landing craft seen on *Navy Log* (abbr.)
44 *All-Star Golf* gadget
45 Impair
46 Black bird
47 Weaken

across

1 Sound
5 Supports
9 Hello!
11 Paradise
12 "In ___"; having difficulty (2 words)
13 Period
15 Host of *Small World* (full name)
18 Jane Wyatt on *Father Knows Best*
19 Richard or Pat
20 Actor Richard ___
23 TV network (abbr.)
24 TV's Mr. Roberts
25 New *Voice of Firestone* host
27 Near
29 Performed
30 Eve of *Mr. Adams and Eve*
31 Fifth sign of Zodiac
32 Mr. Sullivan
33 Presently
34 Spring Byington's television role
35 Communal insect
36 Dick Wesson's role
37 Sgt. Pendleton of Phil Silvers' show
40 Before noon (abbr.)
41 TV's *Combat Sergeant* (2 words)
48 *M Squad* vehicle
49 Composer-conductor David ___
50 Novel by Zola
51 *Dough ___ Mi*
52 Poker stake
53 Trickle

December 6, 1958

across

1 *You ___ Your Life*
4 Sheep bleat
7 Where Susanna works
11 Son-in-law of Mohammed
12 Complaint about TV commercials
13 Grasp
14 TV's Robin Hood
16 *Love of Life* family
17 Pitcher
18 Mining material
19 *Thin Man*'s terrier
22 Shade trees
24 Nurture
25 Affirmative
26 Beverage
29 *Playhouse 90*'s ex-producer (2 words)
33 Sold out (abbr.)
34 Actress West
35 Kind of fuel
36 Ali of "The Arabian Nights"
37 Withered
38 Unit of energy
39 Erase
42 TV's Bilko
44 Public speakers
48 A kick
49 Oscillate
50 Be prostrate
51 *Father Knows ___*
52 Randell's old show
53 He's Wally

down

1 TV Western set
2 Actor Wallach
3 *___ Tac Dough*
4 Past of bear
5 Steve Allen's sister-in-law (2 words)
6 TV commercial
7 Principals on TV
8 *___ Gun, Will Travel*
9 Mr. President
10 It's mightier than the sword
12 Perry Mason's forte
15 Schultzy would like to have Bob's
16 Actress Ruth ___
19 Singer Russell ___
20 Burn
21 Hawaiian root
23 Grassland
26 Toward the sheltered side
27 Teller of tall tales
28 Italian family
30 TV picture
31 Seize
32 Overturn
36 Actor Lomond
38 Yankee outfielder Slaughter
40 Periods
41 Place
42 Abate
43 Fish eggs
45 What TV players hope never to be
46 ___ Grande
47 Baste
49 Thus

December 20, 1958

down

1 *Search for* ___
2 Arabian gulf
3 Helium or neon
4 Opera by Massenet
5 Rattle when breathing
6 Baseball referee (sl.)
7 *Dough Re* ___
8 A fold
9 English school
10 El ___, Kit Carson's pal
11 *Gunsmoke* set
13 There are many such shows this year
18 The Lone Ranger's nephew
22 Shanty
23 Producer McCleery to friends
24 Violinist with Lawrence Welk
26 A Gershwin
27 Boat propellants
28 Sailor
29 More than an amateur
30 Bilko
32 Frank Smith of *Dragnet*
34 Matt Rockford of *Cimarron City*
36 Negative
37 New York opera house
39 *The Verdict Is* ___
41 Leather worker's tool
42 Hunt
43 Defendant's petition on *Traffic Court*
44 Bard
45 Outrigger canoe
47 *Brighter* ___
48 Mr. President (affectionate)
49 United Kingdom network (init.)
51 Newspaper item

across

1 A game for Beaver and Timmy
4 Instrument for Rocky Rockwell
11 Drugstore drink
12 Mr. Burger on *Perry Mason*
14 Actress Teal ___
15 Very high mountain
16 *Zorro*'s time
17 Mr. Welk's favorite Alice
18 Windup for most TV "baddies"
19 Present time
20 *Truth* ___ *Consequences*
21 ___ *the World Turns*
22 TV's Mr. March
25 Hunter constellation
28 Flowers from Holland
31 Mrs. *Thin Man*
32 He fights with a cane
33 Remnant
35 Jack who makes TV films
37 Silverheels' pal
38 Mark of *The Rifleman*
39 Archaic "you"
40 *Down You* ___, TV oldie
41 Egyptian viper
44 Cooking utensil
45 For each
46 Fuse
48 Promissory note (init.)
49 Boast
50 Rusty of *Rin Tin Tin* (2 words)
52 Reward for Lassie
53 Singing group with Sammy Kaye
54 Recent *Millionaire* star

March 7, 1959

across

1 Penny's relation to Sky King
6 Actress Hunter
9 TV marshal
10 Spoken
12 Roman 54
13 Directed
14 TV picture
16 Across
18 Needed for *Highway Patrol*
19 News agency (abbr.)
20 Where 1-Across lives
22 Curve
23 Twenty-third Greek letter
24 Passageway
26 TV special, "___ Little Indians"
27 TV network (sl.)
30 Mike Nelson of *Sea Hunt*
32 Cool beverage
33 A drink for Robin Hood
34 Wally Cleaver, e.g.
36 A trap for game
37 Timmy of *Lassie*
38 TV's Ellery Queen
42 Atop
43 Detetive on *Naked City*
44 Serving container
45 Jody on *Buckskin*
47 Female sheep
50 Before
51 To storm
52 Hamilton Burger of *Perry Mason*

54 Saturated
55 *You ___ for It*

down

1 TV actor David ___
2 French "he"
3 Building addition
4 Producer Fred ___
5 Termination
6 *Man with a Camera*
7 Fleur-de-lis
8 Rabid
9 Prima donna
11 Hired
12 Singer Denise ___
15 Think
17 Color TV pioneer
18 Johnny ___, music director-composer
21 Kept out of sight

22 Man's name
23 Home-school group
25 Actress Simone ___
27 ___ *Train*
28 Betty in *Father Knows Best*
29 Lieutenant on *The Lineup*
31 The younger Burns
35 Epithet for a baddie
37 A Lennon sister
39 Terror
40 Merit
41 Cereal grass
43 Orchestra leader Rose
46 Perry Mason's forte
47 Seventh Greek letter
48 Part of verb to be
49 Large deer
53 Personal pronoun

April 4, 1959

across

1 Existed
4 *Highway Patrol* star
8 Cantor's daughters
12 Mr. Burrows
13 The Hawkeye State
14 Cowboys go that ___
15 TV network
16 Defunct quiz show
(2 words)
18 *Perry Mason's* creator
20 Caviar
21 Nineteenth letter
22 Warrior (obs.)
23 Possessed
26 Wayne of *The Californians*
28 Shang dynasty
29 Gabor sister
30 Wing (Lat.)
31 Villainous
32 Nothing
33 Impair
34 Gene Barry
35 Singer Nelson ___
36 Some
37 Small bit of food
38 Mineral deposit
39 ___ *Love or Money*
40 Meadow bird
42 Paar's pianist
(2 words)
47 Undermine
49 Miss Adams
50 Prong
51 Undivided
52 Composition
53 Ernie Ford's state
(abbr.)
54 Novel

down

1 Pallid
2 An ecclesiastic
3 Della Street's job
4 Stings
5 Tier
6 "Run a tab"
7 Lone Ranger's
nephew (2 words)
8 Alice ___
9 ___ Jima
10 Dick ___ Dyke
11 CBS symbol
17 Actor Rip ___
19 Landing craft (abbr.)
22 Hugh O'Brian's
role
23 Steve Allen's
orchestra leader
24 Eager
25 *What's My Line?* host
26 Peggy Wood's
famous role
27 Ladd often seen
late at night
31 Elizabeth of
Wimpole Street
34 TV studio
equipment
35 Vast age
38 Cub reporter on
Superman
39 *Lamp unto my* ___
41 *Today* director
42 Craft for Canyon
43 Short poem
44 *Twenty-___ Men*
45 Falsehood
46 TV animal trainer
Frank ___
48 Church bench

April 25, 1959

across

1 Baby's napkin
4 Daub
9 ___ *Hunt*
12 Lyric poem
13 Cowboy's pal
14 Katy O'Connor
15 ___ Hale of *Perry Mason*
17 Mr. Bregman
19 A home for Pahoo-Ka-Ta-Wah
20 Lassie, e.g.
21 Reach across
22 Richard Boone's role
26 Cry of triumph
27 ___ *Hearing*
29 Mr. Carney's friend Harvey
30 Denise ___
31 Saltpeter
33 Insect egg
34 Places of refuge
36 ___ Henderson of *26 Men*
37 Nineteenth letter
38 Cuddler
40 German composer
42 ___ *Miss Brooks*
43 *To ___ the Truth*
44 *Father ___ Best*
47 Star of *Decoy*
50 Mr. Hunter, actor
51 *Who Do You ___?*
53 Cereal grass
54 Gets in the hair of many actresses
55 Two of the Rough Riders
56 Mr. Murray, actor

down

1 ___ Cummings
2 ___ Lupino
3 Emcee of *County Fair* (2 words)
4 The D.A.'s Man
5 ___ Sahl, comedian
6 Epoch
7 ___ *the World Turns*
8 Major Mosby
9 Describes soap operas
10 All-night movies never seem to ___
11 No matter what one
16 ___ Benaderet
18 Western state
20 TV discussion group
21 Dinah ___
22 ___ Breck of *Black Saddle*
23 Star of *Deadline for Action* (2 words)
24 Hibernian
25 ABC, CBS and NBC (sl.)
26 Col. Humphrey Flack
28 What Maverick isn't
32 Gale Storm's captain
35 Pack
39 Merman's voice
41 ___-*Star Golf*
43 Acting's one for an actor
44 *Cisco ___*
45 Negative vote
46 *Studio ___*, oldie
47 *Restless ___*
48 Knotts's pal
49 Cozy room
52 Sun god

May 2, 1959

across

1 Shelley Fabares on Donna Reed's show
5 Dinah has lots of it
8 What Jack Smith wants you to do
11 African lily
12 Feeding place for Fury
13 Part of a TV set
15 Fred Asher on *Lineup*
17 Mrs. Robert Sterling
18 Some
19 Upon
20 Supply with weapons
22 Depart
23 Misery
24 Nickname for Mr. Arnaz
25 Indefinite article
26 Descriptive of Mr. Bluster
29 Caesar
30 Gershwin brother
31 Beast on *Bold Journey*
32 Actor Bobby ——
33 Redolence
34 Jada Rowland on *The Secret Storm*
35 Gene Barry's TV role
36 She's Liz Fraser
37 Shannon's boss
38 TV Rough Rider
39 *State Trooper* star
40 *Young —— Malone*
41 *People —— Funny*
42 *For Love —— Money*
43 Falsehood
46 Household appliance
48 —— *Yard*
51 Not any
52 Drunkard
53 Not twice
54 Trap

55 Burro
56 Comedian Orson ——

down

1 Donna to 1-Across
2 TV's Casey Jones
3 The Texan
4 Logical response to Mike Anthony's offer
5 Sky King's "Song Bird"
6 "Extra" on *Sea Hunt*
7 Richard Boone's role
8 Wagonmaster on TV
9 Subject for *Accused*
10 Favorite TV Captain
14 *Naked City* producer
16 Friar Tuck's cowl
21 Clem Kaddidlehopper
23 TV contestants hope to do this

26 Violinist with Welk
27 George Montgomery's TV town
28 A Mouseketeer
29 Took a seat
30 Wedding response (2 words)
32 Mrs. Raven on *Love of Life*
33 —— Ranger of *Death Valley Days*
35 TV Western prop
36 Sgt. Bilko's home
38 A Lennon sister
39 *From These ——*
43 *Superman* reporter
44 Indian of Peru
45 Mrs. Groucho Marx
47 Individual
49 Variety of lettuce
50 Tennis term

June 3, 1959

down

1 Grandpa McCoy's home
2 South African lily
3 Richard Coogan on *The Californians* (2 words)
4 Attempt
5 Background of many *Silent Service* shows
6 Son-in-law of Mohammed
7 TV disc jockey Clark
8 Vivian Vance's role
9 Knight's title
10 Increase
11 Petrol
17 Gone by
19 Young sheep
22 Related
23 *Wagon* ___
25 Francis and Cerf, e.g.
26 Great Lake
27 Harry Von ___
28 Plead
29 Cruise
31 Important in TV scheduling
35 Bridle strap
41 Small bed
42 *Who Do You* ___?
44 Small insect
46 Miss Raines, actress
48 Chair
49 ___ *of Night*
50 TV writer Mosel
51 In debt
52 A *Jack Benny Show* regular
53 Denise ___, singer
54 However

across

1 *Hall of* ___
5 Singer Tom ___
9 Droop
12 Exclamation of pity
13 Dismounted
14 Miss Lupino
15 Decays
16 TV's Jefferson Drum
18 Gold or silver
20 Ale container
21 Mrs. Anderson of *Father Knows Best*
24 Actor Perry ___
28 "Inside ___"
30 Mr. Sahl, comedian
32 *You* ___ *There*, oldie
33 Orchestra leader for Ed Sullivan
34 Caesar's third "wife"
36 Nothing
37 Alcoholic beverage
38 U.S. coin
39 Moray
40 Choose
43 Lois Lane of *Superman*
45 Mineral deposit
47 Clamor
50 Inspector Grebb of *The Lineup* (2 words)
55 Employed
56 Reverent fear
57 Any of various American wild plums
58 Male deer
59 Comedian Moore
60 Small pie
61 Italian family

across

1 Davenport
5 Taxi
8 Lyric poems
12 Mr. Kennedy, actor
13 Be in debt
14 Carry (colloq.)
15 Nick's wife
16 Ellery Queen
17 *Name That ___*
18 Host of *G.E. Theater* (2 words)
21 Thirsty
22 Evergreen tree
23 *Zane Grey ___*
27 ___ *Line*
31 Petroleum
32 Electrical unit
34 New Mexican Indian
35 Perry Mason's secretary
38 Singer of *Pete Kelly's Blues*
41 TV spy show
43 Born
44 Actor in *Wagon Train* (2 words)
50 Peter ___ Hayes
51 Unlucky
52 Small bottle
54 *Lamp ___ My Feet*
55 *Top Pro Golf* gadget
56 Miss Fitzgerald
57 Costar of *How to Marry a Millionaire*

58 Exclamation
59 *The Donna ___ Show*

down

1 ___ *Francisco Beat*
2 Scent
3 Gambling game
4 Blake of *Gunsmoke*
5 Emcee of *Beat the Clock*
6 Daunted
7 *Circus Boy* costar
8 City in Gisele's country
9 Newscaster Edwards
10 Sicilian volcano
11 Observed on TV
19 ___ Linkletter
20 Lamprey
23 The Gray Ghost

24 Hasten
25 Building wing
26 One *Rough Rider* is a "Johnny ___"
28 Utilize
29 *Rawhide*'s Favor
30 ___ March
33 The Texan
36 *Saber of ___*
37 Inquire
39 Weight of India
40 Costar of *Gunsmoke*
42 Costar of *77 Sunset Strip*
44 Air vent
45 Fruit skin
46 Poker stake
47 TV's talking dog
48 Flooring square
49 She plays 35-Across
53 Tommy Nolan, e.g.

July 4, 1959

across

1 Rockford of *Cimarron City*
5 Commercials
8 Dust cloth
11 A *Voice of Firestone* specialty
12 Right for the horse's mouth
13 Dismounted
15 Tear
16 Seldom found in a Western
17 Christmas
18 Rowdy on *Rawhide*
20 "Spectacular" producer
22 The "Perfect Fool"
24 Katy to Olive
25 Featured with Moore
30 Wells Fargo had to have 'em
34 Case for small articles
35 Sweet potato
37 TV Canine
38 Miss Palmer
40 *The Lineup* setting (2 words)
42 Dance (colloq.)
44 Twelfth greek letter
45 Announcer with Allen
49 *Perry Mason* detective
54 Spread for bread
55 Geological time
57 Singer O'Brien
58 Plays *December Bride* son-in-law
59 Sign of a hit show (abbr.)
60 Yugoslav leader
61 Before
62 Blue (colloq.)
63 Summer drinks

down

1 Donna Reed's TV daughter
2 Space on the surface
3 Shade
4 Arthur of *Search for Tomorrow*
5 TV network
6 Part of a TV set
7 *77 Sunset ___*
8 Orchestra leader (2 words)
9 An astringent
10 Monster or river
14 Half a score
19 *Silent Service* setting
21 An organ for TV
23 State not often enjoyed by Mike Nelson
25 Socialite (sl.)
26 North American Indian
27 Groove
28 Mr. Brinegar of 18-Across
29 The Lawman
31 Arabian caliph
32 Producer Jaime ___ Valle
33 The sun
36 Peg on *Life of Riley*
39 *Who Do ___ Trust?*
41 *Beat the Clock* host
43 *Meet the ___*
45 State trooper
46 On the lee
47 Lunar or solar
48 Mrs. Thin Man
50 TV's Miss Shaw
51 Parched
52 Ben Franklin's toy
53 "Country Slaughter"
56 Bow the head

July 18, 1959

across

1. Label
4. ___ Wooley of *Rawhide*
8. Cornelia ___ Skinner
12. Color
13. Ancient Irish capital
14. Kind of meat
15. Tavern
16. Mike Nichols' partner (2 words)
18. Ed's rival
20. David Niven, e.g.
21. *Wild ___ Hickok*
23. Girl's name
27. Mowbray of *Col. Flack*
29. Small island
32. ___ Lupino
33. Jack Kelly's role
34. New (comb.)
35. Flutter
36. Be mistaken
37. Bruin
38. To sheltered side
39. Ty Hardin's role
41. Measure of length
43. ___ Roberts
46. *The Lawless ___*
49. Costar of *Whirlybirds* (2 words)
53. *It Could Be ___*
54. Pronoun
55. Butter substitute
56. ___ Arden
57. *___ Kelly's Blues*
58. Gape
59. Clique

down

1. *___ Is Alice*
2. Female relative
3. Star of *Bat Masterson* (2 words)
4. *U.S. ___ Hour*
5. Mr. March
6. Epochs
7. Fishing lure
8. "Amahl," for example
9. ___ Tully of *The Lineup*
10. Mr. Gershwin
11. ___ *King*
17. ___ *That Tune*
19. John Payne's role
22. *What's My ___?*
24. Was host of *Music Theater* (2 words)
25. ___ Adams
26. TV movies: time, not date
27. Son of Adam
28. State in Venezuela
30. ___ *Hunt*
31. She was in *How to Marry a Millionaire*
35. ___ *the Nation*
37. Star of *The Goldbergs*
40. Din
42. Synthetic fiber
44. Nautical greeting
45. Girl's name
47. Emulate Paladin
48. Hard fat
49. *A Naked City* man
50. Regret
51. ___ Carney
52. Actor Ayres

August 1, 1959

across

1 Lt. Masters of 26-Across
4 ___ *Trooper*
9 Golly!
12 Miss Gabor
13 Integrity
14 Branch
15 Host of *Perry Presents*
17 Ty Hardin's role
19 Dave King's "Z"
20 Costar of *Rough Riders*
21 Leave out
23 TV's Miss Benaderet
25 Watched TV
26 ___ *Tin Tin*
27 Host of *The Price Is Right*
29 Betty in *Father Knows Best* (2 words)
34 Panelist on *What's My Line?*
35 Ibsen character
36 TV's Mr. Kennedy
39 *People* ___ *Funny*
40 ___ Roberts
41 Police show
43 Goddess of healing
44 Disembarks
45 Marvin Miller's handout
49 Silkworm
50 Delightful places
52 Ram's mate
53 Louis ___, comedian
54 *The* ___ *Reed Show*
55 *Amateur Hour* host

down

1 One *Rough Rider* is a Johnny ___
2 ___ *Got a Secret*
3 Pat Harrington Jr.'s alias
4 Lean-to
5 *Romper Room* fan
6 Small insect
7 *Leave It* ___ *Beaver*
8 *Perry Mason* author
9 Merrily (alt.)
10 *Brenner*'s son
11 Make corrections
16 Fishing snare
18 Circus ring
20 *Young Dr.* ___
21 Pay dirt
22 Wire measure
23 Coarse cloth
24 Senior
27 Heart (anat.)
28 Compass point (abbr.)
30 Pleased emcee deWitt
31 Ricky's mom
32 *Jubilee* ___
33 Snakelike fish
36 *Burns &* ___
37 *Detective*'s ___
38 *Tugboat* ___
40 Petroleum
42 Secondhand
43 Party-giver Maxwell
45 *26* ___
46 Tavern
47 Have creditors
48 Man's nickname
51 *Who* ___ *You Trust?*

September 26, 1959

across

1 ___ Merlin of *Rough Riders*
4 Smear
8 Envelop
12 Artificial language
13 ___ *of Night*
14 Whetstone
15 TV comedian (2 words)
17 *The Thin Man*'s dog
18 Border
19 *The U.S. ___ Hour*
20 South American country
23 Local positions
26 Angry
28 In no way
29 *On ___ Go*
32 TV's lively hostess (2 words)
35 Compass point (abbr.)
36 Fish eggs
37 *Johns Hopkins* host
38 *Day in ___*
40 Stained
41 Auxiliary verb
44 Function
46 ___ Albright of *Peter Gunn*
47 *Bachelor Father* niece
52 Mimic
53 Miss Magnani
54 ___ *Got a Secret*
55 Miss McCormack played this "bad girl"
56 *Father Knows ___*
57 A Boone

down

1 ___ Arness
2 Stir
3 And not
4 Lucille's mate
5 *Gunsmoke*'s Doc
6 Indian grunt
7 Babylonian god
8 ___ *My Line?*
9 David ___, conductor-composer
10 Poker stake
11 Resound
16 *To Tell the ___*
19 Arrangement
20 Bishop ___
21 Periods of time
22 Estimate
24 ___ *Sanctum*, an oldie
25 ___ Poston
27 Mr. Flynn, actor
29 City in New York
30 Costar of *Perry Mason*
31 Watched TV
33 *It Could Be ___*
34 Western entertainment
38 Dick ___
39 *As the World ___*
41 Cuff
42 TV comedian
43 Pianist Templeton
45 Scram, cat!
47 Taxi
48 This *Studio* is off the air
49 ___ Masters in *Rin Tin Tin*
50 Miss Gardner
51 Snare

across

1 By way of
4 Roncam's boss
8 Star of *Perry Mason*
12 Kookie
13 *Suspicion* summer host
14 Bewildered
15 Beverage
16 Beauty spot
17 TV newscaster
18 Houseboy in *Bachelor Father* (2 words)
21 Title for Olivier
22 *The Lawless* ___
26 The "Perfect Fool"
28 TV canine star
32 Pinch
33 One of 48-Down
35 Locale for *Men into Space*
36 *Lamp ___ My Feet*
37 Sister to Zsa Zsa
38 Costar of *How to Marry a Millionaire*
40 Nearby
41 Joanna Barnes's job on *21 Beacon Street*
43 Over (contr.)
45 Star of *Black Saddle* (2 words)
51 ___ Wyatt of *Father Knows Best*
54 To sheltered side
55 Payable
56 Frontier for movies
57 A king
58 Unlike Mike Nelson
59 Mrs. Thin Man
60 Seasoning
61 Good answer to Michael Anthony

down

1 The Rough Riders
2 Start of a TV show
3 *Gunsmoke*'s Doc
4 ___ *Three*
5 Musical instrument
6 Solid to liquid
7 Spread for bread
8 Emblem for Brenner
9 *Jubilee* ___
10 Electrical unit
11 ___ Milland
19 Distance measure
20 Louis ___
23 ___ Sothern
24 Miss Hayworth
25 Type of TV commercial
26 Pieced out
27 British King
29 ___ *Francisco Beat*
30 ___ Caesar
31 Wrath
34 *Tic ___ Dough*
36 One who uses
38 Sailor's "yes"
39 Horton or Young
42 NBC has its own company
44 *Ruff and ___*
46 Makes lace
47 Miss Maxwell
48 *The ___ McCoys*
49 Remedy
50 Piano levers
51 ___ Provost
52 Fuss
53 And not

October 10, 1959

across

1 Singer Tommy ___
6 Opera by Verdi
10 Baily of *77 Sunset Strip*
11 Actress Merry ___
13 Star of *Trackdown*
14 Recede
16 One time
17 Increase
18 Contend
19 Make lace
20 Tiny state (abbr.)
21 *Tales of ___ Fargo*
23 Ruthenium symbol
24 Edible bulbs
27 The Lawman
30 Transgresses
31 A pearl
32 Periods of time
34 Pahoo-Ka-Ta-Wha
36 Yard (abbr.)
37 He plays 10 Across
39 That person
41 Veneration
43 Singer Alice ___
44 *Divorce Court* subject
45 Old Irish capital
47 Hold

48 Nucleus
49 *Honeymooners* neighbor
51 Betty Anderson
53 Legal document
54 *Love of Life* family

down

1 TV workshop
2 ___ lang syne
3 Short sleep
4 *Frontier* ___ (abbr.)
5 Peter Gunn
6 Indefinite article
7 Wedding response (2 words)
8 Depression
9 *Naked City* cop
10 Blemish
11 Cain's brother

12 Organization
15 Belonging to Baird
21 *For Better or___*
22 Water vapor
25 Born
26 Bore
28 Operated
29 Unusual
31 Roy or Ernie
32 Margaret Anderson
33 Mr. Binns
34 Forehead
35 Pennsylvania city
38 Field of floating ice
40 Pitcher
42 Lake bordering Ohio
44 ___ *Ranger*
46 Hewing tool
48 104 (Rom.)
50 Contraction of "I would"
52 *Rescue 8* locale (abbr.)

November 21, 1959

across

1 Energy (sl.)
4 He has a black saddle
8 Microbe
12 Scull
13 *The* —— *Ranger*
14 Cleveland's lake
15 *Lassie*'s boy
17 Explain
18 Sherbet
19 *Bourbon* —— *Beat*
20 *Colonel* ——
23 Newscaster Edwards
24 *The* —— *Word*
25 —— Cerf
28 *Lamp* —— *My Feet*
29 Miss Claire
30 Dip water from
32 Star of *Adventures in Paradise*
34 Forearm bone
35 Hamburger rolls
36 *Meet the* ——
37 Over
40 —— Murray
41 Dick ——
42 Morgan's rank
46 A baddie may do this
47 *Amateur Hour* host

48 Pay dirt on *Bonanza*
49 —— *of Night*
50 Printing fluids
51 Tiny

down

1 Soft drink
2 Hearing organ
3 Sports seen on TV (sl.)
4 *Beat the* ——
5 Fail at *Concentration*
6 Emmet
7 Early pronoun
8 TV comedian (2 words)
9 *Perry Mason* author
10 Split
11 —— *McGraw*
16 TV comedian-pianist (2 words)
17 Stupefy

19 Submarine detector
20 Bad "sniffles"
21 —— Jeffries of *Rescue 8*
22 *The Thin Man*'s dog
23 Sand tracts (Brit.)
25 Star of *Brenner*
26 *Wells Fargo* story
27 Cans
31 Spanish article
33 Evening period
36 Emcee Bert ——
37 Tooth complaint
38 Clothed
39 Pealed
40 —— Kelly of *Maverick*
42 *The D.A.'s* ——
43 —— *to Marry a Millionaire*
44 *People* —— *Funny*
45 —— Marvin of *M Squad*
47 *Dough Re* ——

58

December 5, 1959

across

1 The Texan
5 Music director Ayres
13 Great Lake
14 Schultzy (2 words)
15 Necessary for *World Championship Golf*
16 Connecticut (abbr.)
17 Catalogue
18 Mrs. Baird
21 *Rescue 8* setting (abbr.)
22 Girl's name
25 Rocky wears one in *The Alaskans*
28 Loudly
29 Jim of *Wells Fargo*
32 Good height for a TV hero
33 Broadcast
34 Fluctuate
36 Craftiest
38 Thick
39 Large deer
40 Kookie's street
41 ___ *the World Turns*
43 Found on a cowboy
44 *Life ___ Father*, oldie
46 Lorne Greene's role
47 Availed
51 Gunn's gal (2 words)
54 Grandpa McCoy's word for vex
55 Jacoby of *Peter Gunn*
56 Writer Gardner

down

1 *You ___ Your Life*
2 Anger
3 Falsehood
4 He's on *Today*
5 Lily to Ruth on *December Bride*
6 Indian of Peru
7 Useful to the Troubleshooters
8 Defense group (init.)
9 Mr. March
10 Marshals fight it
11 Anna-___ on *Black Saddle*
12 Navy craft (init.)
19 Ancient
20 *Dough ___ Mi*
22 Feline
23 Exclamation of sorrow
24 Rock 'n' ___
25 TV Western prop
26 *For Better ___ Worse*
27 *High ___*, oldie
29 Top TV show
30 Scotch for John's
31 Gaelic
33 Request
35 Still
37 Overhead railway
38 Louis and Keely, e.g.
40 Thus
41 Military assistant
42 Agitate
43 Poet
44 Snare
45 Fowl
46 A score on *All-Star Golf*
48 Olivier's title
49 Building addition
50 Scotch river
52 Exclamation of joy
53 A note on Sinatra's scale

across

1 Bad
5 Small quantity
9 Navy craft (init.)
12 Parasitic insects
13 Land measure
14 Had lunch
15 Hal Peary's TV role
18 Negative
19 Star of *Bold Venture*
20 Garroway's show
23 Hunt
25 Beyond
26 Man seen on *Hennesey*
27 Screen Actors Guild (abbr.)
30 Try out for a role
31 Decompose
32 Give charity
33 Cessation
34 Olivier's title
35 Mrs. Marx
36 Iota
37 *Men into ___*
38 Producer Del Valle
41 Exclamation of surprise
42 Rochester (2 words)
49 Bind
50 Two did on *To Tell the Truth*
51 Weird (var.)
52 Station (abbr.)
53 Czech river
54 Feminine suffix

down

1 A tree
2 By way of
3 Frigid
4 Jack E. ___, comedian
5 Date for a guy
6 NBC's parent company
7 *House Party* host
8 Melody Lee ___ of *Bourbon Street Beat*
9 Fluid rock
10 Agitate
11 East Indian wood
16 Dennis Joel on *The Betty Hutton Show*
17 Class
20 Ripped
21 Kiln
22 *Wanted— ___ or Alive*
23 Susanna Pomeroy
24 Dine
27 Drugstore drink
28 Actor Guinness
29 Bat Masterson
31 River (Sp.)
32 *Hotel ___* (2 words)
34 *Hawaiian Eye*'s Tracy ___
36 Friend to Simone Genet
37 The girl above
38 Modern planes
39 Mine passage
40 Start of a TV show
43 Be sick
44 Pen point
45 President's monogram
46 TV receiver
47 Food fragment
48 Comic Louis ___

February 27, 1960

3 Eliminate
4 Electric current (abbr.)
5 Nicky on *The Betty Hutton Show*
6 Image
7 Adjective for *Alcoa Presents*
8 The rear of *Mr. Lucky*'s ship
9 Persia
10 William ___
11 Kookie's talk
13 *Hotel* ___ (2 words)
18 Her *Person to Person* visit was canceled
19 Turf
21 Cross-examine
23 Dennis the Menace
25 Danny Thomas' producer
26 ___ *Eye*
27 Scandinavian coin
29 By way of
33 Hat (sl.)
34 Posed
37 Seasons for *Continental Classroom*
38 Montana city
40 Charles Lamb's pen name
42 Temptation
43 At that time
44 Lampreys
45 Jaime ___ Valle
47 Crafty
49 ___ *Alaskans*
52 105 (Rom.)

across

1 Show starring Robert Fuller
8 Relief
11 Subject for *Tightrope!*
12 Producer Coe
14 ___ *Three Lives* (2 words)
15 Singer Denise
16 Domesticate
17 Step for the Murrays
18 Pianist with Paar
20 Pile
21 Carbon monoxide
22 An age
24 Sun god
25 Miss Dinah
28 Capital of Delaware
30 Mata's partner
31 Singer Stevens

32 Actor Tom ___
34 ___ *Trooper*
35 Note of the scale
36 Illuminated
38 Express contempt
39 Expire
41 First show of a series
43 Mr. Mack
46 Olive and corn
48 Epithet for a baddie
49 Biblical pronoun
50 Talon
51 Mr. Ayres of music
53 Negative vote
54 *Peter Gunn*

down

1 Edie of *Peter Gunn*
2 A policewoman on *The Lineup*

March 5, 1960

across

1. A Real McCoy
5. Keeps Highway Patrol on the road
8. Singer Molly ___
11. Picture puzzle
13. Mr. Carney
14. ___ of the Plainsman
15. Cheyenne
16. River (Sp.)
17. Salutation
18. Hoss of *Bonanza*
21. Star of 14-Across
24. Command to a horse
25. TV newscaster
26. What *Hennesey* metes
29. *It Could ___ You*
31. A daughter on *Secret Storm*
32. Tries for a TV role
33. TV writer Serling
34. Who's doing this puzzle?
35. *For Better or ___*
36. A sponsor's objective
37. Prohibit on TV
38. TV's skin diver
40. TV host (2 words)
44. *Jubilee ___*
45. Crowlike bird
46. Johnny Yuma
50. Buntline of *Wyatt Earp*
51. Lyric poem
52. *Men into ___*
53. Negative vote
54. Loco wishes she were
55. Poker game for Maverick

down

1. Circle segment
2. Sportscaster Allen
3. Sash for Mihoshi Umeki
4. ___ *Showcase*
5. Dress for the part
6. Seed covering
7. The Three ___
8. Costar of *Gunsmoke*
9. Roof edge
10. Water pitcher
12. *All-___ Golf*
19. Star of *Man and the Challenge*
20. These (Fr.)
21. Gardner McKay's role
22. A star (colloq.)
23. Foxy
27. TV spy show
28. Office worker (colloq.)
29. Philippine knife
30. Actress Barbara ___
32. He plays Beaver's brother (2 words)
33. Headland
35. *Silent Service* background
36. Slumbers
37. Shotgun Slade
39. Flubs a line
40. *Peter ___*
41. Traveling with 21-Down
42. Created
43. Had creditors
47. ___ *Masterson*
48. Early French coin
49. *I ___ Three Lives*

62

March 26, 1960

down

1 Belonging to producer McCleery
2 Short sleep
3 Nothing
4 Cuckoo
5 Permits
6 That girl
7 *Silent Service* man
8 Vases
9 Weapon for Sheena
11 Seen on the Tiki
12 Miss Raines
15 Limb
17 Female sheep
19 ___ Mineo
20 Period
21 Come before ems
22 For the birds
24 McCauley on *Men into Space*
25 Roman emperor
28 Joey on *Circus Boy*
30 Enjoyed a soap opera
33 Another of 31-Across
34 Piece out
35 Place
37 *Who ___ You Trust?*
38 Bob Conrad's role on *Hawaiian Eye*
39 Old-fashioned "hip"
40 ___ *Three Lives* (2 words)
41 Exhausted
43 And
46 Italian river
48 Party for men only
50 Close
51 Rescue
53 ___ Olsen and Chic Johnson
54 Prefix meaning not
55 *Beat ___ Clock*
56 Cereal grass

across

1 A yearly record
6 Mr. Erwin (poss.)
10 *Rawhide* singer
11 She played *Johnny Ringo*'s girl
13 ___ *Personality*
14 Adam on *Bonanza*
16 ___ *Hunt*
18 Auction
19 Perceived
23 Lt. Martha Hale's British counterpart
26 Waste cloth
27 Melody Lee on *Bourbon Street Beat*
29 Northern defense line (init.)
31 TV Western prop
32 Johnny Yuma

36 Writer Mosel
38 Tom of *Hawaiian Eye*
39 Top TV show
42 Sarge on *The Dennis O'Keefe Show*
44 "Three" to Maverick
45 Charles Lamb's pen name
47 Steve Allen's bandleader
49 Pat on *The Betty Hutton Show*
52 Jay Silverheels' role
57 Roy of 49-Across
58 *Hawaiian Eye* hello
59 He was a big Mouseketeer
60 Girl who was on *Five Fingers*

May 21, 1960

across

1. Fawns' moms
5. Mark of a wound
9. A layer of skin
10. Annette on *Hotel de Paree*
12. Musical note
13. *To Tell the Truth* host (2 words)
16. ___ *Got a Secret*
18. Miss Peep
19. An actress must do this easily
20. Bough
22. Cleopatra's nemesis
23. Eggs
24. Johnny Midnight
26. Clay on *The Deputy*
28. Child's toy
29. Corruption
30. Humiliation
32. TV need
35. Companion of "hem"
36. New York opera house
38. ___-Lisa of *Black Saddle*
39. Vast age
40. 150 (Rom.)
41. Mr. Caesar
42. TV's Pat, Nicky and Roy
48. Bronco Layne
49. Rochester
50. Karen Sharpe role
52. Rescue
53. Mrs. Cugat

down

1. Vittorio ___ Sica
2. A celestial sphere
3. Australian bird
4. Downcast
5. Pry in meddlesome way
6. This Man Dawson's rank (abbr.)
7. ___-*Star Golf*
8. He plays Lieutenant Tragg (2 words)
9. A Nelson
11. Bilko has a lot of it
12. *The Walter Winchell* ___
14. TV network
15. Actor Robert ___
17. Annual TV event (2 words)
21. TV studio equipment
22. Tumult
25. TV comic Louis ___
26. Hail
27. Italian money
29. Enjoy a TV snack
30. Females
31. Writer Bret ___
33. Singer with Gobel
34. Wife of a lord
36. Reno of *The Alaskans*
37. Building addition
43. Miss Lupino
44. 104 (Rom.)
45. A wing
46. National Association of Broadcasters (abbr.)
47. Confer knighthood
51. *Dough* ___ *Mi*

June 11, 1960

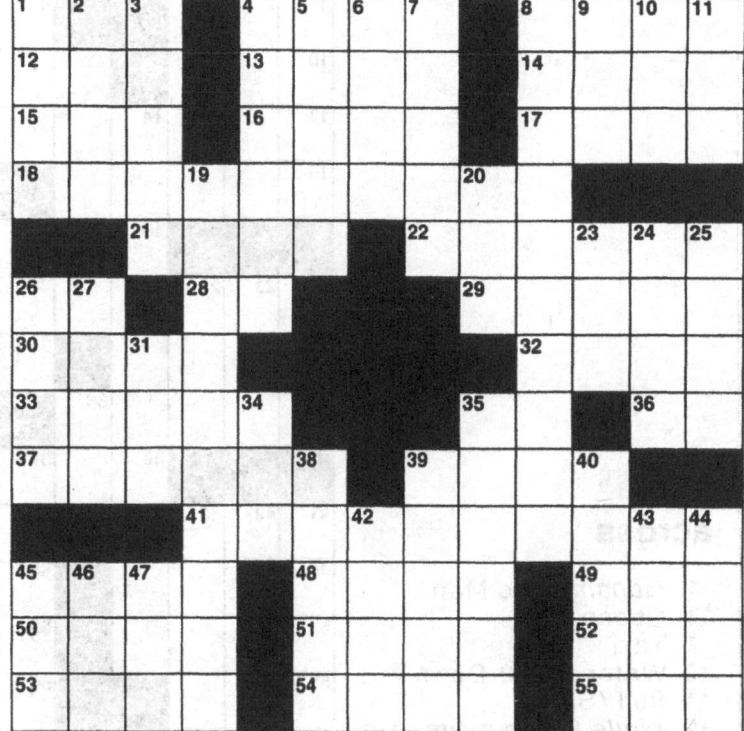

across

1 Church seat
4 Sloping walk
8 *Wanted-___ or Alive*
12 Girl's name
13 Prerequisite for a TV series
14 Creator of Perry Mason
15 Location for *Steve Canyon*
16 A clique
17 Robert Stack's role
18 TV comedian (2 words)
21 Wise man
22 Frightened Miss Muffet away
26 550 (Rom.)
28 Producer Howard
29 Stage whisper
30 Bellow
32 Rosemary on *The Betty Hutton Show*
33 "Candid Camera" man
35 Miss Peep of nursery-rhyme fame
36 Battleship "Big ___"
37 *Untouchables* narrator
39 Slang term for Steele and Lopaka
41 Oliver on *Adventures in Paradise* (2 words)
45 *Music Hall* star
48 Jerome ___, composer
49 Five-dollar bill
50 Smell
51 New York canal

52 Seventh Greek letter
53 Wild growth
54 Stains
55 And not

down

1 Randy's dad
2 Gunn's gal
3 Prevents
4 Randy Towne
5 Austrian psychiatrist
6 Supper
7 Trousers
8 Roy Strickland (2 words)
9 Sooner than
10 Belonged to Capone
11 *Crunch and ___*
19 Groucho's gimmick (2 words)

20 Office of Price Administration (abbr.)
23 Expire
24 Dutch cheese
25 One of The Alaskans
26 *Quick ___ McGraw*
27 She plays 2-Down
31 ___-*Star Golf*
34 Born
35 Kookie
38 Scraped together
39 Uncanny
40 Comes after six
42 Extremely
43 Prohibit
44 365 days
45 Intimidate
46 A poem
47 One of The Three Stooges

October 8, 1960

across

1 *Gunsmoke*'s Matt
4 Obese
7 Taxi
10 Writer for 42-Down
11 Bull (Sp.)
12 *Wells Fargo*'s Jim
13 Kelly in *Bachelor Father*
15 Egyptian goddess
16 Work, as dough
17 ___ Cerf, panelist
19 ___ Collins of *Perry Mason*
21 ___ Hunt
22 Bud ___, TV emcee
26 ___ *My Line?*
30 Scent
31 ___ Hunter
33 Go away!
34 ___ *Loves Mary*
36 ___ Landon of *Bonanza*
38 Electrified atom
40 Card game
41 Ann Sothern's role
45 Pleads with
49 Lasso
50 ___ Welk
52 Irish saga heroine
53 Aid
54 *People ___ Funny*
55 Keenan is Ed's
56 Pen point
57 Wine cask

down

1 ___ Benny
2 Holy image
3 Nothing more than
4 *Queen ___ a Day*
5 Kind of horse
6 Musical sounds
7 Costar of *The Deputy*
8 Dismounted
9 *Father Knows ___*
11 Garroway's TV show
12 TV hostess (2 words)
14 TV actor-writer (2 words)
18 Unlike a rerun
20 Still
22 *M Squad* man
23 Lyric poem
24 Building site
25 Strike against
27 Cry of triumph
28 Pedal digit
29 The sun
32 ___ Baird, puppeteer
35 ___Randell
37 *Day in ___*
39 Costar of *The Real McCoys*
41 Raw minerals
42 Perry ___
43 ___ *End*
44 E. Indian harvest
46 Small fly
47 Light tan
48 Observed on TV
51 TV network (sl.)

May 20, 1961

across

1 Timber tree
4 Wooley of *Rawhide*
8 Sums up
12 Miss Benaderet of *The Flintstones*
13 —— *and Gladys*
14 Booty
15 Audience
16 Young of *Mister Ed*
17 Moon goddess
18 Star of *Acapulco* (2 words)
21 Mr. Wills's
23 Linden tree
24 Storms
25 For each
26 Broadcast Promotion Association (init.)
29 Exclamation of pity
30 The Deputy's boss
31 Tom Ewell's "wife"
32 One of The Americans
33 Attempt
34 Uncanny
35 Scarf for Pinky
36 Fred Flintstone's pal
37 *Garry Moore Show* regular (2 words)
41 Son of Adam
42 The Gunslinger
43 *I've —— a Secret*

46 The Tiki's backbone
47 William —— playwright
48 *People —— Funny*
49 Singer Duane ——
50 Observed on TV
51 Comic Skelton

down

1 Mr. Burrows
2 —— *Hunt*
3 TV attorney
4 Stone chips
5 Assists
6 Greenland town
7 Bachelor Father
8 The Deputy
9 McClure of *Checkmate*
10 Finished
11 *All-—— Golf*
19 Pub drinks

20 —— *Force Story*
21 Sour person
22 Costar of *Perry Mason*
25 Snoop
26 Paul —— of *Rawhide*
27 Peel
28 *The —— Griffith Show*
30 Panelist on *What's My Line?*
31 Flowerless plant
33 Also
34 Star of *The Asphalt Jungle*
35 The Tall Man's pal
36 Pianist-comedian
37 —— *That Spare*
38 Reclining
39 *The Donna —— Show*
40 *The —— Ranger*
44 Raw mineral
45 *Amateur Hour* host

67

July 15, 1961

across

1 —— of Wells Fargo
6 Brother
9 I —— Three Lives
12 Wanted–Dead or ——
13 ——hide
14 Historical age
15 —— Loves Mary
16 Actress Tyrrell
17 Not none
18 Hong Kong houseboy
20 Seven (Roman)
21 Hot —— the Wire
24 34th President
25 Observed on television
26 Have Gun, Will ——
29 Republic of Korea
   (abbr.)
31 Early-morning show
32 Mrs. Flintstone
36 —— Hunt
38 Islanders locale
39 Possible prize on
   The Price Is Right
42 Mr. Skelton
44 Wapiti
45 ——-Star Golf
46 Talon
48 Andy Griffith's auntie
49 Aries
50 Marble
55 Producer Wm. T. ——
56 People —— Funny
57 Nick Adams' role
58 Explosive
59 Queen —— a Day
60 U.S. —— Hour

down

1 Thump
2 Malt beverage
3 Made a campfire
4 Miss Arden
5 Person bound to
   the soil
6 Bringing Up Buddy star
7 The Lone ——
8 Bristle
9 —— It to Beaver
10 Mr. Kovacs
11 —— Court (2 words)
19 Needed in your car
21 Hall of Fame
   ballplayer Mel ——
22 Back
23 Craze
25 Could be fatal on
   Route 66
27 Distance covered by
   the Wagon Train
28 CBS symbol
30 Have
33 Told on To Tell
   the Truth
34 —— Blanc
35 Inquire
37 Naked City man
38 Director Lupino
39 Sebastian ——
40 Ernie Ford (2 words)
41 Like Paladin
43 Mr. Fudd
47 Civil and World
49 British air force
51 Achieve
52 Nickname for
   Mr. Jones
53 Prop for a golf show
54 Building addition

August 19, 1961

across

1 One of The Americans
5 PT on *Whirlybirds*
10 Western setting
12 Iris or Violet on TV
14 Guarantee
15 Calm
16 Fasten tightly
17 Charged atom
19 Long wooden implement
20 *You ___ for It*, TV oldie
22 Lady TV panelist
26 Cowardly color
31 Departure
32 Fabricate
33 Elaine Strich's role
35 *G.E. Theater* host
36 Grandmother in *One Happy Family*
38 And so forth (abbr.)
41 Eve's origin
42 Thorsen of *The Detectives*
46 Dobie Gillis
49 Actress Donahue
51 Actor Tong
52 Mrs. Howard Duff
53 Bring forth
54 Obtains

down

1 Actress Wyatt
2 Miss Maxwell
3 Baseball term
4 *Search ___ Tomorrow*
5 James or Jeanne
6 Street in Paris
7 *National Velvet* mom
8 *Leave ___ Beaver* (2 words)
9 Large lizard
10 Linda to Rusty
11 Jay in *Bringing Up Buddy*
13 Ever (poet.)
18 Good (sl.)
20 Annie Farge's role
21 Actor Martin
22 Time of one's life
23 King (Fr.)
24 Cartoon character ___ Abner
25 Compass point (abbr.)
27 Meadow
28 Linger
29 Egg
30 Skin tumor
34 Actress Corcoran
35 Johnny Yuma
37 Secretary in *The Ann Sothern Show*
38 Wynn and Sullivan
39 Contraction for "it was"
40 Rosemary De ___
42 Seasoned
43 One
44 *My Three ___*
45 Hit-show sign (abbr.)
47 Peruvian singer Sumac
48 Status of many fall shows
50 Haul

August 26, 1961

across

1 Mitchell of *Whispering Smith*
4 Step
8 Gloomy
12 Past
13 Mild oath
14 She's Velvet
15 One half of a TV comedy team
17 Star of *Angel*
18 *Amateur Hour* host
19 Star of *Asphalt Jungle*
20 Of the sun
23 Costar of *Perry Mason*
24 ___ Young of 7-Down
25 *Death Valley* ___
26 An oldie: *Jubilee* ___
29 NBC baseball announcer (2 words)
32 *Route 66* traveler
33 Woody plant
34 Fasting period
35 Lady in *Guestward Ho!*
36 One of The Untouchables
37 ___ Alberoni of *Tom Ewell Show*
40 *Queen for a* ___
41 Star of *Whispering Smith*
42 Star of *Sea Hunt*
46 *Laramie* character
47 Borrowed sum
48 Sailor's "yes"
49 Fedoras
50 ___ Dalton of *Hennesey*
51 Affirmative vote

down

1 Cooking fuel
2 Indian's grunt
3 *It Could Be* ___
4 Bentley's houseboy
5 Old
6 Vehicle for 32-Across
7 *Mr.* ___
8 Dazzling light
9 Costar of *Danny Thomas Show*
10 Plead with
11 Bearing
16 To rest in upright position
17 Untrue
19 The other of 15-Across
20 Seasoning
21 Mixture
22 Magic ___
23 Costar of *Peter Loves Mary*
25 Famous horse race seen on TV
26 Utilizes
27 *My Three* ___
28 Against (prefix)
30 Gazes steadily
31 ___ Bochner of *Hong Kong*
35 Hat edges
36 Showery
37 Movable part of window
38 Hawaiian dance
39 Blue-pencil
40 Dull
42 *Love That* ___
43 Merry
44 *Hawaiian* ___
45 *Victory at* ___
47 *Jack* ___ *Lanne Show*

September 23, 1961

across

1 Donna Reed's TV "son"
5 Group of tents
9 ____ Faces West
12 River in Poland
13 Buckeye State
14 Horse and buggy
15 CBS newscaster
17 Fishhook line
19 Louis ____, comedian
20 One Hawaiian Eye
21 Gunsmoke costar
24 In what way?
25 77 Sunset Strip costar
26 Wagon Train costar
31 Where Hong Kong is
32 ____ Miss Brooks
33 Early Greek theaters
34 Naked City costar
36 Close by
37 Not to tell the truth
38 Little
39 The Deputy
42 Burmese dialect
43 Run away
44 Dobie Gillis' pal
48 Ever (poet.)
49 Romper ____
51 Butter substitute
52 Route 66 traveler
53 Store
54 Like Garroway's old World

down

1 Bonanza son
2 He's Kookie
3 Not many
4 Mystery Theatre host (2 words)
5 System of signals
6 Sighs of relief
7 National Velvet's handyman
8 To Tell the Truth panelist
9 Large plant
10 Have Gun, ____ Travel
11 Make eyes at
16 Cereal plant
18 FCC chairman (2 words)
20 Gather with stiches
21 Tell secrets
22 Mislay
23 Indigo dye plant
26 Changed TV time period
27 Actor's signal
28 Nucleus of a TV show
29 The ____ McCoys
30 A nobleman
35 Drying frames
38 ____ When
39 ____ the Press
40 TV's talking dog
41 He's the Gunslinger
42 ____ unto My Feet
44 Bovine sound
45 Mr. Baba
46 ____ Skelton
47 Female deer
50 Cry of surprise

October 21, 1961

down

1 Musical work
2 Agreement
3 Mr. Candid Camera
4 ___ *It to Beaver*
5 Actress Myrna ___
6 Trouble
7 Durante's outstanding feature
8 John Forsythe's role
9 *Hawaiian Eye* dish
10 Away from center
11 Before
17 One of the Stooges
19 Female sheep
22 Bridge term
24 TV police series (2 words)
25 Single thing
26 An oldie: *The Name's the ___*
27 Young actor Richard ___
28 TV's Velvet Brown
30 Roman 52
31 Where Top Cat lives (var.)
35 Performer likely to be found on *International Showtime*
41 Devour
42 Phyllis and Jack of *Pip the Piper*
44 Ordered on *Day in Court*
46 *Perry Mason* creator
48 Mrs. Robert Sterling
49 Red, Black and Yellow
50 *The Tall ___*
51 ___ *Got a Secret*
52 TV receiver
53 Greek letter
54 A buck (abbr.)

across

1 Precious stone
5 Costar of *Rescue 8*
9 He wrote "The Raven"
12 Wan
13 Aroma
14 ___ *Miss Brooks*
15 California university (init.)
16 A national park
18 *My Three Sons'* dad
20 The self
21 Huntley's forte
23 Species
27 Sprite
29 Singer Fitzgerald
32 Suffix
33 *Who Do ___ Trust?*
34 Tiki canvas
36 Poncie Ponce's role
37 TV's Ford
38 Measure of distance
39 Summer in Paris
40 Rituals
43 Place for a barbecue
45 One of the Hathaways
47 The Rifleman
50 Talking horse (2 words)
55 *What's My ___?*
56 Hail
57 Singing voice
58 Volcano in Italy
59 ABC, CBS, or NBC
60 *The ___ McCoys*
61 Stains

November 25, 1961

across

1 Letters of the alphabet
4 Mike O'Toole's girl Friday
8 Fury's gait
12 *Who Do ___ Trust?*
13 Toward the mouth
14 Ready for gathering
15 Miss on *Password*
16 Miss Albright
17 Sour
18 NBC newscaster (2 words)
21 *Perry ___*
23 A coat (sl.)
24 Miss Markey
25 Miss Williams
27 Dennis the Menace
30 Annex
31 Wooden shoe
32 Drink for Robin Hood
33 Strong alkaline solution
34 Playing card
35 Freight boat
36 Maynard is Dobie's
37 Seizes
38 TV comedian (2 words)
42 Bilko's base, ___ Baxter
43 Feminine suffix
44 Miss Sothern
47 Creator of 21-Across
48 Ladies' parties
49 Affirmative vote
50 Boy actor Richard ___
51 ___ *Grey Theater*
52 Rowe or Skelton

down

1 *Hawaiian ___*
2 And not
3 ___ *6*
4 Costar of *The Real McCoys*
5 Type club used on *All-Star Golf*
6 There's a lot of it on 27-Down's show
7 Gardner McKay (2 words)
8 Ray Collins' role
9 Cereal food
10 Son in 22-Down
11 Mr. Mack
19 Host of *The Twilight Zone*
20 Layer
21 Repast
22 *The ___ Griffith Show*
25 Costar of *The Donna Reed Show* (2 words)
26 Mr. Burrows
27 TV host (2 words)
28 Tropical plant
29 Evergreen trees
31 Remain
35 ___ Paulo, Brazil
36 Bentley's houseboy
37 *From ___ Roots*
38 Star of *Manhunt*
39 Part of a shield
40 Genus of shrubs
41 Mr. Laurel
42 Young Dr. Malone's charge
45 Louis ___, comedian
46 CBS newsman, ___ Calmer

December 23, 1961

down

1 A striking success (sl.)
2 Charley Weaver's Mount ___
3 Robbie of *My Three Sons* (2 words)
4 ___ Kovacs
5 Go down in the ratings
6 *The New Steve ___ Show*
7 Approached
8 *Surfside 6* man
9 Likely to be heard on *NBC Opera*
10 A Maverick
12 One of The Hathaways
18 Acquire
19 Costar of *The Defenders*
20 Huntley's field
21 ___ Roberts
25 Energy (sl.)
27 CBS information show
28 City in Russia
29 *The ___ McCoys*
31 Stitched
33 Collar continuations
36 Lottery
38 Mr. Poston
41 Unripe
43 Old term for blouse
44 *Laramie* man
45 Butter substitute
46 Wilbur of *Mister Ed*
47 Otherwise
51 Self
52 ___ *When*

across

1 ___ *World of Sports*
5 He's Hoss
8 Small portion
11 Scent
12 *Perry Mason* author
13 *Car 54, Where ___ You?*
14 Ed or Keenan
15 Miss Albright
16 By way of
17 Kathy on *Follow the Sun* (2 words)
20 ___ Corcoran of *Bachelor Father*
22 Born
23 Period of time
24 ___ *Cat*
26 Decorative scheme
30 Lumps
32 Electric unit
34 Challenge
35 More foxy
37 The Tall Man
39 Meadow
40 Brandish
42 *The Dick ___ Show*
44 Elma of *Bus Stop* (2 words)
48 Building wing
49 Costar of *87th Precinct*
50 Roman date
53 ___ *Hunt*
54 Minus
55 Heroic tale
56 Opie to Andy
57 Compass point
58 *Adventures in Paradise* man

January 6, 1962

across

1 Perform on TV
4 Top ___
7 ___ Rowlands of *87th Precinct*
11 *Queen ___ a Day*
12 Color
13 The Steve ___ Show
14 Mr. Baba
15 Literary scraps
16 Gathered leaves
17 *The Defenders* costar (2 words)
20 *The ___ McCoys*
21 Father on 39-Across
25 Allude
28 Like father who knows best
29 Voice on *The Flintstones*
32 Rescued
34 Costar of *Leave It to Beaver*
35 Miss Fitzgerald
37 Monkey-like animal
39 *Dobie ___*
41 Costar of 54-Across
44 Another of 54-Across (2 words)
48 *Make That ___*
51 Mr. Gershwin
52 *College of the ___*
53 Como's conductor
54 *___ 54, Where Are You?*
55 Miss Lupino
56 Pleased
57 He's Kookie
58 ___ Brown of 13-Across

down

1 At a distance
2 *Disney's Wonderful World of ___*
3 Indian group
4 ___ Correll, Calvin's voice
5 Frances Bavier's role
6 Rip
7 *Pete and ___*
8 Large deer
9 Born
10 *Ichabod ___ Me*
13 Region
18 Spike of corn
19 A star of *77 Sunset Strip*
22 Dennis the Menace
23 Self
24 *The ___ Bread*
26 Untrue
27 Miss Arden
29 Implore
30 Mr. Wallach
31 ___ *Star Golf*
33 Garry Moore regular
36 ___ *Hitchcock Presents*
38 ___ *Rogers Show*
40 Angers
42 Slow-moving creature
43 Subtly derisive
45 Gaming cubes
46 Mrs. G. hopes to be one
47 Periods of time
48 Screen Actors Guild (abbr.)
49 Jean Vander ___, a *Flintstones* voice
50 Southern constellation

January 13, 1962

across

1 Exclamation
5 Unusual
8 Place for an outlaw
12 Singing voice
13 *Car 54, Where ___ You?*
14 Region
15 Shakespearean king
16 Nickname for one of Steve's three sons
17 ___ Merrynote
18 Ben on *Bonanza*
20 Kukla and Ollie
22 Hamilton Burger
24 Large container
25 Bub to 16-Across
30 Maggie ___ of *Calvin and the Colonel*
34 Atmosphere
35 Go astray
37 ___ *Up and Live*
38 Bout (sl.)
40 Actor Barton ___
42 Possessive pronoun
44 *Mrs. G. Goes ___ College*
45 Gal on *Candid Camera*
49 *Bachelor Father*'s cook
54 Ardor
55 Poisonous snake
57 Composer Edouard ___
58 Charles Lamb
59 An old car
60 Haze
61 Satiate
62 Anger
63 Malt beverages

down

1 Irritate
2 Bread spread
3 Principal actor in a TV show
4 Trumpet or sax
5 Paddle
6 Liquid particle
7 New show premiere
8 Sir Malcolm, boat racer
9 One of the Great Lakes
10 For fear that
11 Scottish girl
19 He's now a private eye
21 Bar in London
23 One of the Hathaways
25 Fuel for cars on *Straightaway*
26 Street in Paris
27 Announcer ___ James
28 ___ *Velvet*
29 Limb
31 Mauna ___
32 Singer Alice
33 Piece out
36 Biggy of *King Leonardo*
39 Ballplayer Mel
41 Gunther Toody
43 Miss Lewis
45 Profound
46 Round cooking jar
47 Metal bar
48 River in Belgium
50 Joan Freeman of *Bus Stop*
51 Lassie has one
52 Otherwise
53 Degenerates
56 Author of "The Raven"

February 17, 1962

across

1 Back of the Tiki
4 Voice of Barney Rubble
7 TV receiver
10 African lily
11 CBS symbol
12 Lassie has one
14 Beaver's dad
15 *King* ___
17 Conclude a TV show
18 ___ Cedric Hardwicke
19 Host of *Password*
20 Cry of sorrow
22 *Rawhide* boss
23 Form of polite address
25 Actor Brynner
26 Cecil the ___ Serpent
29 *The* ___ *Griffith Show*
30 Cowboy Rogers
31 *Price Is Right* host
32 *The Brighter* ___
33 Late comic Costello
34 Friend of Dixie
35 Miss Fabray
36 Marshal Dillon
37 Bob Stack's role
40 *Top* ___
41 Affirmative
44 Chuck Connors' role
46 Largest continent
47 ___ May Wong
48 *You* ___ *There*
49 Filth
50 Sheriff's badge (sl.)
51 TV producer Hiken
52 Woodman's tool

down

1 Voice of Fred Flintstone
2 *Make Room* ___
  (2 words)
3 Hoffman on *Ben Casey*
4 Music director of
  The Jack Paar Show
5 Actor Richard
6 Voice of The Brain
  on 40 Across
7 Place for Fury
8 Actor Holliman
9 Current
10 Wonder
13 ___ Chaney Jr.
16 Small spike
18 Dr. Zorba of *Ben Casey*
21 Place
22 Chris of *Adventures
  in Paradise*
23 Rabid
24 Collection of bits of
  information
25 *It Could Be* ___
26 Follows 65
27 Actor Wallach
28 Tavern drink
30 Bert of *87th Precinct*
31 Part of King's bridle
33 Tardy
34 ___ Harrington Jr.
35 Kate McCoy
36 French painter
37 Vast age
38 Bits of thread
39 African town
40 Gladys Porter
42 Ireland
43 Perched
45 *The Tall* ___
46 Girl's name

April 14, 1962

across

1 Top ___
4 Like Calvin's Voice
8 Some commercials do this
11 Commotion
12 Singer Fitzgerald
13 Indian of Peru
14 Sun god
15 Buddy in *The Dick Van Dyke Show*
17 Kitty in *Gunsmoke*
20 King (Fr.)
21 Cook in fat
22 Food for Popeye
26 Toward shelter
27 Powder
28 Born
29 James McCallion in *National Velvet*
30 Heywood in *Margie*
31 Railroad (abbr.)
32 Finish
34 TV interference
35 Engagement for Margie
37 Father of the Bride
39 Nuggets of knowledge
40 *Hawaiian Eye* dish
41 Nick in *Ben Casey*
44 Ben in *Frontier Circus* (2 words)
48 Negative
49 Mrs. Robert Sterling
50 Arrange methodically
51 ___ *Star Golf*
52 And Griffith's TV aunt
53 Related
54 Strong alkaline solution

down

1 Wife in *Pete and Gladys*
2 Man in *Naked City* (2 words)
3 *Tell It ___ Groucho*
4 Inanimate
5 *Bus Stop* girl
6 High railways
7 The Tall Man
8 Western star
9 NBC parent company
10 Actor Tong
13 Press
16 Man in *Follow the Sun*
18 *You ___ There*
19 Comic Louis
22 Kind of cabbage
23 Till
24 Surely
25 *Frank McGee's ___ and Now*
26 He plays 37-Across
27 Prong
33 Gal on *SurfSide 6*
34 Coasted
35 Hoss in *Bonanza*
36 Actress Doran
38 Not any
41 Comedian Gabe
42 Pieced out
43 Single
44 Punch on *Fight of the Week*
45 *Room for ___ More*
46 Newt
47 Dolores Del ___
51 Foe of Ness

across

1 *Dennis the Menace* star
4 *Top* ___
7 Mr. Sahl, comedian
11 *Room for* ___ *More*
12 Black bird
13 Gertrude Berg's role
14 Star of *Ben Casey*
16 Vestige
17 Myrna ___, actress
18 *Queen for a Day* host
19 ___ Wills of *Frontier Circus*
22 Jason's ship
23 Ore deposit
24 *Hawaiian* ___
25 Pen points
29 On
30 *You* ___ *There*
31 *National Velvet* star
32 ___ *Telephone Hour*
33 TV's Mr. Mack
34 Had creditors
35 Indians of Utah
37 Shipping box
38 *Cheyenne* costar
41 *The Tall* ___
42 Omit a syllable
43 *Bonanza* costar
47 Allude
48 Commotion
49 Lamb's parent
50 Early farm animals
51 Eventually
52 Costar of *Leave It to Beaver*

down

1 *Bonanza* son
2 *Pete* ___ *Gladys*
3 Evergreen tree
4 Regular on *The Garry Moore Show*
5 *The* ___ *Griffith Show*
6 It is (poet.)
7 Another regular on *The Garry Moore Show* (2 words)
8 ___ Roberts
9 ABC's *Wide World of Sports* event
10 Those people
13 Male deer
15 *Password* host (2 words)
18 *The New* ___
19 Society
20 TV and movie comedian
21 Pagan god
22 Como's conductor
24 Consumed
26 Hawkeye State
27 A Maverick
28 *Surf* ___ *6*
36 Layer
37 *Checkmate* costar
38 Leading man in a TV play
39 Carl Betz's role
40 Prevalent
41 Fashion
43 Ed Sullivan's conductor
44 *The* ___ *Skelton Show*
45 *1,* ___, *3, Go!*
46 Stitch

December 1, 1962

across

1 Curved bone
4 Deadly
9 Quick punch
12 Hubbub
13 Defendant's excuse
14 Cockney's abode
15 Costar of *Naked City* (2 words)
18 TV comics try to evoke it
19 Coal compartments
20 He plays O'Toole
22 Stupid fellow
24 ___ Fleming of *Rawhide*
25 Mainstay of a sheep's vocabulary
26 Oriental bishop's title
30 *Sam Benedict* setting, ___ Francisco
31 Vase
32 Playing duration of a Broadway show
33 Killed
35 TV's Mr. Serling
36 Canary
37 He's Mitch in *Wide Country*
39 TV comedian
40 *Hallmark ___ of Fame*
42 Saturate
43 *Today*'s "Fearless Forecaster" (2 words)
48 Pub drink
49 The Untouchables' leader
50 Miss Gabor
51 Affirmative
52 Last inning
53 Eventually

down

1 Cheering shout
2 Wedding reply (2 words)
3 Star of *McHale's Navy*
4 An oldie: *Two ___ West*
5 To sheltered side
6 ___ Considine of *My Three Sons*
7 TV network
8 Place of oblivion
9 He plays Dickens
10 One of The Real McCoys
11 TV medic
16 Man's name
17 Opera by Verdi
20 *Laramie* character
21 Spoken
22 TV's Miss Burnett
23 *The Magic ___ of Allakazam*
25 Star of *Perry Mason*
27 NBC newsman
28 Be on fire
29 *The ___ Williams Show*
34 *The Lawrence ___ Show*
36 Boyfriend
38 *Password*'s host
39 Star of *Hazel*
40 *Wagon Train*'s boss
41 High cards
42 Highlander
43 He's Dennis the Menace
44 Actor ___ Wallach
45 Transgress
46 ___ *Got a Secret*
47 Consume

December 22, 1962

across

1 Cleopatra's pet
4 Star of *Saints and Sinners*
9 Dennis's street
12 View
13 French artist's cap
14 She plays Toody's wife
15 Lady TV star (2 words)
18 ___ Brooks of *Meet the Press*
19 Contend
20 *Jackie Gleason's American ___ Magazine*
22 *Laramie*'s "young un"
25 ___ Disney
26 Costar of *Gunsmoke*
28 Music note
29 An *Empire* industry
30 ___ *My Line?*
31 *Hazel*'s costar
32 *Truth ___ Consequences*
33 Disembodied spirits
34 Repeats noisily
35 *To Tell the Truth* panelist
37 Rub out
38 Owns
39 TV lawyer
40 Costar of *Rawhide* (2 words)
47 Rowing blade
48 TV's "Pea-Picker"
49 Depression agency (abbr.)
50 Wise old bird
51 Tears apart
52 Cozy room for TV viewing

down

1 Cigar residue
2 Habitat of the USS Appleby
3 ___ Roberts of *Bonanza*
4 Put up with
5 She's Mrs. Bobby Darin
6 ___ Linkletter
7 *The Gallant ___*
8 Costar of *Hawaiian Eye*
9 He plays Jed Clampett
10 Father Fitzgibbon on *Going My Way*
11 *Our ___ Higgins*
16 Lease
17 Playboy's smooth talk
20 Descend swiftly
21 Egypt's capital
22 The Morse code uses them
23 Golf clubs
24 Intelligence
26 Avoid
27 Son in *Empire*
30 *Wagon Train*'s cook
31 Selma ___, Como writer
33 ___ Irwin of *Mr. Smith Goes to Washington*
34 *Quick ___ McGraw*
36 Costar of *The Nurses*
37 U.S. Sen. ___ Kefauver
40 Dove-like sound
41 Perry, Sam and Lawrence's field
42 Before
43 *The ___ Sothern Show*
44 ___ Caesar
45 Raw mineral
46 ___ O'Herlihy

January 12, 1963

across

1 Shade tree
4 Circle segment
7 Mirth
11 *Who Do ___ Trust?*
12 Weaving machine
14 How the cowboy traveled
15 Building wing
16 Ear projection
17 Indigo dye
18 He's Adam Shepherd (2 words)
21 ___-Margret
22 ___ Rogers
23 *What's My ___?*
25 Shower
27 Monk's title
30 Common verb
31 Perry Mason's secretary
32 Linear (abbr.)
33 *Going My ___*
34 Train track
35 Tie together
36 A roll of money (sl.)
37 ___ *Cat*
38 TV vocalist (2 words)
44 *Make ___ for Daddy*
45 Close by
46 Robin Hood's drink
48 Miss Magnani
49 Star of 33-Across
50 Floor covering
51 Form of "to be"
52 TV comic
53 Small barrel

down

1 *Hawaiian ___*
2 Lounge about
3 Costar of *Ensign O'Toole*
4 ___ Joslyn of 29-Down
5 Crucifix
6 Costar of *The Virginian*
7 Robbie in *My Three Sons*
8 Lengthy
9 *Here's ___*
10 Snakelike fish (plural)
13 Baritone Robert ___
19 Not many
20 Hebrides island
23 Edmond O'Brien's TV profession
24 Mr. Gershwin
25 ___ *Room*
26 Mr. Baba
27 Larry in *Fair Exchange* (2 words)
28 ___ Tin Tin
29 *McKeever ___ the Colonel*
31 A lawman needs a fast one
35 Feather scarf
36 *Jane ___ Presents*
37 Weary
38 Desert dweller
39 Not any
40 Finished
41 Sinister look
42 Costar of 29-Down
43 Slough
47 Omelet item

March 23, 1963

down

1 Popular profession on TV
2 Desert dweller
3 —— *That Spare*
4 *Meet the* ——
5 Doug McClure's role
6 Not difficult
7 Loses moisture
8 *Search for* ——
9 Persia
10 *The Gallant* ——
13 Our planet
19 —— *Benedict*
20 First king of Israel
23 *Top* ——
24 Malt beverage
25 TV series (2 words)
27 Metal
29 —— *Step Beyond*
30 Moderator of 4-Down
32 *The Beverly Hillbillies* type of humor
34 —— Rust of 19-Down
37 Leases
39 —— G. Carroll of *Going My Way*
42 Costar of *Father Knows Best*
44 Live coal
45 He's Dr. Kildare
46 The Kingston ——
47 Opera by Verdi
48 *Laramie* character
49 Owns
52 French article

across

1 —— *Unto My Feet*
5 *Amateur Hour* host
8 —— Conway of *McHale's Navy*
11 Sandarac tree
12 Uncommon
14 Metallic rock
15 Ship's trail
16 Continent
17 *Our* —— *Higgins*
18 Panelist on *I've Got a Secret* (2 words)
21 Tree fluid
22 Leading TV actor
23 Taxi
26 Wrestling prop
28 Great Lake
31 Mr. Guinness
33 Olivier's title
35 *The* —— *Ranger*
36 Dennis Day's one
38 Nothing
40 Marry
41 Group of TV technicians
43 Alphabet letter
45 TV comedian (2 words)
49 The man's
50 Scarlett O'Hara's home
51 *The Price Is Right* host
53 Veteran TV writer Goodman ——
54 Prison (sl.)
55 *Here's* ——
56 —— *King*
57 *Route 66* character
58 Strikes against

July 20, 1963

across

1 TV picture flaw
5 Fixed charge
8 *Stump ___ Stars*
11 Mrs. Cugat
12 Simple lyric
13 Became larger
14 Star of 8-Down
16 He's McKeever
17 Presses for payment
18 Inheritors
19 ___ *Scouts*
22 TV comedian
23 Fred Astaire's sister
24 Elegant dress
25 *The ___ McCoys*
26 Weep
27 One of *My Three Sons*
31 David's partner
33 TV host
34 Summer ermine
36 Pantry
37 Actress ___ Conway
38 Restrain
39 Residence
40 Costar of *The Dakotas* (2 words)
44 *Combat* service
45 Miss Gardner
46 Story
47 Ruler of Tunis
48 Affirmative
49 Identical

down

1 ___ *Benedict*
2 TV network
3 Japanese sash
4 Dr. Ted Bassett (2 words)
5 Scout of *Major Adams, Trailmaster*
6 Hearing organs
7 *Hawaiian ___*
8 *Wagon ___*
9 Panelist on 24-Down
10 Lambs' mothers
13 Costar of *Route 66* (2 words)
15 Melody
18 Chop
19 Paving material
20 Fruit drink
21 Meadow
22 Mr. Fuller of *Laramie*
24 *I've ___ a Secret*
26 Matched group
28 Coal scuttle
29 Anger
30 For each
32 Mr. March
33 *The Rifleman's* son
34 Costar of *The Virginian*
35 *Lassie*'s boy
36 *The Rifleman*
37 Food fish
38 Grotto
40 He's Dennis
41 *Perry Mason*'s field
42 Mr. Baba
43 *The Gallant ___*

August 17, 1963

across

1 Actor Alan
5 TV Oldie, ___ Stop
8 *G-E College* ___
12 Bread spread
13 Employ
14 Miss Adams
15 Polish river
16 McHale or O'Toole
17 Irritate
18 Crumb
20 He's Fenster
22 Time of Life
23 Yes to 16-Across
24 Gerson on *Dr. Kildare*
27 Singers with Welk
31 She's Miss Brooks
32 Gold in Madrid
33 TV beatnik
37 Actor Anderson
40 Wedding vow (2 words)
41 Commotion
42 Emmy and Oscar
45 Tonto's leader
49 *The Eleventh Hour* costar
50 Toody's vehicle
52 Besides
53 Against (prefix)
54 Sound from the arena
55 Apollo's mother
56 Camera spool
57 "One" in Berlin
58 Think

down

1 Weaving frame
2 Actor ___ Ray
3 One of Elly May's critters
4 At or on the back
5 Our Man Higgins, e.g.
6 Land of the free
7 Daytime TV fare
8 Polly ___
9 *King Leonardo's* page
10 *Have Gun—___ Travel*
11 Cobb and Marvin
19 The self
21 Comic Louis
24 Hoffman of *Ben Casey*
25 Hail! (Lat.)
26 Fanciful desire
28 Prefix "not"
29 Source of lead
30 Correlative of neither
34 ___ P. Stoner of *Ensign O'Toole*
35 Actor Byrnes
36 Man in *77 Sunset Strip*
37 Ves in *Stoney Burke*
38 City in Oklahoma
39 Actor ___ Reagan
42 Actor John ___
43 "Days of ___ and Roses"
44 Poker stake
46 Mirth
47 Famous Italian family
48 *Make ___ for Daddy*
51 Mr. Baba

October 5, 1963

50 ____ Sullivan
51 Finale

down

1 Lamprey
2 Costar of *The Beverly Hillbillies*
3 ____ *Point*
4 Curved supporting structure
5 Dull
6 River in Arizona
7 Son in *Bonanza*
8 Contradict
10 Catch sight of
11 Star of *The Farmer's Daughter*
12 ____ Disney
17 Band leader ____ Brown
18 Use a ladle
21 ____ *Lieutenant*
22 Embrace
23 Costars with 29-Across
24 Period in history
25 He's McHale
26 Miss Merkel
27 ____ *Casey*
29 Volcanic rock
33 Frightening sound
34 Sound for attention
35 *You ____ Say!*
36 Frees from
37 Notion
38 A Red Skelton character
39 *The Patty ____ Show*
40 Thin nail
41 Balanced
45 TV actor ____ Byrnes

across

1 Recede, as a tide
4 TV commercial
6 Wander about
9 Hearing organ
10 Makes mistakes
12 *ABC's ____ World of Sports*
13 ____ J. Cobb of *The Virginian*
14 Begone, cat!
15 ____ Young, costar of *Mister Ed*
16 Star of *The Eleventh Hour* (2 words)
19 Piano lever
20 Large tank
21 ____ *Is the Life*
23 *The Donna ____ Show*
25 *My Three Sons'* grandpa
28 Vandal
29 ____ Greene of *Bonanza*
30 United
31 Omelet item
32 Arabian robes
33 Breakfast cereal
34 Salutation
35 Lassie
36 Host of a new TV show (2 words)
42 Unemployed
43 Move circularly
44 ____ *Got a Secret*
46 Think
47 Card game
48 *Meet the Press* moderator
49 ____ Jaffe of 27-Down

across

1 TV host
5 Cry of triumph
8 Triangular sail
11 Exchange premium
12 *My Three Sons'* grandfather
13 *The Bill ___ Show*
14 He's Barney Rubble (2 words)
16 Prayer ending
17 ___ *Side, West Side*
18 Costar of *Channing*
19 Turn off Route 66
22 Grain for grinding
23 Main artery
24 She's Danny Thomas' TV wife
25 ___ *the Press*
26 Suitable
27 ___ Palance
31 Up above
33 Indian's boat
34 ___ *of Hollywood*
36 Costar of *Bonanza*
37 Rob Petrie's co-worker
38 Jolts
39 Norway's capital
40 Miss Ball is the star: *The ___* (2 words)
44 Active person
45 ___*Step Beyond*
46 Irish Republic
47 Actress ___ Harding
48 *Amateur Hour's* host
49 Require

down

1 Mrs. North
2 Grow old
3 Be ill
4 *The Detectives* star (2 words)
5 Degrade
6 *Sea* ___
7 TV network
8 He's Mr. Novak
9 Inactive
10 Prohibits
13 Star of *The Fugitive* (2 words)
15 Molten rock
18 Be mistaken
19 ___ Jaffe of *Ben Casey*
20 Soap-opera grief
21 Before
22 *I've ___ a Secret*
24 An edge
26 *Word ___ Word*
28 *Arrest ___ Trial*
29 Murmur lovingly
30 One of *The Defenders*
32 Plaything
33 Movie star Grant
34 *Perry ___*
35 *The Steve ___ Show*
36 Intertwined
37 Fizzy drink
38 ___ Lockhart of *Lassie*
40 Building site
41 Hasten
42 Raw mineral
43 Marry

January 18, 1964

across

1 Patty Duke's role
5 Professor in *Channing*
9 Stephen Vincent ___
10 *Here's Edie* star
12 Jenny in *The Travels of Jaimie McPheeters* (2 words)
15 One of Phil's pals
16 Arabic (abbr.)
17 Sellout sign
18 Connors' costar
23 Miss Fabray's
27 She played one of Harry's Girls
28 Mr. Cole, singer
29 ___ Marshall of *My Favorite Martian*
30 A Spanish plateau
31 Not far off
33 A host of *Candid Camera*
36 To point a weapon
39 Upon
40 Western series
44 Uncle on *Petticoat Junction* (2 words)
49 *The ___ Limits*
50 TV wife of 19 Down
51 Casey's club
52 Ova

down

1 TV singing sisters
2 Actress Seymour
3 Boy's name
4 And elsewhere (Latin; 2 words)
5 Used to own
6 Lyrical poem
7 Theme of *Combat!*
8 Printing measures
9 A war (1899-1902)
11 Fly like Sky King
12 Stars of *Breaking Point* (abbr.)
13 Worn-out horse
14 Organization of the 1930s
19 ___ Young, TV comedian
20 *The Twilight ___*
21 Miss Bethune
22 Ancient Roman coin
24 All over again
25 A national space group (abbr.)
26 TV celebrity
30 Novak or Ed
32 Portrays Quince on 40-Across
33 Female deer
34 To open
35 Actress Joanne ___
37 Property of Miss Lupino
38 Principals of *The Lieutenant*
41 What Casey tends to
42 A former American political party
43 String up baddies
45 Something to chew
46 Had breakfast
47 Soak
48 Marx or Smothers (abbr.)

across

1 Away
4 Mr. Wooley
8 Ship's mast
12 And not
13 Like many TV movies
14 She played Gladys
15 Period of time
16 Mister Ed's costar
17 Of the ear
18 Not any
20 *Rawhide* extras
22 Card game
23 Linkletter's fete
24 Son in 37-Across
25 Mr. Arnaz
26 Bobbie Jo of *Petticoat Junction*
29 Self
30 A race or stock
31 Miss Gabor
32 Jack Benny's announcer
33 Catch sight of
34 Set in motion
35 Pale colors
37 *The Donna ___ Show*
38 She's Kitty
40 TV host
41 Raised platform
42 One of *The Beverly Hillbillies*
44 Another Caesar
47 Actress Francis
48 Stuart Erwin's role
49 Miss Arden
50 Come upon
51 Fencing sword
52 Not old

down

1 Single unit
2 Preposition
3 Regular on Jacki Gleason's show (2 words)
4 Slope
5 Costar on *Perry Mason*
6 Greek letter
7 TV medic (2 words)
8 Star of East Side/West Side
9 Costar of 37-Across (2 words)
10 Seed covering
11 Event on *ABC's Wide World of Sports*
19 Clumsy fellow
21 Dry
22 Utah's state flower
23 Chirps
24 Another hillbilly
25 Ralph Bellamy's role (2 words)
27 Eager
28 Paving material
30 Curve
34 Lloyd Bridges' old domain
36 Insertion
37 Cattle land
38 Son in *Bonanza*
39 *Fury*'s neck hair
40 Window glass
43 Yelp
45 I have
46 Type of moisture

October 10, 1964

across

1 Admit frankly
5 Spanish article
8 Lassie
11 Mr. Arnaz
12 Mr. Wallach
13 Ember
14 Vend
15 Be ill
16 Early stringed instrument
17 The Man from U.N.C.L.E. (2 words)
20 Vase
21 Decline
22 Conscious
25 A Defender
29 Writer Serling
30 Motor coach
31 Be in debt
32 Mister Mayor
35 TV comedian
37 Paving material
38 Mr. Pettit, NBC newsman
39 One of The Entertainers (2 words)
45 Klugman in Harris Against the World
46 Mimic
47 Stanley Livingston
49 Wander
50 Fish eggs
51 Gilligan's Island skipper
52 Mr. Marvin
53 Miss Sothern
54 Girl's name

down

1 TV commercials
2 Change direction
3 Norway's capital
4 Alan Young in Mister Ed
5 Find out about
6 Dismounted
7 Another TV comedian
8 Trampas in The Virginian
9 Solemn declaration
10 The Farmer's Daughter's boss
13 Arnold Palmer's work tools
18 Before
19 Mr. Burrows
22 Noah's boat
23 Sorrow
24 Fruit drink
25 Play on words
26 Unit of weight
27 Possess
28 French marshal during Napoleon's reign
30 Betty Anderson in Peyton Place
33 Costar of Gunsmoke
34 Mr. March
35 Tom in Tom, Dick and Mary
36 Host of International Showtime
38 Hilda in The Joey Bishop Show
39 —— Betz of The Donna Reed Show
40 South African lily
41 Kind of review an actor likes
42 On
43 Two of TW3's T's
44 Cause to slope
48 Pod vegetable

November 21, 1964

across

1 Fall month (abbr.)
4 Roman goddess of the harvest
7 Bowling item
10 Sixth Jewish month
11 Aid
12 Hail!
13 Gaze intently
14 Bill of fare
15 Lurch of *The Addams Family*
16 Creator of Perry Mason
19 Negative
20 Climax on *The Defenders*
23 Fairy queen
26 Vane in *Mr. Novak*
29 The Man from U.N.C.L.E.
30 Pub drinks
32 Fighting force
33 English school
34 City in Nevada
35 Cost
37 Perceive visually
38 Character in *The Baileys of Balboa*
40 Cuckoo relative
42 One of the Rogues (2 words)
48 He's Jim, Sam Bailey's son
50 Jai-___

51 Region
52 Exists
53 Alike
54 Departs
55 One of Benny's gang
56 CBS symbol
57 Conclude

down

1 Aroma
2 Lester in *McHale's Navy*
3 Hilda in *The Joey Bishop Show*
4 Actor Philip ___
5 Await judgment
6 Feat
7 AFL team
8 I have (contr.)
9 Moderator Brooks
10 Mimic

11 ___ *Hour*
17 Deity
18 Scottish variation of "Irish"
21 African lily
22 Solitary
23 ___ Antony
24 Opposite of aweather
25 Surly TV doctor
27 King of Judah (Biblical)
28 Mrs. Howell on *Gilligan's Island*
31 Earth
36 Compass point
39 Rental contract
41 TV picture
43 Beautiful boxer
44 Star's ambition
45 Press
46 Require
47 Auto fuel

91

February 13, 1965

down

1 TV space family
2 At the risk of the owner (abbr.)
3 Hasten
4 Allied group (abbr.)
5 Jack and Randy
6 Australian bird
7 —— *College Bowl*
8 *Bonanza* star
9 *Rawhide*'s Rowdy
10 First king of Israel
11 Hart of *Burke's Law*
12 One who keeps a secret (sl.)
18 Commotion
20 To swindle (sl.)
21 School vehicle
23 He's McHale
25 *TWTWTW* bandleader
27 Comic Adams
28 Not good
30 Parker's rank
31 TV ghost
32 High mountain
33 Miss Lupino
34 Simian
35 *My Living Doll*
36 Goes with nonsense
37 Otherwise
39 Mr. Vane of *Mr. Novak*
41 Coin
42 He's Burkhardt on Cara's show
45 *What's This Song?* host
47 Duo
50 Behold!
52 Battleship "Big ——"

across

1 He's Gomez on *The Addams Family*
5 Comedienne Cass
10 *General Hospital*, e.g.
12 —— *Three*
13 Proposition
14 "Summer" in Paris
15 He's Anderson of *Perry Mason*
16 "—— *tu, Brute!*"
17 World power
19 Motion picture award
21 Andy Griffith's TV aunt
22 Vein of ore
24 Panelist Poston
25 Plays on words
26 Bud in *Flipper*
28 *Twelve O'clock High* setting
29 Correlative of neither
30 Corn spike
31 He slew Abel
33 Mingo of *Daniel Boone*
36 Transaction
37 Wynn and Sullivan
38 Raced
40 Cooking abbreviation
41 *Rogues'* family, St. ——
43 Female sheep
44 Not abed
45 Nickname of 15-Across
46 Obtain
48 Mother
49 Catlike
51 Phyllis of *TWTWTW*
53 *World War I* combat zone
54 Portal

February 20, 1965

across

1. Lady soldier
4. He's Hoss
7. Girl's name
11. Persia
13. Mr. Wallach
14. Require
15. Antitoxins
16. TV network
17. FDR's mother
18. Costar of *Flipper*
20. ___ Donahue of *Many Happy Returns*
22. Mouth (comb. form)
23. Cloth fragment
24. Costar of 43-Across
28. Costar of *Peyton Place*
32. Andy Griffith's "son"
33. ___ Young of *The Rogues*
35. Pallid
36. Dennis Day, e.g.
38. Costar of *The Munsters*
40. In no way
42. Paving material
43. *The Bing ___ Show*
46. Leg joints
50. Man's genus
51. *Burke's ___*
53. Nobleman
54. Pertaining to an era
55. Miss Gabor
56. Irritate
57. Beginner
58. Mr. Milland
59. Mr. Skelton

down

1. Desire
2. Region
3. ___ Betz of *The Donna Reed Show*
4. Costar of *Karen*
5. Priest's vestment
6. More agreeable
7. One of *McHale's Navy* (2 words)
8. TV singer-host
9. Roman emperor
10. Jewish month
12. The Man from U.N.C.L.E. (2 words)
19. Mr. Gershwin
21. Inhabitant of Laos
24. *I've ___ a Secret*
25. Gorilla
26. TV canine
27. Accomplished
29. Hearing organ
30. Everyone
31. Zodiac sign
34. Escape
37. Dick Van Dyke's role
39. Is able to
41. Mary ___ Moore
43. NBC newscaster
44. Actor Calhoun
45. Persian poet
47. Den
48. Perry Mason author
49. Toboggan
52. Miss Gardner

March 27, 1965

across

1 Communication (abbr.)
4 Tube
8 Winged mammal
11 Miss Albright
12 Winged
13 Actor Wallach
14 Jewish month
15 Star on *Gilligan's Island* (2 words)
17 Barbara Parkins in *Peyton Place*
19 River (Sp.)
20 One T of *TW3*
22 He's Jed
26 Mr. Burrows
28 TV music man
31 Historical time period
32 That woman
33 Singer Frankie __
35 Edge
36 Actor Ron __
37 Retain
38 Command to a horse
39 Ramond Burr's role
42 Rub
44 For each
46 Great confusion
49 Admiral Nelson in *Voyage*
54 Against
55 Whole
56 Mother of the gods
57 Excite or move someone
58 Informal farewell
59 Secondhand
60 Feminine suffix

down

1 Current fashion or style
2 __ *People*
3 Lee J. Cobb's role
4 American airline (abbr.)
5 Not well
6 Host Jack __
7 Mr. Ford
8 *Petticoat Junction* star
9 Entire
10 Bind
11 Set for *Novak's* Arthur Bradwell
16 Peg in quoits
18 Type of sailboat
21 East Indian wood
23 *No Time for* __
24 Great Lake
25 Appellation
26 Coughing sound
27 Actor Lugosi
29 Falsehood
30 Was aware
34 Heroic poem
40 Open (poet.)
41 Late Indian leader
43 Aspect or facet
45 College cheers
47 Elevator inventor
48 Title of respect
49 Folk singer Dylan
50 One
51 Understand
52 Female ruff (var.)
53 Child (Pogo's word)

April 10, 1965

across

1 Prima donna
5 Restaurant bill (sl.)
8 He's Daniel Boone
12 Sour, biting
13 Possessive pronoun
14 *Tycoon* regular
15 Costar of *The Defenders*
16 Southern constellation
17 Baking place
18 *Broadside*'s Adrian (2 words)
21 Spring month
22 Female deer
23 Top of a wave
26 Karen's Dad
30 Gilligan's alter ego
31 Temporary fashion
32 Teachers' group (abbr.)
33 She's in *No Time for Sergeants*
36 Melts
38 Fruit drink
39 Setting for *McHale's Navy*
40 Costar of *The Man from U.N.C.L.E.* (2 words)
47 Elie ——, NBC newscaster
48 Island (Fr.)
49 Assumed attitude
50 Smooth (phonetics)
51 Convent dweller
52 Arrow poison
53 Whirlpool

54 Golly!
55 Bird's home

down

1 Child's challenge
2 Chilled
3 Landscape
4 Weird TV family
5 A servile flatterer
6 Atmosphere surrounding someone
7 New TV Western
8 Myron —— of the Welk Show
9 Roof edge
10 Swerve or distort
11 Judgment (Fr.)
19 Rodent
20 —— Grady of *My Three Sons*

23 TV network
24 King (Fr.)
25 Recede, as tides
26 Papa
27 Actress Balin
28 Modern
29 Vapor
31 *Rawhide* star
34 Paul Ford's TV role
35 Sum up
36 Orange pekoe
37 *Flipper* costar
39 *American —— Magazine*
40 Welk saxophonist
41 Bedridden
42 Sell
43 Mystery aid
44 Unaccompanied
45 Utilizes
46 —— *the Press*

May 1, 1965

across

1 Southern state (abbr.)
4 Summit
7 Fast plane
10 Among
11 Arabian name
12 English school
14 TV microphone crane
15 Actor Cobb
16 An invisible atmosphere
17 Quint McHale (2 words)
20 River (Sp.)
21 Accelerate (an engine)
22 Occupant
25 In high spirits
29 Spoken
30 Actress Foch
31 Court game
34 *Hector Heathcote's* elephant pal
36 Biblical woman
37 Expert pilot
38 Gal in *No Time for Sergeants* (2 words)
45 Spring flower
46 He's Lurch in *The Addams Family*
47 *Hallmark* offering
48 Bullets in *Combat!*
49 Moray
50 Long ago
51 She's Donna's friend Midge
52 Initials of a former President
53 Baxter or Brown

down

1 "Love" in Madrid
2 TV's Linus is one
3 Richard Basehart's role (2 words)
4 He plays Ozzie's pal Joe
5 Bread spread
6 He's Caje on *Combat!*
7 Wilma Flintstone (3 words)
8 Small case
9 Actor Rip ___
10 Mr. Burrows
13 "No" in Edinburgh
18 "One" in Bonn
19 Jellylike substance
22 Young child
23 Before
24 Miss Fabray
26 Metal from Peru
27 Compass direction (abbr.)
28 *Valentine's* ___
32 Climbing vine
33 Not standing
34 Western prop
35 Diamonds (sl.)
38 She's Allison in *Peyton Place*
39 Girl's name
40 Portray in words
41 Require
42 Red gin
43 Paddles
44 Comic Louis ___

September 18, 1965

across

1 Actor John ___
5 Manufacture (abbr.)
8 Rebounding sound
12 Leave out (printer's instruction)
13 TV oldie: *You ___ There*
14 Bermuda or creeping grass
15 Dreary
16 Mild oath
17 Bitter
18 Before noon
19 MGM symbol
21 Triple
22 *A ___ Called Shenandoah*
24 Legendary birds
26 Part of "TV"
27 Nocturnal noise
29 Small case
31 TV dial position
32 He's Gomer's Sergeant (2 words)
35 Extra on *Hogan's Heroes*
36 Producer Brodkin
37 Lifting implements
39 Breakfast items
41 Jalbert's role on *Combat!*
43 Superlative suffix
44 Greek letter
45 Ralston or Miles
47 Part of canned laughter
48 On top of
50 Address on *Convoy*
51 Cholesterol (abbr.)
53 To tremble (obscure)

54 Ever (poet.)
55 Sewing machine inventor
56 Worthless residue
57 Attempt
58 Not hard

down

1 Family of weirdos
2 Foe on *Twelve O'Clock High* (2 words)
3 Tavern drink
4 Film necessity
5 The nearsighted Mr. ___
6 Andy's aunt (2 words)
7 Mr. Skelton
8 Nelson, Sullivan and Ames
9 Ex-Rouge Robert ___

10 *The Fugitive, Bonanza* and *Slattery's People* (3 words)
11 *Trials of ___*
20 She's Granny
23 Neither follower
25 Comedian Erwin
26 Yugoslavian ruler
28 Sports cheers
30 Speak up
33 Knight of the Rueful Countenance (abbr.)
34 *___ Man's Family*
35 Kimble's pursuer
38 Comedienne Joan ___
40 Boone's Hannibal is one
42 His mother is a car
46 Kildare's concern
49 Nickname for Miss Cass
50 Video receiver
52 Exclamation (dial.)

December 11, 1965

across

1 Greek Muse of history
5 *Voyage to the Bottom ___* (3 words)
13 Shaped like an oar
14 He's Smart (2 words)
15 Snicker ___: knife
16 Meal leftovers
17 Small role
18 Darkens by the sun
19 The Hooterville (abbr.)
20 Portrayed by 2-Down
21 Female animal
22 ___May, a Hillbilly
25 Interjection
26 Clever TV dog
29 Summer drink
32 Series with Ruth Roman (3 words)
35 Lyric poem
36 Skilled person
37 ___ *the World Turns*
38 Son of Isaac
39 Pester
40 Skelton feature: The Silent ___
43 Symbol for cerium
45 Mongolian desert
46 Bearer of acorns
47 Rabbit relative
49 Another time
50 He's Crackerby
52 Title of respect
53 TV's state legislator, beaten at the polls
54 Banner's role on *Hogan's Heroes*

down

1 Roland Winters in *The Smothers Brothers Show*
2 Actress featured on 32-Across (2 words)
3 She's Granny, costar of 22-Across
4 Courtroom cry
5 The nose detects it
6 Sergeant assigned to F Troop (2 words)
7 It's dynamite to play with
8 Claims ownership
9 Mingo of *Daniel Boone*
10 Movie jungle boy
11 Actor ___Jannings
12 The Thin Man's dog
20 Adjective-forming suffix
23 Italian-actress Virna
24 Romanian coins
26 Football position (abbr.)
27 Cries of discovery
28 A wading bird
29 In the morning
30 Dick Kallman's TV role
31 Main character on *The FBI* (poss.)
33 Compass direction
34 Everest, for example (abbr.)
38 ___ al
39 Ancient Grecian district
40 Aims of a soap opera
41 New star of *12 O'clock High*
42 Gumbo
44 Not so difficult
45 Nasty cut
47 Abyss
48 Who's got a secret?
51 Gary Collins portrays one (abbr.)

98

April 9, 1966

across

1 Miss Adams
5 Actor Audie ___
11 Egg-shaped
12 Actress Wood
13 Safe harbor
14 Spanish hero ___ Cid
15 Shout
16 Precious stone
17 Aleutian island
19 High mountain
20 Good golf score
21 Where Pierre is (abbr.)
22 Nineteenth letter
24 On ship
26 Old-fashioned
29 Opposite of gain
30 Scent
32 Ranger Bennett of *Laredo*

35 Quick look
37 Help
38 "I Aim ___ the Stars"
39 Dine
40 Actor Hunter
43 Polluted air
45 Doctor of laws (abbr.)
46 An astringent
48 Atop
49 Miss Seaforth
51 Actress Day
53 Small particles
54 Saga
55 Lairs

down

1 *Green Acres'* Lisa
   (2 words)
2 Skelton's bandleader
   (2 words)

3 Piece of news
4 Even (poet.)
5 Soda-fountain drink
6 Where Odgen is (abbr.)
7 He plays a Martian
8 Entreaty
9 Mound of earth
10 Sharp cry
11 Expression of pain
12 Mesh
17 Total
18 Subject of *This Proud Land*
20 What Joe calls Crazy
21 Senior (abbr.)
23 Portico
25 On the ocean
27 He's Rossi on *Peyton Place* (2 words)
28 Character on *Gunsmoke* (2 words)
31 Retired (abbr.)
33 Family member
34 Actor O'Brien
35 Hope specialty
36 Gerard's rank (abbr.)
40 Lofty
41 Wings
42 Town (colloq.)
44 United
45 Stringed instrument
47 Actress West
49 Downcast
50 A maritime province (abbr.)
52 *Lost* ___ *Space*

June 18, 1966

across

1 Finish
4 Tel ___, Israel
8 Resinous substance
11 Appeal
12 French composer, Edouard ___
13 Harem room
14 Jai ___
15 Mrs. Munster
16 Palmas or Vegas
17 Corbett of *Jesse James*
19 He's Maxwell Smart
21 Charged particle
22 Turkish title
23 Where the Antilles are (abbr.)
24 Sea ___, craft on 7-Down
26 Even score
27 Mr. Mack
28 Poses
29 *Run ___ Your Life*
30 Prying
31 Drama division
32 Ensign Parker
33 Outlaw Black ___
34 Everest, e.g. (abbr.)
35 Devour
36 Felix the ___
37 Harold of *Hazel*
39 Gospel singer ___ Jackson
43 Source of metal
44 Accommodation
46 Cadence
47 Falsehood
48 TV skunk
49 Arrow poison
50 Make lace
51 Skelton and Buttons
52 Actor Byrnes

down

1 Singer Fitzgerald
2 Close
3 *Please Don't Eat the* ___
4 He plays Riley on 7-Down
5 Doff a hat
6 "Under the weather"
7 ___ *to the Bottom of the Sea*
8 Actress Albright
9 Batman (2 words)
10 Lurch on *The Addams Family*
11 Mrs. North
18 In what manner
20 Hamilton Burger, e.g.
22 Aura
24 Character in *The Big Valley*
25 Cousin of the Addams'
26 One of the Smothers Brothers
27 Craggy hill
28 Honey West's partner (2 words)
29 Equip
30 Mom on *The Patty Duke Show*
32 Beautiful Elizabeth
33 Sound of contempt
35 Man on *Green Acres*
36 Walking sticks
38 Borscht ingredient
39 Hazel, e.g.
40 Peter ___ Hayes
41 Oldie, ___ *Three Lives* (2 words)
42 Dined
45 Poem

June 25, 1966

across

1 *Kraft Summer Music* ___
5 Varnish ingredient
8 Cheering shout
11 Shun
13 Miss Lupino
14 Japanese sash
15 Costar of *Fugitive*
16 Deface
17 Crawling insect
18 He's Joe in *Laredo* (2 words)
21 Shade tree
22 Without delay
23 Star of *Petticoat Junction*
26 Likely
28 Snouts
31 Lady in *Flipper*
33 *You Don't* ___!
35 Bird of peace
36 ___ Rigg of *The Avengers*
38 He's Col. Hogan
40 The late Mr. Cole
41 Is drowsy
43 Opening
45 Star of 1-Across (2 words)
50 Turkish title
51 Southern constellation
52 Yawns
54 Not well
55 *The* ___ *from U.N.C.L.E.*

56 Select group
57 ___ Kurty of *Dr. Kildare*
58 The lady
59 Western plateau

down

1 One who overacts
2 Declare openly
3 ___ Saunders of *Petticoat Junction*
4 Cotton thread
5 Large bean
6 Star of *Get Smart*
7 *Tonight Show* host
8 An *I Spy* man
9 Border on
10 *12 O'clock* ___
12 *Perry Mason*'s secretary
19 Little devils
20 State of mind

23 *To Tell the Truth* host
24 Actor Wallach
25 A star of *Gilligan's Island* (2 words)
27 Actor Hunter
29 She's Lisa of *Green Acres*
30 Matched group
32 Soon
34 ___ Bear
37 *The* ___ *Family*
39 Sign of membership or rank
42 Girl's name
44 Sacred song
45 Prison
46 Make eyes at
47 Weathercock
48 Andy Griffith's "son"
49 Fishing snares
53 Ocean

across

1 He plays Nick on *The Big Valley*
6 Great singer Enrico ——
12 The U in U.N.C.L.E.
14 Famous British yachtsman
15 Rural Delivery (abbr.)
16 Atmosphere
17 Basehart's role (abbr.)
18 Football position (abbr.)
19 Impresario Hurok
21 Actress Bette ——
23 Sheep's bleat
24 Pertaining to an age
26 Mrs. Jerry North
27 Plays Gruber on *McHale's Navy*
28 Arouse from sleep
30 Indian garb
31 He's Henry Phyfe
32 Drop of paint
33 Russian girl's name
35 *Peyton Place* star
38 Snicker ——
39 Do wrong
40 Mr. Mack et al.
42 Cut with an ax
43 Young lover or gallant
45 Faucet
46 Three-toed sloth
47 Digit
48 Ever (poet.)
50 Mother
51 —— *Don't Eat the Daisies*
53 One who commands
55 Man on *Peyton Place*

56 Neville Brand's *Laredo* role

down

1 Handbag
2 Samantha's mom
3 Seventh musical note
4 Greek letter
5 Red (Scot.)
6 Maintain or assert
7 Assists
8 Indicates record speed
9 Where Ogden is (abbr.)
10 He's Nagurski in *The Wackiest Ship*
11 Plays Rodney in *Peyton Place*
13 Hung in folds
20 Perry Mason's forte
22 Dick —— Dyke

23 Saloon
25 Huge
27 Actor Sebastian ——
29 New Zealand parrot
30 Actor Mineo
32 Fess Parker's role
33 American dramatist
34 Actor Ayres
35 Miss Farrow
36 Fisherman's need
37 Plays Boone's pal Mingo (2 words)
38 Figure
39 Sugary
41 Bowling score
43 Just passable
44 Never (poet.)
47 Siamese (var.)
49 Gordon Mac——
52 Overhead train
54 Rosemary —— Camp

August 6, 1966

across

1 TV comedian
5 Gerson on *Doctor Kildare*
8 Star of *Trials of O'Brien*
12 Actor Hale
13 Before
14 Star of *I Dream of Jeannie*
15 Petroleum
16 *Batman*
17 Decline
18 Paces
20 Loiter
22 Stomach
23 Blood factor
24 Lawrence on *Gidget*
26 Robert Vaughn's role
29 Body part
31 Grandpa Munster
33 Sound of disgust
34 Either of two Browns
35 Miss Hathaway of *The Beverly Hillbillies*
37 Part of "to be"
38 *Get ___*
40 Andy Griffith's TV son
41 Long time period
42 Cry of surprise
43 TV network
45 Collection of anecdotes
47 The Farmer's Daughter
51 Bald
53 Image
55 Tavern drink
56 Onionlike vegetable
57 TV receiver
58 Otherwise
59 Scottish-Gaelic
60 Monogram of a former President
61 Small, round object

down

1 Foe of 9-Down
2 Landed
3 Plays Jack Dane on *Daktari*
4 Printer's measure
5 A Beverly Hillbilly
6 Russian range
7 Uncle on *My Three Sons*
8 Not many
9 Star of 38-Across
10 Singer Horne
11 Was aware of
16 Shady tree
19 Dancer Juliet
21 Man's nickname
25 Doctor Royal on *Hank* (2 words)
26 Health resort
27 Electrical unit
28 Football position (abbr.)
29 Inclined to stick with relatives
30 Pronoun
31 Cuckoo
32 Heath on *The Big Valley*
36 News agency (abbr.)
39 Large extinct bird
41 *Green ___*
42 Be sick
43 Skilled
44 Another Hillbilly
46 Summer drinks
48 Lucy's Mr. Mooney
49 Miss Lanchester
50 Actress Donna ___
52 Piece out
54 Baseball great, Mel ___
58 Man on 41-Down

November 26, 1966

3 Preposition
4 Railroad
5 Pitcher part
6 Repeated sound
7 Article of clothing
8 Dana Wynter's role
9 Barbara Stanwyck on *The Big Valley*
10 Opinion-researcher Roper
11 Actress Donna ___
12 Moisture
18 Hawaiian garland
19 FBI's Special Agent in Charge (abbr.)
21 Young child
24 *The ___ Patrol*
26 Blood type
27 Follow with TV camera
28 Frank Ferguson on *Peyton Place*
29 Captain of the Seaview (2 words)
30 Pecan
32 Mr. Ford
33 Consume
36 Evil
39 150 in Rome
40 8-Across (poet.)
42 Edge
43 Creek
45 *The Rounders* star
47 Night fliers
48 Dismounted
50 Patrolman's round of duty
52 Uproar
53 Small pie
54 Conjunction
56 Short sleep
58 Collection of anecdotes
62 McCoy of *Star Trek* (abbr.)
63 Football position (abbr.)

across

1 Grandpa on *The Road West*
8 Always
12 Actress Marlene ___
13 Lowly
14 Seventh Greek letter
15 Twenty-first Greek letter
16 Summit
17 Lucy on *Pistols 'n' Petticoats*
20 Table scrap
22 Fox (Scot.)
23 Corn spike
25 Bull (Sp.)
27 Bird
31 *My ___ Sons*
34 Beverage
35 Large container
37 Mr. Gershwin
38 Relative
41 Gary Collins on *Iron Horse*
44 Ball of yarn
46 502 in Rome
47 Musical measure
49 Tease
51 Judy on *Lost In Space*
55 Alfred of *Batman*
57 Meadow
59 Mr. Fleming
60 Ginger on *Gilligan's Island*
61 *He, ___!*
64 Pace
65 Family on *Shane*

down

1 Quote
2 Cure

104

April 1, 1967

60 Yearns (colloq.)
61 Finales

down

1 Mom
2 British actor ____ Guinness
3 Star of *The Avengers* (2 words)
4 Scoff
5 Greek letter
6 Leg
7 *It's About Time* girl
8 Sharpen a razor
9 Star of *Occasional Wife* (2 words)
10 Inactive
11 Sullen
19 A Man from U.N.C.L.E.
21 Costar of *That Girl*
23 Baseball team
25 Be drowsy
26 Sheep's bleat
28 Pruitt's Uncle
29 Price labels
31 White lie
32 Affirmative
35 Plumbing mishap
38 Building wing
42 *Family Affair* girl
44 *Laredo* character
45 Stubborn animal
46 Ship's company
47 Hard to find
48 Star of *I Dream of Jeannie*
50 Peter ____ Hayes
51 Oxen of Tibet
54 Magazine managers (abbr.)

across

1 Charts
5 Shade trees
9 Central
12 He's Gilligan's skipper
13 Cause to slope
14 Wedding reply (2 words)
15 Measure, apportion
16 Cupid
17 Actor Gulager
18 *Green* ____
20 Describing one of the Smothers
22 ____ *Horse*
24 Pod vegetable
25 TV network
27 Yarn fluff
30 Resist openly
33 Timber tree

34 He's Rodney in *Peyton Place*
36 Two of three do it on *To Tell the Truth*
37 Woman (sl.)
39 ____ *of Night*
40 Another TV network
41 Priest's robe
43 Miss Lane of *The Virginian*
45 He plays Trampas
49 An *I Spy* man
52 Vase
53 Lose color
55 Lamb's pen name
56 He's Kato on *The Green Hornet*
57 Star of *My Three Sons*
58 Descended
59 Female sheep

May 20, 1967

across

1 Father
5 Spring
9 Actor Byrnes
12 Comedian King
13 Volcano in Italy
14 Fade away
15 The Green Hornet
16 15-Across's paper
18 Sharkey on *Voyage to the Bottom of the Sea*
20 Word bases
21 Long time period
23 *Bell Telephone* ___
24 TV network
27 Motorist's inn
29 Eb on *Green Acres*
32 Mr. Waverly of U.N.C.L.E.
33 Extinct bird
34 *Love* ___ *Rooftop* (2 words)
35 Obstruct
36 A planet
38 Uncle in Southampton
39 Audacious
41 Part of a wheel
43 Metal
45 Patricia Harty's role
49 Rebecca on *Daniel Boone*
53 Batman
54 Mr. Linkletter
55 Rowboat gear
56 Antimissile missile

57 Distress signal
58 *Star* ___
59 Actresses Sandra and Ruby

down

1 Theatrical role
2 Away from the wind
3 Twins
4 Musician Previn
5 Band leader Brown
6 "Summer" in France
7 That Girl
8 *Rat* ___
9 Carney's role (2 words)
10 Formal assembly
11 Belonging to Monroe of *Voyage*
17 Promissory note
19 ___ Kippur

22 Wanderer
23 Moor
24 Priest's robe
25 Actress Benaderet
26 Chance Reynolds' of *The Road West*
28 Craggy hill
30 Unit
31 Frantic
36 Man on *Peyton Place*
37 Hold close
40 Over (Poetic)
42 Star of *Laredo*
43 Health resorts
44 Tropical plant
46 Actress Adams
47 Capture
48 Mingo of *Daniel Boone*
50 Automobile
51 Anger
52 Inquire

July 1, 1967

across

1 Walk in water
5 Everyone
8 Emperor
12 Dry
13 Actress West
14 French friend
15 Spanish river
16 Lions
17 Manufactured
18 Israel on *Daniel Boone*
20 Wane
22 Mr. Skelton
23 Advertisement
24 Remainder
26 Ed Sullivan, e.g.
29 Bill Cosby on *I Spy*
31 Boxing term
33 He's Batman
34 Haul away
35 Star of *I Dream of Jeannie*
37 Football position (abbr.)
38 Larry Storch on *F Troop*
40 Elizabeth of *The Virginian*
41 Unique person or thing (sl.)
42 550 in Rome
43 Candy Kane of 44-Down
45 Greek letter
47 Actor-folksinger Boone
51 Baked desserts
53 Precious stone
55 Part of the verb "to be"
56 Be gone!
57 Vast age
58 Man's name
59 Slippery
60 Singer Starr
61 O'Hara on *Batman*

down

1 The Boy Wonder
2 Operatic solo
3 Dress designer
4 Mr. Sullivan
5 Doctors' group (abbr.)
6 Tardy
7 Bandleader (2 words)
8 Cap
9 Don Adams role
10 Assistant
11 She's Donna Stone
16 Mrs. Tony Martin
19 Adam West role
21 Wager
25 Star (Lat.)
26 Mr. Holbrook
27 Poem
28 A continent (abbr.)
29 William Shatner show (2 words)
30 Correspondent (abbr.)
31 Captain Parmenter of *F Troop*
32 Unit
36 District Attorney (abbr.)
39 Turn to the right
41 Rodney on *Peyton Place*
42 Thirsty
43 Church part
44 *Captain* ___
46 Atmosphere
48 Title
49 Faucet leak
50 Sharp bark
52 Pig pen
54 Reddish-brown horse
58 Symbol for erbium

July 8, 1967

across

1 Bert ___, comic
5 Fred MacMurray's part
8 Bell sound
12 Jai-___, popular Latin American game
13 Dolores Del ___
14 On the sheltered side
15 ___ Connelly, playwright
16 Arranged (abbr.)
17 Blood vessel
18 National song
20 Baltimore baseball player
22 Actress Gardner
23 Mr. Mosel
24 Stafford Repp on *Batman*
27 Hazel's position (2 words)
31 Thin rope
32 Lad
33 Pottery material
34 Seized opponent, as in football
36 Part of play
37 Electrically charged atom
38 Mrs. Sinatra
39 Jack ___, comic
42 Finally (2 words)
46 Arabian
47 Conclusion
49 Girl's name
50 Textile factory
51 Beverage
52 Persuade
53 Old Harry Morgan role
54 A Smothers Brother
55 Complain

down

1 Tibetan monk
2 Young or King
3 Richard Rodgers' collaborator
4 The Fugitive (2 words)
5 Serious TV play
6 Melody
7 Actress Malone
8 Illya Kuryakin
9 Butter substitute
10 Commissioner Gordon
11 Mr. Rayburn
19 Lisa on *Green Acres*
21 She's Marge Bergman in *Search for Tomorrow*
24 October (abbr.)
25 Exclamation (var.)
26 Kind of light
27 Clump of ivy
28 Malt liquor
29 James Bond's creator
30 Change color of
32 Mr. Cerf
35 Card game
36 Be seated
38 Polite title of address
39 ___ *Unto My Feet*
40 Great Lake
41 Brewing necessity
43 Pertaining to aircraft
44 *The ___ of Western Man*
45 At that time
48 New (comb. form)

across

1 What a cow chews
4 Ben Gazzara's role
8 The Caped Crusader
12 Turkish title
13 In addition
14 Singer Horne
15 Resident of
   Southampton (2 words)
18 To be (Lat.)
19 Poet's abbreviation
20 Receive salary
23 *Daktari*'s Judy
28 Extrasensory perception
31 Door pads
33 Gilligan has one
34 Part of *The Red Skelton
   Hour* (3 words)
37 Girl's name
38 Region
39 Periods of time (abbr.)
40 Camper's shelter
   (2 words)
42 He operates 9-Down
44 The Long Branch, e.g.
46 He's Mingo in
   Daniel Boone
50 Character in *The
   Road West* (2 words)
56 Sioux Indian
57 Glacial ridges
58 Parmenter of *F Troop*
59 He plays The
   Boy Wonder
60 ___ lily
61 Finale

down

1 Apparel for 8-Across
2 Grunts
3 ___ *of Our Lives*
4 Friend
5 Woodcutter Baba
6 Spacecraft on *Star Trek*
7 Vein of ore
8 Whole quantity
9 *Casa ___ Gato, T.H.E.
   Cat* night club
10 One (Dialect)
11 Spoil
16 Actor Marvin
17 Incorporated (abbr.)
21 Friend (Fr.)
22 Thin, sparse (Sp.)
24 Pronoun
25 Espionage series
   (2 words)
26 Character on
   It's About Time
27 Animal friends
28 Volcanic mountain
29 Photograph
30 Father (Fr.)
32 To cut: snick and ___
35 Polish river
36 Faucet
41 TV schedule
   abbreviation
43 Piece of corn
45 Andy's pal
47 TV host Douglas
48 She's Jeannie
49 Dispatch
50 Archer's equipment
51 Greek letter
52 Conjunction
53 A Beverly Hillbilly
54 Small horse
55 In favor of

April 20, 1968

across

1 Skelton character
5 TV network
8 *Felony Squad* man
11 Volcanic rock
12 Murmur lovingly
13 Bail
14 Moslem ruler
15 Rowing instrument
16 Flower
17 Star of *The Guns of Will Sonnett*
19 Music composition
21 Tavern
22 Help
23 Correct
26 Sheriff Ryker of *The Virginian*
30 Female
31 Slice
32 Costar of *The Felony Squad*
33 TV comedian-host
35 Costar of *My Three Sons*
36 Sally Field's role
37 Capuchin monkey
38 Costar of *N.Y.P.D.*
41 Declare
45 Region
46 Japanese sash
48 Man on *The Rat Patrol*
49 Stead
50 Star of *Garrison's Gorillas*
51 Of a wing
52 Youngster
53 Drunkard
54 Fabric

down

1 Cat's weapon
2 Tibetan monk
3 Wicked
4 Costar of *Mission: Impossible* (2 words)
5 Fruit of the oak
6 Large snake
7 Costar of *The Andy Griffith Show*
8 Actress Lane of *The Virginian*
9 Mine entrance
10 High plateau
13 Costar of *The High Chaparral* (2 words)
18 Finale
20 Lubricate
23 Omelet item
24 Wire measure
25 Before
26 Firearm
27 Tibetan antelope
28 Ancient times (Archaic)
29 Costar of *The Flying Nun*
31 Star of *Mannix*
34 Prosecute
35 Cooking fuel
37 Roger Moore's TV role
38 ___ Disney
39 Opera solo
40 TV's Donna ___
42 *Perry Mason* author
43 Sheepskin used in bookbinding
44 Beginner
47 Frightening sound

August 3, 1968

across

1 Chum
4 *Beverly Hillbillies* man
7 TV network
10 Dry
12 Mr. Gershwin
13 Rain heavily
14 Mr. Arnaz
15 Town on *The Andy Griffith Show*
17 Devil
19 Occupied a chair
20 Close by
23 Lawful
27 Likely
29 One of *My Three Sons*
30 Of this kind
31 Lifetime
33 Costar of *The Lucy Show*
34 Follows orders
36 Prevents
38 TV comedian
39 Molten rock
40 Piercing tool
42 Costar of *The Big Valley*
46 TV series
51 Star of *I Dream of Jeannie*
52 Nobleman
53 Distant
54 Costar of *The Virginian*
55 CBS symbol
56 Compass point
57 Floor-cleaning tool

down

1 Cushions
2 Region
3 Catalog
4 Star of *Gunsmoke*
5 Period in history
6 *Death Valley* ___
7 And not
8 Prickly seedcase (var.)
9 Weep
11 Costar of *Peyton Place* (2 words)
13 Costar of *Mission: Impossible* (2 words)
16 Bundle of cotton
18 Bird's beak
21 Wing
22 Royal
24 Small fly
25 Troubles
26 Mr. Majors of *The Big Valley*
27 Machinery oil
28 Freezer
30 Cry
32 Costar of *Green Acres*
35 Stitches
37 Costar of *The Mothers-in-Law*
41 Animation
43 He was Batman
44 Pianist Peter ___
45 ___ *Judgment*
46 Island (Fr.)
47 Star of *The Invaders*
48 Raw mineral
49 He's Hoss
50 Before

111

across

1 Legal document
5 ___ unto My Feet
9 Seedcase
12 The ___ Chaparral
13 Medley
14 Conductor Bloch
15 Siouan Indian
16 TV series
18 Costar of The Flying Nun
20 Western plateau
21 Peculiar
23 Watches
26 Low female voice
29 Miss Lupino
32 Lassie's costar
34 Thin rope
35 Against
36 Miss Fitzgerald
37 Trim
38 Star of 17-Down
39 Emit fumes
40 Costar of The Virginian
42 Make mistakes
44 ___ Baer
47 Conductor on The Hollywood Palace
51 TV series (2 words)
55 Impolite
56 Costar of The Mothers-In-Law
57 Mr. Kazan
58 Jumping insect
59 Furious
60 Repose
61 Fender mishap

down

1 Pronoun
2 Miss Hayworth
3 Mr. Stravinsky
4 New TV series (3 words)
5 Ship's record
6 Astringent
7 Source of coal
8 Sheriff's men
9 In favor of
10 Hardwood tree
11 Stain
17 New TV series (2 words)
19 TV host
22 Costar of Bewitched
24 Perry Mason author
25 Auction
26 Drama division
27 Star of Hawaii Five-0
28 Three singers
30 Female deer
31 Girl's name
33 Tibetan ox
41 ___ Pyle, USMC
43 Sun god
45 Costar of Here's Lucy
46 Spring flower
48 Govern
49 Star of I Dream of Jeannie
50 Chair
51 Jewel
52 Costar of Green Acres
53 Costar of That Girl
54 Make lace

across

1 Place to sleep
4 *Get Smart* star
9 Crow's cry
12 Doctors' organization (abbr.)
13 Easy (sl.)
14 Poem
15 Large number
17 Lung sounds
19 Prompts an actor
20 Song for one
21 Age group
23 *The Hollywood* ___
26 Not common
27 Hillbilly wars
28 District of Columbia (abbr.)
29 Bitter vetch
30 Lone Star state
31 Conceit (colloq.)
32 Toward
33 Type
34 Little quarrel
35 Sewing strands
37 Men's clothing item
38 Shade trees
39 Vessel
40 Top of the head
42 He entertains the troops (2 words)
45 Possessed
46 Alert
48 Comedienne Elaine ___
49 Mr. Sullivan's
50 Passover feast
51 Compass point

down

1 Humbug!
2 Australian bird
3 The June Taylor ___
4 *Green* ___
5 Expires
6 Conjunction
7 Bob Barker's job (abbr.)
8 Covers
9 Pigment
10 Fruit drink
11 Man's nickname
16 Sand hill
18 Alack!
20 *The Felony* ___
21 A delight
22 *Star Trek* crew's home base
23 Male and female
24 Actor Buchanan
25 Bill Cosby role
27 Gives nourishment to
30 Role on *The Virginian*
31 The essence of something
33 Ringing object
34 Iranian ruler
36 Peruses
37 Solemn
39 Dull speaker
40 *He &* ___
41 Blackguard
42 Evil
43 Greek god of forests
44 ___ *Guess*
47 You and me

across

1 Pig
4 The ____ Valley
7 Mournful
10 Actor ____ Sharif
12 Be mistaken
13 Genus of auks
14 Fodder tower
15 Glide on snow
16 Green Acres lady
17 Building for horses
19 Costar of Get Smart
21 Have a TV snack
22 Enemy
23 An Emmy, for example
26 Chief meals
30 Talk noisily
31 Gentle ____
32 ____ Up and Live
33 Man on The Virginian
35 Powdery
36 Lubricate
37 Turf
38 Cask
41 Agnes Moorehead's role
45 Employs
46 Gorilla
48 Narrative poem
49 Irritate
50 TV comedian
51 The ____ of the Game
52 Sullivan's conductor
53 The Doris ____ Show
54 Bandleader Brown

down

1 Bonanza man
2 Leave out
3 Festive
4 Attack
5 Annoy
6 Merv ____
7 Slipped
8 Too
9 Singer Martin
11 Star of That's Life
   (2 words)
13 Password host
   (2 words)
18 Boy
20 An eternity
23 TV's Mr. Carney
24 Armed conflict
25 Collection of anecdotes
26 ____ Moines, Iowa
27 Dawn goddess
28 Decay
29 Firmament
31 Costar of The Mothers-
   in-Law
34 Bakery product
35 Star of Get Smart
37 Shabby
38 Star of Ironside
39 Continent
40 Depend
42 Lustrous gem
43 Hoarfrost
44 High cards
47 Pod vegetable

May 24, 1969

across

1 Highest point
5 Puppeteer Baird
8 Spar
12 Hope Lange's role
13 City in Oklahoma
14 Skillful
15 B.P.O.E. member
16 Group on *Star Trek*
17 Black
18 Bandleader Sammy ___
20 Ed Norton
22 Possess
23 ___ *Three Sons*
24 The Orient
26 Girl's name
29 Actress Douglas
31 Greek letter
33 Comedian King

34 Jeanne d'___
35 Comic Crosby
37 Concerning
38 Italian poet
40 Let fall
41 Jethro on TV
42 Frank Sinatra's son
43 Sailor
45 Friday or Gannon
47 Fervent
51 *The Outcasts* costar
53 Jeff of *N.Y.P.D.*
55 Summer drink
56 Where Ogden is
57 Time of your life
58 Nautical term
59 Melody
60 Man's name
61 Loan

down

1 Leon or Nancy
2 Actor Robert ___
3 Mannix
4 Symbol for erbium
5 Saloon
6 Notion
7 Comedienne Vicki ___
8 Actress West
9 *The FBI* costar
10 Leisurely
11 Mr. Ford's state (abbr.)
16 Shout
19 *Gunsmoke*'s Kitty
21 Summer hue
25 Gladys on *Bewitched*
26 Vehicle
27 Cheer from the arena
28 Sun god
29 *Laugh-In* star (2 words)
30 Morsel
31 Golf star
32 Little devil
36 Otherwise
39 Nuclear energy group
41 *Family Affair* star
42 Buddy Ebsen's role
43 Man at the race track
44 Aleutian island
46 Singer Patty ___
48 Harry on *Here's Lucy*
49 TV genie
50 Jim of *Adam-12*
52 That girl
54 Bolivar Shagnasty
58 Mr. Capone

June 21, 1969

across

1 Small child
4 Carl Betz's TV role
8 Increase
11 Single
12 Miss Adams
13 Vessel (Lat.)
14 Love (Lat.)
15 Agent 86 (2 words)
17 TV comedian
19 Annoys
20 Seat
22 Girl's name
23 Large deer
26 Linda Evans' TV role
28 Sheep's bleat
31 Shaped like V
32 Guided
33 Possess
34 Even (Poet.)
35 TV host
37 He's Carlos
38 A prayer (Archaic)
40 Middle Western state (abbr.)
42 A prefix meaning half
43 Character on *The Queen and I*
47 Tony of *My Friend Tony*
51 Burning
52 Obstruct
53 He's Joshua on *Here Come the Brides*
54 Comedian Wilson
55 Cunning
56 Poker stake
57 Thus far

down

1 Large book
2 Below (nautical)
3 Miss Day
4 Buddy Ebsen's role
5 A Japanese plant
6 To sound
7 Costar of *Land of the Giants*
8 Lisa of *Green Acres* (2 words)
9 Belonging to *Hawaii Five-0*'s Mr. Fong
10 Shaped like an S
11 Actor Mineo
16 Mr. Rowan
18 Alex Mundy's employer
21 City in France
22 A Mother-in-Law
23 Surname of 22-Down
24 Heath on *The Big Valley*
25 Star of *Mayberry RFD* (2 words)
27 Delaware (abbr.)
29 Reverence
30 No matter which
35 She portrays 41-Down
36 Edward's nickname
39 An Australian bird
41 *Family Affair* girl
42 Close
44 Office necessity
45 Glass ingredient
46 Yes (sl.)
47 A network
48 A charged atom
49 To carve
50 Spanish cheer

across

1 Baseball tool
4 Receive audio
8 Festive
12 Formal poem
13 Miss Bancroft
14 Cheese
15 Durable Western
17 Sold by the post office
18 New (pref.)
19 Judy and Cheetah, for instance
20 Artificial; phony
23 ___ *Girl*
24 Fleet animal
25 Declared
26 Resort
29 He interviews kids (2 words)
32 Singer with her own show
33 Former Defender Robert ___
34 *Let's Make a Deal* host
35 Fly
36 Star of 23 Across
37 Typical small town
40 Fiery
41 Gather together
42 Mimic Frank ___
46 Katie on *My Three Sons*
47 Cuts grass
48 Crack pilot
49 Musician Kenton
50 He's in *The Mod Squad*
51 Permit

down

1 He's Hogan
2 Fuss
3 Decade
4 Former "Voice of Mission Control"
5 My Friend Tony
6 Literary collection
7 Regarding
8 Understand a joke (2 words)
9 ___ -12
10 Light
11 Electrical units
16 Heavenly creature
17 Ghost (poet.)
19 Chef Julia
20 Kind of fish
21 One of the Avengers
22 Pretentious
23 Buyer
25 Skulk
26 ___ *Trek*
27 Senator from Rhode Island
28 He sings "Alice's Restaurant"
30 Used on a golf course
31 ___ *Life*
35 ___ Saint James
36 Was star of 31 Down
37 Boone and O'Brien
38 Leave out
39 He's Jose Jimenez
40 Allen Ginsberg poem
42 Gushy stuff
43 "2001" computer
44 The ___ Capades
45 Network (abbr.)
47 Job of 29 Across

August 9, 1969

across

1 Kismet
5 Snake
8 Droop
11 Man's name
12 Pain
13 Coach Parseghian
14 Orchestra leader on
   The Carol Burnett Show
16 Tavern
17 Actress Donna ____
18 Hidden obstacle
19 O'Brien on *Lancer*
23 Actor Carl ____
24 Stern
25 Comic King
27 Comic Paulsen
28 Bury
30 Craggy hill
33 Leg joint
34 Pat or Daniel
36 Liberate
38 Man on *Mission:
   Impossible*
39 Noun suffix
40 Fly upward
42 For each
43 Star of *The F.B.I.*
48 B.P.O.E. member
49 Puppet Danny ____
50 Resound
51 Presidential monogram
52 Ever (poet.)
53 Appear

down

1 Turkish hat
2 French friend
3 Actor Conway
4 Shady tree
5 Highest point
6 Salt-water fish
7 Home for pigs
8 Actress Susan ____
   James
9 *Here's Lucy* costar
10 Group
12 Region
15 Role of 43-Across
18 Japanese coin
19 Cookbook abbreviation
20 Greek "H"
21 Oldie: ____ *Patrol*
22 Symbol for erbium
23 Star of 37-Down

25 Greek goddess
26 Football position (abbr.)
29 Where Maine is (abbr.)
30 Heavy weight
31 Oldie: *Studio* ____
32 Carlos with 36-Down
33 Festus on *Gunsmoke*
35 Gold or yellow in heraldry
36 The Flying Nun
37 Doctor on *I Dream
   of Jeannie*
38 Infant
39 Raced
40 Oldie: *East* ____,
   West ____
41 Actor Sharif
43 Playwright Akins
44 Either of two Browns
45 Diamonds (sl.)
46 Oldie: *He &* ____
47 Eb on *Green Acres*

August 16, 1969

across

1 Mrs. George Gobel
6 Rowan ___ Martin
9 Oklahoma city
12 Hampton on *The Doris Day Show*
13 Female ruff
14 Lassie
15 Granny Clampett
16 Actor Ron ___
17 Commotion
18 Without: French
20 Weather forecast
21 Support
25 Juanita on *The Doris Day Show*
27 Man on *Here Come the Brides*
29 Symbol for sodium
30 Toward the stern
33 Art critic Saarinen
34 *That Girl*
36 Hurried
37 Actor Marshall
39 One of *Hogan's Heroes*
40 Wander
42 Average
43 Woman's dress
46 Actor Byrnes et al.
48 Tavern drink
49 Comic Blanc
50 More domesticated
55 One of Lee's men
56 Cuckoo
57 Brian Keith's role
58 Star of *Hogan's Heroes*
59 New socialite
60 Larry on *Bewitched*

down

1 Mr. Baba
2 Celtic sea god
3 Anger
4 Swindle (slang)
5 Hurricane centers
6 Athletic field
7 Dr. Rossi on *Peyton Place*
8 Algerian governor
9 ___-12
10 Extinct bird
11 Eager
19 Some
20 Yes in Madrid
21 Open
22 Composer Bartok
23 Tabitha on *Bewitched*
24 Decade
26 Mother
28 Oldie: ___ *Millie*
30 *Laugh-In* co-star
31 Insect
32 Actor Rip ___
35 Limb
38 Ben on *Bonanza*
39 Mrs. Tony Martin
40 Symbol for tin
41 Extemporize
43 Clothing
44 Bread spread
45 Buck on *The Doris Day Show*
47 Detachable button
49 Insane
51 Literary collection
52 1105 in Rome
53 Actor Wallach
54 San Fernando ___

	1	2	3	4	5	6	7		8	9	10	11
12									13			
14					15				16			
17			18	19		20		21		22		
		23		24		25		26				
27	28	29			30		31			32	33	
34				35		36			37			
38			39	40		41		42	43			
	44			45		46						
47	48		49		50		51		52	53	54	
55		56		57		58			59			
60				61			62	63				
64				65								

across

1 *Dark* ——
8 Formal assembly
12 Ann Marie (2 words)
13 Old Marie Wilson role
14 Apollo's son
15 Meadow
16 Grandeur
17 Foot lever
20 TV network
22 Comic Louis ——
23 Actress Sandra ——
25 *My Three* ——
27 Jayne or Audrey
31 Bil ——
34 Tavern
35 Corrode
37 Steve on 25-Across
38 Snake
41 Skelton character
44 Mild oath
46 Blackbird
47 Oldie: *Queen* —— *a Day*
49 Footlike part
51 Condemn
55 Miss Maxwell
57 Late comic Costello
59 Falsehood
60 A *Banana Split* character
61 Skelton character
64 *Name of the Game* star
65 Skelton character

down

1 Sandal or pump
2 Former character on *Mission: Impossible*
3 By
4 Actor on 25-Across (init.)
5 Petroleum
6 Song bird
7 Thick pieces of concrete
8 Immerse
9 Ray Burr's role
10 TV award
11 Non-live TV show
12 Gratuity
18 Affix
19 Actor —— G. Carroll
21 Male swan
24 Ram's mate
26 Continent (abbr.)
27 Actress Farrow
28 Remnant
29 Eva on 9-Down
30 Despondent
32 Bandleader Bloch
33 Thirty-fourth President (init.)
36 Oolong
39 Actor Marshall
40 Knock
42 Rowan —— Martin
43 Expire
45 Miss Reese
47 Hat material
48 Potpourri (var.)
50 Consommé
52 Cudgel
53 Frosty
54 Cowboy's "yes"
56 Some
58 Baseball official
62 Uncle on *Bewitched* (init.)
63 Football position (abbr.)

November 22, 1969

across

1 She's one of The Survivors
5 Top of a container
8 Samantha's nickname
11 Cooler
12 Ripped
13 Island (Fr.)
14 Movie "tough guy" (2 words)
16 Former Portuguese colony
17 Regrets
18 First word of Michael Parks' show
19 Miss Reynolds
23 Implements used by Julia Child
24 Astrological sign
25 Comedian Crosby
27 Complain
28 She's a Beverly Hillbilly
30 Consumed
33 Again
34 He stars on *The Bold Ones*
36 Singing family
38 Changes
39 Unfeeling
40 Shade
42 Greek letter
43 *Petticoat Junction* setting (2 words)
48 Lighted
49 Have sympathy for
50 Newsman Abel
51 Actress Sandra or Ruby
52 Donkey
53 Actress Merrill

down

1 Lillian's nickname
2 Crack pilot
3 Born
4 Limb
5 It's the *American Style*
6 Eye part
7 Family room
8 Glimpse
9 Bitter drug made from a plant
10 Intend
12 Real
15 Getting up
18 Singer Jones
19 Mr. Rowan
20 Age
21 Huge
22 Exist
23 Wiggly singer
25 Not old
26 Preposition
29 Concerning
30 Chopping tool
31 Rocky hill
32 Printer's measures
33 Conjunction
35 Toward
36 Character on *My Three Sons*
37 Angry
38 He hails from Wall Lake, Iowa
39 Not released
40 Not that
41 Cereal grain
43 Resort
44 He does "The Silent Spot"
45 Actor Wallach
46 Moral fault
47 Drink

across

1 Actress Parker
8 Tabitha Stephens
12 Police drama
13 City in Nevada
14 Tease (sl.)
15 Beseech
16 She's Granny
17 *Lancer* man
20 Border
22 Born
23 Before (poet.)
25 Single
27 He's Alex Mundy's dad
31 A feminine name
34 New (comb. form)
35 Arab garb
37 Female deer
38 Actress Grimes
41 . . . Then Came ___
44 Mr. Bishop
46 Miss Lupino
47 From (Scottish)
49 Sailor (colloq.)
51 Jed Clampett
55 Columnist Barrett
57 Actor Majors
59 Nebraska (abbr.)
60 She's Jeannie
61 Katie Douglas (2 words)
64 Lucy's boy
65 Costar of *The Mod Squad*

down

1 Newsman Sevareid
2 Timber wolf
3 Printing measure
4 Symbol for arsenic
5 Bird's beak
6 Polish river
7 Announcer for 44-Across
8 Go astray
9 Debbie ___
10 A suffix
11 Not any
12 Internal Revenue Service (abbr.)
18 A beverage
19 Three (comb. form)
21 Lucy to Craig
24 Period of time
26 Chinese measure of distance
27 Picnic companion
28 Ocean
29 TV singer-host (2 words)
30 Decline
32 Card game
33 Desire
36 Mr. Onassis's nickname
39 Missouri (abbr.)
40 In addition
42 Lyric poem
43 Catch
45 Famous World War II conference site
47 Given name of 27-Across
48 Past tense of ride
50 Part of a harness
52 Essential for skiing
53 Lampreys
54 A direction
56 An American bird
58 Finish
62 Unit of surface measure
63 Symbol for cerium

down

1 Existed
2 Before
3 Mayberry's Aunt
4 She's Agent 99
5 Seat
6 Gaucho weapon
7 He's Chip
8 Wept
9 She's Bobbie Jo
10 Send out
11 Netting
19 Free of
20 Relatives
21 Competent
22 Enemies
23 Enthusiastic viewers
26 He's Hoss
27 Army post
28 "Perry Mason" author
29 Game animal
31 Costar of *Mayberry R.F.D.*
32 ___ *Hospital*
34 *Gunsmoke* character
35 To ask earnestly
36 Cancelled show, *The Music* ___
37 *Laugh-In*'s Judy ___
38 Declare in pinochle
39 Opera song
40 Tumult
41 Writer of verse
45 Lyric poem
46 Perched
47 Type measures

across

1 Star of *Dragnet*
5 TV network
8 A Skelton role
12 Region
13 Popular, as a TV star
14 John Forsythe's TV residence
15 Prophet
16 Wing
17 Spring flower
18 Star of 21-Across (2 words)
21 *Family* ___
24 Cover
25 Reside at the Shady Rest
26 Cozy room
27 Nourished
30 Miss Horne
31 Merry
32 Mr. Vidal
33 Feminine suffix
34 Star of *Get Smart*
35 "Mr. Television"
36 The sun
37 *Medical* ___
38 Costar of *Julia* (2 words)
42 Great Lake
43 And not
44 Skelton's conductor
48 King of beasts
49 Star of *Mayberry R.F.D.*
50 ___-*12*
51 Tropical fruit
52 Dined
53 ___ *Make a Deal*

March 21, 1970

down

1 European goat
2 TV comedienne (2 words)
3 Building extension
4 American humorist
5 *Laugh-In* girl
6 Presage
7 Guided
8 A suffix
9 Cicatrix
10 Gain money
11 Actress Francis
14 Adored personage
19 Commercials
20 Fate
22 *The Virginian* costar
23 Friend (Fr.)
24 Ken Berry's TV role
25 An altar (Latin)
26 Used on baby's diaper
27 Dean Martin's real name
28 Comedienne Debbie
29 Yards (abbr.)
31 A Beverly Hillbilly
32 Spanish article
34 Chris to Carol
35 Scottish hat
36 Goals
37 One of the Lennons
38 Argument
39 Famous English school
40 Diminutive for Gertrude
41 Singer Gary
43 Smell
45 Summer (Fr.)
46 Doctor of Laws (abbr.)
47 ___ *Don't Say!*
49 Symbol for ytterbium

across

1 Notion
5 She's Katie Douglas
9 Ocean
12 *The ___ Ones*
13 *Love, ___ Style*
15 Perry Mason creator
16 TV comedian
17 Mend
18 Eleven in Roman numerals
19 *That Girl*
20 Star of *Bonanza*
21 He's Blue
24 Roman sun god
25 Maxwell Smart
26 Boone or Paulsen
27 Arid
30 Rajah's wife
31 Mr. Nabors
32 Fibbed
33 Sailor's reply
34 Japanese coin
35 Property of Mr. Franciosa
36 Soap-opera folk often need it
37 Robert Brown's TV role
38 Announcer Philbin
41 Block
42 Oregon (abbr.)
44 Article
45 Long period of time
46 *The Carol Burnett Show* regular
48 Star of *To Rome with Love*
50 Mineral vein
51 Trinitrotoluene
52 Twisted
53 Twilight

April 18, 1970

down

1 He's French
2 Child actor on *Here Come the Brides* (2 words)
3 ___ Tin Tin
4 Get lost!
5 Men
6 Singer-Actor Ed
7 Educational network
8 Oriental (abbr.)
9 "___ of the Field"
10 Colder
11 Light brown
12 ___ *Life to Live*
20 Sewing instruments
21 Egyptian coin
23 Tennessee Ernie to friends
24 Vegetable container
25 Plays Gabe on *Daniel Boone*
26 Alice Ghostley's role
28 Large cot
32 Corn spike
33 What Don Grady calls Fred MacMurray
35 Ben Cartwright
37 Hire
39 Change
40 Dog's cord
42 Herb Edelman's role
44 Limb
45 Female ruff
46 Flower necklace
48 ___ part; small role
50 Touchdown (abbr.)

across

1 Slavic language
5 Character on *The High Chaparral*
13 TV special, "Who Killed Lake ___?"
14 *The ___ Sportsman*
15 Mr. Crosby
16 Allow
17 Buckley's *Firing ___*
18 Kind of electrical current
19 *The Bold ___*
21 Pastry
22 Script sections
24 French name
27 *My ___ Sons*
28 Snakes
29 Bone (Lat.)
30 Creator of James Bond
31 *Mr. ___ Goes to Town*
33 ___ DeLuise
34 ___ *the World Turns*
35 Happy
36 Torment
38 Closer
40 "Neither a borrower nor a ___ be"
41 Orchestra leader Brown
42 Floating ice
43 Southern state (abbr.)
44 *Laugh-In*'s "dirty old man"
46 Meadow
47 Newsman Elle
49 Goes into again
51 Coat with gold
52 Billie Jo on *Petticoat Junction*
53 Feminine name suffix

125

across

1 Lassie
4 Boast
8 ___-12
12 Mr. Gershwin
13 Julia's son's pal
14 Costar of *Here's Lucy*
15 Chum
16 Cereal food
17 Enthusiasm
18 Star of *Room 222* (2 words)
21 Night birds
22 Perched
23 *Laugh-In* regular
25 The sun
26 ___ Boone
29 Costar of *Green Acres*
30 Part of a play
32 Turkish title
33 ___ *Cards*
34 Mr. Carney
35 Gait
36 Mr. Wallach
37 Scorch
39 Costar of *Marcus Welby, M.D.* (2 words)
43 Sidewalk edging
44 Set of players
45 Jalopy
47 Poker stake
48 Joe ___ Worley
49 Vine
50 Nobleman
51 Sinister glance
52 Sailor's "yes"

down

1 Quick swim
2 Verbal
3 Costar of *Ironside*
4 Emerald
5 Sudden police visits
6 Curved structure
7 TV host-comedian
8 *Get Smart*'s ___ 99
9 Host of *Death Valley Days*
10 Alack!
11 *Hogan's Heroes*
19 Possess
20 Harvard's rival
23 Informed (sl.)
24 Miss Gardner
25 Stage scenery
26 Rebecca on *Daniel Boone*
27 Lifetime
28 Faucet
30 ___ *of the Century*
31 Costar of *The High Chaparral*
35 Salt
36 Live coal
37 Star of 11-Down
38 Baseball feat
39 Costar of *Petticoat Junction*
40 Costar of *Laugh-In*
41 Prayer (archaic)
42 It was *McHale's* ___
43 Boy's hat
46 Cereal plant

across

1 Famous cheese
5 Seaport (abbr.)
8 He's Jethro
12 Foolishly fond
13 Card game
14 Singer on Ray
   Stevens' show
15 False image
16 *That Girl*
17 Related
18 Summer hosts
   (3 words)
21 No (Scottish)
22 *Bonanza* star
26 Lucy's TV son
29 Your (archaic)
30 *The ___ Squad*
31 Actor's part
32 Mr. Linkletter
33 Biography (abbr.)
34 Collection of
   anecdotes
35 Rosemary Prinz'
   TV role
36 Given name of
   22-Across
37 *___ Splits*
39 Cry
40 TV hostess (2 words)
45 First name of
   53-Across
48 Expire
49 Verbal
50 *___-12*
51 American humorist
52 Bucket

53 Star of *Get it
   Together*
54 Japanese coin
55 What must meet!

down

1 Revise
2 Extinct bird
3 Tiny particle
4 Miss Fullerton of
   To Rome with Love
5 He's Blue
6 Small body of water
7 Late evening show
8 *Gunsmoke's* Kitty
9 Diving bird
10 Actor Wallach
11 Move swiftly
19 Horse (slang)
20 Weep

23 An Arabian ruler
24 12 o'clock high
25 *___ of Night*
26 Shellfish
27 Columnist Barrett
28 Comedian King
29 Attempt
32 Property of 8-Down
33 TV comedian
   (2 words)
35 American bird
36 *___ Angeles*
38 Maxwell Smart
39 Brightness
41 Naval assistant
42 City in Algeria
43 Attack
44 Building extensions
45 Son of (prefix)
46 Girl's name
47 Celebration (comb.)

October 17, 1970

down

1 Forbidden
2 Mr. Gershwin's
3 Denise of *Room 222*
4 Stick to
5 Mr. Calloway's
6 In the past
7 Job of Friar's Club
8 Milburn Stone
9 Formerly one of Hogan's Heroes
10 Abbe ___
11 Had knowledge
17 Los Angeles football player
19 Amount paid as rent
22 Movies
23 Dollar bills
24 Relaxed
25 By way of
26 In addition to
27 Scarlett's home
28 What drama appeals to
29 A loud noise
30 Actors' union (abbr.)
36 Having spokes or rays
37 Mr. Parseghian
39 Ignore
40 David Frost goodby (2 words)
41 In the distance
42 Finishes
43 Estimated Times of Departure (abbr.)
44 Declares
46 Bond's creator
47 Diamonds (slang)
48 Small island

across

1 Robbie's Katie
5 Used for cueing
9 Class or kind
12 Dry
13 Money exchange premium
14 Actor Johnson
15 One of music's "Three B's"
16 Colonel Hogan (2 words)
18 Theater guides
20 Over again
21 Natural mineral
22 Structure
25 Karen of *Room 222*
28 McMahon and Nelson
31 Miss Balin

32 Former show, ___ of Wells Fargo
33 Miss Farrow
34 Commercials
35 "Satchmo"
37 Expression of regret
38 Consume
39 Series lead
42 *The Courtship of ___ Father*
45 *Five-0*'s Kono
49 Jot
50 Miss Hagen
51 Sour
52 Williams or Griffith
53 No
54 TV networks (informal)
55 Lifesaving Service (pl.)

January 16, 1971

across

1 Martini item
4 TV network
7 Dandy
10 Weaving machine
12 Look at TV
13 *Goodtime* ___
14 Needle case
15 Star of *Mayberry R.F.D.* (2 words)
17 Costar of *The Beverly Hillbillies*
19 Light brown
20 Inheritor
23 Costar of *My Three Sons*
27 Card game
30 Country in Asia
31 Siouan Indian
32 Transgress
34 One-fourth pint
35 *Another* ___
37 TV comedienne
39 Room
40 Haughty person
41 Full of (suffix)
43 Hollywood award
47 TV singer-host
52 Margarine
53 Miss Adams
54 Cheering shout
55 Roman emperor
56 Baseball necessity
57 Caustic solution
58 *The* ___ *Squad*

down

1 Star of 13 Across
2 Jot
3 Name word
4 Inquire
5 Hairy insect
6 Copper coin
7 *Search* ___ *Tomorrow*
8 *Days of* ___ *Lives*
9 Use a lever
11 Costar of 58-Across (2 words)
13 Regular on *Laugh-In* (2 words)
16 Sacks
18 Affirmative
21 ___ *News to Me*
22 Train tracks
24 Seed covering
25 Pickling herb
26 Harvard's rival
27 Dairy animals
28 Up above
29 Girl's name
33 Sally Field's former role
36 Costar of *Here's Lucy*
38 Dove's sound
42 Julia's son's pal
44 Skelton character
45 Air (comb.)
46 Cross
47 Spider's trap
48 Miss Lupino
49 Illuminated
50 *Hillbillies'* Elly ___
51 Pronoun

across

1 Obstruct
4 *That* ___
8 Actor Gulager
11 Miss Turner
12 Opera melody
13 Not hers
14 Terminates
15 ___ *a Deal* (2 words)
17 City official
19 Withered (poet.)
20 Novel
22 Bottom frame of window
23 Bandleader Brown
26 Lucy's Viv
28 It is (contr.)
31 Miss Gardner
32 Star of former show *Topper*
33 Poem
34 Mayberry's Ken Berry
35 Man's name
37 Miss Fabray
38 Actor Devine
40 Favorite
42 Tangle
43 Actress Reed
47 Beaten
51 Australian tree
52 Ember
53 Unctuous
54 Useful metal
55 Exclamation
56 Cheat
57 Suffix meaning life

down

1 *Bright Promise* star
2 Singer Williams
3 Actor James ___
4 Girl (slang)
5 Anger
6 Scratch
7 Famous TV dog
8 Mr. Heston
9 Similar
10 Employ
11 Nickname for Lemuel
16 Singer Torme
18 Reverend (abbr.)
21 Comedian Cox
22 Ladle
23 ___ Vegas
24 *Green Acres*' Lisa
25 *Bewitched* lady
27 Snare
29 Miss Lupino
30 Japanese coin
35 ___ *Night* (2 words)
36 Sgt. Rivera on *Dan August*
39 The late King Cole
41 Comedienne Fields
42 Belt
44 An Ibsen heroine
45 Midday
46 ___ B. Davis
47 Sheep's bleat
48 Estuary
49 BPOE member
50 Stain

March 13, 1971

across

1 Hogan's camp
4 Cut
8 Sonny's Mrs.
12 "All About ___"
13 Former *Tonight* host
14 Groundhog's home
15 O'Connor of summer show
16 Baxter or Bancroft
17 Director ___ Kazan
18 *The ___*, doctor show
20 Resist
21 Cartoon: ___ *Hawks*
22 Raymond or DeBenning
23 Belonging to Celeste
26 TV enthusiast
27 *The ___ Couple*
30 On sheltered side
31 Plays a Partridge daughter
32 Become member of
33 Miss Grant
34 Campanella or Namath
35 ___, *Fran and Ollie*
36 Miss Rivers
38 Conjunction
39 Kind of nut
41 Too sweet
45 Gene Barry's old role
46 Producer's eternal hope (2 words)
47 Johnson or Heflin
48 Don Rickles' forte
49 Treaty
50 Gabor sister
51 Globes
52 *The Bold ___*
53 TV receiver

down

1 Arnie's buddy
2 What The Galloping Gourmet needs
3 *The Wild Wild ___*
4 Ned of late, late movies
5 ___ *and the Professor*
6 John's (Scottish)
7 Before
8 Rah, rah, team!
9 The Senator
10 Mr. Abel
11 True
19 Girl's name
20 Move rapidly
22 An inlet
23 First name of 9-Down
24 Spanish cheer
25 Star of *The Young Lawyers* (3 words)
26 Mannix's payment
28 Water down (abbr.)
29 Deoxyribonucleic acid (abbr.)
31 Galloway or Knotts
32 Miss Pace
34 Miss Sterling
35 Comedian Don ___
37 Desert's watering places
38 Miss Ghostley
39 ___ Pago
40 Arabian prince
41 Detective Charlie ___
42 Burl of *The Bold Ones*
43 Part of church
44 Tiny insect
46 Mailing address for soldiers (abbr.)

July 17, 1971

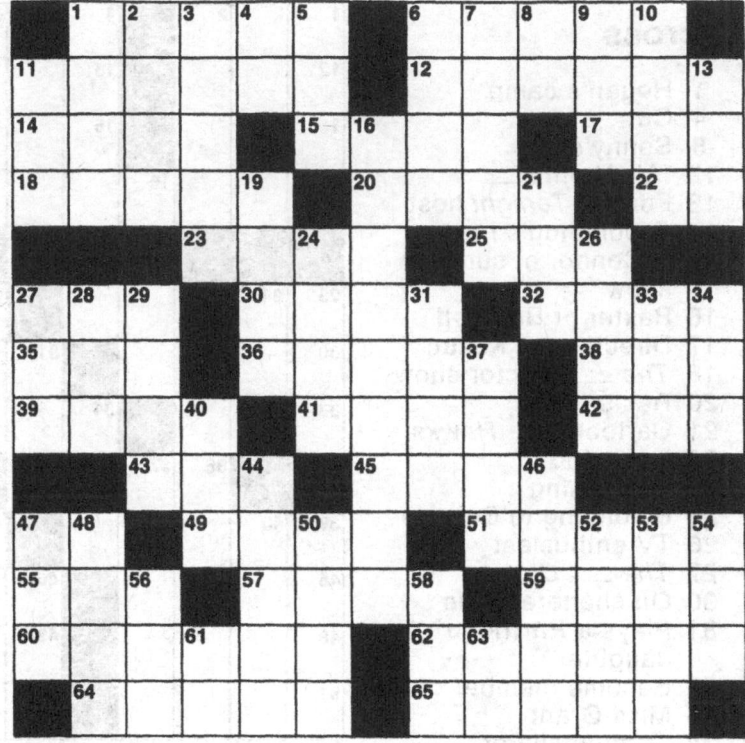

across

1 Miss Finley of *From a Bird's Eye View*
6 *Green* ——
11 Typical summer fare
12 TV role of 1-Across
14 River in Poland
15 The Ohre River (German name)
17 *The* —— *Couple*
18 Mr. Martin's
20 Girl's name
22 The fifth tone of the diatonic scale
23 Mix
25 Star of 8-Across
27 Hail!
30 Ancient Syria (Hebrew name)
32 Actress Francis
35 "Steve" to "Chip"
36 Actor Moore
38 *Music Hall* host
39 Former newsman Abel
41 Egyptian river
42 Affirmative
43 Dine
45 Greek mountain
47 Military policeman (abbr.)
49 Turn over and over
51 Stories
55 Netherlands East Indies islands
57 Harvest
59 Past tense of ride
60 —— *Street*
62 He starred in *The Immortal*
64 Costar of *Love on a Rooftop*
65 Mr. Nuvo

down

1 Foot (comb. form)
2 Region
3 *As the World* ——
4 Tons (abbr.)
5 Adjective forming suffix
6 Prayer ending
7 Costar of *Love on a Rooftop*
8 Football position
9 Self
10 Belonging to Mr. Caesar
11 Mr. Serling
13 Tokyo (former name)
16 Host of *The Memory Game*
19 The featured actor
21 Miss Gardner
24 A metal
26 Singer Williams
27 American humorist
28 TV host —— Doonican
29 Miss Adams
31 Property of 44-Down
33 Born
34 Shaped like S
37 Relax
40 Hearing organ
44 Host of *It Was a Very Good Year*
46 Producer Spelling
47 Celebration (comb. form)
48 Type of school
50 Sly look
52 Feminine name
53 *The* —— *of Night*
54 Observe
56 Employ
58 Professional Golfers' Association (abbr.)
61 Symbol for astatine
63 Symbol for erbium

August 7, 1971

2 The Galloping
Gourmet
3 Angers
4 Get smaller
5 Kind of dog
6 Otherwise
7 Actress Ruby ___
8 Subsided
9 Raymond Burr's role
10 Ogle
11 *Medical Center* star
19 He's on *Adam-12*
20 *Hee* ___
22 One of the Interns
23 To and ___
24 Mr. Skelton
25 *Alias Smith* ___
(2 words)
26 Actor Majors
28 Grow older
29 *Dan August* detective
31 Adams or Rickles
32 A Great Lake
34 Mr. Murray
35 Keepsakes
37 Gary or Buck
38 Work animals
39 Tell a secret
40 Lawrence Welk's Bob
41 Coffee (slang)
42 Spelling contests
43 Swear word
44 Dr. Welby might
order one
46 ___ *Smart*

across

1 Winter sport gear
4 Lean-to
8 ___ *Kingdom*
12 That girl
13 A hollow place
14 Section
15 Mine's product
16 Trick
17 Christmas (Fr.)
18 Mr. Zimbalist's role
20 Mr. Fonda
21 Football position
22 Villains
23 Mr. Blair
26 *Men at* ___
27 James Bond's creator
30 Lease
31 He plays Arnie's son
32 *The* ___ *of Night*

33 *The* ___ *Couple*
34 Mr. Garagiola
35 Cornered
36 Miss Rivers
38 French pronoun
39 In full bloom
41 Featured on *Archie's
Fun House*
45 Buckley's *Firing* ___
46 Mr. Gordon
47 TV set's rabbit ___
48 Arabian seaport
49 Level
50 Greek letter
51 Roger Bowen, to Arnie
52 Soviet news agency
53 Timid

down

1 Footwear

133

November 6, 1971

across

1 What actors do
4 Actor Leon ___
8 *Cade's County* star
12 Indian timber tree
13 Narrow path
14 Plant of the lily family
15 Consumed
16 Barren
17 Man's name
18 Star of *Funny Face* (2 words)
21 Utters
22 Shy
23 Actor McClure
25 "___ Miserables"
26 Ski-nosed comedian
29 Hearing organ
30 Crash
32 Miss Gardner
33 Pig pen
34 That man
35 ___-12
36 Distress signal
37 To smooth or polish
39 He's Nichols (2 words)
43 Spanish painter
44 Electrically charged particles
45 Youth
47 Timeless one (Sanskrit)
48 Upon
49 Miss Gabor

50 Actor Barry
51 Gaseous element
52 Desire

down

1 City in Oklahoma
2 *Bear ___!*
3 O'Hara, United States ___
4 A woman of rank (2 words)
5 Miss Moore's property
6 Girl's name
7 Entices
8 Whimsical
9 Olive shrubs (genus)
10 Chestnut-colored horse
11 He's Richard on *Arnie*
19 Complain
20 Snack (Yiddish)

23 Mr. O'Connor
24 Cereal grass
25 Flight (slang)
26 *The Good Life* regular
27 Ovum (plural)
28 Dull noise
30 Foot cover
31 ___: *Impossible*
35 ___ B. Davis
36 Amused expression
37 ___ Domingo, Dominican Republic
38 Malicious burning of property
39 Professor Howard's grandson
40 Comedian King
41 Departed
42 Talk wildly
43 Former UN president
46 James MacArthur's role

November 13, 1971

across

1 The ___ Couple
4 Coagulate
8 Fast dances
12 Zodiac sign
13 Of a wing
14 Inactive
15 *Hawaii Five-O* man
16 Love to excess
17 ___ *the Press*
18 Star of *The Good Life*
   (2 words)
21 Legal paper
22 Speak
23 Henry Fonda's role
25 Eddie's father
26 TV network
29 Intention
30 Spectacle
32 ___ Majors
33 ___ Stern of
   Getting Together
34 Owned
35 Lion's neck hair
36 Distress signal
37 Leading TV actor
39 Star of *Nichols*
   (2 words)
43 Anklebones
44 Jot
45 Louis ___, comedian
47 Standard amount

48 Fall in drops
49 Stutz Bearcat
50 Girl's nickname
51 Longings
52 Compass point

down

1 Antique
2 *Let's Make a ___*
3 Star of *The Partners*
   (2 words)
4 Framework
5 Star of *Room 222*
6 Solemn declaration
7 Traitor's crime
8 *The ___ Stewart Show*
9 Notion
10 *Goodtime Hour* host
11 Clique
19 Mr. Skelton

20 *The Movie ___*
23 Crow's cry
24 Hasten
25 ___ Baxter of *The Mary
   Tyler Moore Show*
26 Linc in *The Mod Squad*
27 Bonanza man
28 Look at TV
30 Sandal
31 Costar of *The
   Partridge Family*
35 *The ___ and the City*
36 *Alias ___ and Jones*
37 Glossy fabric
38 Snares
39 Donna Mills role
40 Dismounted
41 Skirt inset
42 Robert Conrad's role
43 Washing vessel
46 Before (poet.)

December 18, 1971

down

1. Once possessed
2. A mineral
3. School organization (abbr.)
4. Even (poet.)
5. Singer Martin's nickname
6. Prayer ending
7. Affirmative
8. *Room 222* costar
9. Miss Adams'
10. Greek or Roman temple
12. Mr. Curtis of *The Persuaders*
15. He portrays 36-Down
18. Ghost sound
19. Quick poke
20. Lyric poem
21. A river in China
22. New Mexico (abbr.)
23. Star of *Getting Together*
25. Earth
26. Either
29. Masculine pronoun
30. Actor Ely
31. *The ___ Couple*
32. Sheep's bleat
33. Actor Torn
35. Laugh
36. He's a Treasury agent
37. First name of 5-Across
38. Property of Miss Sothern
39. Man alone
40. White (Lat.)
41. Body part
43. Wander aimlessly
44. Not thin
45. Spanish cheer
46. Mr. Taylor
47. Singer O'Connor

across

1. TV comedian
5. TV comedienne
8. He's Festus
11. Mr. Johnson
12. What a clock tells
13. Girl's name
14. *The Chicago Teddy Bears* costar (2 words)
16. ___ de Janeiro, Brazil
17. Soon
18. Found in a hive
19. Late-night host
23. *My Three ___*
24. Costar of *The Partners*
25. London quarter
27. A Cartwright
28. TV hostess
30. Mr. Reiner of *All in the Family*
33. Donna or Robert
34. Character on *The Mary Tyler Moore Show*
36. Norse god
38. She's Miss Kitty
39. Small store
40. Girl's name
42. Nickname for sailor
43. Star of *Cade's County*
48. Mr. Onassis
49. Property of a TV network
50. South African plant
51. Cars run on it
52. Mail in India
53. Belonging to Mr. Knight

across

1 ___ Mahal
4 Oppressed peasant
8 Actor Young
11 Kind of "monster" lizard
12 Girl friend (Fr.)
13 Mine's product
14 ___-12
15 Durable Western series
17 Belief
19 Mr. Knight's
20 Samantha's nickname
22 Complete
23 Comic DeLuise
26 Extra pay
28 "___ Capades"
31 Miss Gabor
32 Old show: ___ for Your Life
33 Admirer
34 Armed conflict
35 Thomas or Kaye
37 Age
38 Spirit
40 Affirmative
42 Avoid
43 Leonard Nimoy's recent role
47 Rod Taylor's series
51 Lease
52 Building wing
53 Sector
54 The Funny Side host
55 ___ in the Family
56 Not sloppy
57 Belonging to Mr. Ames

down

1 Ebb and flood
2 Comedian ___ King
3 Actor Brolin
4 Droop
5 Flightless bird
6 ___ Tin Tin
7 Matt's helper
8 Series about domestic workers The ___ (2 words)
9 Annoys
10 Golly
11 Narrow ship channel
16 Singer Torme
18 ___ Hunter
21 Ethical
22 "___ Face"
23 Morning dampness
24 Eggs (Latin)
25 Peter or E.G.
27 Sally Field's former role
29 Auto
30 Actress Hartman
35 She stars in 22-Down
36 Yeah
39 Days of ___ Lives
41 George Kennedy's role
42 Exchange for money
44 He plays Mike Brady
45 Hotels
46 Female saint (abbr.)
47 Miss Lillie
48 You ___ There
49 Beverage
50 Occupied a chair

across

1 Supply weapons
4 Sprite
7 Baked dessert
10 Starring role
12 Zodiac sign
13 *To ___ the Truth*
14 Against
15 Host of *The Hollywood Squares*
17 V-shaped cut
19 Female deer
20 Osculate
23 Disturbed
27 Late-night TV host
29 Ointment
30 *My Three Sons'* Katie
31 Actor ___ Brynner
33 Regretted
34 Short jackets
36 *Medical ___*
38 Comedian Paul ___
39 Sharp
40 Edible tuber
42 *The Chicago Teddy ___*
46 Star of *Hawaii Five-O* (2 words)
51 Man on *The D.A.*
52 Singer Miss Lane
53 Locale for *Primus*
54 Norse story
55 Costar of *Getting Together*
56 Former show: *I ___*
57 Informed (slang)

down

1 *Laugh-In* regular
2 City in Nevada
3 *Gunsmoke* man
4 Shade tree
5 Meadow
6 Star of *Cade's County*
7 Green vegetable
8 Not well
9 Building wing
11 TV comedian (3 words)
13 Don Adams' series (2 words)
16 French coins
18 Hasten
21 Pigpen
22 Adhered
24 Twist about
25 Always
26 Costar of *The Mary Tyler Moore Show*
27 *The Man and the ___*
28 Soon
30 ___ Aviv
32 Costar of *Owen Marshall*
35 Christmas stamp
37 Bird's beak
41 Green plant
43 Nursemaid in India
44 Storm
45 Ginger cookie
46 Facial bone
47 Man's name
48 TV network
49 Corded fabric
50 *The Doris ___ Show*

across

1 That girl
4 Paddles
8 Fathers
12 Fruit drink
13 Exchange
14 Baseball player Matty ___
15 Mr. Caesar
16 Walking stick
17 Kind of light
18 He's on *The Mary Tyler Moore Show* (2 words)
21 Glenn ___
22 Miss Medford
23 South African plant
25 Singer Torme
26 Writing tool
29 Mr. Harrison
30 Bowling term
32 Former show: ___ *Patrol*
33 Wally ___
34 Make a mistake
35 Miss Buzzi
36 Former show: *It Takes* ___
37 Mimicked
39 He plays Jimmy Stewart's colleague (2 words)
43 Opposite of "yep"
44 Southwest Asian country
45 It's now PBS
47 Phobia
48 Satisfy
49 Stutz Bearcat was one
50 Carol's costar
51 Female sheep
52 Mr. Wallach

down

1 Possesses
2 ___ Adams
3 Comedian (2 words)
4 Felix's roommate
5 Emmy, for instance
6 Philosopher Ayn
7 Lecturer
8 ___ Bonaduce
9 To the sheltered side
10 Entrance
11 Center of our solar system
19 Sorrow
20 ___ *of the Century*
23 Rainbow's shape
24 Astrological sign
25 Blemish
26 Kim Richards' role on *Nanny and the Professor*
27 Consume
28 To the "___" degree
30 Stitched
31 *Bright* ___
35 Race (an engine)
36 *You Are* ___
37 Marble
38 Longs for
39 ___ Bishop
40 October birthstone
41 Bird's crop
42 Actual
43 Football league
46 Three: prefix

February 26, 1972

across

1 *O'Hara, United ——— Treasury*
7 Dejected
10 *Love, —— Style*
12 Cool drinks
14 David Frost, e.g.
15 Falsehood
16 Mother
17 O'Hara is one (abbr.)
18 Actress Field
20 Tibetan ox
21 Top TV show
22 Boy
24 Egyptian sun god
25 Spank
27 Painter Edouard ——
29 Weird
30 Passport endorsement
31 Challenged
33 English statesman
34 Welby or Kiley (abbr.)
35 Drunkard
37 Actor Knight
38 Diamonds (sl.)
40 Blouse
42 Youth group (init.)
45 Rest
47 Peer Gynt's mom
48 Color of a horse
49 Jack Lord for one
50 Katie on *My Three Sons* (2 words)
52 She plays Lil Nuvo
53 Mitchell on *Nichols*

down

1 Smoke and fog
2 Trial
3 Actor Metrano
4 Musical note
5 Brilliance
6 Jib or main
7 Sheriff Cade
8 Daily (2 words)
9 Uncle on *My Three Sons*
10 Exclamation
11 Girl's nickname
13 Asian actor Harold ——
18 Perch
19 Sweet potato
21 Actress Helen ——
23 *Good Life* costar
25 Rod Taylor's show
26 Make a mistake
28 Young insect
29 *The Courtship of —— Father*
32 Two (Sp.)
33 Favorite
36 Definite article
37 Child actor Lehman
39 Isaac's son
41 Egyptian goddess
42 Dullard
43 Old sailor (sl.)
44 Sue —— Langdon
46 Before
48 Record company
51 Symbol for gold

140

1	2	3	4		5	6	7	8		9	10	11
12					13					14		
15					16					17		
18				19		20			21			
		22			23			24				
25	26			27		28	29		30		31	32
33			34				35		36			
37		38		39					40			
	41		42		43		44					
45	46			47	48		49			50	51	
52			53			54		55				
56			57					58				
59			60					61				

across

1 Comedienne Meara
5 Book of the Bible
9 Total
12 Command to a dog
13 Ink stain
14 Actress Farrow
15 Busy place
16 Car
17 Building wing
18 Sues and King
20 Wife on *My Three Sons*
22 Comic Lynde
24 Actor Wallach
25 Body of water
27 Portal
30 Cicatrix
33 Actor Carney
34 Wash
36 *Arnie*'s wife Sue ___
37 Mr. Dillon
39 Director Preminger
40 Nothing
41 Lamprey
43 Dan Blocker's role
45 Consuelo on *Marcus Welby, M.D.*
49 Slogan
52 Belonging to Mr. Sullivan
53 Musical ending
55 Actor O'Neal
56 Spanish river
57 Press
58 Otherwise
59 Desire
60 Spooky (var.)
61 Minus

down

1 Villain's cry
2 One of *The Bold Ones*
3 Ma on *Nichols* (2 words)
4 First name of 45-Across
5 Arabian garment
6 Kind of sandwich
7 Convey
8 Range
9 *Love,* ___ (2 words)
10 Kind of pickle
11 *Medical Center* costar
19 Foam
21 Elevated railways
23 Crazy
25 Cade of *Cade's County*
26 Age
28 Scrap of food
29 Woman on *Nichols*
31 Cuckoo
32 Actor, critic ___ Reed
35 TV equipment
38 Mike on *Me and the Chimp*
42 Miss Arnaz
44 Don Rickles' TV wife
45 Exceedingly
46 Miss Adams
47 Writer Vidal
48 Scent
50 Russian news agency
51 *The Bold* ___
54 Some

141

across

1 Sack
4 *Sesame Street* subject
8 Competent
12 *Three ___ Match* (2 words)
13 Disable
14 Mr. Martin
15 He's Arnie
17 Ranch worker
18 *___ Life to Live*
19 *You Are ___*
21 Extreme pain
24 Sonny's mate
25 Citrus fruit
26 *___ Williams III*
30 Tennessee's Mr. Ford
31 Roller derby site
32 Ordinary (abbr.)
33 J.D. Cannon's role
35 Snug bug's home (2 words)
36 ___ and file
37 Fire
38 Petula or Roy
40 Miss Peggy ___
41 Give temporarily
42 Series set in San Francisco
47 Mr. Sevareid
48 Sea bird
49 *Adam-12* vehicle
50 ___ Rayburn
51 Whirlpool
52 CBS logo

down

1 *Concentration* host
2 Sue ___ Langdon
3 Needlefish
4 *Love Is ___ Splendored Thing* (2 words)
5 Unfurnished
6 Heston role: El ___
7 *Alias ___ Jones* (2 words)
8 Stick
9 *The Hair ___ Bunch*
10 Pianist Ken ___
11 Stop
16 Not any
20 Queen of the gods
21 Actor Guinness
22 Female
23 Prefix for all
24 Town official
26 Newsman Walter
27 Girl's name
28 He plays Eddie
29 *The ___ of Night*
31 At a distance
34 Miss Nuyen
35 Strong drinks
37 Jack ___
38 Center
39 Reclined
40 *Hawaii Five-O* star
41 Limb
43 Mr. Buttons
44 ___ skating
45 Lynda ___ George
46 Before

across

1 He's McCloud
7 Make free of
10 Lady on *Longstreet*
12 Miss Lupino's
14 Iroquois Indian tribe
15 Garden tool
16 Confined
17 Actor Romero
18 He's Columbo
20 Exist
21 Sailor
22 Socialite
24 Either
25 Emcee Parks
27 *Laugh-In*'s Johnny
29 Entice
30 Exclamation
31 Old Show: *Green* ___
33 Actress Barbara ___
34 Blood factor
35 Comic Caesar
37 Some
38 Sheriff Cade
40 Movie coils
42 Happy
45 *The Bold* ___
47 Friend (Fr.)
48 Mrs. Roy Rogers

49 Allied group (init.)
50 Liz on *Room 222*
52 Novel
53 Mike on *All in the Family*

down

1 Telegram
2 Actress Markey
3 Era
4 Versus (abbr.)
5 Anesthetic
6 Cheer for
7 Comic Taylor
8 Notion
9 *Laugh-In* host (2 words)
10 Pianist Lane
11 Require
13 After parts of ships

18 Actor Hingle
19 Confederate soldier
21 Ash and beech
23 *The* ___ *Bunch*
25 J.J. on *Cade's County*
26 Make a mistake
28 Arena cheer
29 Teddy on *The Jimmy Stewart Show*
32 Title of respect
33 Printers' measures
36 Singer Martin
37 Maid on 23-Down
39 Allot
41 Turkish title
42 Harry on *Here's Lucy*
43 Winged
44 Affirmative
46 Plant
48 Mark on *Ironside*
51 Greeting

December 2, 1972

across

1 Insurance-investigator series
8 Leer
12 Bob Newhart, for instance
13 What Monty Hall offers
14 Number
15 Metric unit of measure
16 Belonging to Mr. Mitchell
17 Miss Day
20 TV receiver
22 Female ruff
23 Chilled
25 Hop ___ *Bonanza* cook
27 Landon or Cole
30 Devotion
33 Zsa Zsa's sister
34 At a distance (archaic)
36 "The Raven" author
37 ___ Day George
40 Location for new series in San Francisco
43 Scottish chemise
45 String instrument
46 Quantity (abbr.)
48 So!
50 Recorded
53 Dennis and Doris
55 In the manner of (2 words)
57 Gone by
58 Capri, for instance
59 Captain ___
62 At that time
63 Internal parts (colloq.)

down

1 Sonny's last name
2 *Love* ___ (2 words)
3 Opposite of SW
4 Commercial
5 Secret agency (abbr.)
6 Fruiting spikes
7 Joints
8 Strange
9 Star of 1-Across (2 words)
10 Former pianist for Dean Martin
11 Otherwise
12 Fish
18 I (Ger.)
19 Ocean
21 Pointer
24 Actress Susan ___
26 Symbol for nickel
27 ___ Brooks
28 Climbing plant
29 Spanish article
31 Small child
32 Affirmative
35 To the ___ degree
38 Prosecutor (abbr.)
39 Notre Dame coach
41 Rodent
42 Period
44 Military garb
46 Mine entrance
47 New comedy series
49 Star of 47 Down
51 Individuals
52 *The New Scooby-___ Movies*
54 He plays 25-Across
56 Jo ___ Pflug
60 Southern state (abbr.)
61 Airline schedule (abbr.)

December 9, 1972

across

1 Tige Andrews' role
5 Gear tooth
8 *Room 222*'s half year
12 ___ Arnaz Jr.
13 Lyric poem
14 Basic to a TV show
15 Monty Hall's trade
16 Soap-opera specialty
17 Small fly
18 TV psychologist
21 Disobedient
24 Rodent
25 TV comedienne
26 Paul Sims is a member
27 Period of time in *America* series
30 Panelist Orson ___
31 ___ Air, home of the stars
32 Costar of *Ironside*
33 Ancient
34 Sprinted
35 Explode
36 Lew Grade's title
37 *Mission: Impossible* man
38 Costar of *Search* (2 words)
42 ___ *Domini*
43 Air (comb. form)
44 Great Lake
48 Leading actor
49 Actor ___ Buttons
50 Costar of *The Odd Couple*

51 Sally Ann ___
52 TV commercials
53 A patient of Dr. Jamie's

down

1 Sum up
2 Actor Billy ___ Williams
3 King of Judah
4 *Gunsmoke*'s Doc
5 Variety-show host
6 Supreme Norse deity
7 Rank on *M*A*S*H*
8 Close-fitting
9 Miss Ferber
10 Bring up children
11 *Gunsmoke* man
19 Spanish cheer
20 Seen on the news
21 Knob of a shield
22 Christmas song

23 Highway
26 *Bonanza* man
27 To gain
28 Stratagem
29 Overly esthetic
31 *Today* lady
32 TV comedienne
34 Late-show movie, "Road to ___"
35 Bleat
36 TV morning-show hostess
37 Zoo-show stars
38 Football term: ___ mark
39 Until (poet.)
40 Emulate a rodent
41 Costar of *The Brady Bunch*
45 Cowboy ___ Rogers
46 Printing fluid
47 CBS logo

February 10, 1973

down

1 Korean War series
2 Motor vehicle (abbr.)
3 James Brolin's role (abbr.)
4 Suffix meaning small
5 Antelope
6 Land measure
7 Necessities
8 Strange
9 An Alp
10 Shelley Fabares' role
11 One of *The Brady Bunch*
12 Bandleader Brown
18 Existed
19 Perch
21 McCloud's other name
24 Allow
26 French article
27 A craze
28 Mouth (comb. form)
29 Actors Boone and Widmark
30 He plays Archie's son-in-law
32 Route (abbr.)
33 Aero (variant)
36 Edith is to Archie
39 Knockout (abbr.)
40 Government agent
42 First name of 41-Across
43 Born
45 Poet Poe
47 Withered
48 Bucket
50 Structure for grain storage
52 Stupid fellow
53 Wanders aimlessly
54 Age
56 Actor Majors
58 Chatter
62 Neon (abbr.)
63 Argon symbol

across

1 Richard Widmark's TV role
8 Mr. Sharif
12 Star of *The Delphi Bureau*
13 Accomplished
14 Superlative suffix
15 British actress Mary ___
16 Ridge of sand
17 Many new ones in the fall
20 Belonging to actor Buchanan
22 He plays Uncle Moe
23 Be ill
25 Sodium chloride
27 He played Banyon
31 Stiller's better half
34 Onassis's nickname
35 Mr. Tryon
37 Suffix meaning native
38 Martin and Cavett
41 Star of *Anna and the King*
44 Actress Lange
46 ___ Ane Langdon
47 Mineral spring
49 Yards (abbr.)
51 Reef
55 ___ Holliman
57 Actor Young
59 Scull
60 Be borne
61 Star of 1-Down
64 Otherwise
65 Actors Sampson and Forster

March 10, 1973

across

1 — Nelson Reilly
8 Government agent (2 words)
12 *M*A*S*H* costar (2 words)
13 Beige
14 Rhoda to Mary
15 Mr. Baird
16 Send out
17 Sandy Duncan's home town
20 Sprite
22 GIs' cards
23 Actor Chaney
25 Shout
27 Role of 12-Across
31 Greek letter
34 Exclamation
35 Shady tree
37 Trouble
38 Female servants
41 Bob Newhart's TV wife
44 Beech or plum
46 Performed
47 Water barrier
49 Sues and Alda
51 Columbo
55 Andy's partner
57 Owen Marshall's forte
59 In debt
60 Money in Rome
61 One-time *Laugh-In* regular (2 words)
64 Actress Barbara —
65 Public roads

down

1 Modeling material
2 *Let's Make a Deal*'s host
3 Any one
4 Sun god
5 Law degree
6 Miss Adams
7 Wife on 9-Down
8 Golf gadget
9 — *and Wife*
10 Dry
11 Crazy (sl.)
12 Likely
18 B.P.O.E. member
19 Caviar
21 Nourished
24 Comic Louis —
26 Football position (abbr.)
27 Drone
28 Eastern title
29 *Temperatures Rising* star
30 Overhead railways
32 Light metal
33 Malt liquor
36 Moist soil
39 Man on 29-Down (abbr.)
40 Red or coral
42 Area code
43 Sweet drink
45 Miss Fitzgerald's
47 Mrs. Roy Rogers
48 Among
50 Old sailor
52 Sell tips
53 Ram's mates
54 Things in law
56 Mateo or Pedro
58 Conflict
62 Symbol for neon
63 Compass point (abbr.)

April 14, 1973

across

1 Bartender in *Gunsmoke*
4 Elevated railways
7 Raise
11 Raw mineral
12 Airplane maneuver
14 Beehive state
15 Armed conflict
16 Egg-shaped
17 Persian elf
18 ___ *Rising*
21 Female deer (pl.)
22 Affirmative reply
23 Comedian Wilson
25 Miss Arthur's nickname
26 ___ *Ramsey*
29 Decay
30 Songstress Bailey
32 Goof
33 Fire residue
34 Emmet
35 Heavy cart
36 Paddle
37 Mimics
39 *The Streets of ___* (2 words)
44 Nautical mile
45 Mr. Lynde
46 Successful show
48 Concerning (2 words)
49 Yugoslav leader
50 Mr. Wallach
51 Man of *The Little People*
52 Allow
53 Alkaline solution

down

1 Scatter seed
2 Smell ___, be suspicious (2 words)
3 Miss Baxter
4 Run away to wed
5 *Bridget ___ Bernie*
6 Fly high
7 Strong man of *Mission: Impossible*
8 Roman route
9 Paying passenger
10 ___ *Is Your Life*
13 Performer
19 Swab
20 River duck
23 Friar
24 Spanish article
25 Baseball club
26 Mr. Bernardi
27 Historical period
28 Weep
30 Late night TV host
31 Engrossed
35 ___ O'Connor
36 Frequently
37 Sharp
38 Try-out show for a series
39 Snow runners
40 Girl in *The Little People*
41 Ibsen heroine
42 Spike
43 Unctuous
47 An equal score

across

1 Geraldine's creator
5 Astern
8 One of the Waltons
12 Base
13 *Lamp Unto My Feet* host (abbr.)
14 Girl's name
15 He's Lou Grant (abbr.)
16 Appear
17 Trade
18 What Monty Hall offers
20 Secret agent
22 Insect
23 That is (abbr.)
24 Acting sisters; Betty and Jane ___
26 Obligation
29 Mr. Cooke
33 Descended
34 District in Sweden
35 He's Che Fong
36 Five-0 member
38 *Queen for* ___ (2 words)
39 Incline
40 ___ *the World Turns*
41 Feminine (abbr.)
43 Doze
45 Actor Graves
49 Comedian King
51 Netting
53 Unlock (poetic)
54 Louse (plural)
55 Bestow title
56 Property of Bernie's uncle
57 Singer-comedienne Ballard
58 Belonging to actor Eben
59 Let it stand!

down

1 Sanford's other name
2 Ore deposit
3 Johnny Carson's birthplace
4 Pint (abbr.)
5 Mellow
6 Tips
7 *Search* actress
8 Sullivan, Asner and Begley
9 ___ *Martin's Laugh-In* (2 words)
10 Persia
11 Greer's title (abbr.)
16 Compass point
19 *The* ___ *People*
21 Affirmative
25 A bother (2 words)
26 Crow
27 ___ Wallach
28 He's Walter Findlay
29 He's Dr. Pierce (2 words)
30 Beat
31 She's "sweet as apple cider"
32 Cowboy Rogers
37 Hunter or Fleming
40 Mimic
41 Star of *Columbo*
42 Essayist
44 A Hollywood Square
46 Sound the horn
47 Fencing sword
48 Pause
50 Born
52 Cronkite's network
56 Title for woman's libber

149

August 18, 1973

4 —— *the Family*
   (2 words)
5 Give in small portions
6 —— carte (2 words)
7 He is Gage in
   Emergency!
8 Irish actor Peter ——
9 Forbidden (variant)
10 *De* ——; superfluous
11 —— *Life to Live*
16 Folksinger-actor
   Burl ——
20 Reva —— of
   Temperatures Rising
21 Character actor
   Jack ——
22 —— *of Life*
23 Prevaricator
24 Shallow, round dish
26 Chief detective of
   McCloud
27 A single thing
28 Michael Cole on
   Mod Squad
29 Featured player
31 Miss Adams
34 Stimulating tonic
35 Pro ——
37 Evil spirit
38 To cut short
39 Greek goddess of youth
40 Actress Turner
41 Sleeveless Arab cloak
43 Born
44 Baxter on *The Mary
   Tyler Moore Show*
45 ——-Magnon man
46 —— *Ramsey*

across

1 Make lace
4 ——-12
8 Mr. Preminger
12 Kimono sash
13 Miss Falana
14 Mountain lake
15 Rock Hudson's role
17 Woodwind instrument
18 Contend
19 Bobby —— of
   Emergency!
21 Actress —— Corby
   of *The Waltons*
24 Small pond
25 Miss Nettleton
26 TV GUIDE feature
30 Miss Gardner
31 To fill with joy
32 Meshed fabric

33 Burgess —— of *Search*
35 Miss Moreno
36 *This Is Your* ——
37 *Dating Game* winner
38 Title for Ironside
40 Allow
41 Man's nickname
42 *Three* —— (3 words)
47 Actress Osterwald
48 City in Nevada
49 Before
50 Imitator
51 Mr. Martin
52 Milburn Stone's role

down

1 One of the Smothers
   brothers
2 TV network
3 Mr. Conway

October 13, 1973

across

1 Lt. Arthur Tragg
5 *Lotsa Luck* star
8 Female
11 Askew
12 Miss Sinatra
13 No
14 He's Mike Stivic
   (2 words)
16 Grandchild (Scot.-var.)
17 Property of Mr. Majors
18 Belonging to Calucci
19 Brawls
23 Tears
24 She's Consuelo
25 ___-12
27 Ignited
28 Sister of 12-Across
30 Not young
33 *Five-O*'s McGarrett
34 Girl's name
36 Grandpa Walton
38 Actor O'Connor
39 Sole of foot (comb. form)
40 Win
42 Prefix meaning "single"
43 He's Howard Borden
   (2 words)
48 Snare
49 Egg-shaped
50 Joy
51 Adjective suffix
   meaning "of"
52 *Five-O* member
53 *M*A*S*H* actor

down

1 Daughters of the
   American Revolution
2 Past
3 Cornhusker's state
   (abbr.)
4 Ever (poet.)
5 Have dinner
6 Singles
7 Damage
8 *The ___ Sisters*
9 Star of 8-Down
10 Watches
12 Fastens
15 Actress ___ Parker
18 Billy ___ Hawkins
19 *Roll Out!* star
20 Mr. Wallach
21 Allow
22 Printer's measure
23 Actor Burr
25 Conjunction
26 White House locale
29 Argon symbol
30 Anglo-Saxon money
31 "___ Abner"
32 Archie to Gloria
33 Wreath
35 Indefinite article
36 Mr. Rayburn's property
37 Archie's Mrs.
38 Pickle
39 Dr. Jamison's nurse
40 Donate
41 Comedian King
43 ___ & Carol & Ted
   & Alice
44 Turkish ruler
45 Not well
46 Guided
47 Affirmative vote

151

November 3, 1973

across

1 What Archie is to Gloria
5 Twelfth month (abbr.)
8 Margaret ___
12 False god
13 Before (poetic)
14 Useless
15 Comedian Lynde
16 Miss Farrow
17 Legal claim on another's property
18 Property of Raymond Burr's TV character (2 words)
21 Prefix meaning "not"
22 Mistake
23 Actor Torn
26 Insecticide
28 Nickname for actor Howard
32 Nomad
34 Signature (abbr.)
36 Dean Martin's nickname
37 He's Columbo
39 What Amanda is to Adam Bonner
41 Eric Scott's TV role
42 Complain
44 Purpose
46 Oscar's Felix (2 words)
51 Uncivil
52 India (abbr.)
53 Whirl
55 Assist
56 Familiar (abbr.)
57 Solitary
58 Examination
59 Southern state (abbr.)
60 Wise to

down

1 Fruit seed
2 ___-12
3 Rain hard
4 ___ the Family (2 words)
5 Belonging to *Sanford and Son* actor
6 One of the Waltons
7 Stop
8 *The Snoop Sisters* star
9 Miss Adams
10 Malt liquors
11 Lair
19 ___ Steiger
20 Annoy
23 Talk (slang)
24 Anger
25 Actor Harrington
27 Comedian Conway
29 Pen point
30 Compass point
31 At a distance
33 Singer Tony
35 *The Waltons'* Ellen Corby
38 Actor Walston
40 Comedian Caesar
43 Lorne Greene's new role
45 Miss Thomas
46 Every TV set has one
47 Poems
48 Analysis (abbr.)
49 Mr. Ames
50 Period of penitence
51 Rodent
54 MGM lion

The crossword grid with numbered cells (1–60).

across

1 Lou is to Mary Richards
5 Lysergic acid (abbr.)
8 *Here's Lucy* actor
12 He's Capt. Pierce
13 Over (Poetic)
14 Wicked
15 Nevada city
16 Tumeric
17 Paintings
18 Belonging to *Banacek* star (abbr.; 2 words)
21 —— Paulsen
22 Work unit
23 Nickname for actress Britton
26 Sainte (abbr.)
28 *Kojak* star
32 Mr. Sevareid
34 High mountain
36 Prophet
37 *M*A*S*H*'s O'Reilly
39 Anger
41 Boy's name
42 Born
44 The Brady's Jan
46 He stars as 46-Down (2 words)
51 Sonny and Cher ——
52 Adjective suffix
53 He's Felix
55 Presage
56 Zodiac sign
57 New York waterway
58 Fish
59 Desire
60 Cincinnati ball club

down

1 Last summer's series *The Corner* ——
2 Designer Cassini
3 Rational
4 *The* —— *Sisters*
5 She's "Hot Lips"
6 Ooze
7 Curtain
8 Mr. Apple's property
9 Eager
10 Belonging to Lillian
11 Overhead trains
19 Dance step
20 Mr. Linkletter
23 Via
24 Screw pine
25 Center
27 Actor Wallach
29 Mr. Ayres
30 He's Steve Austin
31 Years (abbr.)
33 Belonging to Bill Conrad's character
35 Dick Van Dyke's role
38 Alejandro ——
40 Miss Gabor
43 Dr. Bob Hartley's wife
45 Go in
46 Detective in disguise
47 Singles
48 One who uses
49 Ripped
50 Feminine name
51 —— Barker
54 Affirmative

July 13, 1974

across

1 He's "Hawkeye"
5 Brood of young animals (dial.)
9 Bread spread
12 Fly
13 Alan ___
14 Lincoln's nickname
15 "The ___," Jackie Gleason movie
17 Natives of Copenhagen
19 Rooster's mate
20 *The Outer* ___
21 First showing
24 Shoestrings
25 Actor Sharif
26 Brass wind instruments
27 Musical note
29 "To ___ with Love"
30 ___ Burnett
31 Beetle
32 And (Fr.)
33 TV movie: "The Alpha ___"
34 ___ *222*
35 Drills
36 Lassie's master
37 Smudges
39 Drink like a cat
40 Lone Ranger's side-kick
41 Movie based on a novel by Arthur Hailey
45 Actress Sothern
46 *One Life to* ___
48 Great Lake
49 Actor Milland
50 Thin
51 Donna ___

down

1 Fire residue
2 Mary Richard's boss
3 The (Ger.)
4 Actor Hill
5 ___ *Came Bronson*
6 Hearing organ
7 ___ Jolson
8 ___ *Center*
9 *The Odd Couple*'s Gloria
10 Aid criminally
11 *M*A*S*H* meal
16 Allow
18 Singer Ed ___
20 Toil
21 Measured amount
22 Send forth
23 The Long Branch is one
24 Entices
26 Strips of cloth or recordings
27 Weaving machine
28 *M*A*S*H* personnel
30 Actor O'Connor
31 ___ DeLuise
33 Protective garment
34 Jack the ___
35 Comedian Jack ___
36 Pave
37 ___ *Trek*
38 Girl's name
39 Legal claim on property
41 Actress Gardner
42 Raw mineral
43 Sport, obsolete
44 Comedian Knight
47 For example (abbr.)

August 10, 1974

across

1 Commercials
4 She's Edith
8 Junkyard owner
12 Illuminated
13 Beach hill
14 Miss Horne
15 ___ Trucking Company
16 ___-relief
17 "The Wizard of ___"
18 Ted Baxter's job
22 Measure of weight
23 ___ lift
24 ___ Smith
26 Prohibit
29 Approves
31 Mrs. Bunker
33 CBS commentator
35 Stitch
37 South African plant
38 Hawaiian greeting
40 Tiny ___
42 Actor Ayres
43 Negative
44 Electric unit
46 Aunt (Sp.)
48 Dr. Bob's field
53 He's Reverend Leroy
56 Fish eggs
57 Glop
58 Assistant
59 Possessive pronoun
61 Cloth scrap
62 Rip
63 Promontory
64 Actor Wallach

down

1 He is Hawkeye
2 Chop fine
3 Beef-vegetable dish
4 *McCloud*'s Cannon
5 *The Newlywed Game* host
6 Literary collections
7 Cozy retreats
8 J.J.'s mother
9 Mr. Buttons
10 Cancel
11 German article
19 Jill ___ John
20 Bill and ___
21 Augment
24 Nebraska Indian tribe
25 Bite
26 Orson ___
27 ___ Guthrie
28 Wayne's movie "___ Bravo"
30 TV ___
32 Unwell
34 ___ *One*
36 Former child star Jane ___
39 Exclamations
41 My (Sp.)
45 Mr. Cohen
47 *Hawaii Five-O*'s Harrington
49 Positive thinking psychotherapist
50 Monster
51 Score in hockey
52 Bear or Berra
53 ___ *Albert and the Cosby Kids*
54 Prevaricate
55 Mountain near ancient Troy
60 Baseball position (abbr.)

across

1 Mike Stivic
4 He's Nakia
7 Anita Cramer's sweetheart
11 Rhoda's mother
12 Kansas senator
13 Capable
14 Early's profession (abbr.)
15 Hawkeye
16 Average
17 *Kojak*'s Stavros
20 Composer-conductor Johnny
22 Legal matter
23 *Movin' On* trucker
24 One of the *Sons and Daughters*
26 Laboratory
29 French summers
30 Goddess of speech
31 Actor Gordon
32 Negative
33 *Planet of the Apes* astronaut
34 Inspires dread
35 Far (dialect)
36 Begets
37 Appleton's solid citizen (2 words)
42 Woven silk fabric
43 Member of *The Sonny Comedy Revue*
44 National Editorial Association (abbr.)
47 Girl's name
48 Hurry
49 Actor Ronny ___
50 Mr. Fonda
51 Truckie to Zack Wheeler
52 Compass point

down

1 Edge
2 Poem
3 *Maude*'s new maid
4 Punch or knife
5 American automotive pioneer
6 Miss Arthur
7 He's Rockford
8 *Hawaii Five-0* actor
9 Flea (Scot.)
10 Swamps
12 Curse
18 Morays
19 ___ *Haw*
20 She's Molly Lundstrom
21 Miss Hayworth
24 Chad's property
25 Tub
26 *Kodiak* creator
27 To shelter
28 Mrs. Harry Truman
31 She's Peggy Fair
33 *Hawaii Five-0*'s Jenny
35 Friend of "Hot Lips"
36 Skewer
37 Deep cut
38 Man's name
39 State in Arabia
40 Relating to aircraft
41 Pronoun (abbr.)
45 Age
46 Cutting tool

September 28, 1974

across

1 He's McMillan
5 *Police Woman*'s Detective Styles
8 *Nakia* star
11 Vocal solo
12 Ireland
13 Sue ___ Langdon
14 Miss Moore (2 words)
16 Exclamation
17 Hades
18 Edith Bunker
19 David Hartman's TV role
23 "Pepper" Anderson's boss
24 Valerie Harper series
25 *The Texas Wheelers*' star
27 Devour
28 ___ *Moon*
30 Maude
33 Raw hide
34 Chico's "Man"
36 Afternoon socials
38 He's Carl Kolchak
39 Nuisance
40 Entrance
42 He's Sheriff Sam Jericho
43 *Apple's Way* actor
48 Actress Mary ___
49 On the lee
50 Comply
51 Fleur-de-___
52 Band man Brown
53 Masculine

down

1 Stuff
2 Anglo-Saxon money
3 Circa (abbr.)
4 Miss Ballard
5 *The Rookies* regular
6 Russian city
7 Ever (poet.)
8 Ring-shaped roll
9 Child actor Tatum
10 Existed
12 One who eyes
15 *Planet of* ___ (2 words)
18 *The Rockford Files* star
19 Prefix meaning "town"
20 Exclamation
21 ___ *for Women Only*
22 Midwest state (abbr.)
23 Lee McCain's role
25 Excess-profits tax (abbr.)
26 French article
29 *Petrocelli*'s Pete Ritter
30 Borough (abbr.)
31 Female sheep
32 ___ B. Davis
33 Comedienne ___ Carroll
35 Railroad (abbr.)
36 He's Broadhurst
37 Park in Colorado
38 Information
39 Mr. Sand
40 Roy Rogers' partner
41 Singles
43 Actor Bisoglio
44 *Happy Days*' Mr. C
45 To Be Announced (abbr.)
46 Snakelike fish
47 Humorist Louis

across

1 Petrocelli's chief investigator
5 Rights (abbr.)
8 Girl's name
11 Rip
12 Painful
13 Loiter
14 *Chico and the Man* star
16 Leave (abbr., var.)
17 Kiln
18 Mildred to McMillan
19 Star of *Little House on the Prairie*
23 *Paul ___ in Friends and Lovers*
24 Actor John ___
25 She's Jill
27 Senora (abbr.)
28 Archie's neighbor
30 Bill Crowley is one
33 Miss Stapleton
34 Trapper John
36 Mr. Apple's property (abbr.)
38 He's Mike Stone
39 Combining form meaning recent
40 Shakespearean king
42 Glutton
43 Esther Rolle series (2 words)
48 Land measure
49 Sea gull
50 Greater
51 Jeff Reed's marital status (abbr.)
52 Football scores (abbr.)
53 Young Caine

down

1 Parent-teacher group
2 Lamprey
3 Actor Hunter
4 Before
5 Marion on *Happy Days*
6 Hurry
7 Japanese coin
8 Creator of 23-Across
9 He's Harry O
10 Ancient
12 Baseball great ___ Musial
15 Terry, Mike and Chris
18 Miss West
19 Latter-day Saint (abbr.)
20 Prefix meaning air
21 National Recovery Administration (abbr.)
22 Actor ___ Fore

23 McMillan's first name
25 *The Manhunter* star
26 Indefinite article
29 Sun god
30 Miss Charisse
31 ___ *Life to Live*
32 Indite
33 Rhoda's boyfriend
35 He plays 1-Across (nickname)
36 Terry Webster
37 Ted Baxter's Georgette
38 Created
39 Role for 19-Across (abbr.)
40 McGarrett
41 Ages
43 ___ *Christie Love!*
44 Demon
45 Boy's name
46 Mistake
47 Ocean

December 14, 1974

across

1 Theresa Merritt's role
5 Addie thinks Moze is hers
8 *Hawaii Five-O*'s Doc
12 French islands
13 Self
14 French cheese
15 Meadow
16 Mr. Guinness
17 Poet
18 *Kojak* star
20 Nakia's boss
22 Civil engineers (abbr.)
23 "That is" (abbr.)
24 *The $10,000 Pyramid* host
26 *The Guiding Light* actor
29 Perennial comedy "___ Aunt"
33 Leave out
34 Margin
35 Noun suffix (plural)
36 Actor Gavin and family
38 Store
39 Heron (archaic)
40 Producer Fred ___ Cordova
41 Arabian garment
43 Supplement
45 *The New Land*'s Molly
49 Kolchak's first name
51 Golf club
53 Erie, Pa. airport code
54 Be borne
55 Can
56 Sheep genus
57 Else (Scot.)
58 Compass point
59 Jack Elam's recent role

down

1 Comedian ___ Kamen
2 Toward shelter
3 Repast
4 Adverb
5 Boy's name
6 Eras
7 Milburn Stone (2 words)
8 Decline
9 *Emergency!* regular
10 Ireland
11 Romero and Glass
16 Affirmative vote
19 ___ *House on the Prairie*
21 Middle Irish
25 Nearer
26 Anna Larsen to Tuliff
27 Doctor's group
28 Miss Moore's TV role
29 CBS anchorman
30 Secreted
31 Yeomanry
32 Compass point
37 Before
40 News correspondent ___ Rather
41 Field
42 *Maude* actor
44 Jim-Bob's sister
46 Actress Patterson
47 He's Steven Apple
48 Danger
50 Barnaby's Betty
52 ___ *Life to Live*
56 "The Wizard of ___

159

across

1 A prop for Carol's cleaning lady
4 Stitch
7 Hurried
11 Actress Hartman
12 Uninteresting, dull
13 He plays young Caine
14 Mary's boss
15 Ireland
16 By mouth
17 ___ on the Prairie (2 words)
20 Matt might lead one
22 ___ Chaney Jr.
23 Semiprecious stone
24 Rod McKuen, for instance
26 ___-relief
29 Match Game '74 host
30 Karel Capek play
31 Living quarters for Hawkeye
32 The ___ Couple
33 Word on a towel
34 Pro ___
35 ___ Rather
36 In ___ space
37 David Hartman series (2 words)
42 Golf club
43 Dies ___, Latin hymn
44 Rhoda's mother
47 Principal
48 ___ and Daughters
49 He's Apple

50 Confederate
51 Black or Red
52 Compass point

down

1 The 2000 Year Old Man
2 Yoko ___
3 Friends and Lovers' star (2 words)
4 Cut
5 ___ Holliman
6 The Texas ___
7 Eating tool
8 South American country
9 Historical periods
10 Mr. Robertson
12 Beast (Fr.)
18 Capri, for instance
19 "___ Lips"

20 Cartoon opossum
21 Unlocked (poet.)
24 Jessica Walter's Amy ___
25 Days of ___ Lives
26 ___ Arthur
27 Poker stake
28 ___ Trek
31 Faithful
33 Possesses
35 Steve McGarrett's partner
36 Change for a five
37 Capital of 8-Down
38 European mountain chain
39 Twist
40 Indonesian islands
41 Zola novel
45 ___ Meredith
46 Cutting tool

February 22, 1975

52 Actor Romero
53 ___ *Life to Live*

down

1 Harvest
2 *The Girl ___ Life* (2 words)
3 Will ___
4 Betsy ___
5 Expect
6 Paul ___
7 Curved moldings
8 ___ *Tune* (2 words)
11 Linear measurement (abbr.)
13 951
14 Remained inactive
19 He plays J.J.'s father
20 Jim-Bob, to John
22 Fish
23 Graduate degree
24 Host of 25 Down
25 Long-running quiz show
26 *Celebrity Sweepstakes'* host
28 CBS symbol
30 ___ *My Children*
31 Stingy
32 *Truth ___ Consequences*
34 Sea bird
35 Fastened
37 Ex-bandleader Shaw
38 Chop finely
39 *Gambit's* network
40 Meadow
41 Keenan ___
42 Toward and within
43 Kind of light
44 *The Newlywed ___*
46 Behold!

across

1 Sonny drives one
4 A step for Nureyev
7 *Movin'* ___
9 Direction
10 Not at home
12 Lasses
15 Soul (Fr.)
16 ___ *of the Lost,* children's show
17 Mrs. Peel's first name
18 *The $10,000 ___*
20 *Now You ___* (2 words)
21 Tom Seaver, for instance
22 It keeps rising
23 Primary
26 Jason Walton

27 Pronoun
29 God of war
30 Assistance
31 He plays Grady
33 Preposition
34 Heidi's mountain pasture
35 Host of *The Hollywood Squares*
36 ___ Lynde
38 Miss Farrow
39 Host of 18 Across
41 ___ *Streak*
45 Host of *Tattletales*
46 Loretta ___
47 Educational association (abbr.)
48 Persian poet
49 Fairy-tale opening
50 *Split Second* host
51 Old pronoun

across

1 He's Dr. Joe Gannon
5 Club
8 Plant disease
12 Appeal
13 River (Sp.)
14 Scholarly book
15 One who employs
16 Mr. Asner (abbr.)
17 *Baretta* star (abbr.)
18 Miss Valentine plays her
21 10th letter of Hebrew alphabet
22 Child actress Melissa ___ Anderson
23 Ampere (abbr.)
26 Actor Mineo
28 Inspector Keller
32 Producer of 50-Down
34 Ocean
36 Steve Forrest series
37 Dr. Simon Locke
39 Sea bird
41 Compass point
42 Version (abbr.)
44 Whale (Comb. form)
46 *Khan!* star (2 words)
51 *Maude* actor
52 Unrefined metal
53 Cat's ___
55 Other (Sp.)
56 Daughters of the American Revolution (abbr.)
57 French paste
58 Existed
59 Mornings (abbr.)
60 Wide-mouthed jar

down

1 Mr. Gulager
2 Shell
3 Region
4 County in Northern Ireland
5 Belonging to sister of 43-Down
6 An opera
7 San Remo and Walnut Grove
8 *The ___ of San Francisco*
9 Chill
10 Early pulpit
11 Wager
19 Goddess of dawn
20 Masculine name
23 Angular (abbr.)
24 Morocco (abbr.)
25 Golf instructor
27 Miss Meriwether
29 Female sheep
30 Late actor Heflin
31 French summer
33 Claude Akins' series (2 words)
35 Belonging to Brian Keith's TV character
38 *Sunshine* actress
40 National Elevator Industry (abbr.)
43 She's Mrs. Joe Gerard
45 Pace
46 *The Rookies*' Jill
47 Employ
48 A small drink
49 Congeal (Dial.)
50 ___ *Baltimore*
51 *Caribe* actor
54 Workers Educational Association (abbr.)

April 12, 1975

across

1. —— Murray
4. Inquire
7. Cameron Mitchell, for short
10. —— Alda of *M*A*S*H*
12. Hawaiian food
13. —— Lockhart, actress
14. *That's My* ——
15. Play on words
16. —— Johnson, comedian
17. Actress Vaccaro
19. TV game show
21. Mountain pass
22. Gaming cube
23. Woodland deity (Myth.)
26. He was Nakia
30. Afresh
31. River barrier
32. Green plum
33. *The $10,000* ——
35. *The* —— *Burnett Show*
36. Loiter
37. The Long Branch, for example
38. Bob ——, TV host
41. Star of *Gunsmoke*
45. Tropical plant
46. Be mistaken
48. —— Sevareid
49. TV headliner
50. —— Charles Chaplin
51. —— Hayworth, actress
52. *Sanford and* ——
53. An oldie: *I* ——
54. Fishing snare

down

1. Side post of a doorway
2. Of a wing
3. —— *That Tune*
4. Shock
5. Former French coin
6. *Wild* ——
7. Sidewalk edging
8. Against
9. —— *the Press*
11. Rhoda's mother (2 words)
13. Star of *The Rockford Files* (2 words)
18. Beetle
20. Broadcast
23. Tree fluid
24. Some
25. Territory (abbr.)
26. Temporary fashion
27. Paving material
28. Self
29. Electric unit
31. Ramble
34. —— West, actress
35. Jalopy
37. He's Petrocelli
38. Food fish
39. Low female voice
40. Parti-colored horse
42. One of the Waltons
43. Location
44. Begone, cat!
47. —— Torn, actor

May 24, 1975

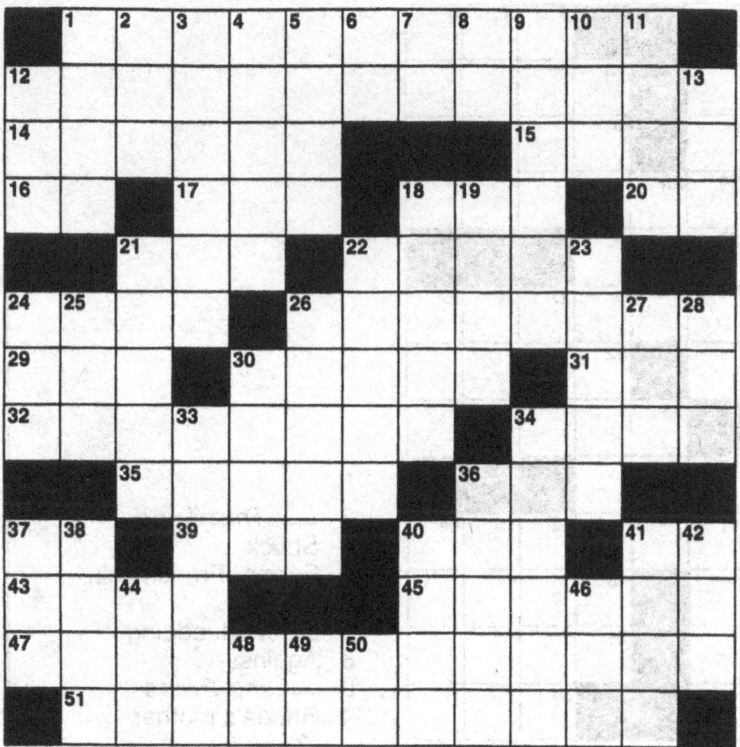

3 Movie great Orson
4 Biblical city (Joshua 12:2)
5 Actress Foch
6 Al ___ Rogatis
7 Exclamation
8 Family member
9 Come up
10 Family doctors (abbr.)
11 Long fish
12 ___ Johnson
13 Soak flax
18 Room's furnishings
19 Invites
21 Highly skilled
22 Charges
23 Lake resort
24 Kelsey runs one
25 Hockey game requirement
26 Early invaders of England
27 Propel a boat
28 ___ Buddhism
30 Operatic highlight
33 TV detective Harry
34 Energetic person
36 Crane in ship's bow
37 Kind of wood
38 Store
40 Summerall and Hingle
41 ___ Ellen Walton
42 Plural of is
44 The ear (prefix)
46 High, rocky hill
48 Twice (prefix)
49 Type of current
50 French article

across

1 Lamont's Aunt Esther (2 words)
12 She plays Joe's wife (2 words)
14 Singer Frankie ___
15 Gilligan had one
16 Symbol for sodium
17 Meadow
18 German article
20 Jill ___ John
21 Gas (prefix)
22 Position again
24 *The Price Is Right* contestants make them
26 *Now You See It* host (2 words)
29 ___ Trucking Company
30 Chico fixes them
31 Garden tool
32 Kolchak's occupation
34 Lower
35 Attempts
36 Permanent color
37 ___ *the World Turns*
39 Lived
40 Peter ___
41 Edith to Gloria
43 Oxford or brogan
45 Embodiment
47 Offbeat comedy series (3 words)
51 Series with no regular cast (2 words)

down

1 Molten rock
2 Chicken ___ king

June 28, 1975

across

1 Mitzi of *We'll Get By*
5 Jim-___ Walton
8 Burned remains
11 Song for Sills
12 To prepare the way
13 Expert (colloq.)
14 Sister of 5-Across ___ (2 words)
16 Esther Rolle is one on *Good Times*
17 Conceited
18 Permits
19 Minstrel showman (2 words)
23 Roster of actors
24 Precocious Master Reese
25 Term of approval
27 One: Italian
28 *The Secret* ___
30 Pikelike fish
33 *The Brady Bunch* dad
34 Michelangelo masterpiece
36 Those in favor of
38 Ralph ___, *Good Times*' Michael
39 Mournful utterance
40 Miserly or malicious
42 Vessel
43 Comedy series set in the '50s (2 words)
48 Federal agency (abbr.)
49 ___ Moran, *Happy Days*' Joanie
50 Pre-Richie role of 33-Down
51 Antagonist
52 Gotham (abbr.)
53 Negative reply (sl.)

down

1 Posturing performer
2 Openings: Latin
3 Atmosphere
4 Blithe
5 Indonesian island
6 Cooking compartment
7 *Gentle* ___
8 Willie of *We'll Get By*
9 Young actor Jacoby
10 Skirt borders
12 Scheme
15 *Good Times* family
18 Boy
19 Flightless bird
20 Girl's nickname
21 British military decoration (abbr.)
22 Harry Truman's state (abbr.)
23 Group, firm
25 Deity
26 Conjunction
29 *Good Times* daughter monogram
30 Obtain
31 Consumed
32 Monogram for child actor Rippy
33 ___ Howard
35 Erin (abbr.)
36 ___ Rico (var.)
37 Another acting Howard
38 Short title for Bob Keeshan
39 One of the Platts in *We'll Get By*
40 Laura's older sister in *Little House on the Prairie*
41 Heroic
43 Female fowl
44 *Happy Days*' Ralph
45 Military address (abbr.)
46 Bark
47 Observe

165

across

1 He's Joe Gerard
5 Man of patience
8 Hindu prince
12 Mr. Lugosi
13 Unlock (poet.)
14 Kiln
15 Prophet
16 Ocean
17 Actor Orson
18 Ida ___ on *Rhoda*
21 Yes (sl.)
22 Territory (abbr.)
23 Era
26 Article
28 *Caribe* star
32 Girl's name
34 Sound on film (abbr.)
36 Headliner
37 Man on *The Odd Couple*
39 Soak
41 Belonging to Mr. Brown
42 Knock
44 Female ruff
46 She's Florida Evans (2 words)
51 Dutch cheese
52 Foot part
53 Carbonated soft drink
55 Actress ___ Dietrich
56 Letter "S"
57 Greedy
58 Bird
59 Retain (abbr.)
60 Try for an acting job

down

1 Monogram for British playwright
2 Unicorn (Biblical)
3 Butter substitute
4 Mr. Orwell
5 Belonging to Rockford's dad
6 Reveal
7 Brute
8 Property of *Baretta* star
9 Assert
10 Miss Stapleton
11 Girl's name
19 ___ *Christie Love!*
20 French pronoun
23 River in Venezuela
24 Showman Edwards
25 And so forth (abbr.)
27 Goddess of dawn
29 Consumed
30 Heel
31 Time periods (abbr.)
33 He's Lucas Tanner
35 *S.W.A.T.*'s Hondo Harrelson
38 Cheer
40 *Hot l Baltimore* resident (abbr.)
43 Mr. Falk
45 Actor Dana ___
46 River in Germany
47 Rational
48 *Upstairs, Downstairs* head maid
49 ___ *of Life*
50 Charles Lamb pseudonum
51 Mr. Asner (abbr.)
54 Total

1	2	3	■	4	5	6	■	7	8	9	10
11			■	12			13	14			

across

1 Picnic pest
4 Baseball club
7 Real estate map
11 Zack's daughter
12 Mr. Kazan
14 Miss Barrett
15 Moving piece of machinery
16 Costar of *The Waltons*
17 Wicked
18 TV sportscaster (2 words)
21 Rave
22 Owns
23 ___ Tyler Moore
25 Evergreen tree
26 Small rug
29 Hubbub
30 *What's My Line?* panelist
32 Compass point
33 Modern
34 Use a lever
35 Costar of *M*A*S*H*
36 Mr. Mineo
37 Mr. Griffin
39 TV newscaster (2 words)
44 Soft, light fabric
45 ___ Wolfe, sleuth
46 Zodiac sign
48 *Gunsmoke* man

49 City in Oklahoma
50 An oldie: *Burke's* ___
51 Opening for coins
52 Golf gadget
53 Building wing

down

1 TV network
2 Ark's skipper
3 TV late show
4 Started
5 Wide-awake
6 Fastened
7 *Meet the* ___
8 ___ *of Life*
9 Indigo
10 Lofty
13 *All in the Family* man
19 Route
20 Rowing blades

23 *Chico and the* ___
24 Fruit beverage
25 Move on wings
26 Costar of *The Rookies*
27 *Sammy* ___ *Company*
28 Orange pekoe
30 Health resorts
31 *What's My Line?* panelist
35 Have being
36 Costar of *The Waltons*
37 Rose ___
38 Wear away
39 Shade trees
40 Genuine
41 Within
42 Outlet
43 *Let's Make a* ___
47 Nocturnal bird

October 18, 1975

across

1 *Joe Forrester* star
8 Actor Leon
12 She's Fay (2 words)
13 Miss Gerritsen
14 River in China
15 —— Grande
16 Oliver Hardy's partner
17 *Holvak* regular
20 Tuck's title (abbr.)
22 Billiard rod
23 Mr. Carney
25 Yes
27 He's Dr. Jake Goodwin
31 Actor —— Forrest
34 Girl's name
35 Bark
37 Miss Ullman
38 *On the Rocks* inmate
41 Cloris Leachman series
44 Minstrel ——-A-Dale
46 Scottish var. of do
47 Ed to Chico
49 Forest humus
51 Hood of Sherwood Forest
55 One time
57 Narrow inlet
59 Fuss
60 Chemical suffixes
61 Sally's Mac
64 Daughter of 41-Across
65 He's Cable

down

1 Mr. Lugosi
2 Restrain
3 Inspector general (abbr.)
4 On *Emergency!* staff (abbr.)
5 Needlefish
6 Fixed star
7 *Medical* ——
8 Actor Harrington's property
9 He's Jeremiah Worth
10 Isaac's eldest son
11 Sensible
12 Mae West role
18 Headgear
19 Epoch
21 Roman bronze
24 Attempt
26 In
27 Tony to Frank Montefusco
28 Highest note
29 Belonging to *Bronk*
30 Ladle
32 Seven in Rome
33 English versions (abbr.)
36 Doctoral degree
39 Suffix meaning of
40 He's Chin Ho
42 Yare (var.)
43 Man's name
45 Producer Lear's property
47 Utah town
48 She's Kate McShane
50 Comedian Little
52 Bundle
53 Indian city
54 Prefix meaning not
56 The letter "S"
58 Medical organization
62 Pronoun
63 Sports announcer (abbr.)

down

1 Constellation
2 Isinglass
3 Unbleached
4 Requires
5 TV cop series
6 Follow orders
7 Lady in *Barnaby Jones*
8 Costar of *Chico and the Man*
9 Dismounted
10 Go by train
11 Mimic
19 The —— Grande
20 Rowing blade
23 Costar of *Joe Forrester*
24 Be mistaken
25 Phillippine peasant
27 Mr. Conway
29 —— *Adams Screen Test*
30 Miss Gardner
31 Mr. Bolger
33 *The Carol —— Show*
35 Claude Akins' series (2 words)
38 Cushion
40 Accomplished
43 Costar of *Ellery Queen*
45 Costar of *The Mary Tyler Moore Show*
46 Quick punches
47 Butter's rival
48 Villain's foe
49 Change direction
50 Leak out slowly
51 Ointment
55 Owns

across

1 So be it!
5 Mr. Newhart
8 Brenda Vaccaro's role
12 Tarzan creator: Edgar —— Burroughs
13 Costar of *Barney Miller*
14 Paper holder
15 Land measure
16 Soak, as flax
17 Assists
18 *Medical Center* nurse (2 words)
21 Perch
22 Edible tuber
23 Baretta's Fred, for example
26 Mel ——, former baseball player
28 Man in *M*A*S*H*
32 Bedouin
34 Intention
36 PBS series
37 Costar of *Emergency!*
39 An oldie: —— *Squad*
41 Negative vote
42 Uncooked
44 By way of
46 TV singer (2 words)
52 To sheltered side
53 Longing
54 Costar of *The Rockford Files*
56 —— D'Angelo/ *Superstar*
57 New (comb. form)
58 Old Testament book
59 Black dust
60 Sea eagle
61 Belonging to Mr. Buttons

169

down

1 Possess
2 Defunct Lee Grant series
3 Belonging to Mr. Prinze
4 Additional
5 Mr. Sevareid
6 *Gunsmoke* and *Bonanza*
7 The Six Million Dollar Man
8 Ski Nose
9 Chemical suffixes
10 Permanent color
12 Former series, *Naked* ___
18 Singer ___ Arnold
19 Old series, *Halls of* ___
20 Eastern ruler (var.)
21 God of love
24 Don ___
25 *Joe* ___ *Sons*
26 *Gambit*, for one (2 words)
27 McGraw and Muhammad
28 Son of Adam
31 Actress Miles
33 Lick up
35 ___ *O*
36 Lamont's "Pop"
37 Norse epic
38 Evangelist Roberts
39 Patti ___
40 Level
41 What Leroy Brown was
44 Historical period
45 ___ Reed

across

1 ___-Broadway
4 Cat sound
7 Lean-to
11 Combat
12 Center
13 He was Matt Helm
14 Comedian Louis ___
15 Beverlee McKinsey role on *Another World*
16 Sword
17 Ellery Queen, et al.
20 Songstress Helen ___
22 Miss Arden
23 Dry
24 ___ Crosby
26 Chico sells it
29 Frequent stand-in for Johnny
30 Sue ___ Nevins, the Happy Homemaker
31 Singer Jerry ___
32 Beast of burden
33 Doctor of Laws degrees (abbr.)
34 Discharge
35 ___ Linden
36 Adjective for Schneider
37 Daytime fare (2 words)
41 Actor Patrick ___
42 Gesture of farewell
43 Heraldry (abbr.)
46 Actor John ___
47 Ancient
48 Unrefined mineral
49 Longtime host of *What's My Line?*, John ___
50 Hankering
51 Paraffin

down

1 Float
2 Singer ___ Guthrie
3 Elsa and the MGM trademark
4 Singer ___ Tucker
5 Comedian Bob ___
6 Musical instrument
7 Jay Silverheels' role
8 Whole
9 ___ Fontane of *Joe and Valerie*
10 Bachelor of Engineering Science (abbr.)
13 Cartoon: *Sylvester and* ___
18 Prefix meaning three
19 Chew
22 ___ *du lieber!*
23 ___ Na Na
25 To plant seed
27 ___ *Day at a Time*
28 Compass point
30 The pig in *Green Acres*
31 Bambi, e.g.
33 They have a peacock named Rover and a cow named Chance
36 Contralto ___ Anderson
38 Cheer
41 She's Alice
43 Canine star
44 The horse of 7-Down
45 Florence to *The Jeffersons*
46 Oldie: *One ___ Beyond*
47 ___ Bancroft
48 Rain torrentially
49 Compass point

across

1 ___ Disney
5 "Johnny One ___"
9 Children's show: ___ *Bears*
11 Solo for 36-Down
12 Ebony
13 Charlie ___ Tuna
14 Flin ___, Manitoba
15 Will not
16 *How the West ___ Won*
17 He says "Gr-r-r-r-reat!" (3 words)
20 Actress ___ Allgood
21 District in France
22 ___ *the World Turns*
24 Internal Revenue (abbr.)
26 *Upstairs, Downstairs* house: ___ Place

29 ___ Everett
32 Ski rope
34 Keenan ___
35 Group of females
37 "___ and Peace"
39 Actor Horton's first two initials
40 Actress Patricia ___
42 Dogs like Sam
45 He's finicky (3 words)
49 Actor ___ Viscuso
50 Within
51 Nothing
52 ___ Caesar
53 Arabian gulf
54 Carter or Lockhart
55 ___ McMahon
56 Short sleeps
57 Tidbit for Rona Barrett

across

1 Late TV host, Ted ___
5 Movie
9 Pigpen
12 The Kingston ___
13 Den
14 Actor Bosley
15 Sophia in *Viva Valdez* (2 words)
18 Stage actor's finish
19 North Atlantic Treaty Organization (abbr.)
20 Dr. Early of *Emergency!*
23 Policewoman
25 Actress Marsha ___
26 Actor Dabbs ___
27 Note well (abbr.)
29 Employ
30 Game-show regulars
31 ___ Ane Langdon
32 Movie star Hamilton (init.)
33 Raw vegetable dish
34 Monty ___
35 Early film star Lupe ___
36 Singer ___ Reese
37 Best Picture of 1958
38 Baseball's McGraw
39 He plays Luis Valdez
44 Mr. Gershwin
45 Singer Abbe ___
46 ___ Sevareid
48 Producer ___ Brooks
49 Director Preminger
50 Actress ___ Thompson

down

1 Mountain (abbr.)
2 Joan of ___
3 Central Intelligence Agency (abbr.)
4 Gymnast Olga
5 "One ___ over the Cuckoo's Nest"
6 Singer Janis ___
7 ___ Torres
8 Carl Reiner in *Good Heavens* (2 words)
9 Colorado, e.g.
10 Dorothy's dog
11 Peruvian singer ___ Sumac
16 Cleaning implement
17 Two of a kind
20 Hoodlum
21 Actress Barbara ___
22 ___ *Day at a Time*
23 Desi ___
24 Require
26 Actress ___ Storm
27 Invalid
28 ___ Lugosi
30 He's Horshack
31 ___ Mineo
33 Type of lily
34 Epstein of *Welcome Back, Kotter*
35 "Myra Breckinridge" author
36 Batman and Robin: The Dynamic ___
37 First name of 35-Down
38 Kojak's first name
39 Edge
40 Cosby character: ___ Albert
41 Canadian province (abbr.)
42 Openings (anat.)
43 ___ Caesar
47 West Coast state (abbr.)

September 11, 1976

59 Man's name
60 College degree (abbr.)
61 Crowley of *Police Woman*

down

1 Oldie: ___ *Masterson*
2 Greek god of war
3 Tidy
4 Comic Milt
5 Robert Blake's role
6 King of Norway
7 Used in relay race
8 *Match Game* regular
9 Oldie: ___ *Come the Brides*
10 Mr. Carney's
11 Rod McKuen
19 *C'est la* ___
20 ___ Taylor
23 Nickname for *Kojak*'s Dobson
24 Miss Arden
25 Healthful food (abbr.)
27 ___ Gulager
29 ___ Hunter
30 *Green Acres* star
31 ___ Skelton
33 Belonging to Hardy's friend
35 *Kukla,* ___ *Ollie* (2 words)
38 ___ and the Family Stone
40 Same
43 Costar with 5-Down
45 *Mary Hartman, Mary Hartman* regular
46 Kind of fish
47 Dash
48 Pianist Peter
49 Suffix (chem.)
50 Singer Fitzgerald
51 Back of anything
55 Automobile engine part (abbr.)

across

1 *Break the* ___
5 He's Dr. Hartley
8 Edward of *Upstairs, Downstairs*
12 Region
13 The "cotton state" (abbr.)
14 Superman
15 Philadelphia Phillies, for example
16 Oldie: *The* ___ *Patrol*
17 Comic Johnson
18 Hondo of *S.W.A.T.* (2 words)
21 Egg
22 Nothing
23 Unit of energy
26 And all that (abbr.)
28 *Hollywood Squares* host
32 Motorcyclist Knievel
34 Man's name
36 Keep safe
37 Dean Martin's roast location
39 Psychic ___ Geller
41 Adjective for Leroy Brown
42 Diminutive suffix
44 High mountain
46 Fonzie of *Happy Days* (2 words)
52 To sheltered side
53 Seventh letter of Greek alphabet
54 Mr. Guinness
56 *Streets of San Francisco* star
57 Film star Chaney
58 He lived at the Shiloh ranch

November 27, 1976

across

1 Doorway post
5 *All in the Family's* Mike
8 Polio-vaccine doctor
12 Great Lake
13 Not well
14 Tropical plant
15 Fruit pastry
16 Labor union (abbr.)
17 Alter
18 Costar of *Alice* (2 words)
21 Affirmative vote
22 Nickname for Struthers
23 Pod vegetable
26 Twisted
28 He's *Serpico*
32 ___ Sevareid
34 German article
36 FDR's mother
37 *To Tell the Truth* host
39 Mild rebuke
41 Negative vote
42 Not at home
44 Turf
46 One of *Charlie's Angels* (2 words)
51 Star of *Columbo*
52 Falsehood
53 Name word
55 ___ *of Night*
56 Building wing
57 Costar of *Rhoda*
58 Darling
59 Relating (abbr.)
60 Long walk

down

1 Fast plane
2 Bedouin
3 Mud
4 Costar of 43 Down
5 Costar of *Executive Suite*
6 Medley
7 Moves, as wind
8 Star of *Kojak*
9 Costar of *M*A*S*H*
10 Star of *Hawaii Five-0*
11 Lock opener
19 Chop
20 Boy
23 Wooden pin
24 Period in history
25 Ventilate
27 Thus far

29 ___ *Dyke and Company*
30 Lyricist Gershwin
31 *One ___ at a Time*
33 *Kojak* man
35 Costar of *The Quest*
38 Mr. Brynner, actor
40 Costar of *Baretta*
43 *The Mary ___ Moore Show*
45 TV hostess
46 Green gemstone
47 Seaweed
48 Egypt's river
49 ___ Tennille
50 Chunk
51 Nourished
54 Born

174

December 18, 1976

down

1 Policeman
2 Past
3 ___ in the Family
4 Charles ___ Reilly
5 Olivia Walton's husband
6 Mountain (comb. form)
7 Druggist's salt
8 Executive Suite's Stephen ___
9 Morning show
10 ___ Alda
11 1940's film actor Turhan ___
16 Hither and ___
17 Singer Burl ___
20 ___ Lugosi
21 He was Batman
22 ___ Harrison
23 Belongs to Grandpa Walton
24 Horse feed
26 He plays Tony Randall's son
27 Graham ___
28 Detective's assignment
30 Columnist Rona ___
31 Also
33 Famous bear
34 Hawaii Five-0's Khigh ___
35 ___ news
36 Cry
37 Cover with concrete
38 Actor's part
39 Aries the ___
40 ___ Jacobi
41 "The Meathead"
42 Comedienne Charlotte ___
43 ___ bit
44 ___ and the Family Stone

across

1 Actor James ___
5 Actor ___ Ferrer
9 ___ Hunter
12 Make eyes at
13 Evangelist Roberts
14 That Good ___ Nashville Music
15 She plays Flo in Alice (2 words)
18 Sanford and ___
19 ___ the Terrible
20 The Red ___
23 Sticky
25 She was Jeannie
26 Sounds of a drum
27 Knights of Columbus (abbr.)
29 Careless
30 Match Game regular
31 "___ for Two"
32 Morning
33 Belongs to Jack of late-show fame
34 British actress Diana ___
35 Belongs to Hawaii Five-0 star
36 Dinah
37 Rich Man, ___ Man–Book II
38 French for king
39 Tony Randall's house-keeper (2 words)
45 ___ Gardner
46 Instrument
47 He's Wojo of Barney Miller
48 Alice's boss
49 Part of a TV set
50 ___ Lamarr

February 26, 1977

across

1 Inquires
5 Enjoy a soaper
8 Costar of *Family*
12 Costar of *The Rockford Files*
13 He's Fish
14 Among
15 Not out of
16 French for no
17 Contended
18 Host of 4-Down (2 words)
21 Overly
22 The sun
23 Pub drink
26 Miscalculate
28 Costar of *The Waltons*
32 The ___ Show
34 He's CPO Sharkey
36 Winter flakes
37 Account examination
39 Lorne's old role
41 Comedian Louis ___
42 Guided
44 Soaked
46 *Who's Who* hostess (2 words)
52 To sheltered side
53 Wing
54 Potential steel
56 ___ *Trek*
57 Deface
58 Cereal plant
59 Kind or class
60 Picnic pest
61 Body of water

down

1 Black bird
2 Music for singing
3 She's Sabrina
4 ___ *for the Stars*
5 Costar of *The Jeffersons*
6 Woodwind instrument
7 Curves
8 Star of *Kojak*
9 Moslem ruler
10 Perished
11 Sums up
19 Enemy
20 Cry of surprise
23 Turkish title
24 Edward Asner's role
25 Finale
27 Costar of *All in the Family*
29 Tavern
30 Plaything
31 Ram's mate
33 Costar of *Little House on the Prairie*
35 *The Bob ___ Show*
38 Jasmine
40 New (comb. form)
43 *Executive Suite* is one
45 Spin
46 Male singer
47 Low female voice
48 Raising children
49 He's Hawkeye
50 Opera air
51 He's McMillan
55 Born

March 5, 1977

across

1 What Donny and Marie do
5 TV "opera"
9 One of Pappy's group
12 Former late-show host Jack ___
13 Joint
14 Hockey organization
15 "Huggy Bear" of *Starsky & Hutch* (2 words)
18 Top dog (abbr.)
19 Actor Nick ___
20 Georgette of *The Mary Tyler Moore Show*
23 Mickey ___
25 "___ Window"
26 TV roles
27 Roosevelt's first two initials
29 Chart
30 Centers
31 Actress's neckpiece
32 Molinaro of *Happy Days*
33 Stops
34 ___ Griffin
35 Anne's *Rhoda* role
36 One of The Jacksons
37 *Police* ___
39 *Days of* ___ *Lives*
40 Norma Zimmer's title
46 Broadcast
47 Stage light
48 Mr. Stravinsky
49 Registered nurses (abbr.)
50 ___ Preminger
51 Six o'clock show

down

1 Health resort
2 Lord Peter Wimsey actor
3 ___ "King" Cole
4 *Sesame Street* character
5 Hop
6 Singer Yoko ___
7 American Expeditionary Force (abbr.)
8 Charles Schulz comic strip
9 Camera position
10 Talk
11 Otherwise
16 None
17 Singer Diana ___
20 *Good Morning America* humorist
21 Actress Patricia ___
22 Space
23 Allen or Ingels
24 Metallic rocks
26 Survey
27 Tennessee Ernie ___
28 Former Monkee ___ Jones
30 Cousteau's boat
31 Actor Gazzara
33 Injure
34 *Wild Kingdom's* Perkins
35 Flies
36 McClanahan of *Maude*
37 Mark of a wound
38 *The* ___ *Man*
39 Upon
41 Suitable
42 Obtained
43 The ___ of Aquarius
44 Beaver's brother, Tony ___
45 Years (abbr.)

April 9, 1977

across

1 Malt beverages
5 ___ Angeles, Cal.
8 Mr. Kotter
12 ___ Disney
13 ___ Got a Secret
14 ___ Mountains, USSR
15 ___ Stanley Gardner
16 Scold
17 Gossip-column tidbit
18 Squiggy of Laverne & Shirley (2 words)
21 Greek goddess of the dawn
22 Hawaiian wreath
23 Movie: "Room at the ___"
26 Snatch
28 Georgia ___
32 Dress designer Cassini
34 Tibetan ox
36 Donate
37 Sally of Rhoda
39 ___ in the Family
41 Command to a horse
42 Art to Caesar
44 Comparative ending
46 Saturday morning cartoon (2 words)
51 Tennessee Ernie
52 England (abbr.)
53 ___ Roberts
55 Excerpt from a film
56 Compass point
57 Opera star
58 Florentine house
59 German article
60 Again

down

1 Fearful respect
2 Dana Elcar's role
3 Singer ___ Fitzgerald
4 Lee Majors' part
5 Bionic Woman
6 The President's ___ Office
7 Actor George ___
8 ___ Light
9 Comedian ___ Johnson
10 He played Jethro Bodine
11 Tree
19 Electrified particle
20 Born
23 Today host Brokaw
24 Grand ___ Opry
25 Garden vegetable
27 ___ Baa Black Sheep
29 Actor ___ Young
30 ___ Arden
31 ___ Meriwether
33 Will Geer's role
35 Jamie Farr's M*A*S*H role
38 Children's show ___ II
40 Allow
43 Cartoon: ___ Buggy
45 Valerie Harper's role
46 Silent star ___ Negri
47 Beverlee McKinsey in Another World
48 First name of 37-Across
49 Happy Days teenager
50 Good review
51 Federal Communications Commission (abbr.)
54 Sirota's profession

June 4, 1977

across

1 Mountains (abbr.)
4 Jewel
7 —— the World Turns
9 ——raja
10 Movie: "—— the Wild Wind"
12 Stub
14 Lawrence and Gorme (3 words)
17 Containers
18 Artery
19 Belonging to MHMH actor Mullavey
21 Therefore
22 One —— to Live
23 To Tell the Truth regular Kitty ——
27 Sprite
28 Hindu garments
29 —— Simcox of Code R
30 Children's show: The —— Company
32 Cold hands, —— heart
33 Play: "The —— of the Greasepaint..."
34 The —— Boys mysteries
35 "Fat Albert" creator Bill ——
37 The —— Show
38 Basketball team: The Harlem ——
43 The Streets of —— Francisco
44 Lard of Baa Baa Black Sheep
45 And others
46 Old Blue Eyes (init.)
47 Girl
48 Wartime medal (abbr.)

down

1 Welcome ——
2 Sherman Hemsley and Isabel Sanford (2 words)
3 Brad —— of The Tony Randall Show
4 Mardi ——
5 Even (poet.)
6 Grizzly Adams' —— Jack
7 James Sutorius's series (2 words)
8 Law case
9 Woman's title
11 Belongs to singer Bailey
13 She's Maude
15 Bitter vetch
16 —— Berra
19 Song group: —— club
20 Small brook
21 —— Sevareid
23 Singer Vikki ——
24 The late —— Onassis
25 Hawaii Five-0 star
26 TV award
28 Remained
31 Late actor Lee J. ——
32 Most ——
34 "Some Like It ——"
35 Centimeter-gram-second (abbr.)
36 Norwegian king
37 Football objective
39 Children's game
40 Nucleic acid
41 Aries the ——
42 Oliver Hardy's partner (init.)

June 11, 1977

across

1 Mouths
4 He's Hawkeye
8 ___ *Sharkey*
11 ___ *Who*
12 Not any
13 Attila was one
14 A Bunkerism
15 J.J.'s self-description
17 Another Bunkerism
19 Joan of ___
20 Sanford Sr.
22 Kunta was one
26 "The Man ___ Came to Dinner"
28 Something forbidden (2 words)
31 Teacher's organization
32 *Days of ___ Lives*
33 A TV tube
35 Wildlife photographers ___ and Jen Bartlett
36 Elderly
37 Next
38 Presidential monogram
39 Goldfinger's weapon
42 Hindu god
44 He's Dog of *Dog and Cat*
46 A lament
49 Feather
54 Harrison or Coward
55 Exclamation
56 Author Lardner
57 Red Skelton character
58 Famous opera house
59 Unescorted
60 Asner's

down

1 Paul Newman was born here
2 Garner and Berry
3 Requester
4 *Sonny ___ Cher*
5 Actress Myrna
6 Soprano Moffo
7 Comes close
8 "The Windy City" (abbr.)
9 Place
10 ___ *Life to Live*
11 What reason?
16 1150
18 Loan
21 An order (2 words)
23 Plus Father (2 words, see 49-Across)
24 Letters
25 Direction
26 Sheep's hair
27 Occasional dance on *Hawaii Five-0*
29 Japanese drama
30 Poems
34 Feminine name
40 Mischievous child
41 What MGM's lion does
43 He was Ben Casey
45 A group
47 Thousands (sl.)
48 Shade tree
49 Samantha to her friends
50 *Chico and ___ Man*
51 Dine
52 Actress Balin
53 Breakfast dish

July 23, 1977

across

1 Revolutions per minute (abbr.)
4 Grape brandy
8 ___ Disney
12 Paddle
13 Film actor John ___
14 Margarine
15 Tibetan ox
16 "Othello" character
17 Madam (contr.)
18 She plays Mrs. Ike Godsey: ___ Edwards (2 words)
21 Richie on *Happy Days*
22 Related
23 Eartha ___
25 He played Chicken George
26 Polly Holliday's role
29 Arthur Godfrey's instrument (colloq.)
30 Bowling term
32 ___ Abner
33 For each
34 ___ Parseghian
35 Chess play
36 Curie or Bovary (abbr.)
37 ___ Rabbit
39 Larry, Curly and Moe: The ___ (2 words)
44 Actress Martha ___
45 Covers with pitch
46 Born
48 ___weiss
49 Andy Taylor's son
50 Bounder
51 Ancient inhabitant of Asia
52 Chief of *The Untouchables*
53 "The West ___ Horror"

down

1 ___ Clark of *Hee Haw*
2 Jack ___
3 The Sweathogs' teacher (2 words)
4 "As ___ goes, so goes the Nation."
5 One more time
6 Fury
7 Kevin Dobson's *Kojak* role
8 *Wonder* ___
9 Jai ___
10 Producer Norman ___
11 Scholarly book
19 National Educational Television (abbr.)
20 *The Onedin* ___
23 Irv Kupcinet
24 ___ Eisenmann of *The Fantastic Journey*
25 *Baa ___ Black Sheep*
26 Mrs. Brady
27 Actress Ullmann
28 *That Good ___ Nashville Music*
30 Identical
31 Actor Robert ___
35 One of the "Little Women"
36 Singer ___ Haggard
37 ___ Karloff
38 The Tournament of ___
39 "Let ___ eat cake!"
40 "Dr. Jekyll and Mr. ___"
41 Robert, Donna or Rex
42 Video ___
43 ___ Connery
47 ___ "Kookie" Byrnes

181

October 22, 1977

across

1 PBS's ___ Beat
5 Roger Mudd's network
8 Whirled
12 ___ and the King
13 He's Barney
14 ___ Mostel
15 Patricia ___
16 White House daughter
17 Berra or Bear
18 Archie's refuge, Kelcy's ___
20 Lou Grant
21 Oblong (abbr.)
24 TV dentist
27 Della ___
29 Vindicated
33 Tilt
34 Rachel's mother on Another World
35 A ___ at the Top
36 She plays Bob's wife
38 Official decree
39 Whiskers
41 Mr. Buttons
42 As the ___ Turns
45 Singer Janis ___
47 American novelist James ___
48 The Better ___
50 Walton daughter
54 Stare
55 In the past
56 ___ World of Sports
57 Belonging to Mr. Knight
58 He's CPO Sharkey
59 Quarrel

down

1 Prohibit
2 ___ Day at a Time
3 Old show, Three ___ Match (2 words)
4 Newsman Marvin ___
5 One-name singer
6 Cartoon sound of a blow
7 ___ and the Family Stone
8 Ethnic miniseries
9 Peasant worker
10 Encourage
11 Black, in Paris
19 He's Fish
20 Exist
21 Killer whales
22 Actor Bridges
23 Actress Kay ___
25 Consumer advocate
26 ___ Marie Saint
28 Belonging to quarterback Ken
30 First or reverse
31 Relieve
32 The ___ Scott Decision
34 Literary collection
37 ___ Beatty
38 Miss ___ Contest
40 Psychic Jeane ___
42 Mr. Disney
43 Curved molding
44 Actor Robert ___
46 Chancellor's program
48 Morose
49 Personality
51 Comic Taylor
52 Rhoda's mom
53 Hockey equipment

down

1 "___ How She Runs"
2 Gymnast ___ Korbut
3 Arkin or Alda
4 *The Tony ___ Show*
5 ___ Davis
6 Indian nurse
7 Actress ___ Balding
8 Sebastian ___
9 Bedouin
10 Farm structure
11 Stop
19 Years (abbr.)
20 ___ *Petrol*
23 ___ Na Na
24 *Please Don't ___ the Daisies*
25 Maugham's "Cakes and ___"
26 American Institute of Architects (abbr.)
27 ___ Zeppelin
28 Before (poet.)
29 *How the West ___ Won*
31 Nearsighted cartoon character (2 words)
32 Actor ___ Price
34 The late ___ Onassis
35 *Husbands, Wives ___ Lovers*
36 Actress Sharon ___
37 Ire
38 At that time
39 Actress Janice ___
40 ___ Chase
41 Opera
42 ___ Montand
43 Greek letter
47 Soviet Socialist Republic (abbr.)

across

1 Fly
5 Archie's Place
8 Singer Johnny ___
12 Singer ___ Fitzgerald
13 *Richie Brockelman, Private ___*
14 Solo for Beverly Sills
15 Actor Richard ___
16 Actor ___ Hunter
17 Lucille ___
18 Bobby Porter's *Quark* role (3 words)
21 *You ___ There*
22 Morris the ___
23 ___ & Crofts
26 Perform in a play
27 Actor ___ Ayres
30 Monty ___
31 ___ Farrow
32 Alice's co-worker
33 Consumed
34 ___ Parseghian
35 Assistants
36 Movie: "The Man with the Golden ___"
37 Allyn ___ McLerie
38 Betty I & II (3 words)
44 *The Incredible ___*
45 Actor ___ Young
46 Belongs to actress Arden
48 ___ Sommer
49 Poem
50 Basketball team
51 Close by
52 Paddle
53 Russian ruler

August 19, 1978

down

1 Skirt edge
2 Costar of *CHiPs*
3 To sheltered side
4 She's Laverne
5 She's *The Waltons'* Olivia
6 Butter's rival
7 Pares
8 Costar of *Welcome Back, Kotter*
9 Among
10 Davenport
11 Playing card
19 Snakelike fish
20 Captain Kirk's diary
23 *The ___ Couple*
24 Meadow
25 River barrier
27 Spike of maize
29 Southern constellation
30 *Quincy* fellow
31 Foxy
33 She's Hot Lips
35 TV comedian (2 words)
38 Negatives
40 Instrumental duet
43 Vessels for heating liquids
45 Costar of *Charlie's Angels*
46 Girl's name
47 *In Search of the ___ America*
48 Ointment
49 Operating at a distance (comb. form)
50 Site of the Taj Mahal
51 He's Hutch
55 Soak, as flax

across

1 Pile
5 Swab
8 Time gone by
12 ___ Stanley Gardner
13 Island (Fr.)
14 Cupid
15 Manner
16 Alphabet letter
17 *Love of ___*
18 Costar of *Carter Country* (2 words)
21 Affirmative
22 Sun
23 Ancient
26 Costar of *Barnaby Jones*
28 Costar of *Barney Miller*
32 *Let's Make a ___*
34 Sam's breed (abbr.)
36 ___ Roberts
37 Costar of *Soap*
39 ___ Serling
41 Oldie: ___ *Prentiss*
42 Caviar
44 Motor coach
46 Costar of *What's Happening!!* (2 words)
52 Filet mignon
53 New (comb. form)
54 Composer Stravinsky
56 Market
57 High mountain
58 Not false
59 Star of *M*A*S*H*
60 *Studio ___*
61 Stop

September 16, 1978

down

1 TV network
2 *Romper* ___
3 Low female voice
4 Costar of *The Rockford Files*
5 Costar of *M*A*S*H*
6 Absent
7 Thick
8 TV host
9 Assistant
10 One who ices
11 Meadow
19 Costar of *Barnaby Jones*
20 ___ *My Children*
23 Wager
24 Gold (Sp.)
25 Auction offer
27 Poisonous snake
29 Indicates maiden name
30 *One* ___ *at a Time*
31 Dined
33 Costar of *The Hardy Boys Mysteries*
35 Costar of *The Jeffersons*
38 Tibetan ox
40 Oldie: *See It* ___
43 Interoffice notes
45 Costar of *Eight Is Enough*
46 Zoo enclosure
47 Costar of *M*A*S*H*
48 Shout
49 Jot
50 Ridicule
51 Cot
54 *Meet* ___ *Press*

across

1 Bedouin
5 Nicholas on *Eight Is Enough*
8 Costar of *Barney Miller*
12 Tree trunk
13 Have creditors
14 Cereal plant
15 Sheep shelter
16 Sprinted
17 Notion
18 Costar of *60 Minutes* (2 words)
21 Thus far
22 Sprite
23 ___ Hope
26 Greek letter
28 She's Alice
32 ___ Sevareid
34 Timber tree
36 Adjective for Felix Unger
37 TV morning show
39 Writing implement
41 One network's symbol
42 *Quincy* fellow
44 Extinct bird
46 Costar of *Project U.F.O.* (2 words)
51 Island east of Java
52 Alice's boss
53 Debatable
55 Mild oath
56 Bullring cheer
57 Engrave with acid
58 Contradict
59 Nickname for actor Stallone
60 Benefit

185

October 21, 1978

across

1 Sabrina, Kelly and Kris
7 Kind of oil
13 Bugs Bunny food
14 ___ Francis
15 Sharif and Bradley
16 Mary's middle name
17 ___ Charles
18 Expire
21 Harem room
22 Part of the Bible (abbr.)
23 ___ *Goes to Washington*
27 Article
28 ___ Reddy
30 ___ Fields
32 Actress Farrow
33 *Apple* ___
34 *The Brady* ___
36 "The ___ Time I Saw Paris"
38 Father
39 "___ the merrier" (2 words)
41 ___ Dorado
43 Bullfight cheer
45 Court
46 Profound respect
47 Late great rock-and-roll star
50 African friend of Kunta Kinte
52 Wobble
54 *Rockford Files* actor
55 *Sesame* ___
56 *Battlestar Galactica* star

down

1 Squirrel food
2 Joe ___
3 Drab color
4 Bobble a baseball
5 ___ Alamos
6 Jill ___ John
7 Western state's postal abbreviation
8 ___ Hindle of "Clone Master"
9 Nickname of "Rocky" star
10 Combining form meaning "end"
11 ___ *at a Time* (2 words)
12 Broadcast again
18 Robert Urich's role on *Vega$*
19 *WKRP* ___ *Cincinnati*
20 Belonging to Johnny's sidekick
23 Gleam
24 Extend to
25 *The* ___ *Chase*
26 *America* ___ !
29 Ostrich-like bird
31 Christopher ___
34 Nureyev's field
35 Chop
36 Jack ___
37 Wayne ___
38 Rod McKuen and colleagues
40 Sports biography: "Little ___"
42 Rental document
44 At any time
46 Poker call "___ up!"
48 Resident (suffix)
49 *Studio* ___
50 Distant
51 Sue ___ Langdon
53 "John-Boy" actor's monogram
54 Specific gravity (abbr.)

December 2, 1978

across

1 Extrasensory perception
4 TV network
7 Estimate
11 Recompensed
13 Basis for *M*A*S*H*
14 Chilled
15 Beginning of a TV show
16 Some
17 Steep, rugged rock
18 Costar of 46-Across
20 Globe
22 Island (Fr.)
23 What Dandy Don drinks
24 *The ___ Boys*
27 He's Archie
31 Newsman ___ Sevareid
32 "My ___ Sal"
33 Sturdy cart
34 Johnny Carson's aide
36 Dinah ___
37 Costar of *Barney Miller*
38 ___ *Na Na*
39 Rubbed out
42 Animal's confining rope
46 TV comedy series
47 Period in history
49 Perry ___, singer
50 Fastened
51 Dick ___ Patten
52 Makes a murmuring sound
53 Costar of 46-Across
54 Finale
55 Cereal plant

down

1 Heroic
2 Star of *Family*
3 Wharf
4 Conscious
5 Prohibit
6 Costar of *Soap*
7 Costar of *Battlestar Galactica* (2 words)
8 Land measure
9 Rip
10 ___ *of Night*
12 ___ *Man Undercover* (2 words)
19 England's cathedral town
21 ___ capita
24 Skirt edge
25 Curved line
26 Basketball hoop
27 Is able to
28 Gold (Sp.)
29 Roman household god
30 Caustic solution
32 Costar of *Eight is Enough*
35 Garden tool
36 The lady
38 "Please ___ By"
39 Sundance Kid's girlfriend
40 Shower
41 Killed
43 An oldie: *Amateur ___*
44 TV award
45 ___ Marie
48 Sprinted

187

across

1 Stitch
4 Skirt edge
7 In compasrison with
11 ___ Wallach, actor
12 Wild hog
13 Actor's part
14 ___ My Children
15 Costar of Happy Days
16 Actor John ___
17 He's the Hulk (2 words)
20 Task
22 Not in
23 ___ Roberts
24 Recording strip
26 Chico's motto: "It's not my ___"
29 Of a sour fruit
30 Female sheep
31 Singer Patti ___
32 Harvest goddess
33 River in Poland
34 Land measure
35 He's Barney Miller
36 The ___ of Hazzard
37 Costar of M*A*S*H (2 words)
42 Important appliance for Julia Child
43 Late-show fare: "High ___"
44 Grand ___ Opry
47 Change direction
48 "Chariots of the ___"
49 He's Kaz

50 Catch sight of
51 Type measures
52 Defective bomb

down

1 Cousteau's field
2 Building wing
3 He's Mork
4 Mr. Ed's foot
5 "___ on down the Road"
6 Lady in Three's Company (2 words)
7 Characteristic
8 Boss ___ in 36-Across
9 Star of M*A*S*H
10 Pianist Peter ___
12 Dry, as wine
18 Not for Women ___
19 Actress ___ McClanahan

20 Man from U.N.C.L.E.
21 Stumble
24 Costar of The Love Boat (2 words)
25 Reverence
26 Star of Hawaii Five-O (2 words)
27 Monster
28 "Killer ___"
31 ___ Lynde, comedian
33 Lout
35 He's the Fonz
36 Lairs
37 Budge
38 Burl ___, singer
39 Retain
40 Romper ___
41 Stewart and Taylor
45 ___ Grant
46 Finale

across

1 Incline
5 Shakespeare's fairy queen
8 Part in a series
12 Sword
13 Metallic rock
14 ___ Alda
15 Ancient Scot
16 ___ Tin Tin
17 Shields or Yarnell, for example
18 Jay Johnson's *Soap* role (3 words)
21 BernNadette ___
22 Within (comb. form)
23 The ___ Wars
24 Sam of *Quincy*
25 Quincy's workroom
28 Assam silkworm
29 "___ on a Hot Tin Roof"
30 Scott or Jimmy
31 Winter month (abbr.)
32 "Peter ___"
33 Singer Lou ___
34 John Schuck's *Turnabout* role
35 Swords
36 Gary Cookson's *Delta House* role
39 ___ Griffin
40 French King
41 TV interference
43 "Some ___ Running"
44 "The ___ and the Pussycat"
45 Skin condition
46 ___ Laurel
47 Born
48 TV ___ pattern

down

1 Representative (abbr.)
2 As pretty as ___ (2 words)
3 Latka's job in *Taxi*
4 Porky Pig's girlfriend
5 Belongs to Mindy's friend
6 Operatic solo
7 Patrick O'Neal's *Kaz* role
8 Actor Dack ___
9 Potpourri
10 "Mary Had a Little ___"
11 Compass point
19 Counter Intelligence Corps
20 Distinguished Service Order (abbr.)
21 Rushed
24 ___ Saynor of "The Corn Is Green"
25 *Family* family
26 Movable parts of an airplane wing
27 Sorrell Booke plays ___ Hogg
29 John ___ Swayze
30 Took care of the kids
32 Cushion
33 Charlotte ___ of *Diff'rent Strokes*
34 ___ Anne McDonald
35 "___! You're on *Candid Camera*!"
36 Tidy
37 *My Friend* ___
38 Actress Misty ___
39 Masters of ceremonies
42 "Dangerous When ___"

July 7, 1979

across

1 "The Defection of ____ Kudirka"
6 He's Lou Grant
11 Captain ____ of *Battlestar Galactica*
12 "The Darker Side of ____"
14 "Gunga ____"
15 Nebraska city
17 ____ Paulo, Brazil
18 Advertisement
19 Magazine show
21 He played Eliot Ness (init.)
22 Net
24 *Logan's* ____
25 ____ Sommer
27 *How the West Was Won* star
29 Fighting forces
31 Ever (poet.)
32 "____ Blu, Depinto Blu"
33 Famous river
36 Prime-time Texas soap opera
39 Cooking show: ____ Kerr
40 Summer in France
42 Actress ____ Bethune
43 "____ Baskin"
44 Actress ____ Arquette
47 India's first woman Prime Minister (init.)
48 Robert ____ of *Quincy*
50 "____ Suspicion"
51 Medical association
52 ____ Rodriguez (2 words)
54 BJ of *BJ and the Bear*
56 Aleutian native
57 "Bolero" composer

down

1 *The Amazing* ____*-Man*
2 Electrically charged atom
3 *Little House on the Prairie* star (init.)
4 Medicinal plant
5 She's Chrissy
6 Maren Jensen's role
7 ____ Connery
8 Comedian Russell's initials
9 Bitter vetch
10 Montalban's role
11 Lorne Greene's role
13 "The Subject Was ____"
16 "Aku ____"
19 A Little Rascal
20 *Poldark* heroine
23 ____ *Previews*
26 Actress ____ Palmer
28 Standing Room Only
30 Ribonucleic acid
33 "Toys in the ____"
34 Actress ____ Scott
35 Author of "The Railway Children"
36 Singer John ____
37 Daryl Anderson's role
38 Dr. Carl ____
41 Chinese philosophy
45 Hawaiian island
46 Actress ____ Patterson
49 Source of the Clampetts' wealth
51 ____ *of Uncertainty*
53 *Medical Center* star (init.)
55 *Emergency!* treatment

November 17, 1979

across

1 "Li'l ——"
6 Baseball, hockey or tennis e.g.
11 *The Prime of Miss Jean ——*
13 Meredith Baxter ——
14 "The Cat in the ——"
15 Donahue of *Soap*
17 Fuel
18 "The Wizard of ——"
19 Dolores —— Rio
20 Compass point
21 Edge
23 Musical instrument
25 "Take ——, She's Mine"
26 Danny DeVito's role
28 Thespian
30 *The Streets of —— Francisco*
31 —— Aviv
32 "—— Johnny!'
34 —— & Crofts
36 *Faux ——*
37 *American Band——*
39 Affirmative answer
41 He was Mr. Brady (init.)
42 Fruit drink
43 Eleven (Roman)
44 Man's name
46 *The Secret ——*
48 —— Club
49 Mickey Mouse's girlfriend
51 —— Boone
53 Patty Duke ——
54 Actor Cliff ——

down

1 Detest
2 South American country
3 The —— Ready for Prime Time Players
4 He's Lou Grant
5 "Adam's ——"
6 "To —— with Love"
7 Public Relations
8 Singer Yoko ——
9 Rob or Carl
10 Mary —— Moore
12 —— Gorme
13 —— Abzug
16 Prefix meaning new
22 *A Woman Called ——*
23 "Our —— Have Tender Grapes"
24 Performed
25 "The Buddy —— Story"

27 United Arab Republic
29 "—— and Sympathy"
32 Ron Glass's *Barney Miller* role
33 —— of the Union
34 Edgar Bergen's Mortimer ——
35 A group of six
36 He sang with Keeley Smith
38 "Much —— About Nothing"
40 Beverly ——
45 Insect
46 "It's a —— to Tell a Lie"
47 Chart
48 "The —— and the Pendulum"
50 Nickel (chem.)
52 "River of —— Return"

across

1 *The Dukes of Hazzard*'s "Boss"
5 Drummond
9 Chosen (abbr.)
12 Flivver
13 She's "Shirley's" daughter Debra
15 ___ small world (2 words)
16 It is
17 Resort city and spa in S.W. England
18 International language
19 Assistance
20 Dallas quarterback
21 *Struck by Lightning* role
24 Not
25 Another *Struck by Lightning* role
26 ___ Walston
27 World War II vehicle
30 Ms. Fabares, for short
31 Summer skin color
32 Panelist and singer ___ P. Morgan
33 First name of 25-Across
34 ___ Chamberlin
35 *Vega$*'s private eye
36 ___ Holbrook
37 ___ Janssen
38 Lorenzo ___
41 ___ Flanagan
42 Beatle monogram
44 Scent or smell
45 Step, for Nureyev
46 Halt
48 *Detective School* star
50 *Hawaii Five-0* role
51 Quantity (abbr.)
52 Predator's victim
53 "___ a man who wasn't there" (2 words)

down

1 Rock musical

2 ___ *Blue* (3 words)
3 Units of weight (abbr.)
4 Former Portuguese enclave in India
5 Method of dyeing
6 Dull, dry
7 Mental ability (abbr.)
8 Greek letter
9 Guys' gathering
10 Diminutive suffix
11 Singer Zella ___
14 Black, to a poet
19 Raggedy ___
20 Thinnes of *From Here to Eternity*
22 Actor Robert ___
23 Feel poorly
24 Girl's name
25 The Concorde is one (abbr.)
26 Mrs. Garrett

27 ___ O'Grady
28 *The Lazarus* ___
29 Beverage
31 Comb. form for communications
32 Indonesian (abbr.)
34 ___ Cruces, N.M.
35 Knot lace
36 ___ *to Hart*
37 Actor Bob
38 Hill with broad top
39 Mary Ingalls is Mrs. ___ Kendall
40 ___ Blanc
41 ___ *Loves a Mystery*
43 Commercial
45 Spanish preposition
46 What to do at Aspen
47 He's *WKRP*'s Venus Flytrap
49 Opposite (abbr.)

May 10, 1980

down

1. ___ Foyt
2. Moo
3. "Moby Dick" captain
4. Gretchen Kraus
5. Canine star
6, 29 & 44. Jay Thomas and Gina Hecht
7. ___ Parseghian
8. "The Secret Life of Walter ___"
9. Bailiwick
10. "To ___, with Love"
11. Truman's first two initials
16. ___ Life to Live
17. La ___, Ill.
20. ___ Topper
21. Singer ___ John
23. Don Murray's role
24. Buck Rogers' pal
25. Actress Jo Van ___
27. Command to a horse
28. He played Fish (init.)
29. See 6-Down
30. Becoming like (comb. form)
32. Electronic Numerical Integrator and Computer (abbr.)
33. At the age of (abbr.)
34. Yard (abbr.)
39. "War and ___"
40. 19-Across character
41. Tolkien character
43. The Gong ___
44. See 6-Down
45. Radar O'Reilly's home state
46. Galway Bay Islands
47. Theater sign
48. Aborigine of Laos
49. "Gunga ___"
50. Rob's dad (init.)
53. ___-Tanisha

across

1. Jai ___
5. Part of a swimsuit
8. Series about the 4077th
12. Trapper ___, M.D.
13. Ever (poet.)
14. Beverlee McKinsey's Another World role
15. Mitchell Ryan is ___ Hawkins in The Chisholms (2 words)
18. Musical instrument
19. One Day ___ Time (2 words)
20. Civil Engineer (abbr.)
22. Extra-illustrated (abbr.)
23. Stone or Stallone
24. Task Force (abbr.)
26. Gymnast Korbut
29. Trouble
30. Night bird
31. Lawrence and Gorme (3 words)
35. Actor ___ Keale
36. Sparks or Beatty
37. Dick Van ___
38. Little House ___ the Prairie
39. "The ___ and the Pendulum"
40. "I" in France
42. "Play ___ As It Lays"
43. "The ___ Chase"
44. Chef ___ Child
47. He's Gary Ewing
50. Short for crocodile
51. "Bali ___"
52. "___ Until Dark"
54. Actress Misty ___
55. Sue ___ Langdon
56. ___ Maria Alberghetti

193

July 12, 1980

59 *Dallas*'s Crosby
60 59-Across's father (init.)
61 Belongs to McMahon
62 Revolved

down

1 Hebrew "K"
2 Sufficient, to a poet
3 Egyptian god of creation
4 ___ Shire
5 Jack and Chris
6 Jason's ship
7 ___ Manilow
8 "___ Joey"
9 Younger Arkin
12 Raymond ___
13 "___ of the Road"
18 ___ la-la
19 To take notice of, to a Cockney
23 Victory letter
24 Alfred (abbr.)
25 Negative conjunction
27 John Raitt to Bonnie
29 Scholastic Aptitude Test (abbr.)
30 ___ du Diable
31 "___ and the Single Girl"
33 ___ Weaver
35 John, Juliet and Hayley
38 "C'est ___"
40 Actress ___ Wallace
43 Climb up or over
45 Minute particles
46 "Cakes and ___"
47 Lee J. ___
49 Was in debt
50 "The Parent ___"
51 Beige
53 TV network
56 ___ Rand

across

1 Retained
5 Workshop for Quincy
8 ___ Kettle
10 Theatrical organization (abbr.)
11 Time period
12 "There'll Be Some Changes ___"
14 Young horse
15 Manager (abbr.)
16 Elder Arkin
17 James Sr. and James Jr.
20 *Trapper John*, ___
21 Nigerian tribe
22 "___, Sir, That's My Baby"
23 Vincent ___ Patten
26 "Harry ___ Tonto"
28 Arnaz Sr. and Jr.
32 Electric force
34 ___ Bottoms
36 Ivy League university
37 Zimbalist
39 "What ___ You Do in the War, Daddy?"
41 John Ritter's father
42 Spanish personal pronoun
44 Meadow
46 Whodunit authoress (init.)
48 ___ Goulet
52 She plays WKRP's receptionist
54 Air Weather Service (abbr.)
55 Killer whale
57 Recedes
58 ___ Grant

down

1 Telegram (abbr.)
2 *60 Minutes* humorist (init.)
3 "This program was recorded live on ___"
4 ___ *Resort* (2 words)
5 Made of oats
6 "Damien: ___ II"
7 Continent
8 Martin or McQueen
9 The 4077___ MASH
10 Listen
11 Age
13 Barrymore and Mertz
17 Author/TV hostess Barbara ___
18 Max of *Hart to Hart*
19 Susan Lucci's role in *All My Children*
20 Isinglass
25 "The ___ Dumpling Gang"
27 "___ Had to Be You"
29 He's Sheriff Lobo
30 ___ Waggoner
32 ___ Pacino
33 She's Mrs. Jefferson
34 "Play ___, Sam" (2 words)
39 Actor Richard ___
41 Inspirations
43 "Freebie and the ___"
44 Employed
45 "___ Small World" (2 words)
46 ___ Stanley Gardner
47 *Edward and ___ Simpson*
51 Luxury liner: ___ II (abbr.)
53 *Truth ___ Consequences*
54 *Untouchables* actor (init.)

across

1 Mr. Roarke's assistant
7 ___ *World Turns* (2 words)
12 Talk-show hostess Virginia
13 Rolle or Williams
14 Baseball's ___ Rose
15 "___ a Yellow Ribbon"
16 *M*A*S*H* star (init.)
17 Libby of *United States* (2 words)
20 Mrs. John Dean
21 "Make Me ___ Offer"
22 ___ Deum
23 FDR's wife (init.)
24 "___ a Teen Age Frankenstein" (2 words)
26 "The Greatest"
28 Adjective suffix
31 *Real People* crimefighter (2 words)
35 French artist
36 Leased (abbr.)
37 "___ Gunner Joe"
38 Judy Garland's daughter (init.)
40 Agricultural Engineer (abbr.)
41 Radar O'Reilly's home state (abbr.)
42 Compass point
43 Richard of *United States* (2 words)
47 "___ and My Gal"
48 Compass point
49 Rip
50 Actress ___ Welch
52 "Sinbad the ___"
55 Bergen's "Mortimer ___"
56 Actor Ed's

August 2, 1980

across

1. Quincy's workshop
4. ___ diem
7. ___ Ladd
11. In a frenzy to kill
13. Mountain (comb. form)
14. *What's My ___?*
15. "___ with a Halo"
16. Ad ___
17. Thought
18. Costar of 23-Across (2 words)
21. Twisted
22. Actress Charlotte ___
23. Stars Donna Pescow
26. British Thermal Unit (abbr.)
27. Small Asiatic deer
30. Star of *Diff'rent Strokes*
31. "Classical ___"
32. "Rag ___"
33. "The ___ and I"
34. ___ Carney
35. ___ Williams
36. ___ Wallach
37. Fifth musical note
38. Light plays Wolek on ___ (4 words)
45. Bonnie Parker, for one
46. Polly Holliday role
47. Black-___ Susan
48. Jai ___
49. Sick
50. "The ___ Breed"
51. *The ___ of the Game*
52. No (Scot.)
53. Norse sea goddess

down

1. "Angel" Kris
2. Friend (Fr.)
3. A failure (sl.)
4. Actress Bergen
5. One of the Great Lakes
6. He's Trapper John
7. Linda Lavin series
8. Italian island resort
9. Trapeze artists usually use one (2 words)
10. Tidy
12. Birdie on *The Misadventures of Sheriff Lobo*
19. "Where the Boys ___"
20. Sow (Ger.)
23. ___ Vigoda
24. Complain
25. ___ Young
26. Rod Carew uses one
27. Given name of 29-Down
28. "___ Acquaintance"
29. New Miss America host
31. Merv ___
32. Phyllis ___
34. ___ MacGraw
35. Pigeon's sound
36. *Dallas* character
37. Fur piece
38. Region in S.E. Arabia
39. Kim Hunter's role
40. Actor Jack ___
41. Singer Fitzgerald
42. Jewish month
43. Character on 7-Down
44. She played "Jeannie"

August 9, 1980

across

1 Exclamation
4 "___ Frome"
9 ___-CIO
12 Mrs. Barney Miller (2 words)
15 Great Lake
16 Time
17 Electrified atoms
18 ___, U.S.A.
21 Julius ___ Rosa
22 Affirmative vote
23 Greek letter
26 "To Be ___ Not to Be"
27 "___ Without a Cause"
32 She's Chrissy (2 words)
36 ___ Papas
37 ___ the World Turns
38 ___ Zeppelin
39 Society for Applied Spectroscopy (abbr.)
41 Audio-visual (abbr.)
43 The ___ (3 words) stars Charlotte Rae
49 Carmine's nickname: "The Big ___"
50 Singer Yoko ___
51 Actor Wallach and inventor Whitney
53 J.R.'s wife (3 words)
56 ___ in a Million
57 Pianist/comedian Victor ___
58 "Freeway," to the Harts

down

1 ___ Vigoda
2 Angel's instrument
3 Solo for Pavarotti
4 Each (abbr.)
5 "A ___ Grows in Brooklyn"
6 Newsman (2 words)
7 Degrade
8 Sha Na ___
9 In a line
10 "Huckleberry ___"
11 ___ Nessman of WKRP news
13 "___, Book & Candle"
14 "___ Lobo"
19 "___ & Pa Kettle"
20 Edible root
23 Greek letter
24 "Ben ___"
25 Verb suffix
26 "One ___ One"
28 "You Can't Win ___ All"
29 Barbara ___ Geddes
30 Before (poet.)
31 Leased (abbr.)
33 "___ Act of Murder"
34 "One Flew Over the Cuckoo's ___"
35 She was Gloria (init.)
40 Song sung by one person (2 words)
41 ___ Molinaro
42 "The ___ from Pompey's Head"
43 "Prelude to the Afternoon of a ___"
44 Author James ___
45 Actor's ___ cards
46 Actor Kam ___
47 Comedian ___ Wilson
48 One, in Germany
49 Railway Sorting Office (abbr.)
52 "___ T.K. Yu"
54 ___ Mayer (init.)
55 Ponch of CHiPs (init.)

October 4, 1980

across

1 "___ Andy" (3 words)
14 *Marlo and ___ Machine*
15 Hearing organ
16 "___ 109"
17 "The Way ___ Were"
18 ___ *Kind of Family* (2 words)
22 Iowa (abbr.)
24 Continent (abbr.)
26 Timothy Van Patten's role
28 "My ___'s Place" (2 words)
31 Indian bean
32 "___ Nine from Outer Space"
34 Telephoned
35 Actress Kate ___
37 "Gunga ___"
38 Impel
39 Volcano
40 Actress Barbara ___
42 Comparative suffix
43 "___ Between the Tates" (2 words)
45 Ethel ___
47 You (slang)
48 Serial number (abbr.)
49 ___ Freberg
50 Laugh sound
52 Shoe width
54 Battery (abbr.)
57 "___ of Beau Geste" (3 words)
63 *The New Adventures ___* (3 words)

down

1 Route (abbr.)
2 Exclamation
3 Flip Wilson character
4 *To Tell the Truth* host (init.)
5 Each (abbr.)
6 Decigram (abbr.)
7 Lyricist ___ Harburg
8 On-the-spot coverage (2 words)
9 Mrs. Pynchon (init.)
10 "Apocalypse ___"
11 Avenue (abbr.)
12 Nickel (chem.)
13 Danny ___ Vito
19 Sha Na ___
20 Empire (abbr.)
21 "The Adventures of the ___ Family"
23 ___ Jolson
24 "Portrait of a Rebel: The Remarkable Mrs. ___"
25 Infuriates
26 Guaranty
27 ___ Franklin
29 Joanne ___
30 "Last Year at ___"
33 Assist
36 Jackdaw
41 Turner or Cole
44 "___ You Like It"
46 Target area (abbr.)
50 Playmates' playmate
51 ___ *My Children*
53 Ethics (abbr.)
55 Boxing term
56 Desire
57 *Hart ___ Hart*
58 "Gideon's Trumpet" star (init.)
59 Hawkeye (init.)
60 Mrs. Garson Kanin (init.)
61 Ex-officio (abbr.)
62 "Looking for ___ Goodbar"

December 20, 1980

across

1 Actor Sam ___
6 Tommy of *Eight Is Enough*
11 Actor Mike ___
12 Dan Tanna of *Vega$*
13 Chou ___-lai
14 Mouth (comb. form)
15 ___ Moody
16 *Truth ___ Consequences*
18 She was Lana on *Three's Company*
22 Prongs
23 *Fish* star (init.)
24 Peau de ___
25 Jeane Dixon, for one
26 "The Boys ___ Brazil"
28 ___ *Life to Live*
29 *Tinker, Tailor, ___, Spy*
32 Actress Rita ___
35 He was Jethro
36 Loop (anat.)
40 ___ Alda
42 Joanne Woodward's husband (init.)
43 Makes a sweater
44 *Benson*'s Taylor (3 words)
47 Former
48 Cha-___
49 ___ *Takes ___ Thief* (2 words)
50 He was Ben Casey (init.)
51 ___ *signo vinces* (2 words)
53 *Barney* ___
55 Smooth
56 Vends

down

1 "The Two Worlds of ___ Logan"
2 ___ Jolson
3 "___ for Algernon"
4 Discharges
5 City in Oklahoma
6 French farewell (2 words)
7 In a line (2 words)
8 Son of Zeus and Europa
9 Grandma Walton (init.)
10 "A ___ the Dark" (2 words)
11 Poet John ___
17 Syngman ___
19 Compass point
20 "The King of Marvin ___"
21 Kanga's offspring
26 Pancake
27 ___ *and Maxx*
30 Obstetrics (abbr.)
31 Actor Tony ___
32 Storm or Gordon
33 Actress Smith
34 Gullet
37 None
38 Hanks and Allen
39 He's Lou Grant
41 Nook
43 Critic Kelly
45 *Tenspeed and Brown* ___
46 Conway and O'Connor
52 Famous TV producer (init.)
54 She's Alice (init.)

January 17, 1981

across

1 Priestly robe
4 Cowboy ___ Carson
7 *Gunsmoke*'s ___ Dillon
11 Actor ___ Garrett
13 Actor ___ Wallach
14 Birds (Lat.)
15 Preposition
16 Shade tree
17 Hayworth or Moreno
18 Pendant ornament
20 Mr. Reed
22 Plaything
23 Telegram (abbr.)
24 Songstress Reddy
27 Cried in a loud voice
31 "___ Since Eve"
32 *Dallas* foreman
33 "Hail ___!"
34 Roamed
36 Acquire knowledge of
37 Comic ___ Taylor
38 Mr. Gazzara
39 Conditional release
42 Sci-fi actor Michael ___
46 Butter substitute
47 New, recent
   (comb. form)
49 Like an eel
50 SS Poseidon fate
51 Having three parts
52 Yard tool
53 Concludes
54 ___ Mineo
55 "___: A Dog"

down

1 Dismounted
2 Songstress ___ Horne
3 Small pieces
4 ___ Smith
5 Sick
6 He's Salami
7 She's on *Taxi* (2 words)
8 Tel ___, Israeli city
9 Tete-a-___
10 Russian ruler
12 "Loveable Lush" actor
   (2 words)
19 Age
21 ___ Durocher
24 *The, His and ___ of It*
25 She's a Gabor
26 Short for Lemuel
27 Unhappy
28 "___ and Sympathy"
29 To be wrong
30 ___ Stewart of
   Guiding Light
32 Regrets
35 ___ Abner
36 ___ Meriwether of
   Barnaby Jones
38 Grill
39 Bodily attitude
40 Comedian King
41 Tear apart
43 Actress Patricia ___
44 Actress and author
   Chase
45 Watched
48 Epoch

200

February 14, 1981

across

1 ___ *of China* (3 words)
13 "13 Great Disasters That ___" (3 words)
14 Midland Heights, for example
15 Original John-Boy (init.)
16 Ponch of *CHiPS* (init.)
17 Amount (abbr.)
18 Short for ammunition
21 At a distance
23 "The Seven Faces of Dr. ___"
24 Garland for Magnum
25 Adjective for 25-Down
26 "Songbird of the South" (init.)
27 "Well," in France
28 Lyric poems
29 ___ Phillips
31 Ripened cheese
32 Tear down
33 He was Dr. Ben Casey (init.)
35 Chooses actors for a play
36 "QB ___ "
37 "The Velvet Fog"
38 Football team
39 "I Was a ___ War Bride"
40 "Joan of ___"
41 Bushel (abbr.)
42 "Little ___"
43 ___ code
44 "Tinker, ___, Spy" (2 words)
49 "A Guide for the ___" (2 words)

down

1 Danny or Marlo
2 "___ Marry a Millionaire" (2 words)
3 Period of time
4 *Carol Burnett Show* regular (init.)
5 Utah (abbr.)
6 Louise Lasser's role (init.)
7 Air (comb. form)
8 Canadian territory (abbr.)
9 Fee, fi, ___, fum
10 "Butterflies ___" (2 words)
11 Clarifies
12 ___ Asner
13 Stick of celery
18 Mel's waitress's
19 Submissive
20 Mrs. Chisholm
21 Actor/hero Murphy
22 *Father Knows Best* star (init.)
25 Muppet bear
27 Goads maliciously
29 *The Ghost and ___* (2 words)
30 Fastener
31 "___ Black Sheep" (2 words)
33 Tenspeed
34 Actor Dana ___
35 Rob's dad (init.)
37 Callas or Montez
39 Additional
42 "Me," in France
43 Admiral (abbr.)
44 He's married to Cyd Charisse (init.)
45 "Haywire" star (init.)
46 Broadway's Peter Pan (init.)
47 Michael Learned's role (init.)
48 Tony ___ Bianco

down

1 Opponent
2 Bonnie Franklin's role
3 *Dan August*'s Rivera (2 words)
4 Cowboys' coach (init.)
5 Exclamation
6 She played Mary Stone (init.)
7 Cheer
8 "___ Mad, Mad World" (4 words)
9 "___ Big"
10 Doctor of Laws (abbr.)
11 U.S. ___ Force
12 Western state (abbr.)
13 Brandon ___ Wilde
19 ___ *Takes Two*
20 He flies through airports (init.)
21 Sophocles and Aeschylus
23 "Et ___ Brute!"
24 Emcee Bill ___
25 Glass bottles
26 Absorbent sea animal
27 Actor Gould
29 "A Pocket Full of ___"
30 Norton-Taylor's role
33 Women's group
36 Cutting tool
41 ___ carte (2 words)
44 Former spouse
46 Good witch in "The Wiz" (init.)
50 Before (prefix)
51 "Soul" in France
53 "Mrs." in France
55 Sea bird
56 Donkey
57 Nickel (chem.)
58 Acceptable
59 South American sloth
60 One
61 ___ *a Big Girl Now*
62 *CHiPs*' city (abbr.)

across

1 Stars Montalban (2 words)
14 Daytime serial (4 words)
15 Burt Reynolds movie "The ___"
16 ___ *the World Turns*
17 ___ *Kildare*
18 "___ in Cell Block 11"
22 *One Day ___ a Time*
24 "It Happened One Night" star (init.)
26 What Kristin did (2 words)
28 Whisper
31 ___ Dawber
32 ___ Thompson
34 Korean river
35 Mine products
37 Jacob's seventh son
38 Perry Mason's creator
39 Nick and ___ Charles
40 ___ Bombeck
42 Nevertheless
43 Gave off light
45 Woody and Steve
47 *Mister* ___
48 1977 Super Bowl
49 Arlene ___
50 ___ Kettle
52 She's Veronica (init.)
54 Meadow
57 Belongs to author of "Marilyn" (2 words)
63 Belongs to child actor in "Escape to Witch Mountain" (2 words)

May 16, 1981

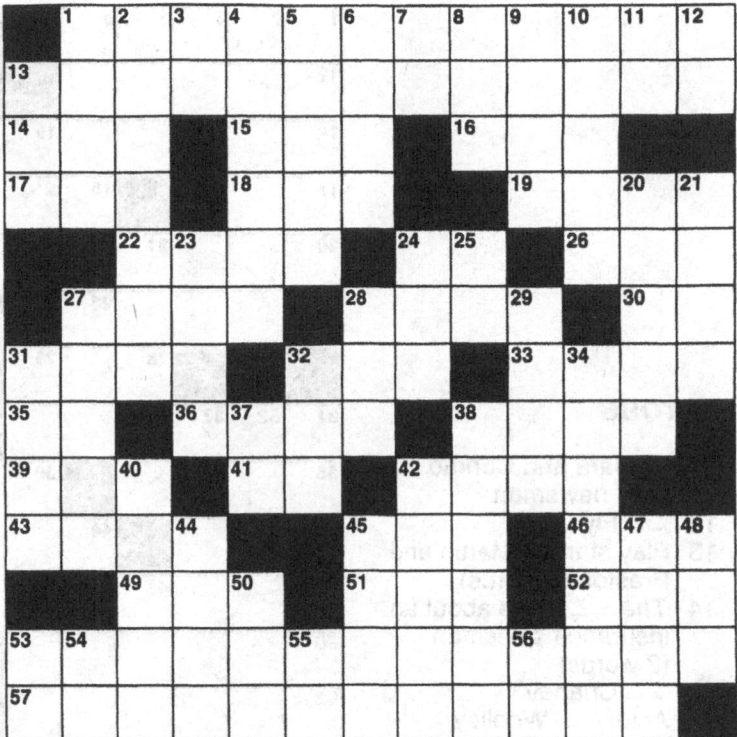

across

1 Daytime serial (2 words)
13 Stars Bonnie Franklin (5 words)
14 "The Ox-___ Incident"
15 Small rug
16 ___ Caesar
17 The ___ and the outs
18 ___ a Living
19 "___-Tough"
22 "Who's Minding the ___?"
24 ___ a Big Girl Now
26 Unit of radiation
27 Phyllis Diller's "husband"
28 ABC's ___ World of Sports
30 "Little ___"
31 Penny
32 "Bali ___"
33 "___ Gunner Joe"
35 He's Fish (init.)
36 Sharif or Khayyam
38 "The Diary of ___ Frank"
39 Religion (abbr.)
41 "Love ___ First Bite"
42 Cereal
43 Mild oath
45 Brother (abbr.)
46 ___ Marie Saint
49 Chi ___ Rodriguez
51 ___ Grant
52 "The Dark at the ___ of the Stairs"
53 ___ Bean (3 words)
57 Stars Hanks and Scolari (2 words)

down

1 Immediately (archaic)
2 Rather or Chancellor
3 Ruby Dee's husband (init.)
4 "The ___ of the Shrew"
5 Alice's last name
6 Dines
7 Right (abbr.)
8 "How the West ___ Won"
9 ___ Redding
10 "Easy ___"
11 Garland's daughter (init.)
12 Rosemary ___ Camp
13 Japanese sash
20 ___ Van Doren
21 Image
23 "Long Day's Journey ___ Night"
24 Shakespeare's "Richard ___"
25 Trapper John ___
27 WKRP's Johnny ___
28 "___ and Peace"
29 Sicilian volcano
31 Jack or joker
32 "Top ___"
34 ___ Funicello
37 ___ Kettle
38 "___ the World in 80 Days"
40 Shoe ties
42 Wide
44 Kojak's first name
45 French cheese
47 '50s actress Joan ___
48 "The Ivory ___"
50 Business-machine company
53 Hot Lips' old flame (init.)
54 She's Bonnie on CHiPs (init.)
55 "Anastasia" star (init.)
56 Diameter (abbr.)

May 23, 1981

across

1 Barbara and Conrad
6 CBS newsman
12 ___ Flynn
13 Play starring Martin and Preston (4 words)
14 *The* ___: oldie about an insurance salesman (2 words)
17 ___ Chaney
18 Actor ___ Woolley
19 Three (comb. form)
20 Ogled
22 Twosome
23 Hawaiian chant
24 Swiss mountain song
26 Aegean island
28 Oldie: *Navy* ___
30 Pistachio or cashew
31 PGA Hall of Famer Tommy ___
34 Ricky Nelson hit: "___ Baby"
38 Horse color
39 "I ___ Camera" (2 words)
42 The Cowardly Lion: Bert ___
43 Unit of weight
44 Bergen's Mortimer ___
46 "Flying Down to ___"
47 Stars Canova (5 words)
50 Bush is its president
51 Zones
52 "___ Horn"
53 Rogers or Newton

down

1 Actor Ed of "Sweet Bird of Youth"
2 Soprano Martina
3 Pressed
4 "___ Voyager"
5 Actor ___ Pickens
6 He played Carlo Ponti (2 words)
7 "___ at the Races" (2 words)
8 Item in Hellman's attic
9 Dropped a clue
10 Swimmer Gertrude ___
11 Belongs to "runner" Ruiz
15 Sign of affirmation
16 African antelope
21 Actor Alain ___
23 Travelers' lodging
25 Costello or Gehrig
27 Center of activity
29 Actor Farley ___
31 "A Portrait of the ___ as a Young Man"
32 Lodger
33 It's soon enough for Peggy Lee
35 ___ *Miller*
36 President Taft, for one
37 Actress Juliet ___
40 Oldest of the "Little Women"
41 "Exodus" hero
44 Location
45 Bring forth; elicit
48 *The* ___ *News Bears*
49 Labor Research Association (abbr.)

across

1 Actress ___ Tewes
7 Matthau or Cronkite
13 ___ Toscanini
14 ___ Lansbury
15 She plays Mrs. Garrett
16 Linda Lavin's role
18 Walter's replacement
19 He was Baretta (init.)
20 Oldie: *Noah's* ___
21 Sid Caesar's longtime
   partner ___ (init.)
22 Exclamation of surprise
25 Negative vote
26 Cher's former husband
28 ___ Field
30 Helen and Stanley ___
31 "Cakes and ___"
32 "___ Buttermilk Sky"
33 The Jeffersons,
   for instance
35 ___ Day
38 Religious image
39 Juice of a plant
42 Frame of a sliding
   window
43 She was Madame X
   (init.)
44 "On ___ Majesty's
   Secret Service"
45 Note of diatonic scale
46 Sass
48 Silent
50 Swiss river
51 Star of *BJ and the Bear*
53 Stephen Foster's
   "___ River"
55 Yankees slugger
56 Former Yankees
   superstar

down

1 Belongs to Hagman
2 Asian peninsula
3 Shoshonean tribe
   member
4 He's Tanna on *Vega$*
   (init.)
5 The ___ of Good Feeling
6 Pitcher ___ Ryan
7 Erratic (sl.)
8 Sue ___ Langdon
9 Asner's role (init.)
10 He's Henry Rush
11 Marilu Henner's *Taxi* role
12 Malice
17 Irish Republican Army
   (abbr.)
23 Greek philosopher
24 ___ Burstyn
26 Philippine knives

27 "The Phantom of the ___"
29 "___ We Have No
   Bananas"
30 Taylor or Steiger
33 Hal Linden is Barney ___
34 Lively
36 *Masada* locale
37 Edie on *I'm a Big
   Girl Now*
39 Western starring
   Alan Ladd
40 Atomic Energy
   Commission (abbr.)
41 Light refractor
47 Charlotte's friend Wilbur,
   for one
48 ___ Babilonia
49 Two (Scot.)
50 Pismire
52 He's Buck Rogers (init.)
54 "___ Act of Murder"

October 10, 1981

down

1 Billy Crystal role
2 "___ One" (2 words)
3 Height (abbr.)
4 Note well (abbr.)
5 *Wall $treet* ___
6 Tommy Bradford
7 The Hulk (init.)
8 "The flowers that bloom in the spring, ___ la"
9 Paddle
10 Louse egg
11 "Baby ___"
12 Shore and Washington
16 ___ Gorme
18 Mimi Kennedy role
20 "___ Girl?"
24 Throat sound
25 Sha Na ___
28 He was Rhoda's husband
30 Cubic (abbr.)
31 Distend
32 Actress Louise ___
33 Year (abbr.)
35 "___, poor Yorick!"
39 Jessica Tandy's husband (init.)
41 Radiation dosage
44 Bo or John
46 Actor Albert ___
47 "The Purple ___"
48 Stitched
51 ___ Tennille
54 *Tic ___ Dough*
55 Her Royal Highness (abbr.)
56 "___ of the Devil"
60 *I Spy* star (init.)
61 He was Dennis the Menace (init.)
62 *Tinker, Tailor, Soldier, Spy* star (init.)

across

1 Ralph Waite role (2 words)
11 "___ of the Dark" (3 words)
13 "___ to Billy Joe"
14 "Leave ___ Laughing"
15 Bandleader Shaw
17 "The ___ in Winter"
19 Coach Reeves of *The White Shadow*
21 Empire state (abbr.)
22 ___ Horne
23 Livia of *I, Claudius*
26 Advertisement
27 No good (sl.)
29 Scott Baio's role
31 Stone or Stallone
34 Egyptian sun god
36 Ponch of *CHiPs* (init.)
37 "The Pad and How to ___ It"
38 Pop artist Andy ___
40 "Looking for ___ Goodbar"
42 French conjunction
43 Actor Everett
45 Snakes
49 He's J.R. (init.)
50 "Desk ___"
52 Robertson or Evans
53 "The ___ of Heaven"
57 Tatum's father (init.)
58 "Hellinger's ___"
59 Michael Learned role (2 words)
63 Starred Marla Gibbs (2 words)

October 17, 1981

down

1. Stars Mimi Kennedy: *The* ___ (3 words)
2. Leading lady
3. Time
4. "Santa ___ Trail"
5. "One if by land and two ___ sea" (2 words)
6. Irish actress McKenna
7. "The Time Machine" author (init.)
8. "Ordinary People" actor (init.)
9. Heights (abbr.)
10. "Strategic ___ Command"
11. Ton (abbr.)
13. Grandpa Walton
18. Ruby ___
20. He was Dr. Gannon (init.)
21. "The ___ Principle"
23. Singer Julius ___
25. "One ___ One"
26. Laurel or Freberg
27. "___ Lady"
29. Additional
32. Britt or Zetterling
33. ___ Muggeridge
34. MacDonald-Eddy movie (2 words)
35. "The Ballad of the ___" (2 words)
37. Percy Kilbride's Kettle role
39. Metal-bearing rock
40. ___-made man
42. Marlo's dad (init.)
45. "___ Named Charlie Brown" (2 words)
48. Her Royal Highness (abbr.)
49. *One Day ___ Time* (2 words)
50. *WKRP* newsman
51. Hawaiian garland
53. Old Testament (abbr.)
54. *WKRP* ad salesman (init.)
55. Carol Burnett's "sister" (init.)

across

1. "___ Saved Pittsburgh" (3 words)
12. "___ Back" (2 words)
14. Plural of os
15. "The Ox-___ Incident"
16. Longtime Speaker of the House (init.)
17. Talking horse, Mister ___
19. Extinct Hawaiian bird ___-___
20. Actress Shepherd's nickname
21. Billy ___ Williams
22. "The Ipcress ___"
24. Singer Don ___
26. Dinah ___
28. Merkel or O'Connor
29. "___ of La Mancha"
30. ___ Conway
31. ___ on the Mount
33. Morning prayers
36. Paddle
37. "Peter ___"
38. Teachers' association (abbr.)
39. *With ___ & Ruby*
41. ___ Molinaro
42. Mike Douglas's real name
43. Rose Burton on *The Waltons*
44. "___ Ballou"
46. She's Kristin (init.)
47. "___ Cid"
48. Exclamation
50. Tennis stroke
51. Mauna ___
52. "___ Benji" (4 words)
56. Show hosted by Bob Barker (3 words)

207

November 21, 1981

down

1. Country conquered by Pizarro
2. Receptacle for baking
3. Striplings
4. A kind of poplar tree
5. Frenzied
6. Hunter or Fleming
7. Scarlett's Butler
8. John ___ Swayze
9. Evangelist Roberts
10. Talk-show host Griffin
11. A center of operations
16. "___ of Life"
17. "___ for the Seesaw"
21. Idolize
22. "The ___ and the Pussycat"
23. Seventeenth letter of Greek alphabet
24. "Butch Cassidy and the Sundance ___"
27. "___ of the Heart"
28. "After ___ Fox"
29. Bad-luck spell
31. Capable of being defended
32. "Some Like It Hot" star
33. Actress Ekberg
38. Indisposed
39. Memorable soprano Alma ___
40. "The Adventures of ___ March"
41. ___ boy!
42. Harris or Rizzuto
43. Soccer great
45. Cape ___, in S.W. Portugal
46. The Love ___
47. English legal societies, ___ of Court
49. Before (poet.)

across

1. First name in movie vamps
5. Evergreen
8. To search thoroughly
12. Le Gallienne and Gabor
13. Cheer
14. A part of the earth's surface
15. Peter Graves sci-fi movie (3 words)
18. 1945 Joel McCrea movie, "The ___"
19. "___ O'clock High"
20. Esther Williams or Buster Crabbe
22. Mork's planet
25. Comic actor Caesar
26. Solemn vow
30. 1968 Joseph Cotten Western (2 words)
34. A vein of ore
35. "They ___ for Their Lives"
36. John Ritter's father
37. Lagos is its capital
41. Horrify
44. Pianist Jose ___
48. 1949 Donald Houston movie (3 words)
50. "___ the Clouds Roll By"
51. "___ Havoc"
52. "___ Get It for You Wholesale" (2 words)
53. Leeward
54. Murray or Berry
55. Meals (colloq.)

December 26, 1981

across

1 Preliminary (abbr.)
7 ____ *Living* (2 words)
11 Fran of *Aloha Paradise* (2 words)
14 ____ *a Big Girl Now*
15 He's Hawkeye (init.)
16 "____ Terror"
17 *Live from the* ____
18 Gelatin
20 Cheer
22 Each (abbr.)
23 Whitman or Pickens
25 ____ West
27 "____ Joey"
29 Anatomical (abbr.)
31 "____ Cid"
32 ____ Stanley Gardner
34 ____ Giant (3 words)
37 ____ *Wolfe*
38 Pacino or Corley
39 Actress Didi ____
40 Neither
41 *The World at* ____
43 Coward or Harrison
45 Archie's Gloria (init.)
46 ____ *When*
48 "A Tale of ____ Cities"
49 Politician Landon
51 BPOE member
53 *The Two of* ____
55 "King Henry ____"
56 His cola commercial won a Clio (3 words)
60 "Jane ____"
61 He was *Lassie*'s Jeff

down

1 Sandy of *240-Robert* (2 words)
2 The original John-Boy (init.)
3 Age
4 "Dear ____"
5 *Your Show of Shows* comedienne (init.)
6 Brian Benben's *Gangster Chronicles* role (2 words)
7 "____ Trovatore"
8 ____ Selleck
9 J.R.'s wife (3 words)
10 Nick Charles' dog
11 "The Three Little ____"
12 *60 Minutes* humorist (init.)
13 Kentucky (abbr.)
19 Jeannie ____
21 "I ____ a Camera"
24 Margaret Houlihan's rank
26 TV Tarzan
27 "Evita ____"
28 "We ____ Alone" (2 words)
30 *Hart* ____ *Hart*
33 Chou ____ Lai
34 Ton (abbr.)
35 *The* ____ *and Mr. Jones*
36 Monty Python member (init.)
42 "The ____ Expeditions"
44 *The* ____ *Boat*
45 "____ Time Next Year"
47 Home for a Mongol
50 "____ from the Madding Crowd"
51 Actress ____ Peaker
52 Tony ____ Bianco
54 "Desk ____"
57 Compass point
58 ____ *Theater*
59 Plural of -eus

across

1 She played Florida
7 He's "Ponch"
11 *Rich Man, ___* (2 words)
13 Actress Garr
14 Dandy Don Meredith's alma mater (abbr.)
15 Archie Bunker's nickname for his son-in-law
17 Actor-comedian ___-Thomas
19 Belonging to actress West
20 Eagle's nest
21 He was Rhett Butler
22 *Our ___ Brooks*
23 He's Sam on *Quincy*
24 "___ the Beach"
25 Johnny's sidekick
29 Cubic (abbr.)
31 A destructive sea goddess
32 Love god
34 City editor of the "Trib"
36 Genetically identical descendant of a single organism
37 Overwhelming craving
38 She played Marva Collins
39 Belonging to Actress Karen of *Little House on the Prairie*
42 ___ *Day at a Time*
43 "One Flew Over the Cuckoo's ___"
44 He plays 34-Across (2 words)
46 To circulate
47 Stylish

down

1 Robert Hegyes' role on *Welcome Back, Kotter*
2 She was Chrissy Snow
3 Hawaiian industry
4 He wrote "79 Park Avenue" (init.)
5 Television award
6 She's Edna Garrett
7 Vivian Vance's longtime TV role
8 She was Della Rogers on *Chico and the Man*
9 Actor Angustain of *The White Shadow*
10 Elvis Presley was ___ Galahad
12 Quarterback turned actor
16 Forbidden by tradition
18 He played Tarzan (init.)
20 I love (Lat.)
21 1956 James Dean movie
26 Grossly stupid
27 Yankee great
28 Ozzie and Harriet
29 "Goldfinger" star
30 To partake of
33 Belonging to ABC's Arledge
34 He's Harris on *Barney Miller*
35 Corrodes
36 Baseball's ___ Young
38 A Russian emperor
39 Gross national product (abbr.)
40 She's *The Waltons'* Rose Burton
41 He was "Kookie"
45 "Murder in Texas" star (init.)

February 13, 1982

across

1 "___ Girl in the World" (3 words)
14 Series about the Novak family (2 words)
15 *Strike Force* star (init.)
16 *BJ ___ the Bear*
17 Singer Diana ___
18 Olivia ___ Havilland
19 *The Shakespeare ___*
21 Algebra (abbr.)
24 "Hot Lead and Cold ___"
25 Centigram (abbr.)
27 Actress Diana ___
30 Actress Blackman
33 Tatum ___
34 "___ Gay"
35 ___ Oakes
36 *Ryan's Hope* actress Kelli
38 *Good Times'* Florida (init.)
39 Livia of *I, Claudius*
41 Forerunner of the CIA
42 *Cousin ___*
44 "___, I Love You"
46 ___ Lenska
47 Grand ___ Opry
48 "Let's ___ It Again"
50 *The Six ___ Man* (2 words)
54 He was the Sundance Kid (2 words)

down

1 Sticky substance
2 "___ Pinafore"
3 Ponch of *CHiPs* (init.)
4 Nickname for Dillman
5 "___ Kleine Nachtmusik"
6 Doctor of Science
7 Priscilla Barnes role (init.)
8 *Star Trek*'s Spock (init.)
9 "___ Be Rich" (2 words)
10 Actor Donahue
11 "___ of the D'Urbervilles"
12 "___ Vegas Lady"
13 Printer's measure
19 Through
20 French article
21 Love in Rome
22 Of the moon
23 Singer Campbell
24 Dr. ___ Manchu
25 Belonging to Porter
26 Linda and Dorian
28 Tex Ritter to John
29 *Masterpiece Theatre* host
31 Yoko ___
32 "___, Nanette" (2 words)
36 Actress West
37 "___ Unmarried Woman"
40 *Leave ___ to Beaver*
42 "The Floating Light ___"
43 She, in France
44 Trudge
45 Ego
46 "___ Lobo"
47 "___ to Billy Joe"
48 Patriotic organization (abbr.)
49 Ordinance (abbr.)
50 "Goodbye, ___ Chips"
51 Old Testament (abbr.)
52 She was Amy in *Ladies' Man* (init.)
53 Tony ___ Bianco

March 27, 1982

across

1 Ted Lange's role
6 Arthur Miller's "___ the Fall"
11 Michael Learned series
12 Wood patterns
13 *Star* ___
14 Caught (colloq.)
15 "For ___ a jolly good fellow"
16 Opera star Beverly ___
17 Over (poet.)
18 Beer containers
19 Male child
22 Abbreviation for 11-Across
23 Mr. Bunker, for short
24 Actor Scott
25 Miss Piggy's beloved (3 words)
29 Troubles
30 Sheet of paper
31 Tony ___ Bianco
32 Knight's title
33 Jazz trumpeter
34 Comedian ___ Caesar
35 ___ Cara of movie "Fame"
37 Monotonous routine
38 Not loose
40 Dawson's role
41 Tattoo's abode
42 The Erie was one
43 To cheat (sl.)
44 Make level

down

1 Kids' news-brief series (3 words)
2 More certain
3 God of war
4 Inquire
5 "Magnum Force" star (init.)
6 Seed covering
7 Shakespearean comic hero
8 Deadlock
9 Burt Reynolds movie, "The ___"
10 Star of "Jaws" (init.)
12 "Buffalo ___"
14 Late-night news show
16 Religious group
17 Mork's home
18 Mr. Kristofferson
20 Broadcast
21 "My Fair Lady" heroine
23 ___ *Bandstand*
24 Policeman's route
26 King, in Nice
27 *From ___ to Eternity*
28 George Burns movie, "Oh, ___!"
33 Cattle group
34 Actress ___ Howard
36 Ladder part
37 Miss Barrett
38 Supersonic transport
39 Actor Wallach
40 He's Barney
41 *Eight ___ Enough*
42 Country singer (init.)

July 10, 1982

across

1 Trite
6 *Ryan's Hope's* Dr. ___ Coleridge
11 Zodiac sign
12 Ruled
14 *Too Close for Comfort*'s Sara (2 words)
16 Pertaining to cities
17 Pacino and Molinaro
19 *Love Boat*'s Gopher
23 Archaic pronoun
24 Saclike structure
25 Jeweled headdress
27 She's Louie's girlfriend
30 NBC board chairman (2 words)
34 Rounded handle
35 French painter
37 Sloping bank (Scot.)
40 Tony ___ Bianco
42 "Peppermint ___"
43 *Days of ___ Lives*
44 Silly
47 Belonging to *Lou Grant*'s Billie (2 words)
53 Determine
54 Embankment
55 Actress Dunne
56 Concerning

down

1 Viscuso or Mineo
2 Endeavor
3 Assist
4 Hawaiian wreath
5 Isaac's son (Bible)
6 "Huckleberry ___"
7 Grow older
8 To set into a surface
9 Discloses
10 Sheriff Semple (init.)
12 He was Baretta (2 words)
13 Period of time
15 "___ Rape"
18 Street (abbr.)
19 Twelve inches (abbr.)
20 To equip
21 Hearing organ
22 Explorer Sir Francis ___
24 "___ and Ale"
26 ___ Jillian
28 Greeting
29 Finish
31 "___ Catch a Thief"
32 Self
33 Actor ___ Daly
36 Original *Tonight Show* host (init.)
37 Derek or Hopkins
38 Straight edge
39 "___, My Love"
41 ___ *Day at a Time*
44 Inactive
45 Naval (abbr.)
46 Fitzgerald or Raines
48 Negative prefix
49 Senator (abbr.)
50 "All About ___"
51 Desire
52 "Desk ___"
53 Smallest state (abbr.)

October 2, 1982

across

1 Miss Sommer
5 CBS anchorman
8 Actor Lorne ___
10 Feminine name
12 Wanda on *Harper Valley* (2 words)
15 Author Fleming
16 Honorary (abbr.)
17 She was *WKRP*'s Jennifer (init.)
18 Upon
19 He's Dusty Farlow
22 He was Columbo
24 Inquiry
26 She was Kate Lawrence
27 Among
28 *Eight Is Enough*'s Mary
29 Told a fib
30 Brief journeys
32 Is victorious
33 Sorrowfully
34 Hawaii's Don ___
36 *WKRP ___ Cincinnati*
37 Edge
38 ___ *Hunt*
39 *Barnaby Jones'* Betty (2 words)
45 *Flamingo* ___
46 *Good Times'* Florida
47 Actor Beatty
48 Actress Natalie ___

down

1 Actress Moran
2 Showed the way
3 Small barrel
4 Chemical suffix
5 Newsman Morton ___
6 *Making a Living*'s Jillian
7 Nothing
8 NBC chairman
9 Volatile liquid
11 Miss ___ Reese
12 Combining form meaning life
13 Coal scuttle
14 Asian wild ox
19 He's Bret Maverick
20 Sour
21 Comedian Skelton

22 Actress Brice
23 Mine entrance
25 "The ___ People"
26 Author Bellow
28 "___: A Dog"
29 Ocean-going conveyance
30 He's Klinger
31 Transparent
32 Kin Shriner's brother
33 "To ___ with Love"
35 Boat paddle
37 Comedian ___ Foxx
38 To cast off
40 Period of time
41 Actress West
42 Compass point
43 World War II war zone (abbr.)
44 Though (clipped form)

November 27, 1982

across

1. ___ Bridges
5. ___ Hutton
8. Novelist Vidal
12. Nastase
13. Genetic material (abbr.)
14. Irish Rose's love
15. Miss Whelchel
16. ___ Byrnes
17. Producer Norman ___
18. Violetta's story (2 words)
21. Roves
22. Baseball stat (abbr.)
25. "Where the ___ Grows" (2 words)
29. American Revolution's Allen
31. Operatic melody
32. Vapor
33. Actress Oakes
35. Belonging to Miss Miranda
38. Greek letter
39. *Taxi*'s Elaine
41. Ponchielli opera (2 words)
46. Marceau, for example
49. European country (abbr.)
50. Oldie: ___ *222*
51. Actor Hale
52. Anger
53. "___ of the Thousand Days"
54. Miss Barrett
55. Compass point
56. ___ *Make a Deal*

down

1. Actress St. John
2. Lamb's pen name
3. Stallone movie
4. "Cape ___"
5. ___ Howard
6. Ocean
7. "___ Satan"
8. Big party
9. Order of the British Empire (abbr.)
10. Inlet
11. Ever (poet.)
19. "Butterflies ___ Free"
20. Mao ___-tung
22. Madlyn of the movies
23. Nickname for Captain Miller
24. Belonging to Miss Balin
25. "The ___ Breed"
26. He was (Lat.)
27. Actress Merrill
28. Trend
30. Hat
34. "___ Lonely Place" (2 words)
35. Weepers
36. Renée ___
37. Fabulous bird
40. A marble
41. ___ Horne
42. TV evangelist Roberts
43. "___ but the Brave"
44. "___ Make Waves"
45. Character actor Leon
46. Damage
47. Labor organization (abbr.)
48. Oldie: *The ___ from U.N.C.L.E.*

215

December 11, 1982

across

1 Healing ointment
5 *Dukes of Hazzard* props
9 Mischievous one
12 Vegetable-oil spread
13 Garfield, for one (2 words)
14 Actress McClanahan
15 Western satire (4 words)
18 Shade
19 Belonging to emcee Martindale
20 *60 Minutes* correspondent
23 Stage
25 Scent
26 Distress signal
27 Setting for *Dukes* (abbr.)
29 "From a ___ Country: Pope John Paul II"
30 NBC board chairman
31 Writing instrument
32 ___ *America*
33 Mr. Sinatra
34 He was Dr. Rose
35 Actress Keaton
36 He's Colonel Potter
37 King and Alda
39 "Salem's ___"
40 Hart on *The Paper Chase* (2 words)
46 Consumed
47 King of beasts
48 "___ Since Eve"
49 *In medias* ___
50 Humorist Bombeck
51 Redecorate

down

1 Mr. Newhart
2 Archie's Place beverage
3 Orchestra leader Brown
4 "___ Is a Freshman"
5 Coffeehouse
6 "___ of Love"
7 Cheerleader shout
8 Actor Granger
9 Actress Cara
10 Animal scent
11 Favorites
16 *Days of* ___ *Lives*
17 Sagacious
20 Couch
21 ___-12
22 *Search* ___ *Tomorrow*
23 Grumman Goose, for one
24 ___ Williams Jr.
26 ___ Tarkenton
27 He was Grandpa Walton
28 Gary Sandy role
30 *Little House* actress
31 For each
33 Excellent
34 Anchorman Dan ___
35 Matrons
36 Informal dance
37 Unclosed
38 "The ___ Show"
39 ___ Horne
41 "To ___ with Love"
42 *Tomorrow* host
43 Actress Plumb
44 Actor Romero
45 Standing Room Only (abbr.)

January 8, 1983

down

1. "The 39 ___"
2. "See ___ She Runs"
3. Art, to Ovid
4. She was Kate in *The Real McCoys* (init.)
5. ___ Scrooge
6. "Que Sera, ___"
7. *Harper Valley* ___
8. *M*A*S*H*'s Flagg (init.)
9. He's Andy Quinn (init.)
10. Follows Do
11. Finales
13. Greek letter
16. Language of "Beowulf" (abbr.)
18. Indiana (abbr.)
19. Victoria Principal's role (init.)
20. Before, to a poet
21. Star of 32-Across
23. ___ *Five-O*
24. *WKRP* ___ *Cincinnati*
27. Shoe width
28. "The ___ Man"
30. He was Captain Greer in *The Mod Squad* (init.)
31. ___ *Elsewhere*
32. Tony ___ Bianco
33. "I ___ a Camera"
37. ___ Tin Tin
39. Pamela ___ Martin
40. He was Ben Walton (init.)
42. *Eight* ___ *Enough*
44. Gridiron gradations
45. ___ Pacino
46. Stars in 47-Across
47. Hence
49. Larry Hagman's role
51. Enemy
52. ___ West
53. Answer (abbr.)
55. Johnny Fever (init.)
56. He's Ponch (init.)
57. 12 months (abbr.)
58. He was Goober (init.)

across

1. *The* ___ *Plays* (PBS series)
12. "___ Two Lovers" (2 words)
13. Roger Mudd reports it
14. Equal Rights Amendment (abbr.)
15. "Breaking Up Is Hard to ___"
17. "___ in Smoke"
18. Actress Balin
19. *Search for Tomorrow*'s Cissy: Patsy ___
22. "___ On, Harvest Moon"
25. Make a mistake
26. "X, Y ___" (2 words)
29. Tolkien creatures
32. *McClain's* ___
34. Moray
35. "___ My Dust!"
36. Actor Sharif
38. Della and Mason
41. 3 to Caesar
43. ___ willow
45. He was Lobo
47. ___ *Greatest American Hero*
48. Jameson Parker is ___ Simon
50. *WKRP*'s Jennifer (init.)
51. Federal Housing Administration (abbr.)
52. Golf commentator Dave ___
54. Daytime series starring Melody Thomas (with 59-Across)
59. Daytime series starring Melody Thomas (with 54-Across)

February 19, 1983

59 Lorne Greene series (2 words)

down

1 Starred in "To Catch a Thief" (init.)
2 *Truth ___ Consequences*
3 "Oliver" star Mark
4 Bruce or Peggy
5 Crucifix initials
6 "___ on Sunday"
7 ___ Lanka
8 Fling
9 ___ *Don't Eat the Daisies*
10 Famous cowgirl (init.)
11 He is Luke Duke (init.)
15 Prison denizen
16 Belongs to actress MacRae
19 *Match Game PM* host
21 *Adam's ___*
23 Molars
26 He's Ray Krebbs
28 *Alice*'s Mel (init.)
30 "Long Day's Journey into Night" author (init.)
31 Former *Saturday Night Live* trouper (init.)
33 Do, ___, mi
34 Devoured
37 Marilu Henner's role
40 Cable-TV mogul
42 Down quilt (Fr.)
44 "___ and Juliet"
48 In the middle of
51 Curve segment
52 Avenue (abbr.)
53 She was Tina Dearborn (init.)
54 *One Day ___ a Time*
56 He was Tarzan (init.)
57 Rapid City state (abbr.)

across

1 She's Alexis on *Dynasty*
8 Petty quarrel
12 "The Grass is ___"
13 Farm implement
14 Served, in Paris
15 Anger
16 ___ *Elsewhere*
17 That is (abbr.)
18 Close
20 "___ Highness and the Bellboy"
22 He was John Boy Walton (init.)
24 Flat-topped mountain
25 He's Ponch on *CHiPs*
27 She's Zsa Zsa's sister
29 "An ___ for an Eye"
31 Prince Charles' wife, for short
32 Robert Blake series
35 ___ Derek
36 Beerlike beverage
38 Snare
39 "___ Brute!" (2 words)
41 He's Hawkeye Pierce
43 *60 Minutes* newsman (init.)
45 A continent (abbr.)
46 Author Bellow
47 On account (abbr.)
49 Noted consumer activist (init.)
50 Kind of league
51 Capital of Jordan
53 "Citizen ___"
55 Faulkner novel and McQueen movie, "The ___"
58 Proofreader's notation

218

March 12, 1983

3 Painters, sculptors, etc.
4 He was John Boy (init.)
5 He was Mingo
6 Entertainer Mineo
7 Disney movie about
  an Indian
8 South African medicinal
  plants
9 "To —— with Love"
10 Mayday signal
12 "Wait Till the Sun
   Shines, ——"
16 IRS review
18 Johnny's sidekick (init.)
20 Agency for small
   businesses (abbr.)
21 Declares
26 —— of Cawdor (Macbeth)
27 Tree products
28 Bowzer's group
29 The Not Ready for
   Prime Time ——
30 —— My Children
33 Actor Stevens of "The
   Bastard"
34 Emmett Kelly, e.g.
35 Actor Greene of Bonanza
36 CHiPs' state (abbr.)
38 Played Tom Buchanan in
   "The Great Gatsby"
39 "Sunrise at Campobello"
   subject (init.)
40 —— Grant
41 Greek letter
45 Chicago Story state
   (abbr.)

across

1 Silent star Bow and
  Bewitched's forgetful
  aunt
7 Soviet news agency
11 Morning-show host
13 Musical medley
14 Umpire's cry
15 Actress Powell and
   First Lady Roosevelt
17 Snoops
19 General Hospital man
20 Uncontrolled movement
21 Robert and Alan
22 —— of the West
23 Seven, to Caesar
24 60 Minutes humorist
   (init.)
25 The —— of San Franciso
29 —— Kettle

31 "Leave —— to Heaven"
32 Game-show host
   Monty ——
34 School group
36 Pollution site, Love ——
37 Actress Anderson
38 "Yankee Doodle ——"
39 Actress Henderson
42 People —— Funny
43 "Up the —— Staircase"
44 Country humorist
   Herb ——
46 Old Norse poem
47 Alan Arkin movie,
   "The ——" (2 words)

down

1 M*A*S*H word
  for helicopter
2 Belonging to Mrs. Wilder

down

1 *Code Red* star
2 Over (poet.)
3 Paddle
4 Marlo's dad (init.)
5 Fred and Ethel ___
6 Order of St. Augustine (abbr.)
7 Routes (abbr.)
8 New line (abbr.)
9 Greek island
10 Nativity of the Virgin Mary (abbr.)
11 "To Sir with Love" actress Judy ___
12 Indian mountain pass
13 Raises
18 "Please Don't ___ the Daisies"
20 Country singer Sheppard
23 Whelan and Ireland
24 "___, the Gay Blade"
26 Archie's Barney Hefner
27 "BJ and the ___"
29 "Run Silent, Run ___"
31 Musical note
34 "Love ___ First Bite"
36 Quell
37 Vote
39 "All the President's ___"
40 *Trapper* ___ (2 words)
42 He's Ponch (init.)
44 "___ and Bess"
46 Baseball's Pete ___
49 *Young* ___ *Boone*
53 Twosome
54 German exclamation
56 ___ *Club*
57 Exclamation
58 Pay court to
60 Famous cowgirl (init.)
61 John-Boy's mom (init.)

across

1 ___ *America* (2 words)
12 "The World's ___" (2 words)
14 Mister, in Germany
15 She's Edna Garrett
16 Hook's sidekick
17 Aged (abbr.)
18 "___ tu, Brute!"
19 Jill ___ John
21 Continent (abbr.)
22 Ton (abbr.)
23 "All That ___"
25 Zsa Zsa ___
28 Revise
30 *Best* ___ *the West*
32 Camera part
33 "___ Cid"
34 ___ Parseghian
35 Southern California city (abbr.)
36 Actor Walter ___
38 "___ Baskin"
39 Actress Dusay
41 Small error
43 ___ *All Night*
45 *Truth* ___ *Consequences*
47 *Alice* star (init.)
48 He was Lou Grant
50 *Little House* ___ *the Prairie*
51 "Gung ___!"
52 He was Hawkeye
55 Spring month (abbr.)
57 Possesses
59 Thomas Wolfe's "___ Again" (4 words)
62 "Goldie and the Boxer Go ___" (2 words)

June 11, 1983

59 Compass point
60 Crowded-theater sign (abbr.)

down

1 *The Thorn Birds* star (init.)
2 A moon of Jupiter
3 She was Lady Marchmain
4 Priscilla Barnes role
5 Inga Swenson role (2 words)
6 *Magnum, ___*
7 "Knock on ___" (2 words)
9 Candidates' dialogue
11 Ewe's mate
13 "___ and Sympathy"
14 "To Each His ___"
17 "___ Dolce Vita"
19 *Hee Haw*'s Lulu ___
20 The late Mrs. Bunker
21 Note well (abbr.)
22 Actress Foch
27 Carrie Fisher's dad (init.)
28 Broadcasting medium
30 *Cagney & ___*
31 Egg colorer
33 Mississippi city
34 Ji-___ Cumbuka
35 Actress Franklin
41 "Gunfight at the ___ Corral"
43 Actor Greene
44 "Sophisticated ___"
45 "The Elephant ___"
46 "___ Station Zebra"
47 "___ Cid"
48 Japanese money
53 *Laugh-In*'s co-host (init.)
56 *Truth ___ Consequences*
57 "Dr. ___"

across

1 *Adam's ___*
4 Country singer Sheppard
6 ___ Kettle
8 "The Spy Who Came In from the ___"
10 Make a mistake
12 "Journey ___ Fear"
15 Language of "Beowulf" (abbr.)
16 ___ *People*
18 Evergreen shrub
19 *Private Benjamin*'s Fielding (2 words)
22 Wandering
23 Derek or Duke
24 "___ No Angel"
25 Musical note
26 "Take ___, She's Mine"
29 Aged
32 She's Grandma Romano (2 words)
36 Santa ___
37 What Attila was
38 "___ Not Disturb"
39 *Medical Center* star (init.)
40 *9 ___ 5*
42 Jamie Farr's role
45 *One of the Boys* star (2 words)
49 ___ *Du Lieber!*
50 Norman or King
51 *WKRP ___ Cincinnati*
52 Require
54 *The Flying ___*
55 Famous English public school
58 "The Producers" star (init.)

221

September 24, 1983

across

1. ___ Lanza
6. "The ___ Seed"
9. Lance of *Falcon Crest*
11. ___ Moreno
13. The San Diego Sports ___
14. Little Jack Horner's prize
16. Trigger's owner (init.)
18. *Fame* actor ___ Anthony Ray
19. The distance between two points
20. *Sha Na* ___
21. Jill ___ John
22. He was Ike Godsey (2 words)
25. Deserve
26. *At* ___
27. Lilimae of *Knots Landing* (2 words)
31. Part of an egg
32. City in Oklahoma
33. Rudolph ___
36. "___! Wilderness"
38. He was Dr. Michael Rossi (abbr.)
39. ___ Bombeck
40. Lincoln and Vigoda
42. Yes, in Spanish
43. Adams or McClurg
44. "___ & Ivory"
45. "Happily ___ After"
47. *Match Game* host
49. *Victory at* ___
50. Fleshy

down

1. Manners
2. Are not (cont.)
3. ___ Auberjonois
4. Actress Balin
5. "The Wizard of ___"
6. Lee Curreri's *Fame* role
7. Objective
8. Marlo's dad (init.)
9. Fall behind
10. Stars Sam Waterston
12. *McClain's Law* star
15. "The Children of An ___"
17. Comedienne Martha ___
19. Painful
22. ___ alai
23. Jennifer DeNuccio was not one
24. Chou En-___
25. ___ Sommer
27. ___ *Loves Chachi*
28. Norse god
29. ___ Maria Alberghetti
30. "___ Lobo"
31. ___ Montand
34. Actress ___ Volz
35. Prefix meaning three
36. "Much Ado ___ Nothing"
37. ___ Winkler
40. A Swedish rock group
41. Synonym (abbr.)
43. Shoe width
44. "An ___ for an Eye"
46. "The People ___ Jean Harris"
48. "I ___ a Camera"

down

1 "___ Came a Spider"
2 Actress Flynn
3 He's innkeeper Dick Loudon (init.)
4 Garrett or DeFazio
5 Charlotte ___
6 Myrna Clegg of *Capitol* (2 words)
7 "Diamonds ___ Forever"
8 Captain Hook's sidekick
9 Dudley Moore's girl friend (init.)
10 "___ Love Call"
11 Bergen and Poe
13 Laurie Morgan (2 words)
20 Rifle club (abbr.)
22 Insect egg
24 Mauna ___
26 Native of Serbia
29 Yes, in German
30 New Zealand parrots
34 "Ride '___ Cowboy"
35 J.R., Ellie, Bobby, etc.
36 Northern region
37 "The Catcher in the ___"
39 National Association of Rocketry (abbr.)
40 ___ *Big Girl Now* (2 words)
41 Ozzie and Harriet ___
45 38-Across star
47 Carmine Ragusa's on closed-circuit TV nickname: "The Big ___"
49 *The Jack ___ Show*
52 Religion (abbr.)
54 "___ for Two"
57 Author Lawrence
59 She sings "For Your Eyes Only" (init.)

across

1 "Forever ___"
6 ___ Cranston in *It's a Living*
12 Kelsey and Lavin
14 Actor Assante
15 *Truth ___ Consequences*
16 *The ___ Zoo Revue*
17 Arikara
18 Decigram (abbr.)
19 Actress Foch
21 Yoko ___
23 Film director Kazan
25 Kind of fish
26 Dirt
27 Paddle
28 Charles Bronson movie, "Mr. ___"
31 Answer (abbr.)
32 Onassis
33 Born (Fr.)
35 "A Flea in Her ___"
38 *Private ___*
42 Droll
43 Maxwell Smart's foe
44 Alice's boss
46 Froster
48 Vase
49 ___ Alto, Cal.
50 New Testament (abbr.)
51 Arrives (abbr.)
53 Greek letter
55 She played Susan Bradford (init.)
56 Sally Field's old TV role
58 "The Mating ___"
60 Charlie Brown's creator
61 Boxing ring

across

1 "The Lavender Hill ___"
4 Actor Carney
7 Suit
10 "I ___ Camera" (2 words)
11 Seven ___
13 Columnist Bombeck
14 Singer Johnny
16 A high mountain
17 "King ___"
18 Features Sarah Purcell (2 words)
21 Boy Scouts of America (abbr.)
22 Yes (Fr.)
23 Yes (Ger.)
25 Gather
27 Author/actress Maya
29 ___ of the Century
30 Words (abbr.)
31 "___ On Down the Road"
32 "Wait ___ Sun Shines, Nellie" (2 words)
34 Proprietor
35 Soaps creator (init.)
36 ___ Haw
37 Porky ___
38 He's Scarecrow
42 "Fiddler on the ___"
44 Likely
45 Singer Campbell
47 Norwegian king
48 Actress Talbot
50 Horace Rumpole
51 You ___ Your Life
52 Ronny or Wally
53 Total

down

1 Singer Davis
2 Mr. Sharif
3 The national pastime
4 ___ the World Turns
5 "___ the Wild Wind"
6 "A ___ of Two Cities"
7 "Born ___"
8 "___ Yankee Doodle Dandy" (2 words)
9 Sticky substance
12 Silver ___
13 Barbara Bel Geddes role (2 words)
15 Knight Rider star
19 "___ Vegas Lady"
20 Kind of dog or nose
23 Actor Ferrer
24 '40s actor Mischa
25 Nick Charles' dog
26 "The ___ Event"
27 Fruit drink
28 Actor Frank
30 Vicki of 38-Down
33 John Ritter's dad
34 Choose
38 The Love ___
39 Heroic poem
40 Leave ___ Beaver (2 words)
41 Robert or Rex
42 A Reiner
43 Grand ___ Opry
46 "Wynken, Blynken and ___"
49 Woodsman's tool

January 7, 1984

across

1 Donna Mills role
5 *Adam's* ___
8 A sailor (sl.)
12 He's Chachi
13 "Much ___ About Nothing"
14 Judd Hirsch series
15 Comment from Arnold of *Green Acres*
16 Loretta Swit role
18 Tony Randall role
20 McCulloch or Fleming
21 Swoosie Kurtz series (2 words)
27 Life (comb. form)
30 *The* ___ *News Bears*
31 Renter's contract
32 Columnist Bombeck
34 Actress Ullmann
36 She's Violet Newstead
37 Vestige
39 "___ Pan Alley"
41 Richard Sanders role
42 Robert Wagner series (3 words)
45 "Twelfth Street ___"
46 He was Ricky Ricardo
50 J.R. keeps her in a tizzy (2 words)
55 ___-de-camp
56 Stuttering actor Roscoe
57 "All About ___"
58 Distinguishing mark
59 ___ Diner, where Alice works
60 Mr. Cunningham to Richie
61 "A ___ Ain't Nothin' But a Sandwich"

down

1 "___ Ben Adhem," Leigh Hunt poem
2 Barbara or Conrad
3 Crooner Crosby
4 A rustic
5 Los Angeles football player
6 "___, Sweet As Apple Cider"
7 Actor Karloff
8 He's Max of 42-Across
9 "___ of the Planets"
10 Tree-chopping tool
11 Very small role
17 *Barney Miller*'s "Wojo"
19 He's Mike Stivic
22 Gary Ewing's wife
23 Archie's "Dingbat"
24 To capture or intercept (colloq.)
25 Villa d'___
26 Affirmative votes
27 She's Vera Gorman
28 Opera singer Petina
29 Actor Sharif
33 Bette Davis or Katharine Hepburn, for example
35 By way of
38 And others (Lat.)
40 National Recovery Administration (abbr.)
43 Made eyes at
44 Rubbish
47 Durocher remark: "___ guys finish last."
48 Month of the Hebrew calendar
49 "Fiddler on the Roof" star
50 Veteran golfer Snead
51 Shoshonean Indian language
52 Snakelike fish
53 Actress Le Gallienne
54 Actor Beatty

January 14, 1984

across

1 He's Venus Flytrap
5 ___ Lanka
8 Viscuso and Mineo
12 She's Simka Gravas
13 Carrier for bricks
14 An alumnus (colloq.)
15 Plural of os
16 Past of bid
17 Relief
18 Talk-show host
   (2 words)
21 Ned or Warren
22 *One Day* ___ *Time*
   (2 words)
23 Evangelist Roberts
24 Trapper John and
   Marcus Welby
26 "___ Who Gets
   Slapped"
28 She's Joyce
   Davenport (2 words)
33 "Love ___ First Bite"
34 "Dead ___"
35 Julie of *Fame*
36 Schneider of
   22-Across
38 Academy Awards
41 Medical series with Ed
   Flanders (2 words)
44 Dorothy's dog
45 "Baby, the ___ Must
   Fall"
46 *It Takes* ___
49 Word for 23-Across
50 "___ Cry Tomorrow"
51 ___ En-lai
52 "The ___ Breed"
53 Building wing
54 A propensity

down

1 Movie studio
2 "A Flea in Her ___"

3 "A partridge ___ tree"
   (3 words)
4 Danny ___ Vito
5 "Thou ___ Not Kill"
6 He played Bon
   Chance Louie
   (2 words)
7 Idea (comb. form)
8 Late Egyptian
   president
9 ___ *Paradise*
10 *Hee Haw*'s ___
   Roman
11 Pirate boatswain in
   "Peter Pan"
16 Small acting role
19 Nimbus
20 Donald Duck's voice
21 Maverick brother
23 Plural of ovum
25 Howard ___ Silva

26 "___ to Hold"
27 Invented the cotton gin
29 New Jersey basketball
   team
30 "Going ___ Style"
31 Winglike
32 "The ___ merrier"
   (2 words)
36 Graves or Cook
37 "And I ___ Survived"
39 Con man's
   confederate
40 Century (abbr.)
41 ___ *of the Family*
42 Starred Tony Musante
43 Great Lake
47 "How the West
   Was ___"
48 "___ of the Blue"
51 She's Daisy Duke
   (init.)

March 10, 1984

51 ___ *Elsewhere*
52 "Don't Go ___ the Water"

down

1 Alice's boss
2 Seed covering
3 Storage bin
4 "The ___ and the Black"
5 Arthur Fonzarelli
6 Mrs. Livingston on *The Courtship of Eddie's Father*
7 Mr. T is a member of this group
8 Wander
9 Actress Lanchester
10 Malt beverages
12 Cat with a hidden tail
18 Ever (poet.)
19 "The Great ___"
22 Japanese sash
23 Mauna ___
24 Newsman Rather
25 "The Man Who ___ Tomorrow"
26 Carol Burnett's ___ Lady character
27 Representative (abbr.)
28 Stallone or Stone
30 *Dynasty*'s Matthew Blaisdel
31 Game show starring Betty White (2 words)
33 Compass point
34 "Harper Valley ___"
35 Stated further
36 "___ It Shocking?"
37 Oriental sleuth Charlie
38 Theater section
39 "I Want to Hold ___ Hand"
40 Organized group
41 ___ *of the Century*
42 Swedish actress Jacobsson
46 "A Flea in Her ___"

across

1 Bulk
5 He was Robbie, Chip and Ernie's dad (init.)
7 ___ code
11 Commentator Sevareid
12 Miss Piggy, referring to herself
13 A single stroke of the bell
14 Actress Kedrova
15 "___ Which Way You Can"
16 "___ On Down the Road"
17 Lance of *Falcon Crest*
20 5-time Tarzan, Barker
21 Movie Scrooge, Alastair
22 "You're not getting ___, you're getting better."
25 "___ Loves Me Not"
26 *Scarecrow and ___ King*
29 *The Love ___*
30 "Bali ___"
31 Higgins or Grey
32 McKellen or McShane
33 Plant seed
34 "___ Love"
35 Cleopatra's snake
36 "___ Not for Me to Say"
37 Ali of *Bring 'Em Back Alive*
43 "Little Red Riding ___"
44 The Loudon's place
45 "The Making of a ___ Model"
47 Chills and fever
48 Louse egg
49 Jazz singer Fitzgerald
50 Word used by 5-Down

April 14, 1984

across

1 She played Kelly Garrett
6 He is Barnaby Jones
11 Binzer on *Vega$* (2 words)
14 Porthos' partner
15 Red planet
16 "From Here —— Eternity"
17 Mickey ——
18 He's Barney Miller
19 Flo's comeback, "Kiss my ——"
21 Price
22 "The —— of Anne Frank"
23 *Emergency!* star
24 Actress Keaton
25 Elongated bass drum
26 —— Ole Opry
27 Belonging to actress Cheryl
28 Declaim violently
29 Pam Dawber role
30 "The —— of Innocence"
31 Funny lady Mabley
32 "—— Cold Blood"
33 Sticky substance
34 "—— McKee"
39 Alumnae of *The Lawrence Welk Show* (2 words)
42 French city on the Loire
43 Actors James and Eddie

down

1 Posed
2 Jonathan Hart to Max
3 Sam on *Quincy*
4 Tablespoon (abbr.)
5 He played Paul Martin (init.)
6 Roy Rogers' wife
7 Swiss capital
8 Upperclassmen (abbr.)
9 Starred in "A Case of Rape" (init.)
10 She was Amy on *Ladies' Man*
11 Mr. T's role
12 Friendship
13 Star of *Rich Man, Poor Man*
17 "Friendly ——"
18 Belonging to Sorrell Booke's character
19 James Dean's last film
20 "The Fountainhead" author
21 She's Shirley
22 Actress Ladd
23 *Hee Haw*'s Lisa
24 Jack Webb series
25 Containers
26 "Monty Python and the Holy ——"
27 Moves unevenly
29 "The —— Our Home"
31 Marshy wasteland
33 African antelope
34 Compass direction (abbr.)
35 *One Day —— Time* (2 words)
36 Lair
37 Income-tax agency (abbr.)
38 Sonny Shroyer role (init.)
40 Ian Fleming's "Dr. ——"
41 The same (Lat.)

April 21, 1984

2 George Wendt role
3 Goodbye (Brit.)
4 He played Danny Novak (init.)
5 Actress Cardille
6 Belonging to Hal Linden character (2 words)
7 She played Susan Bradford (init.)
8 "The War Between the ___"
9 To be (Fr.)
10 Musial or Kenton
11 To weaken
19 Comedian Little
20 He's Tom Magnum (init.)
21 A strainer
22 ___-and-toe
25 Newt
26 "___ Wind in Eden"
27 *Quincy*'s Sam
28 "I Love You ___"
29 "A Flea in Her ___"
30 Revolutionary Guevara
31 Olive ___
33 River in Westphalia
34 He's Michael Archangel
38 Dreads
39 He's Capt. Adam Greer (init.)
40 Hawkeye's home: Crabapple ___
41 Supporting actress in "Some Came Running"
42 Actress Turner
43 "___ Heart"
44 She's Kate Lawrence
45 Political acronym
48 He's Gary Ewing
50 *Switch*'s Frank McBride (init.)
51 She plays Eunice (init.)

across

1 Leafcutter insects
5 Pounds (abbr.)
8 Hardy heroine
12 Director Pitlik
13 Old Arabic (abbr.)
14 "___ girl!"
15 Singer Garfunkel
16 He played Bob Woodward (init.)
17 "The Parent ___"
18 Starred in *Kennedy* (2 words)
23 "___ Paris Burning?"
24 Summers on the Seine
25 *Mama's Family*'s Buzz
28 Ancient Phoenician city
29 Environment (comb. form)
32 William Christopher role (2 words)

35 "___ Flags West"
36 Dutch measure of length
37 City in central Russia
38 *Teachers Only* regular
39 She plays Julie Rogers (init.)
40 Belonging to an "Angel" (2 words)
45 Spanish painter
46 Starred in 8-Down (init.)
47 "___ My Dust!"
49 "___ the Edge"
50 Sea bird (var.)
51 "The Sins of Rachel ___"
52 Person (abbr.)
53 A king of Judah
54 *Saturday Night Live*'s Hall

down

1 Actress Alicia

September 1, 1984

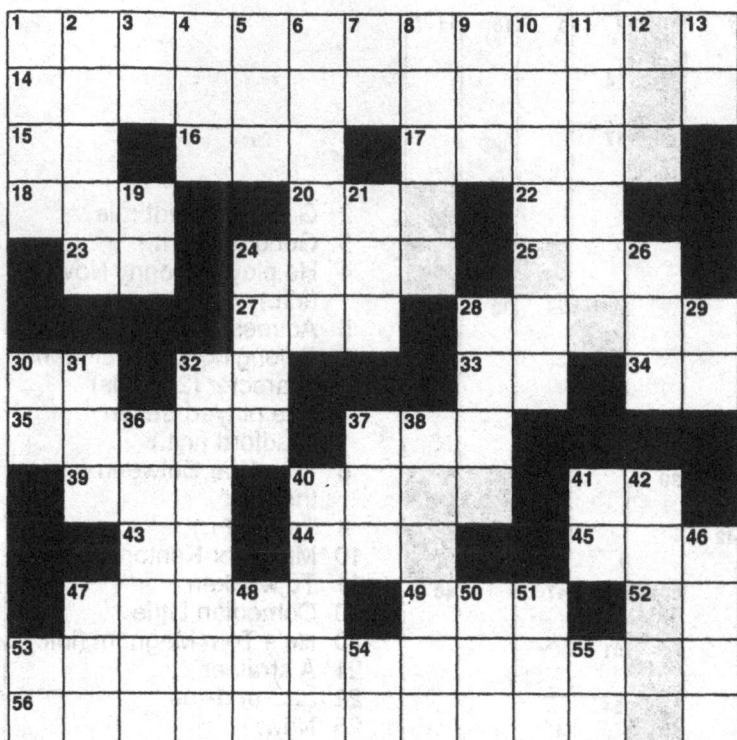

down

1 Egyptian goddess
2 "Ship of ___"
3 Yen (abbr.)
4 "___ 117 Double Agent"
5 United Arab Republic (abbr.)
6 Hundred-dollar bills (sl.)
7 Right eye (abbr.)
8 Miss Jacobsson's
9 Card game
10 Kind of compound word
11 John Gabriel role
12 Hesitations
13 Ben Walton (init.)
19 "Hanta ___"
21 Age
24 Head wear (pl.)
26 Hallucinogen
28 English river
29 *Hart ___ Hart*
30 Eastbound (abbr.)
31 *Guestward Ho!* star
32 Mae West's "___ grape!" (3 words)
36 Lincoln: "I never knew a man who wished himself to be ___" (2 words)
37 Charged atom
38 ___ *Squad* (2 words)
40 ___ the Hutt
41 ___ *Ease*
42 *Hee Haw*'s Minnie
46 Soccer league
47 Saul's Biblical uncle
48 Interest (abbr.)
50 "___ My Turn"
51 Unit of electrical resistance
53 Specific gravity (abbr.)
54 Registered nurse (abbr.)
55 Each (abbr.)

across

1 "___ What I Hear" (4 words)
14 *Masterpiece Theatre* series (3 words)
15 One of Jupiter's moons
16 Theater sign
17 Lends
18 Stone or Stallone
20 "___ and Sympathy"
22 Compass point
23 "___ This Is Love"
24 "Divorce His—Divorce ___"
25 Doctor of Civil Law (abbr.)
27 Al Jolson's real first name
28 Nautical command
30 Actor Asner
32 "___ 109"
33 Virginia (abbr.)
34 "How ___ I Love Thee?"
35 Hillsides (Scot.)
37 *Quincy*'s Sam
39 Employ
40 *Trapper ___, M.D.*
41 Associated Press (abbr.)
43 *Alice* star (init.)
44 Sue ___ Langdon
45 "The ___ Commandments"
47 Desert in Africa
49 "O Sole ___"
52 Hawkeye (init.)
53 *Seven Brides for ___* (2 words)
56 *All Creatures ___* (3 words)

September 29, 1984

across

1 Starred Ron Glass *The ___* (3 words)
13 *Profiles ___* (3 words)
15 City in Nevada
16 Soprano
17 "The ___ Is Green"
19 New (prefix)
21 Employ
22 "___ to Billy Joe"
23 Native of Serbia
24 Puff the Magic Dragon's Land of ___ Lee
26 "Don't Go ___ the Water"
29 She's Chris Cagney (init.)
31 *60 Minutes* humorist (init.)
32 *The Garry Moore Show* vocalist Denise
34 Vivian on *Maude*
35 Compass point
36 Daughter of singer Frank (init.)
37 ___ *Play*
39 Alleviates
41 *B.J. and the ___*
43 *Please Don't ___ the Daisies*
44 Time zone (abbr.)
47 Yonder (abbr.)
48 Cook in an oven
49 "You ___, Father William" (2 words)
51 Blob
53 Christina Crawford's story (2 words)
57 ___ *Neighborhood* (2 words)

down

1 Northern Ireland (abbr.)
2 Dr. Wise of *Doctors' Private Lives* (init.)
3 Actor Beatty
4 "Damien—___ II"
5 Lair
6 Male bee
7 Cirrus (abbr.)
8 "First Monday in ___"
9 United Arab Republic (abbr.)
10 Pneumatic (abbr.)
11 Short for laboratories
12 Writer Stanley Gardner
14 Billy Truman on *Baretta* (init.)
17 Actor and songwriter George M.
18 Fragrances
20 Sea eagle
23 Go away!
25 Short for Alfred
27 '30s actor Mischa
28 Actress Peggy
29 ___ *Previews*
30 "Beau ___"
33 Alma Miles of *Peyton Place*
38 Baseball's Durocher
40 Construction battalion member
42 "Look Back in ___"
44 "___ Night"
45 Half (prefix)
46 Selleck and Poston
48 Tennis great Bjorn
49 Natalie Jastrow on *The Winds of War* (init.)
50 Lighted
52 Laotian
54 Played Gloria Munday on 37-Across (init.)
55 Lt. Ralph Raines of *The Thin Man* (init.)
56 He was Kojak (init.)

November 17, 1984

across

1 Series captained by Hondo Harrelson
5 She was Maude
8 Channel selector
12 Sea eagle
13 Distinctive theory
14 Singer Fitzgerald
15 She was *CHiPs'* Kathy
16 Overwhelming defeats
18 Actor Keach
20 Actor Wallach
21 He was Sam Stone (2 words)
27 NBC's parent company
30 *The ___ Odd Couple*
31 Eagle's nest
32 Roof edge
34 Exclamation of disgust
36 "___ the Tiger"
37 "___ a Crooked Road"
39 She is Mrs. Garrett
41 "___ It Be"
42 He's Richard Channing (2 words)
45 Ruby ___
46 Actress Davis of *Hotel*
50 Relied on
55 Seed covering
56 *Silver Spoons'* Kate
57 "Long ___ Tomorrow"
58 Actress Ward
59 "They ___ That-a-Way and That-a-Way"
60 Prefix meaning not
61 "___ Angel"

down

1 Puts
2 Legal document
3 Actress Lee
4 Educate
5 Offer an amount
6 Compass point
7 "Forever ___"
8 Reaches a decision
9 Not well
10 "Cakes and ___"
11 ___ Vegas
17 *M*A*S*H*'s Hawkeye
19 Yonder (archaic)
22 Network
23 Cognizant
24 Mountain range
25 "Nine to ___"
26 *Lamp unto My ___*
27 Actor Foxx
28 Actress Williams
29 Tel ___
33 Clear
35 He was Barney Miller
38 She was Stella Johnson
40 Recede
43 Closed auto
44 Used in bread
47 "A ___ Grows in Brooklyn"
48 Mah-jongg piece
49 Verve
50 Condensed moisture
51 Before
52 Safety, clothes or cotter
53 The self
54 He was Ralph Furley

January 12, 1985

down

1 Domesticated animal
2 Eager
3 Pertaining to a mansion
4 Wading bird
5 Gives forth
6 Comedian Little
7 Cart driver
8 Belonging to author Zane
9 Wander
10 Margaret Culver in *The John Forsythe Show*
11 Singer Campbell
19 Decay
20 A contour
23 Artificial hairpiece
24 Jackie's former husband
25 Ralph of *Three's Company*
26 Island or ribs
27 A car necessity
28 She was Maude
30 Short sketch
31 Furnaces
35 Wreath of flowers
36 Terence Knox role
37 Desirable thing
38 Native of Scandinavia
39 Actress Diane
40 Woodwind instrument
41 Actress Lee
42 Region
43 Rational
47 Snare

across

1 She was Mindy
4 Group of cattle
8 B.J. in *B.J. and the Bear*
12 Actress Gabor
13 Ruler
14 ___ Out
15 Rin ___ Tin
16 Costa ___
17 Freedom from effort
18 Opal Gardner
21 Howard and Ely
22 Prefix meaning wrong
23 "___ Until Dark"
25 Newsman Rather
26 Trouser pocket
29 Lyricist Gershwin
30 Glowed
32 Recline
33 He was Capt. Buck Rogers
34 *Mama's Family*'s Vint
35 Singer/dancer Falana
36 Ingrid Bergman's daughter
37 On the sea
39 Belonging to "Hot Lips" actress (2 words)
44 Border on
45 Gaelic
46 Author Fleming
48 Be excessively fond of
49 Donna or Rex
50 Compass point (abbr.)
51 "___ Heart"
52 Gratify
53 ___ *Smart*

233

February 2, 1985

50 Loud, continuous noises
51 "___ Witness"

down

1 "True Grit" star
2 Lyricist Gershwin
3 "___ Little Indians"
4 *Simon &* ___
5 Verve
6 Former English measure of length
7 Leo Heatherton in *Phyllis* (init.)
8 *Mama's* ___
9 Building for sports events
10 Wire measure
11 Dine
16 Belonging to Lupino
17 She was the Flying Nun
19 Buffalo football team
20 A kung-fu star
21 Gossip
22 Small demon
23 Sly tricks
24 Point anew
25 Marlo's dad
27 Belonging to Tuesday
30 Fork prongs
31 Robert Burns' poem "___ O'Shanter"
33 Leatherneck
34 *Rich Man,* ___ *Man*
36 "Rally ___ the Flag, Boys"
37 Elms, oaks, etc.
39 FBI agents
40 To recede
41 ___ *Close for Comfort*
42 Actor Wallach
43 Biblical boat
44 He plays the Fall Guy
45 "The ___ After"
47 Starred in "Land Raiders" (init.)

across

1 *The Adventures of* ___ *Carson*
4 Prophet
8 Billy Hufsey's series
12 Anger
13 Woes
14 Opera solo
15 Starred Anderson and MacCorkindale
17 Small fish
18 Maxwell Smart
19 Cinnamon Carter on *Mission: Impossible*
20 He's Hardcastle
23 *Today*'s weatherman
26 Liquors
27 Wicker basket
28 *Green Acres*' Oliver Douglas (init.)

29 Baseball official
30 He was *Kojak*
31 Summer skin tone
32 Business organization (abbr.)
33 "___ to Go Before I Sleep"
34 Strong discomfort
35 Small jobs
37 One of the Smothers Brothers
38 Raw minerals
39 Twelve dozen (abbr.)
40 Ornamental cases
42 ___ *Point N.A.S.*
46 Capital of West Germany
47 To leeward
48 Rose Burton on *The Waltons*
49 Predict

February 9, 1985

across

1 Open
5 She's Soon-Lee Klinger
9 Life (comb. form)
12 Western nation alliance
13 Lisa and Elizabeth
15 Survey
16 "___ High"
17 She's Kraus
18 *Webster*'s George (init.)
19 Joan Van ___
20 Tony Randall role
21 Don Adams role
24 Mork's planet
25 "___ Your Blessings"
26 Chou En-___
27 Baseball abbreviation
30 Before (prefix)
31 Pad
32 Faulkner's "___ Burning"
33 Mao ___-tung
34 "The Cincinnati ___"
35 Robert Urich series
36 Actor Cariou
37 Eddie Van ___
38 "Goldengirl" star
41 "How the West Was ___"
42 She played Sonny Lumet (init.)
44 Carrie Fisher role
45 "A Flea in Her ___"
46 French fashion designer
48 Lamont and Fred
50 Geraldine Chaplin's mother
51 Shout of triumph
52 "Bury My Heart at Wounded ___"
53 "Baby the Rain ___ Fall"

down

1 Looped handle
2 Michael and Tito
3 Indian meal
4 He played Kaz
5 Map
6 She's Tiffany Welles
7 "___ Husbands Necessary?"
8 Overtime (abbr.)
9 "___ the Drum Slowly"
10 "Bus Stop" playwright
11 Eskers
14 "Make Mine ___"
19 "The ___ of Crime"
20 William Tell site
22 Dampen
23 Chemical suffix
24 Grain
25 "___ on a Hot Tin Roof"
26 "A Shropshire ___"
27 "___ of Angels"
28 Tartikoff and DeWade
29 Inches (abbr.)
31 Minute (abbr.)
32 Barbara ___ Geddes
34 He's Cliff Barnes
35 Deborah ___ Valkenberg
36 Loiter
37 "The ___ Soldiers"
38 "The Sun ___ Rises"
39 "Hud" actress
40 Prong
41 Priscilla Beaulieu Presley role
43 Mild expletive
45 Sea bird
46 Comedian DeLuise
47 I owe you (abbr.)
49 Approve

235

April 6, 1985

across

1 *Leave It to* ___
7 Shakespeare tragedy
13 Actress Francis
14 Comic Shecky
15 "___ Window"
16 Actress Derek
18 Walked
19 *Bringing Up Buddy* star
22 At the suit of (abbr.)
25 Book of the Bible
26 *Eight* ___ *Enough*
28 Cuban revolutionary Guevara
29 Company (abbr.)
30 "___ of the Union"
33 Actress Hunt
36 *The Rat* ___
37 "Dinner at ___"
38 "Ma & ___ Kettle"
39 Refuge
40 *CHiPs'* Ponch (init.)
41 Actress Hayworth
43 Garden tool
44 ___ *& Shirley*
47 Ponder
49 New England state (abbr.)
50 Beat
54 Texas city
56 Basil in *Fawlty Towers*
58 U.S. journalist
59 U.S. zoologist

down

1 Oppose, forbid
2 Before (poet.)
3 Southern state (abbr.)
4 Beth Howland role
5 Printer's measure
6 "___ of Sunnybrook Farm"
7 Mercury (chem.)
8 Actor Johnson
9 *Square Pegs'* Butrick
10 British actor Genn
11 Finish
12 Tellurium (chem.)
17 Director Preminger
20 California city (abbr.)
21 *Knots Landing's* Gary (init.)
22 Summit
23 Official language of Thailand
24 Twilled fabric
27 Singer Vaughan
30 South America (abbr.)
31 Bull (Sp.)
32 Actress Sommer
34 Actress Winters
35 *The Fall Guy's* Jody (init.)
36 Actor Duffy of *Dallas*
38 Heavy column
41 Harlan on *Emerald Point N.A.S.* (init.)
42 "___ Eye for an Eye"
45 Actor Ray
46 She was Jeannie
47 Mau ___ (secret society in Africa)
48 "Ode on a Grecian ___"
51 Residence (abbr.)
52 Utilize
53 Turkish title of respect
54 Played Ann in *House Calls* (init.)
55 *Little House* ___ *the Prairie*
57 Island in New York (abbr.)

June 29, 1985

across

1 WWII Bogart classic
11 Florence Harding in *Backstairs at the White House*
12 Gun ammunition
13 Europium (chem.)
14 Hal Smith role in *The Andy Griffith Show*
15 Writer Edgar (2 words)
21 *Amanda*'s star
22 Surrender
23 Ricky and Lesley Webber's adopted daughter on *GH*
24 Positive
25 Mary Beth Lacey
26 Representative
29 Research paper
31 *Queen for* ___ (2 words)
32 William Powell starred in "___ Man" pictures
33 Latin (abbr.)
34 French impressionist painter
36 Chemical Warfare Service (abbr.)
39 "Stayin' Alive" star
41 Level
42 Overtime (abbr.)
43 Agreement
45 "Murder ___ Express" (3 words)
49 "All the ___ Men"

down

1 Actress Johnson
2 "___ Well That Ends Well"
3 ___ *It Now*
4 Ginger's dance partner
5 Female officer on *Hill Street Blues* (init.)
6 Krystle on *Dynasty* (init.)
7 Forward
8 Part of speech
9 Phyllis on *The Mary Tyler Moore Show* (init.)
10 Morning (abbr.)
11 Attractive
12 Comedian Hope
16 Actress Remick
17 She's Alice (init.)
18 "The Cold Room" star Amanda ___
19 All (comb. form)
20 Organs of sight
22 Actor Brynner
24 "The ___ Who Loved Me"
25 "The ___ Commandments"
26 Seasoning
27 Sixth month of Jewish year
28 German spy Hari
29 *Masterpiece* ___
30 *Your* ___ *Parade*
32 An explosive (abbr.)
34 Cloth-eating insects
35 Singer Jolson
36 Scottish societies
37 Former Secretary of the Interior
38 Pen for pigs
40 Cast ballot
41 Walking agents
44 ___ Tin Tin
45 Directed "Anatomy of a Murder" (init.)
46 Near (abbr.)
47 East Indies (abbr.)
48 Officer of the Day (abbr.)

July 13, 1985

across

1 —— for Tomorrow
7 —— Woman
13 To last
14 "An —— Perfect Affair"
15 —— Elsewhere
16 Likeness
18 Weight (abbr.)
19 Sign of the zodiac
22 Actress Claire
23 Exclamation
25 Actress Moore (2 words)
27 Precious stone
28 Pete on Benson (init.)
29 "Jane ——"
30 Jeremy Irons role on Brideshead Revisited
32 Greek letter
33 Curmudgeon on 60 Minutes (init.)
34 Beg
37 Actress MacGraw
39 "Ma and —— Kettle"
41 Lyricist Gershwin
42 Actor Burt
45 Pouchlike part
46 Biography (colloq.)
47 Synthetic fiber
48 Tantalum (chem.)
49 Finished
51 Played Megan Cushing on Lovers and Friends (init.)
52 Witty reply
54 Ethics
57 "—— Boy Floyd"
58 Joins

down

1 —— Street
2 Deceive, trick
3 Julia Cumson on Falcon Crest (init.)
4 Vega$ star (init.)
5 "The Count of Monte ——"
6 Border on a garment
7 Hart to Hart star
8 Alice Brady role in "In Old Chicago"
9 Plays Jo on The Facts of Life (init.)
10 A widow of means
11 Actress Williams
12 He was John Boy (init.)
17 To be sick
20 She played Granny on The Beverly Hillbillies (init.)
21 Singer Gorme
24 Endora on Bewitched (init.)
26 You (archaic)
31 Catherine Bach role on The Dukes of Hazzard
32 Pacify
34 Chatterer
35 Actor Finney
36 Delicately pretty
37 He played the first Steven Carrington (init.)
38 Highway to Heaven star
39 "The —— Next Door"
40 Gunsmoke's Marshal Dillon
41 This —— Your Life
43 Sign of agreement
44 Ginger Grant on Gilligan's Island (init.)
50 Australian bird
52 Bingo on Joanie Loves Chachi (init.)
53 Overtime (abbr.)
55 He played Quincy's Sam (init.)
56 One Day —— a Time

August 10, 1985

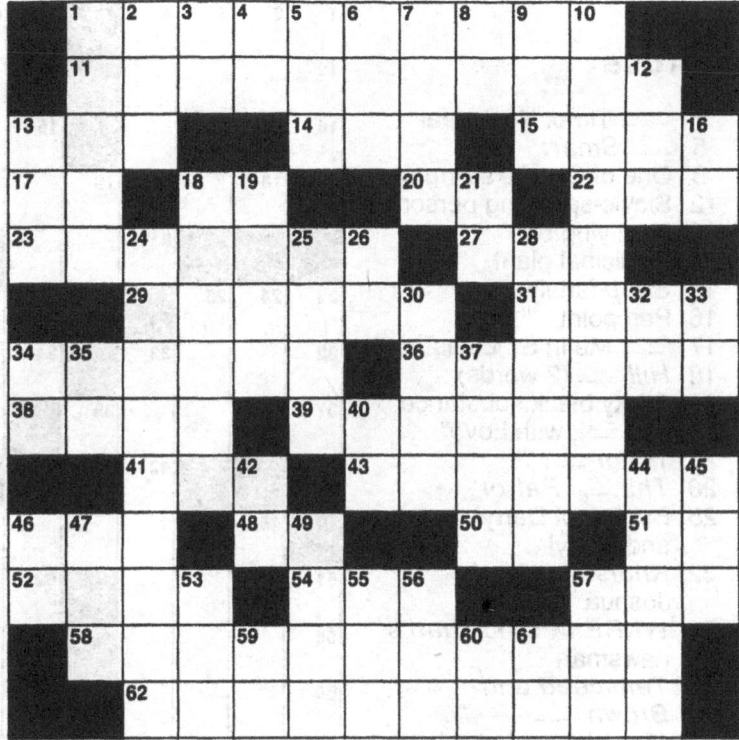

across

1 Kerrie Keane series
  (2 words)
11 *Finder* ___ (3 words)
13 Fore and ___
14 "Victory at ___"
15 "East of ___"
17 "___ This Be Sin"
18 He's Tom Willis (init.)
20 "___ and Pa Kettle"
22 She was Celia Warren
23 Belonging to actress
  Raye
27 ___ *King*
29 *The* ___ *Trail*
31 Woodwind
34 Repeat
36 Serve
38 "Pepe Le ___"
39 "Autumn ___"
41 Ephesians (abbr.)
43 John ___ Swayze
46 *Addams Family* cousin
48 "Gunfight at the ___
  Corral"
50 Elliott Gould series
51 "Sweethearts" star (init.)
52 Plenty
54 Actress Lupino
57 Employ
58 ___ *Craziest Things*
  (3 words)
62 Goldie Hawn movie
  (2 words)

down

1 Robert Blake role
2 Often (poet.)
3 *The Love Boat*'s Isaac
  (init.)

4 He was Jim Harrigan Sr.
  (init.)
5 ___ Enterprise
6 Route (abbr.)
7 "Grand ___"
8 University of Oregon
  (abbr.)
9 ___ *Got a Secret*
10 What Radar slept with
  (2 words)
12 "___ How She Runs"
13 Intention
16 The Big Apple (abbr.)
18 Forrest Tucker series
19 "Mask" star
21 "___ You Like It"
24 Radio City Music Hall
  dancers
25 "Rock of ___"
26 "___ Fine"
28 *Welcome Back,* ___

30 Sha ___ (2 words)
32 "One ___ One"
33 Actor Flanders
34 He's Joe Coffey (init.)
35 "Dr. ___"
37 Domesticated
40 He was Stuart Hibbard
  (init.)
42 "Tiny Bubbles" singer
44 Beginning
45 Indicates maiden name
46 "___ Trovatore"
47 "___ Banana"
49 Firing oven
53 Scatter
55 Degree (abbr.)
56 Advertisements (colloq.)
57 Ultrahigh frequency
59 *Magnum* ___
60 ___ *Madeline*
61 Titanium (abbr.)

September 28, 1985

across

1 "___ Time, Next Year"
5 ___ *Smart*
8 One of Charlie's Angels
12 Slavic-speaking person
13 Nonflying bird
14 Medicinal plant
15 *Soap* family
16 Pen point
17 "___ Me in St. Louis"
18 *Hill* ___ (2 words)
21 Sticky black substance
22 "To ___, with Love"
23 Tit for ___
26 *The* ___ *Patrol*
28 Brother of Darryl
   and Darryl
32 *Knots Landing*'s
   Joshua
34 *WKRP in Cincinnati*'s
   newsman
36 *Tenspeed and
   Brown* ___
37 Chocolate substitute
39 Columnist Landers
41 Offs' opposite
42 Meadow
44 Officers' training school
   (abbr.)
46 Dr. Craig practices here
   (2 words)
51 "___ me up, Scotty"
52 Trademark (abbr.)
53 Beth Howland role
55 Geena Davis character
56 Rhoda's mother
57 Joanie Cunningham
58 Former late-night host
   Thicke
59 Nancy, for short
60 "I ___ You Now"

down

1 Supersonic transport
  (abbr.)

2 "___! poor Yorick"
3 Lee Horsley role
4 1976 women's
  Wimbledon champ
5 ___ *Hospital*
6 Send out
7 Philip Michael Thomas
  role
8 Belonging to *All My
  Children*'s Mark
9 Leeward
10 Female deer
11 Lacey's rank (abbr.)
19 "A Flea in Her ___"
20 "___ Abner"
23 *Tic* ___ *Dough*
24 In the manner of
25 Territory (abbr.)
27 "___ and Sympathy"
29 Seventh letter of Greek
   alphabet

30 Actor/director Howard
31 "___ Giorgio"
33 Steven Carrington
35 Frosty is one
38 In Babylonian myth, god
   of heaven and earth
40 A degree
43 *The Addams Family*
   patriarch
45 "The ___ Little Foys"
46 "___ it with a kiss"
47 Scarlett O'Hara's home
48 Energy Research and
   Development
   Administration (abbr.)
49 Subsequent
   (comb. form)
50 One of the Great Lakes
51 Boy Scouts of America
   (abbr.)
54 *Rocky* ___ *His Friends*

March 8, 1986

down

1 Dick Smothers plays one
2 *Hee Haw* performer —— Roman
3 At the apex
4 St. Gregory, for one
5 Actor Holbrook
6 Tokyo (former name)
7 *The* —— *of Life*
8 Denver Carrington competitor
9 "—— to Billy Joe"
10 Meadow
11 "To —— is human"
17 —— *& Allie*
19 Clear away
22 Dr. Loveless to James West, for example
23 Concluded
24 *Daniel Boone*'s home, essentially
25 Singer Fitzgerald
26 Appear to be
27 Monty Python trouper Eric
28 Past tense of tread
29 Egotist's concern
33 *20/20* co-host
35 Jeanne d'Arc, for one (abbr.)
38 Geena Davis role
40 Carney or Linkletter
43 Actor David ——
44 Rick or A.J.
47 *We Got It* ——
48 A Great Lake
49 "The Bad ——"
50 Selleck or Poston
51 Harem room
52 Garden tool
53 Actress Arden
54 —— King Cole

across

1 Dull, uninteresting
5 *Playboy* publisher (nickname)
8 *Mod Squad* alumnus
12 KITT or General Lee
13 Constance Ford's *Another World* role
14 River in Central Europe
15 —— machine
16 *T.J. Hooker* costar
18 Cartoon series —— *Friends*
20 Actor Hunter
21 —— *of the Rich and Famous*
27 —— *a Living*
30 Actor Knotts
31 School (Fr.)
32 Actress Barrymore
34 Asner and McMahon
36 Make eyes at
37 Belonging to Miss Falana
39 Estimated time of arrival (abbr.)
41 *Cheers* owner
42 *St. Elsewhere* costar (2 words)
45 Three (comb. form)
46 *Good* ——
50 *Highway* —— (2 words)
55 Actress Winningham
56 Aroma
57 —— Marie Saint
58 Garfield's buddy
59 Miss West's
60 ABC, CBS or NBC (sl.)
61 Necessity

May 24, 1986

across

1 "____ Wore a Yellow Ribbon"
4 "Hondo" Harrelson was its C.O.
8 "A ____ Is Born"
12 Demure
13 ____ *Is Your Life*
14 Weary
15 "Tarzan the ____ Man"
16 OPEC concern
17 Very shy
18 Rent anew
20 Type of drawing
21 Lacking
23 "____ Nellie"
25 Farewell in Madrid
28 ____ Carney
29 *The ____ News Bears*
30 ____ Hogg
31 ____ Gardner
32 "The ____ Hell of St. Trinian's"
33 "A Nightmare on ____ Street"
34 "Butterflies ____ Free"
35 Italian food
36 Compass point
37 Cat's mustache
39 Actress Natalie ____
40 Used for sewing
44 He's J.R.
46 Curtsy
47 Do away with
48 ____ Knievel
49 Compainon
50 ____ Godsey
51 Take care of
52 Gaelic
53 Pig ____

down

1 Cicatrix
2 Bob ____
3 Ogler
4 The Rolling ____
5 Betty ____
6 Be sick
7 Initials for Eliot
8 Redford-Newman movie: "The ____"
9 "The ____ Machine"
10 Onassis
11 ____ Buttons
17 Soft color
19 Sonny Shroyer's role
20 Italian money
22 Belonging to Brubeck
23 *Hart to ____*
24 Notion
25 Vigoda et al.
26 Republican senator Bob ____
27 Doctrine (suffix)
29 "____ Stop"
31 Very dry
32 Peel
34 Sailors' call
35 Baseball's Reese
37 *As the ____ Turns*
38 ____ *Landing*
39 Bird
41 Faucet leak
42 "Some ____ It Hot"
43 She was Jeannie
44 "____ It Be"
45 Roman greeting
46 "Cheers," for example
49 ____ *and the Chimp*

May 31, 1986

down

1 Newsman Rather
2 He played Fish (init.)
3 Nickel (abbr.)
4 Mrs. Garrett, et al.
5 Football's ___ Marchetti
6 40th U.S. President (init.)
7 Rocker Adam ___
8 Singer Diamond
9 She's Lacey (2 words)
10 ___ Ameche
11 Setting for *Cheers*
12 Smallest state (abbr.)
15 Bryant or Gillette
17 Denver Carrington competitor
18 Miss Bacall's
20 ___ Stetson's "The Scarecrow"
21 He's Webster (init.)
23 "W.C. Fields and ___"
25 He's Spencer (2 words)
26 "All of Me" star (init.)
28 "Smooth Talk" star
30 Southeast (abbr.)
32 Amount (abbr.)
34 "___ The Extra-Terrestrial"
36 "___ and Pa Kettle"
39 Jeered
41 Mort ___
43 "___ Kelly's Blues"
44 *Hotel*'s Julie Gillette (init.)
45 Commercials
46 "___ Big "
48 Monetary unit (abbr.)
50 *One Life to Live* character
52 Yes, to Cisco and Pancho
53 The original "10"
54 "___ Golden Pond"

across

1 *Fortune* ___
5 *Tribune* editor Lou ___
10 *Glitter* costar (2 words)
12 Ely or Howard
13 Miss Fabray, for short
14 Yothers or Turner
16 "Blume ___ Love"
17 ___ Burnett
19 Actor Cariou
20 G. Carroll and Durocher
22 TV's Blanche DuBois (init.)
24 Princess ___
25 Feature of *Barney Miller* set
26 Actress Lyon
27 "Room ___ the Top"
28 "___ Apartment"
29 Star of "Yentl" (init.)
31 ___ T
32 ___ mode (2 words)
33 ABC News prez (init.)
34 CBS symbol
35 TV award
37 Johnny's sidekick
38 Magnum buddy
39 Small insect
40 Molinaro and Pacino
42 Sight (comb. form)
45 ___ *the World Turns*
47 Froglike animal
49 "___ Tide"
50 "Much ___ About Nothing"
51 Tony Danza sitcom (3 words)
55 *Dallas*'s Miss ___
56 "___ Flor and Her Two Husbands"

August 23, 1986

down

1 Pop singer Scaggs
2 Actor Wallach
3 Lunar vehicle
4 Tennis stroke
5 *The Life of* ___
6 Kate on *Silver Spoons*
7 "Two Years Before the ___"
8 Canadian province (abbr.)
9 Mary on *227*
10 "The ___ Field"
11 *The ___ of Night*
16 Bruce Willis role
19 Dr. Ruth's specialty
20 Command (abbr.)
21 Source of J.R.'s wealth
22 Lionel Stander role
23 Johnny Carson's sidekick (init.)
24 John Forsythe series
26 *Miami Vice* star (init.)
27 "Dr. ___"
30 She's Louise Jefferson (init.)
31 ___ mode (2 words)
32 Writing instrument
33 "___ of the Road"
34 She was Mindy
36 She's Alice (init.)
37 Jane Curtin role
38 *Falcon Crest*'s Lance Cumson
39 Small island
40 Mysterious
41 *The Mod Squad*'s Pete Cochran
42 Michael J. Fox role
44 Dr. Seuss's "The Cat in the ___"
45 "___ Willie Winkie"
46 *The ___ Couple*
47 ___ *Life to Live*
48 John Larroquette role

across

1 "For Whom the ___ Tolls"
5 Jay Thomas role
9 One of the Three Stooges
12 Margarine
13 "On Wings of Eagles" setting
14 *Sanford* ___ *Son*
15 *Remington Steele*'s Laura Holt
17 Equip
18 Bucky ___, baseball player
19 Wild plum
20 *George Burns* ___ *Week*
24 *MacGyver*'s Richard ___ Anderson
25 ___ Dolphins
26 Hill in Athens
28 560 (Roman)
29 Rick or A.J.
31 "The Naked ___"
34 *Night Court*'s Markie ___
35 Marty or Steve
37 Jason on *Growing Pains*
39 *Fantasy* ___
40 Zack Wheeler on *The Texas Wheelers*
41 All the actors in a show
43 Shade tree
44 ___ *Beat*
49 Inlet
50 To leeward
51 Charlotte Rae role
52 "___, Giorgio"
53 Scripture passage
54 TV's Jeannie

down

1 "___ of Eden"
2 "Mafia ___"
3 One (Ger.)
4 Belonging to the talking horse
5 Glide on ice
6 "A ___ of Two Cities"
7 *One Day ___ Time* (2 words)
8 He plays Starman (init.)
9 "The Way We ___"
10 "If You Could See What I ___"
11 "___ When I Laugh"
14 *The ___ Boat*
19 ___ *in the Family*
20 Direction (abbr.)
22 Skills
23 "Bye ___ Birdie"
24 Ursula Andress flick
25 One of the Stooges
26 Bartender Sam Malone
27 Batter, mutilate
28 Louis Malle's "___ City"
29 WKRP newsman Nessman
31 Arvid on *Head of the Class*
32 Kind of snake
34 "The Burning ___"
35 Brother (abbr.)
36 "The ___ and I"
37 "___ of a Mad Housewife"
38 "___ Your Best Shot"
39 Natalie Ross role on *All My Children*
40 "On Golden ___"
41 ___ *People*
43 Surrender
45 Selected (abbr.)
46 He played Barney Miller
47 Welby and Kildare are members (abbr.)
49 He plays Lucy's son-in-law (init.)

across

1 Fencing sword
5 "A ___ Is Born"
9 *Doctor ___*
12 Dry
13 "Romancing the Stone" actress
15 Joan Collins miniseries
16 In the manner of
17 Evangelist Roberts
18 Silvio on *Detective School* (init.)
19 Ingested
20 "___ Day's A Holiday"
21 HBO, for example
24 Direction (abbr.)
25 "Out of Africa" star
26 *Who's ___ Boss?*
27 News correspondent Goode
30 Bone (comb. form)
31 ___ Wallace Stone
32 Lessen
33 Shaped like an S
34 "The ___ News Bears"
35 Heats
36 He's *Dynasty*'s Garrett
37 Theatrical performance
38 Lukewarm
41 "That Night in ___"
42 Sheriff Taylor's home state (abbr.)
44 At another time
45 "The ___ Wolves"
46 Detest
48 Shakespeare tragedy (2 words)
50 Among
51 *77 Sunset Strip*'s Kookie
52 Actress Sheedy
53 Phoebe Cates movie

November 15, 1986

down

1. "A Nightmare on ___ Street"
2. Loud noise
3. Against
4. Situation comedies (colloq.)
5. Actor Sharif
6. "___ on the Roof"
7. *Riptide*'s Cody
8. "___ at the Races" (2 words)
9. Former Yugoslavian leader
10. Prophet
12. Hebrew month
18. Color
19. Chicken or small
22. One of the networks
23. ___ Speedwagon
24. Dick and Joanna own one
25. *The ___ Patrol*
26. Receptacle
27. ___ *Life to Live*
28. Pavarotti movie, "___, Giorgio"
30. Robert and Lindsay
31. Karras and Clark series
33. Former waitress at Mel's
34. George Burns movie role
35. *Get Smart*'s Smart
36. *Hill Street* color
37. Petty quarrel
38. "The Four Seasons" star
39. "The ___ Season"
40. ___ 'n' Andy
41. Unctuous
42. Space agency (abbr.)
46. *The Streets of ___ Francisco*

across

1. Periods in history
5. *The Dukes ___ Hazzard*
7. Harrington and Sajak
11. *Easy Street*'s Anderson
12. French "friend"
13. Actress-singer Adams
14. ___ *Houston*
15. Steven Keaton, to Alex
16. Speed of action
17. Star of "The Toy" (2 words)
20. *Days of ___ Lives*
21. Actress Myrna
22. Michael Mann's ___ *Story*
25. *At the Movies*' Reed
26. "A ___ and His Dog"
29. Vereen and Gazzara
30. *The Winds of ___*
31. *Falcon Crest* product
32. Theo, to Cliff
33. ___ *Albert and the Cosby Kids*
34. Shalit and Wilder
35. High-school subject (abbr.)
36. Game-show host Barker
37. ABC White House correspondent (2 words)
43. Entreaty
44. Ostrich-like bird
45. Spanish aunts
47. Police show ___-12
48. Fish eggs
49. Actress Lanchester
50. Yellowish-brown colors
51. She was Chrissy Snow (init.)
52. Tatum's dad

April 11, 1987

across

1 Dr. Westheimer
5 He's Downtown Brown
8 One-time partner of Sonny
12 Sheriff Taylor's son
13 A place for (suffix)
14 *The Greatest American* ___
15 Connery and Moore role
16 She's Emma Channing
18 Hidden difficulties
20 Its capital is Oslo (abbr.)
21 He played Vincent Danzig (2 words)
27 Presidential economic advisers (abbr.)
30 ___ *Bet Your Life*
31 Make Late
32 McDowall played one in "Alice in Wonderland"
34 Nuclear Regulatory Commision (abbr.)
36 Star of *Friends and Lovers*
37 Cake frosting
39 *Amerika*'s Andrei
41 Indicates maiden name
42 Rae and Rampling
45 Over (poet.)
46 Michael Learned series
50 Mallory and Alex attended these
55 He married Madonna
56 *Kane &* ___
57 *Falcon Crest*'s Melissa
58 Against (prefix)
59 Missles for Soupy Sales
60 Otto Leo in *Celebrity*
61 Require

down

1 Lowe and Reiner
2 *Once* ___ *a Tune*
3 *Family Ties'* Jennifer
4 Avoid answering
5 Newhart handyman George
6 Lyricist Gershwin
7 Marshall's *Odd Couple* role
8 ___ *in Charge*
9 "___ Husband's Affairs"
10 Before (poet.)
11 Decay
17 *Benson*'s Katie Gatling
19 Stallone's nickname
22 Charged atom
23 Sausage
24 Jason on *Growing Pains*
25 Walking stick
26 *The Associates'* Wilfred ___ White
27 Alexis' wardrobe, e.g.
28 *We've Got* ___ *Other*
29 Opera solo
33 Enlists
35 *Top* ___
38 Merriment
40 *The* ___ *from Shiloh*
43 The Phantom of the Opera played one
44 Anspach or Day
47 Ray of *Hill Street Blues*
48 Satisfy
49 Elizabeth on *You Again?*
50 Baseball player's headgear
51 Japanese sash
52 *The Fall Guy*'s Colt
53 Compass direction (abbr.)
54 "The ___ Sack"

247

June 13, 1987

across

1 Lance Cumson on *Falcon Crest*
6 Bengali Hindu caste
11 "——, My Lovely"
12 Mental pictures
14 Outer layer of a tooth
15 *Dennis the* ——
16 Songwriter Paul
17 Alan Alda movie, "Paper ——"
19 Not well
20 Gordon Hathaway of the "Man on the Street Interviews"
21 "Bad Boys" star
22 To slight
23 *Off the* ——
24 She played *Benson*'s Katie
25 *Gimme a* ——
27 "Gremlins" director
28 Cliff Huxtable's wife
29 She was Marion Cunningham
30 Loan
31 Disorderly crowd
32 "—— Wednesday"
35 Increase
36 She played Diane Chambers
37 Domesticated
38 Customary practices
40 —— and Hardy
42 Dissolved substance
43 Gary Coleman role
44 Pop star John
45 Fragrance

down

1 Squiggy's friend
2 Not asleep
3 Vicki Lawrence character
4 *Car 54, Where* —— *You?*
5 *Magnum, P.I.* star
6 Rick or A.J.
7 Sherman Hemsley series
8 *Chico and the* ——
9 "—— All Odds"
10 Hermit
11 *Freebie and the* ——
13 Richard Channing on *Falcon Crest*
18 Writing fluid
21 Johnny Carson's predecessor
22 Joan Collins miniseries
23 He was Venus Flytrap
24 Tall spar
25 *The Cosby Show*'s Vanessa
26 *Love, Sidney* star
27 *Knots Landing*'s Ben Gibson
28 "Santa ——: The Movie"
29 *Barney Miller*'s Detective Harris
31 Burt, Leonard or Ira
32 Producer Spelling
33 Salmonlike fish
34 Detained
36 Apollo's mother in Greek mythology
37 *Name That* ——
39 To burn out
41 Curved line

August 29, 1987

across

1 "The Burning ___"
4 ___ the Music
8 Mr. Drysdale was president of one
12 Fuss
13 "The Black ___"
14 Woodwind instrument
15 "To ___ with Love"
16 "The ___ of the Affair"
17 He played Ralph on *Happy Days*
18 ___ *Burke*
20 *The Newlywed ___*
21 George Hamilton's is famous
22 He's Mike Seaver
25 He plays Blake
27 *Duet*'s Laura might do this
28 ___ *and the Chimp*
29 "___ Which Way You Can"
30 Hamlet and countrymen
31 *Hee ___*
32 Direction (abbr.)
33 King of Judea
34 Emcee Parks
35 Actress Getty
37 "Coffee, ___ or Me?"
38 Shazam's female counterpart
39 He played Jack Tripper
42 Eartha and Knight Rider's car
44 Jerry is one on *Down and Out in Beverly Hills*
45 Hasten
46 Folk singer Guthrie
47 To be foolishly fond
48 Before (poet.)
49 ___ *Wolf*
50 Cheerleader's yells
51 Buttons or Skelton

down

1 Fresh-water fish
2 What Lou Grant does
3 She shared the road with Bob and Bing
4 He starred in "Platoon"
5 *Who's the Boss?* housekeeper
6 *This ___ House*
7 Victoria Principal role (init.)
8 Morrison's nickname on *St. Elsewhere*
9 Husband of nosy Gladys on *Bewitched*
10 Prefix meaning not
11 Door opener
17 "___ at Sea"
19 Miss Fabray, for short
20 Confined
22 Light boat
23 Actor Sharif
24 Eft
25 Co-host of *Today*
26 *The Bold ___*
27 Reiner and Sagan
30 Cold-cut shops, for short
31 Jody on *The Fall Guy*
33 He was patriarch of *The Colbys*
34 *You ___ Your Life*
36 Descriptive name
37 *Good ___*
39 Dr. Westheimer
40 Gaelic for Ireland
41 He was Mike Brady
42 *Krazy ___*
43 Anger
44 Large snake
47 ___ *Kildare*

September 26, 1987

across

1 Tom Bosley role
5 "Little ___ of Horrors"
9 *Family Ties* creator (init.)
12 Jacqueline on *Falcon Crest*
13 She's Mary Beth Lacey
14 ___ *House*
15 Raymond Burr role
17 Angela's mom on *Who's the Boss?*
18 "A ___ of Two Cities"
19 He's Willie on *Valerie*
20 Cookie Monster's street
23 Waxman and Molinaro
24 Untruth
25 Scott, Sim and Mr. Magoo played him
29 Time spans
31 Stage prompt
32 *Cheers* barfly
33 *Gunsmoke* or *Bonanza*
35 Small dog, for short
36 "Ask ___ Girl"
37 Ilene's *Mr. Belvedere* role
40 Singing waitress at Mel's
43 Peggy, on *Dukes of Hazzard*
44 He played "Face"
45 He's "Beans" Baxter
49 She won a Tony for "Carnival" (init.)
50 Maggie on *Emerald Point N.A.S.*
51 He played the Skipper
52 "All the President's ___"
53 Gary's *WKRP* role
54 Rosebud was one

down

1 Natalie in *The Winds of War*
2 Tarnish
3 Yoko ___
4 ___ *Barbara*
5 Step used for climbing
6 *Buck Rogers'* Wilfrid ___-White
7 ___ *Life to Live*
8 Victoria's role on *Dallas* (init.)
9 Thug
10 Nora of *SNL*
11 Kate Stratton of *Silver Spoons*
16 Lara Jill Miller part
17 James or Perry
19 Formerly of Van Halen (init.)
20 "Who ___ Auntie Roo?"
21 Gaelic name for Ireland
22 Caspian and Mediterranean
23 *Reilly: ___ of Spies*
25 "The ___ Also Rises"
26 Exclamation
27 *Rhoda's* Joe Gerard
28 John Steed's *Avengers* partner
30 He played Eliot Ness
31 "I'll ___ Tomorrow"
34 Direction (abbr.)
37 Robert Wagner role
38 Winglike structure
39 Westheimer and Buzzi
40 He played Batman
41 ___ *Street*
42 Tehran is its capital
43 Noisy
45 Middle Brady girl
46 He played captain of the 12th Precinct
47 Fermented drink
48 Actor Beatty
50 *Lou Grant's* Charlie Hume (init.)

250

November 14, 1987

across

1 He's Skippy on *Family Ties*
5 Carl Sagan series
11 *Frank's Place* bartender
12 Belonging to actress Susan
13 Corporal Klinger's hometown
14 His friends include Jambi and Miss Yvonne
15 *Gunsmoke*'s Kitty
16 Elf
17 "You ___ Take It with You"
18 Bruce Lee's *Green Hornet* role
20 Wave, in Madrid
23 *SCTV* regular Rick ___
25 Hometown for Hawkeye of *M*A*S*H* (3 words)
31 Rosalind Russell film, "The ___"
32 "Beverly Hills ___"
33 *The Nancy ___ Mysteries*
35 Book of the New Testament
39 Alec Guinness, for one
40 Agnes Moorehead role
42 St. Francis of ___
45 Ensnared
46 *Mystery!* series, *Strong ___*
47 Actress Kim of "True Grit"
48 Baer's *Beverly Hillbillies* role
49 ___ *Stand Accused*

down

1 Italian city
2 Patrick McGoohan's *Secret ___*
3 *Sanford and Son* star
4 Frog sound
5 Daytime soap opera
6 Peter Lawford film, "___ Time" (2 words)
7 *One ___ Beyond*
8 Cut the lawn
9 ___ *Day at a Time*
10 Compass direction (abbr.)
11 Tony Musante's police series
13 *Tic ___ Dough*
19 Abundant
20 Yoko ___
21 Actress Ullmann
22 Enzyme suffix
24 She was Penny on *Lost in Space* (init.)
25 300 (Roman numeral)
26 "Blame It on ___"
27 Found in muscle tissue (abbr.)
28 Mr. T's role on *The A-Team*
29 Bruce Willis role
30 Lex Luther's girlfriend in "Superman"
34 *Cheers*' Norm Peterson
35 Idolize
36 He plays Cliff Huxtable
37 He's David on *A Year in the Life*
38 "The ___ Sack"
39 Yes-man's response in Madrid (2 words)
41 He was Rocky on *The Rockford Files*
42 Police broadcast this (abbr.)
43 He was Yemana on *Barney Miller*
44 Buntz's *Hill Street* sidekick

across

1 *Hill Street* snitch
4 ___ Lugosi
8 ___ *Trek*
12 "Much ___ About Nothing"
13 Utah city
14 Katherine on *Who's the Boss?*
15 He's The Karate Kid
17 *Laugh-In*'s Judy
18 The ___ Ridge Boys
19 Kercheval role
20 Fred Sanford's buddy
23 "True ___"
24 Assistant
25 "The ___ Hunter"
26 "Uncle Tom's Cabin" author (init.)
29 Mistress of Tara (2 words)
32 Garment border
33 Help in wrongdoing
34 Alda or King
35 He's Perry Mason
36 ___ *Landing*
37 Singer-actress Pia
40 Large deer
41 Pat Morita series
42 *The Chisholms* star
46 *WKRP*'s Jennifer
47 ___ Tennille
48 "___ Deadly Summer"
49 Affirmative votes
50 ___ *All Night*
51 Theo Huxtable (init.)

down

1 Robert Ito role
2 Actress Lupino
3 ___ *Elliot*
4 She's *Hotel*'s Megan
5 Ponch on *CHiPs*
6 He plays Rumpole
7 ABC sportscaster (init.)
8 Don Adams role
9 Actor Rip
10 She's Rae on *Everything's Relative*
11 Actress Charlotte, and others
16 Former Martin Kove series (2 words)
17 "The Purple Rose of ___"
19 *Match Game* regular
20 Long, deep cut
21 Media favorite Donna ___
22 Nicholas on *Eight Is Enough*
23 "Guilty of Innocence: The Lenell ___ Story"
25 "Terms of Endearment" star
26 "The Kid with the Broken ___"
27 Unruly child
28 Without, in Paris
30 Stephanie on *Remington Steele*
31 *Bosom Buddies*' Kip Wilson
35 Bullwinkle's nemesis
36 Comedian Robert
37 Author Emile ___
38 Popeye's greeting
39 Actor ___ Clark
40 White-tailed eagle
42 Jason Seaver to Mike
43 Poston or Cruise
44 "Xanadu" songstress (init.)
45 *The ___ Adventures of Beans Baxter*
47 Sang with Dawn (init.)

February 20, 1988

across

1 Mayberry's mountain man
5 Reagan movie, "Brother ___"
8 Lisa on *Green Acres*
11 Straight (comb. form)
12 ___ *Got a Secret*
13 The President's office
14 Entreat
15 Lacey or Torello, for example
16 Star of *The Ropers*
17 Talk-show queen (2 words)
20 "Strangers ___ Train" (2 words)
21 Ruby or Sandra
22 Chuck or Jimmy
26 Worn by one of the Bosom Buddies
30 Profound respect
31 Milburn on *Gunsmoke*
33 Sportscaster Parseghian
34 He's Michael on *Newhart*
37 Redford film, "The ___"
40 Confederate soldier, Johnny ___
42 *Happy Days*' Richie
43 He's Blake on *Dynasty* (2 words)
49 Jai ___
50 *Doctor* ___
51 Kim's *Guiding Light* role
53 He's Tyler on *Matlock*
54 Evening (poet.)
55 Geller and others
56 19th letter
57 Hamilton Burger and Dan Fielding, for example
58 Snakelike fishes

down

1 Jazz style, for short
2 Folk singer Guthrie
3 Stair
4 She's Chris Cagney
5 Widmark or Thomas
6 Declare openly
7 Lukewarm
8 "___ in My Heart"
9 Singer Jerry
10 "WarGames" actress
13 Bid or proposal
18 A year in Spain
19 Actor Beatty
22 Head covering
23 Be indebted to
24 Court divider
25 Alex, to Steven
27 Hearing organ
28 Spanish lady (abbr.)
29 Actor Mineo
32 *Tonight Show* host, and others
35 Bert's Muppet pal
36 Sports official, for short
38 Richard Pryor film, "The ___"
39 False
41 Bent in respect
43 ___ *and the Fatman*
44 Bullfighting cries
45 Harrison's "Star Wars" character, et al.
46 She's Carla on *Cheers*
47 ___ *Come the Brides*
48 "___ Under the Sun"
52 Donkey

June 18, 1988

down

1. Robert Wagner series (4 words)
2. Meadow
3. Curmudgeonly Jack Paar guest (init.)
4. "Nola" bandleader (init.)
5. *Green Acres* star (init.)
6. Secluded valley
7. ___ *Got a Secret*
8. Jeanette MacDonald's partner (init.)
9. Valerie Bertinelli series (5 words)
10. "The Cat in the Hat" author
11. Double cross
12. *Family* ___
13. You play them in *Vega$*
18. She's Jaleesa on *A Different World* (init.)
19. "___ Shrugged"
20. Show assent
21. Actress Brennan
23. He was *Daniel Boone*'s Mingo (2 words)
24. "The ___ Horizons"
27. Grand Fenwick in "The Mouse that Roared," for example
29. Residence (abbr.)
31. *I ___ of Jeannie*
32. *Addams Family* butler
33. Yuppie's TV necessity
35. *The ___ Sisters*
37. "Black ___"
38. Waxman or Molinaro
40. *My Two ___*
43. Compass point
44. Small piece
46. Subject of "The Greek Tycoon"? (init.)
47. He plays *The Equalizer* (init.)
48. *The Facts of Life*'s Edna Garrett (init.)
49. Singer Don

across

1. ___ *Lucy* (2 words)
6. Fred Flintstone's pet
10. She played Ben Casey's love interest (2 words)
14. Estimated Time of Arrival (abbr.)
15. Bathroom floor covering
16. He played *Webster* (init.)
17. Bond woman in "Dr. No" (init.)
18. Norman on *St. Elsewhere*
21. A people of the Benin province
22. Belonging to comedian Red
24. Authorization
25. Sediment (abbr.)
26. She was Casey on *Mission: Impossible* (init.)
27. Tyne and John
28. Geena Davis series
30. Carbamide
31. "___ at Sea"
32. He was *The Master* (init.)
34. Belonging to Spielberg's alien
36. 66 and others (abbr.)
37. *Crossfire* host
39. Inquiring sounds
40. Either of Larry's brothers
41. *Highway ___ Heaven*
42. Star of "Anastasia: The Mystery of Anna" (init.)
43. Slang term for Sonny Crockett?
44. Life story, for short
45. Series with Ted Bessell and a primate (4 words)
50. Enemies
51. *Murder, She ___*

July 2, 1988

down

1 Joan Van ___
2 He's *Max Headroom*'s Cheviot
3 "Cat on a Hot ___ Roof"
4 *Marcus* ___, *M.D.*
5 Kristofferson or Munroe
6 He plays the Beast
7 He was Sergeant Bilko (init.)
8 Mick Belker's trademark
9 *MacGruder &* ___
10 Director Preminger
11 "___ Wolf"
16 She's queen of the talk shows
17 "Broadcast News" star
19 She was Roseanne Roseannadanna
20 "Mata ___"
21 *Silver Spoons*' Kate
22 Nolte or Charles
23 He played *Barnaby Jones*
25 *The* ___ *Bunch*
26 *Wiseguy* star
27 Evangelist Roberts
28 Feminine suffix
30 He was *Lou Grant*
31 She's Susan Silverman on *Spenser: For Hire*
35 Concerning
36 Balboa or the Flying Squirrel
37 Flat-bottomed boat
38 "___ la Douce"
39 "Deathtrap" star
40 *Falcon Crest*'s Vickie
42 "The Bell ___"
43 "Empire of the ___"
44 Yoko ___
45 ___ King Cole
47 Daphne's role on *Frank's Place* (init.)

across

1 What Ann Marie wanted to do on *That Girl*
4 ___ *in Cincinnati*
8 *Vega$* machine
12 Louis XVI, for example
13 It's rampant on *The Love Boat*
14 Memo
15 *thirtysomething*'s Michael Steadman (2 words)
17 *Couture* or *cuisine*
18 Home to *Nova* and *Frontline*
19 Adam on *Dynasty*
20 Ted's role on *Too Close for Comfort*
23 *Courtship of Eddie's Father* star
24 Placido Domingo forte
25 *Night Court* bailiff
26 Sorrow
29 He's Leland McKenzie on *L.A. Law* (2 words)
32 The ___ Spots
33 *Family*'s Kate
34 *Name* ___ *Tune*
35 Griffith or Williams
36 She was *Good Times*' Florida Evans
37 *Love,* ___
40 Johnny's bandleader
41 "Pretty in Pink" star
42 She played Mrs. King
46 Arabian region
47 Williams or Aaron
48 Actress Merkel
49 "I ___ to Live!"
50 She's Sue Ellen Ewing
51 "Batteries ___ Included"

August 20, 1988

down

1 Spock's were pointed
2 "A ___ to a Kill"
3 Horror hostess and namesakes
4 *Ten Who ___*
5 In a frenzy
6 Jean's twin sister
7 Flanders or Begley
8 Webb's sergeant
9 Merlin's Amish character
10 Fasten with string
11 Climax
17 Simmons movie, "___ Crane"
19 Poston or Smothers
20 Squiggy's pal
22 Mrs. Fletcher's home state
23 *This kind of type* (abbr.)
24 Charlotte on *The Facts of Life*
25 Stephanie's concern on *Newhart*
26 "___ the Night"
27 Makes less dense
30 Word with "coal" or "laundry"
31 *Beauty and the Beast*'s beast
33 Looked fixedly at
34 Actor Chaney
36 "Superman" star
37 Rhea's spouse
39 ___ *Phoebe*
40 Mr. Kazan
41 Dabney's crusty sportswriter
42 Horror maven Craven
43 Occur by chance
44 Dorothy of *The Golden Girls*
47 "Arthur" star (init.)

across

1 Arden or Plumb
4 He was J.J. Starbuck
8 "___ Takes a Hand"
12 Be sick
13 Among
14 "Singin' in the ___"
15 Race a motor
16 *Night Court* matron
17 "The ___ Hand"
18 Michael Talbott role
20 Welk violinist Bob
21 Serling or Steiger
22 *thirtysomething*'s Melissa
25 Setting for *Anna and the King*
27 Cronyn's wife
28 He plays Sam Malone (init.)
29 Pulver's rank (abbr.)
30 ___ *Beach*
31 Lee ___ Cleef
32 She was Julie on *The Love Boat* (init.)
33 Glossy
34 She played *Mama Malone*
35 *Wheel of ___*
37 Boxing promoter King
38 Dines
39 Jigs
42 "___ the Lilies Bloom"
44 Andy on *Matlock*
45 Building addition
46 Part of a roof
47 Martin or Jones
48 *Fame* star Peeples
49 Rushed
50 Lani O'Grady role
51 Séance sound?

55 Stallone, to pals
56 Sea bird
57 It's prevalent on *The Love Boat*

down

1 Time for the credits
2 *Facts of Life* star
3 Doctrine or theory
4 *Me and the* ____
5 Richard Mulligan's new series (2 words)
6 1975 Stacy Keach show
7 Yoko ____
8 Hitchcock movie compass-style
9 *Sonny* ____
10 Carson sub
11 Sophia, for example
19 Stammer word
20 Nell ____, mistress to Charles II
21 Bruce's *Hill Street* role
22 Donny and Marie's home state
23 He plays the Beast
24 Pierce played him
25 "____ to Billy Joe"
28 Reiner or Weathers
29 Actress Sommer
31 Beverlee's role on *Texas*
32 Cambodian leader Lon
34 Nicotine's partner
37 TV-movie, "A Girl Named ____"
39 *Let's Make a Deal* host
40 Eric on *Head of the Class* (init.)
41 Like *The Twilight Zone*
42 "____ of Laura Mars"
43 Actress Patricia ____
46 *Addams Family* cousin
47 *Murder,* ____ *Wrote*
49 Make a mistake
50 Comedian Philips
51 "____ Boot"

across

1 *Monty Python*'s Idle
5 Alex Keaton's favorite subject (abbr.)
9 "Patty Hearst" organization (abbr.)
12 Crosby and Stills partner
13 *Miami Vice* executive producer
14 *Married...with Children* wife, for short
15 Mrs. Bruce Willis
16 Forward part of a ship
17 ____ *Man's Family*
18 Successor to Ormandy
20 ____ *Morning America*
21 Candice Bergen series (2 words)
26 He played Fujiyama on *Quincy*

27 Poor
28 *Medical Center* star (init.)
30 Like Lassie or Boomer
33 *The Completely* ____ *Misadventures of Ed Grimley*
35 Coach Reeves on *The White Shadow* (init.)
36 Lou Grant's star reporter
38 Joan Van ____
39 "Mr. Television" (2 words)
42 Hazzard County deputy
44 Man-eating giant
45 Money for Mifune
46 "____ It Romantic?"
48 She played Donna Stone
52 What you do at *Tattinger's*
53 Malcolm-Jamal's role
54 *My Friend* ____

December 24, 1988

down

1. He plays Ben Matlock
2. New Judd Hirsch series (2 words)
3. "The Man with the Golden ___"
4. One of the Stooges
5. *Almost* ___
6. She was Diane Chambers
7. Compass point
8. Jeanette MacDonald partner (init.)
9. Suzanne Somers role
10. Gretchen on *Benson*
11. Jones or Martin
14. *The ___ Ant Show*
19. John ___ Passos
20. Actor Dotrice
22. On the ocean
23. ___ Hunt
24. He was Hoss
25. Mary on *Little House on the Prairie* (init.)
26. ___ *Albert and the Cosby Kids*
27. La Fiamma on *Houston Knights*
28. Barbara Weston on *Empty Nest*
29. Arnold Palmer prop
31. ___ *L Baltimore*
32. He played Inspector Clouseau's nemesis
34. "The ___ After"
35. "Salem's ___"
36. *Wheel of Fortune* creator
37. ___ *from the Darkside*
38. *The ___ Guy*
39. Garfield's pal
40. Abbe or Charles
41. *Midnight Caller*'s Killian
43. She plays Kate on *ALF*
45. J.R.'s secretary
46. Tom on *Bosom Buddies*
47. ___ Parseghian
49. That is (abbr.)

across

1. Bernie's *Love Boat* role
5. Singer Campbell
9. *Hill Street* snitch
12. ___ *Wolfe*
13. John Goodman plays her husband
15. Title for Edith Evans
16. ___ *Day at a Time*
17. "Animal House" party
18. Year (abbr.)
19. "Birth of a Nation" director (init.)
20. Martin's *Laugh-In* partner
21. Actor Bateman
24. *The ___ DeLuise Show*
25. *Falcon Crest*'s Cole Gioberti
26. Lee Grant series
27. He plays Tubbs (init.)
30. He was Mark on *Hotel*
31. *Murphy's Law* actress
32. Phoebe Cates TV-movie
33. ___ -Alicia
34. Gail's role on *It's a Living*
35. He was Ben Cartwright
36. Floor covering
37. *China Beach*'s Garreau
38. ___ *Square*
41. Felix or Sylvester
42. He played Sheriff Lobo (init.)
44. Hebrew month
45. Impresario Hurok
46. Star of *Oh Madeline!*
48. *M*A*S*H*'s Burns
50. "The ___ Mask"
51. Star of *Paradise*
52. Mastroianni's "Dark ___"
53. "___ Rider"

January 7, 1989

across

1 Mr. Griffin
5 *The —— News Bears*
8 She's Lilith on *Cheers*
12 Nautical term
13 *Kate & Allie*'s Emma
14 Comedian King
15 "The —— of the Cave Bear"
16 *The Tonight Show —— Johnny Carson*
18 South Pacific islands
20 *China Beach*'s Cherry
21 Blanche Devereaux on *The Golden Girls*
27 *Quincy*'s Dr. Asten (init.)
30 —— *Close for Comfort*
31 Archie Bunker's neighbor
32 Water pitcher
34 "Dim ——"
36 *Nancy —— Mysteries*
37 Frost or Brenner
39 Person who does (suffix)
41 Lori on *Nothing Is Easy* (init.)
42 He played Mike Hammer (2 words)
45 Norse goddess
46 Rick or A.J.
50 Horsley's new Western
55 *Midnight Caller*'s Killian
56 —— *Crazy*
57 Pester
58 Cheryl Ladd role
59 Candy Lightner TV-movie subject (abbr.)
60 Comedian Philips
61 Dispatched

down

1 Singer Davis, et al.
2 Jazz artist Fitzgerald
3 Paper quantity
4 "SSSSSSS" poison
5 Belonging to *The A-Team*'s Baracus
6 *People Are Funny* emcee
7 She's Sandy on *Throb*
8 He plays Pop Cavanaugh
9 Actor Wallach
10 Prohibit
11 Home to *Upstairs, Downstairs* (abbr.)
17 Rajah's wife
19 "—— of Love"
22 Huxtable actor, for short
23 Danny's *Taxi* role
24 Group of cattle
25 "—— Leaf" (2 words)
26 Brokaw's forte
27 Clampett patriarch and namesakes
28 Steve Forrest series
29 Kim on *Guiding Light*
33 He plays Bull
35 She was Mary on *Little House on the Prairie* (init.)
38 Colored
40 Belonging to Mosley's *Magnum* character
43 Larry Dallas on *Three's Company*
44 Catherine or Hilly
47 "—— than Friends"
48 Michael Steadman on *thirtysomething*
49 *Empty* ——
50 She was the first Fallon (init.)
51 *One Day —— Time* (2 words)
52 Relieve of
53 Fritz on *Baby Boom*
54 Conceit

April 1, 1989

across

1 *Hee* ___
4 Actress Keanan
9 "___ Loves Me Not"
12 Actress MacGraw
13 Raymond Burr role
14 Election month (abbr.)
15 He played Magnum
17 It's the final frontier
19 A light rhythm
20 Connors and Norris
21 Allow to run over
23 His place was Chez Louisiane
24 "___ It Again, Sam"
25 "Laura Lansing ___ Here"
26 *The Wonder Years'* Karen (init.)
28 "___ the Walrus" (2 words)
29 Steal
30 Business degree (abbr.)
31 He was down and out in Beverly Hills (init.)
32 *Rawhide*'s Rowdy
33 Peter Pan's "I Won't ___ Up"
34 Item
35 "Mars Needs ___"
36 Pepe LePew has one
38 Song for Pavarotti
39 "Sound of Music" family, von ___
40 Steed or Mrs. Peel
43 "Ready, ___, fire!"
44 Dickens character Drood
46 ___ *Day at a Time*
47 Their convention was last August (abbr.)
48 Donna and Robert
49 *The* ___ *Couple*

down

1 "Who ___ Seen the Wind"
2 *Cheers* drink
3 Shatner or Conrad
4 Aroma
5 Delicate sensibility
6 ___ *Dr. Ruth*
7 He played Archie Bunker (init.)
8 Jane Fonda can help you get this way (2 words)
9 Light meal
10 Pawn
11 Arden and Plumb
16 Munsters matriarch
18 Fourth-down decision
20 Moved furtively
21 *Wheel of Fortune* contestant's task
22 Scheme
23 Toss
25 Pigs
26 Woodwind instrument
27 "Each ___ I Die"
29 Cinderella lost hers
30 Myopic cartoon star (2 words)
32 Douglas son played by Stanley Livingston
33 "___ Cocoanuts"
34 "Lady and the ___"
35 Early sitcom ___ *Nest*
36 Bambi's father, e.g.
37 The Kingston ___
38 Enthusiastic
40 Reverent fear
41 Burt Reynolds movie "The ___"
42 ___ Skelton
45 Cecil B. ___Mille

May 27, 1989

across

1 "I Saw What You ___"
4 *Dear John* boor
8 Escaped
12 Fuss
13 Tabitha's brother
14 Drove
15 *Hazzard* car's namesake (init.)
16 *Hee Haw* host
17 Bea's brassy broad
18 Dean of *Nightline*
20 Loud noises
21 She played Segal's roommate
22 Davy, Micky, Mike and Peter
25 *M*A*S*H*'s Houlihan
27 "Like ___ through the hourglass. . . "
28 Tatum's dad (init.)
29 Horror star Chaney
30 Belonging to Capt. Nelson's employer
31 He was Buck Rogers
32 Rick Simon's brother
33 Archie Bunker, for one
34 Chastity's dad
35 *Rich Man, ___* (2 words)
37 ___ Speedwagon
38 Aquatic bird
39 *Highway to Heaven* star
42 Gilda's ___ Litella
44 Nothing
45 Mary on *Little House* (init.)
46 Bon ___
47 *Jump Street*'s Hanson
48 He's "The Greatest"
49 Arthur Hill role
50 *ET* host
51 Former Cambodian leader, Lon ___

down

1 ___ *Shadows*
2 Idea (comb. form)
3 Flipper, for one
4 Michele Lee role
5 Rocker Billy ___
6 *Wiseguy*'s Sonny
7 *Hill Street*'s LaRue (init.)
8 ___ *Place*
9 Eddie Haskell, for example
10 *Sunset Strip*'s Kookie
11 Ruby or Sandra
17 *Meeting of ___*
19 Arsenio's competition
20 Actor Peter ___
22 Raymond Burr role
23 *Happy Days*' Joanie
24 Robert Vaughn role
25 *The ___ Maxwell Story*
26 Gail's *Barney Miller* role
27 *Cosmos* host
30 He's *Star Trek*'s Spock
31 He's *Roseanne*'s hubby
33 He played Kiley to Young's Welby
34 *Gentle ___*
36 Popeye's ___ Oyl
37 Jackie on *The Honeymooners*
39 Character nickname for 25-Across, "Hot ___"
40 Capital of Norway
41 Hammer's mate
42 *Miami Vice*'s Castillo (init.)
43 Cut grass
44 Born, in Paris
47 Marlo's dad (init.)

July 22, 1989

across

1 Stephen Schnetzer role
5 "___ Stop"
8 *Medical Center* star
12 Incite
13 Collection of anecdotes
14 Singer Horne
15 "___ Window"
16 Patrick McGoohan series
18 Bel Geddes *Dallas* role
20 Earned run average (abbr.)
21 Russ on *9 to 5* (2 words)
27 Suitcase
30 He was the Phantom of the Opera
31 Weird
32 Evangelist Roberts
34 "The ___ and I"
36 Gossip reporter Barrett
37 ___ Ness on *The Untouchables*
39 Ever (poet.)
41 Pallid
42 *Beauty and the Beast's* Vincent (2 words)
45 International Relief Organization (abbr.)
46 *Designing* ___
50 Doralee on *9 to 5*
55 "___ in the Afternoon"
56 Dismounted
57 Rhoda's mother
58 Type of rug
59 Actor O'Shea
60 Tennis necessity
61 *Gimme a Break* star

down

1 *The ___ Bears Family*
2 *Kane &* ___
3 "The Seventh ___"
4 "Riot on Sunset ___"
5 Setting for *Cheers*
6 Actress Merkel
7 *60 Minutes'* Morley
8 Ward, June or Beaver
9 "A Flea in ___ Ear"
10 Picnic pest
11 ___ *by Day*
17 "Born ___"
19 Snakelike fish
22 Foot digit
23 She was Georgette
24 "Pretty Maids All in ___" (2 words)
25 Actress Arvesen
26 "Goldfinger" star
27 South African of Dutch descent
28 Singer Guthrie
29 Profit
33 She was Samantha on *One Life to Live*
35 Jewel
38 She was Mr. Mom's wife
40 "___ Wind in Eden"
43 What a violinist uses on his bow
44 She was Kate McCoy
47 "___ Than Friends"
48 Daredevil Knievel
49 "The Fountainhead" star
50 Water barrier
51 Actor Wallach
52 Nothing
53 "___ to Billy Joe"
54 ___ "King" Cole

July 29, 1989

across

1 Reese Watson on *Designing Women*
4 She was Allison on *Peyton Place*
7 Judge Reinhold film, "___ Beat"
10 Vanity
11 Take care of
12 Watch chain
13 He's Michael Harris (2 words)
16 Prefix for three
17 "We ___ the World"
18 Hooperman's pet
21 Actress Berger, et al.
25 "Much ___ About Nothing"
26 "The Snake ___"
28 Singer Guthrie
29 Carlos Ramirez in *The Flying Nun*
30 "___ of Endearment"
33 Trouble
34 Mr. Rambo
36 Delicious!
37 DIII + DIII
38 "The Lion ___ Tonight"
41 Run-DMC did this in "Rock Box"
43 Strong drink
44 NFL player, e.g.
45 Bruce Willis series
51 ___ *My Children*
52 Arthur Miller work
53 New (comb. form)
54 *Nightline* host
55 Stage arrangement
56 "___ of a Kind"

down

1 With it (sl.)
2 *Coming of* ___
3 Bingo game
4 Quincy and others (abbr.)
5 Peruvian Indian tribesmen
6 Idolize
7 "Death ___ Salesman" (2 words)
8 "Requiem ___ a Heavyweight"
9 "In the Line of Duty: The ___ Murders"
11 Mrs. Ed Norton
14 Explode
15 Singer Horne
18 Poets
19 "An ___ Husband"
20 11-Down actress Randolph
22 Charlie Chaplin classic "The ___"
23 "It's ___!"
24 ___ *Gold*
27 "___ to Remember"
31 Comic Eddie
32 *Designing Women*'s Charlene Frazier
35 Composer Jerome
39 Edible parts of oranges
40 Allen Funt's command
42 *Knots Landing*'s Lotus ___
45 Gym pad
46 Bullfight cheer
47 *This ___ House*
48 Gangster's gun
49 "A ___ Leaf"
50 Gunk

December 2, 1989

across

1 *Atom* ___
4 "Das ___"
8 "Little Bo ___"
12 "___ Hard"
13 The Beowulf tale, for example
14 Plays John Ross Ewing III
15 PBS newsman
17 Carriage
18 Crude metal
19 Co-worker of 15-Across
20 Borgnine classic
23 "___ and Spars"
24 Braeden or Sevareid
25 Wrongful act: law
26 Bikini part
29 Secretary of Defense (2 words)
32 Dutch city
33 She played Rose in *The Bill Cosby Show*
34 ___ *Night with David Letterman*
35 Heed
36 Ballet movements
37 A blacksmith does this
40 Prefix denoting "three"
41 "If ___ meet ___" (2 words)
42 Star of "Wet Gold"
46 Neurosurgeon Freeland in *Ben Casey*
47 Mint
48 Utensil for Jeff Smith
49 Young or Penn
50 Smallest in a litter
51 Curved planking

down

1 Naval officer (abbr.)
2 Nicole in *Fame*
3 Chan or Spade (sl.)
4 Wallace or Noah
5 Ron Howard role
6 Subject of "Oklahoma Crude"
7 Helicopter pilot on *Magnum, P.I.*
8 Winnie, et al.
9 Arabian chieftain
10 Gaelic
11 ___ Angeli
16 Cowboy's tally
17 City down under
19 Character actor, John ___
20 Nothing more
21 Dry
22 Staple on *Yan Can Cook*
23 NBC morning show
25 Found in Redwood National Park
26 ___ B'rith
27 Nerve-fiber network
28 Certain votes
30 Westminster ___
31 Mrs. Farlow
35 David ___ Stiers
36 To publish
37 Singer Domino
38 One of the woodwinds
39 Columnist Barrett
40 "The ___ Man"
42 Old French coin
43 Belonging to *Private Benjamin* star (init.)
44 Johnson or Ho
45 Pen
47 *Your Show of Shows* star (init.)

SOLUTIONS

Solution to: June 9, 1956

```
RED . DESI . POOL
ADO . IRON . IDEA
TIN . PRODUCERS
STAGS . NEST .
. LO . TEX . UNDO
PAD . EAR . ORSON
AN . TON . HUE . NL
STERN . VAT . STY
SEMI . BAD . AW .
. . GAIL . ADAGE
KILGALLEN . YAK
ERIE . KENT . ZEE
NEER . OYES . EDS
```

Solution to: June 16, 1956

```
STOP . BEA . PETS
LIFE . IRE . EDIE
IDAS . LIFETIME
PER . IKE . DETER
. RENO . BAR .
SHEEN . HAM . CAL
HALL . DON . PHIL
ELL . BUT . GRAND
. TIE . DEEM .
SHIRE . RAM . PAD
WATERMAN . LIRA
ALEE . ANN . TOIL
TOMS . DAY . ANDY
```

Solution to: June 30, 1956

```
IDAS . ISNT . FIE
ROCHESTER . END
EMERY . ALE . ADE
. IE . GLEASON
ALAN . LEI . ST
GISELE . EH . HA
EVERY . . INNER
DE . EM . STUART
. SO . ASH . AGES
SOTHERN . SN
AVA . ATE . OCTET
MEN . CHALLENGE
ERG . HAKE . STOA
```

Solution to: July 7, 1956

```
. ESAU . ELLS
. DRESS . LOOP
PARCH . TVGUIDE
EVER . FEES . RIG
TIDE . INS . SING
ES . TORN . RATES
. DALEEVANS
SWORD . SEED . AP
LILY . SSR . EASE
ALL . OPEN . RUSE
BLACKIE . ASTER
. RARE . SPORT .
. SPAS . DENY
```

Solution to: July 21, 1956

```
OAK . HOGAN . GEE
FIR . ERASE . ROY
FRAWLEY . SCENE
. MAES . OBOE .
RODIN . DRINKER
ABET . TASTE . MI
BEN . DIVOT . GET
IS . ROBIN . PLEA
DEVINES . TIERS
. ISNT . AREA .
SPREE . EMERSON
ERG . LIVES . ONE
TOO . LIENS . NAT
```

Solution to: August 4, 1956

```
RAG . RAMAR . EVA
ELL . ALICE . TIN
DEE . YALE . WHEN
. APER . BEE .
APSE . MCNELLIS
SHORE . HERD . NO
TAN . DRAWL . MAR
IS . ODES . ELOPE
RESPITES . ARTS
. TEE . TOWN .
LION . STEM . ILL
ERR . WEAVE . NEE
DAM . EATEN . GET
```

Solution to: August 25, 1956

```
LAB . DRAB . MEET
IDA . MIRE . ERDA
BEST . PANELIST
SNEER . BATON .
. BEAD . DON . OB
JEANHAGEN . APE
ILLS . NOR . SMUT
LIL . OGDENNASH
LA . EVE . TOOT
. OVERT . TRESS
MAKEROOM . TUNE
EARN . UNTO . REE
GRAS . SEAR . SEN
```

Solution to: September 8, 1956

```
SEAM . HALF . FIE
ARIA . AREA . ODD
MARCH . TAR . NED
. RAG . FRIDAY
GLEASON . EVA
LOVE . BERLE . NO
ONE . NEWEL . SEA
WE . GALES . COST
. BAN . REPASTS
DORSEY . TEE .
ALI . TAB . ASTER
RED . TRIM . AWAY
TOE . EDGE . ROTE
```

Solution to: September 22, 1956

```
RICH . MENU . CAR
ELLA . AMOS . RIO
SKIT . ROSEMARY
TAM . ACT . SOB .
. ARCHER . OBEY
BOXER . SIR . EVA
OR . DEW . DIM . EL
SAD . SIP . LAINE
SLOP . TALENT .
. LAM . RAY . CEE
SULLIVAN . SHAD
INA . SIDE . HERD
TAR . SEES . ESPY
```

Solution to: October 13, 1956

```
SEA . ADAM . AMOS
ART . LINE . PINE
PRESLEY . PASTE
. LED . CARSON
ROBIN . ALIT .
ARID . STAG . FAT
TALENT . SEARCH
ELL . EARP . BARE
. DARE . MONEY
ROGERS . DAD .
EVANS . LORETTA
EELS . BING . WAR
KNEE . EDGE . ONE
```

Solution to: October 20, 1956

```
TWO . RAPS . GOES
HAG . ORAL . LURK
ILL . GENEAUTRY
STEVE . EDGE .
. SIRS . EDGAR
ED . ASTERS . AHA
WILL . AVA . OBEY
ERE . DRENCH . ME
STONE . GAIN .
. USES . ROOMS
RINTINTIN . ROW
EDIT . DONE . TRI
DALY . SWAY . HEM
```

Solution to: November 10, 1956

```
ART . HIGH . CLAW
RAW . IDEA . RICH
AYE . ROT . VIDEO
BENGAL . AIM .
. TAM . DRSPOCK
DAYS . SIDE . HUE
ADO . LIVES . SPY
VAN . ALAN . FUSS
EMERSON . SOS .
. ITS . PARADE
OVALS . BOB . NED
WIDE . DALE . NAG
LADY . ODOR . ARE
```

Solution to: November 24, 1956

```
BAD.STAG.IVAN
ACE.HERA.RAYE
RHEA.AMI.ANEW
BERLE.SLOTS..
..ITS.DUE.DR.
SIDCAESAR.FEE
ALEE.CIV.ALAN
IKE.ERNIEFORD
DA.ARE.SET...
.WHATS.LEWIS.
ERIE.ALL.RIDE
LOLA.ROOM.DEN
MELD.YEAR.EAT
```

Solution to: December 1, 1956

```
WELK.ACT.STOP
AREA.GOODLUCK
RAINBOW..ART.
..GIG.HOBNOB.
GREAT.AIR..PO
ADORE.STANDUP
.NO.AH.TOYS..
TA.OER.PETE..
OIL.ALAS..DE.
PLOTTED.SHEEN
.WIN..TACIT..
ELAINES.ELATE
DYING.O.MO.YR
```

Solution to: December 29, 1956

```
FLAW.MAD.BEST
ROSEMARY.ARIA
AN.BERLE.KINK
NET.AXE.DENSE
..HIT.NEAR...
AMEN.BEAT.BAG
PARADE.CAMERA
EYE.ETCH.ANTS
..DESI.ANN...
HIRAM.RAH.YET
OVEN.ACRES.DO
MEAN.CUMMINGS
ESPY.ESS.DOES
```

Solution to: January 5, 1957

```
KING.THIS.PAD
ERIE.OUCH.ONE
GABOR.EER.INN
..RAM.DISNEY.
DRAGNET.NIT..
EASE.TUBER.PA
SIP.TENOR.AIR
IN.THREW.ALEC
.PIE.SILVERS.
THOMAS.EYE...
HAL.TOE.ERNIE
ARK.EDGE.TUNA
TEA.RAGS.STAR
```

Solution to: January 26, 1957

```
SPAN.VOW.DAVE
TUBA.ADO.AREA
AMEN.LOR.NEXT
GALEGORDON...
..TAR.WYATT..
WHATS.CAN.GOO
EIRE.BUT.FURY
SKI.BET.TREES
TEASE.PEA....
.HEYJEANNIE..
ERIE.OAT.CORA
LOVE.UNA.ERIC
KEEN.REL.SASH
```

Solution to: February 23, 1957

```
TOT.EARP.BOLO
IVE.RIOT.IRAN
MEN.ANY.PLEBE
ERNEST.ARK...
.ERE.CLOONEY.
MESA.CHAP.ADO
YDS.WHIMS.RIN
NAE.RENO.FRED
AMERICA.VIA..
.INK.DEXTER..
STANG.LOR.IRE
GRIT.WEDS.OIL
TIDY.WIDE.NEY
```

Solution to: March 9, 1957

```
HOBO.DAB.EYES
ORAL.ILL.LOVE
WERE.TEE.SUET
.ROCHESTER...
DAY.RE.SO.HOD
ALS.YRS.NEILL
.CUT.SAL.LTS.
SOLOS.NAT.PEA
HAL.IS.NO.ANN
.INSPECTOR...
RIVA.ERE.DANE
ADAM.AIR.IDEA
MANE.RES.NEWT
```

Solution to: April 13, 1957

```
TEA.STAR.LETS
ALL.NAME.EARP
CLIMAX.CAESAR
.SOP.OUR.TIE.
ALTO.PARTY.LE
SEA.SAT.HAL..
KAISER.LUPINO
.ROC.AIR.BUD.
MA.BRENT.TEND
APT.EAT.JAR..
SPORTS.PARADE
KATE.EDEN.CAW
SLED.LONE.EYE
```

Solution to: May 11, 1957

```
SERF.ATS.VCS.
ARIA.SRI.BELT
CISCOKID.AREA
KNEEL.OCONNOR
..SEP.ANG....
OLD.GENEAUTRY
REED.RAS.PAAR
DESIARNAZ.CYS
..SPY.RIN....
CONNECT.NOAHS
EDIE.ORIGINAL
TONY.MID.SOLO
IRE.OPA.ENOW
```

Solution to: July 20, 1957

```
ORTS.APT.LENT
MART.LEA.OLEO
AGUE.ANDERSON
REEVES.KEENE.
.LED.DUET....
AMI.BUMSTEAD.
DOFF.RAP.ALSO
EMERSONS.IKE.
.AIDE.MEG....
SCANT.SERIAL.
ALICELON.ABLE
WIDE.IDO.SLAV
SPAS.LEW.EERY
```

Solution to: August 3, 1957

```
HAMS.ALP.THAT
ALAN.RIO.HOBO
RENO.ARISE.LO
PECOS.ANT.MEN
.APER.TOGA...
ALL.AIR.PATTI
SOLE.PAT.STET
STEVE.YIP.DES
.DALE.SAKI...
COX.LAS.WELLS
OR.PARTY.ELIA
DEAR.LOU.PONT
ESSE.YAM.SNEE
```

Solution to: September 7, 1957

```
SHIES..BREWER
RALPH.QUIVIVE
OLLIE.UNCAGED
..CAPITA.....
STU.FEZ.RYES.
HOLT.AMADONNA
ONTHECAROUSEL
WIRELESS.RUED
.SAME.TOE.ERA
...GLENDA....
DEADAIR.IRADE
OLDONES.TENOR
GIANTS..HAYES
```

Solution to: October 19, 1957

```
GUS   DAVE  ADAM
ETA   ARID  MADE
TAB   NEE   MELON
SHEENA  PANE
   RAY   DANDREA
SHOT  CARD  ODD
OAF   PARTY BED
ALL   URNS  TENS
PEOPLES  WAR
   NOSY  DOCTOR
EDDIE  PER  SKI
BOON  ORAL  ORO
BENT  FOND  NAT
```

Solution to: November 2, 1957

```
PEG   COMO  FORD
ADO   ALAN  RAYE
NIB   MEL   BAKER
STEVEALLEN
   LOR   OAKLEY
HA  TALENT  IDA
ESTE  ERG   REAL
ATE   LASSIE  ME
RANGER  GAP
   RONRANDELL
TRAIN  AMI  TOE
EARP  RIOT  EVA
APES  ELSE  RED
```

Solution to: December 7, 1957

```
   BBC  ART  MAID
ORAL  LEE  ONCE
NORA  LEA  ODES
EDDYWALLER
   TIN   VERNA
WAGON  FOE  EAR
EVEN  OUR  GAME
SON   ANN  JAMES
TWEED  LOR
   TOMDANDREA
PATH  AIR  NETS
ERIE  TAR  ENOS
PEEL  SLY  RON
```

Solution to: January 4, 1958

```
   LOS  GEM  MAMA
HELP  IDA  IVAN
ANDY  VET  KENT
MAR   DENISE
   AKA  NO  JAR
HENNY  JESSICA
ARGO  JOE  OMIT
LIEBMAN  SANDS
TER  AN  APE
   WESLEY  WAC
MARY  SID  ETNA
ALAN  ELI  TOOT
TENN  NIT  ANN
```

Solution to: February 8, 1958

```
   MOAN  TRUK
   SOUTH  HIRE
SNORE  BENNETT
CERF  BIRD  SHE
AREA  ALE  CHIN
RD  TELL  GRANT
   CHRISTIAN
ASHER  TONI  PA
CHAR  DEN  GROW
ION  AIRY  HOLE
DONOVAN  MILLS
   ERIN  SALLY
   LEDA  SOLO
```

Solution to: February 15, 1958

```
AMES  ELM  SHAD
ROSE  SEA  TALE
EASE  SIS  OVEN
STONE  FORREST
   LA  NOD
MAURICE  YALTA
ELSE  TAC  HEAD
GLASS  ROWLAND
   TAD  PA
COLLYER  COSTA
ALOE  VON  PAUL
PENS  ODE  ELBA
TOES  LED  NEAR
```

Solution to: March 8, 1958

```
LAMP  HERE  DOE
AREA  IDEA  ERA
BETTY  GAS  BAR
   ROBERTCULP
DETOUR  HOT
REAL  AHEAD  PA
ART  STORM  MAN
MY  BASER  DEAD
   SID  OHENRY
MATTDILLON
ADO  LOU  PITTS
MAR  ETCH  SOAP
AMY  SAKE  EDDY
```

Solution to: May 10, 1958

```
SPA  PALM  ACT
KANGAROO  NORA
IGOR  ELS  TRIS
PENAL  LEA  COS
   COP  LIDO
LORETTA  LOREN
EWE   AID  AVE
TEXAS  MATINEE
   AMOS  NOR
ALL  NAP  DINAH
BALI  NED  SOME
EVEN  DAUGHTER
ANN  SLOE  END
```

Solution to: May 24, 1958

```
SAL  GREY  ELL
TEA  EAVE  LOIS
ARM  ONE  BURNS
ROBERTSAUDEK
   SAG  BRET
AM  REAGAN  TAR
HEAP  GET  FATE
ANN  CAMERA  ED
   NEAT  ERA
   KENNETHTOBEY
BETTY  RUE  ARA
RETE  JILL  SIR
PER  OPAL  END
```

Solution to: June 14, 1958

```
WAC  ADAM  WEST
ELL  LINE  HAIR
BEA  LOT  PARTY
BERGEN  BIT
   KEN  PRESTON
WAKE  BAIT  EVE
ARE  TANDY  LEE
RIN  RITE  HERD
MATHERS  RIP
   AND  FATHER
DAVID  TAM  ODE
AXEL  NORA  NEE
BETA  ODOR  END
```

Solution to: June 21, 1958

```
FRED   WELLS
RODEO  MARION
IN  IS  CORA  MA
ANN  SWORD  TOP
RIOT  ART  MAN
   EDWARD  BOND
   IVE  GUS
CASE  PAMELA
ACT  FLO  LINE
BEE  SEALS  EST
AS  ALAN  AT  AH
RANGER  MOORE
BROOD  ORAL
```

Solution to: August 2, 1958

```
   KIND   DOW
LINEUP  TRIAL
EL  DEANMILLER
ALL  SLEEP  TEA
REEK  MAN  EDDY
   RENDER  TRIS
   GEAR  TONS
   COLD  LUPINO
TROT  TAM  EERY
NOD  TENOR  YES
TOMDANDREA  GE
NAILS  SAILOR
   NEE  PLAN
```

Solution to: August 23, 1958

WIN	METE	SLOT
ADE	AVID	HOUR
SEW	JIM	TERRY
PATROL	ERA	
	AIR	MURROW
BALD	KIT	ODE
IRE	SMITH	BOB
FIN	TAD	HERB
FATHER	HER	
	IVY	BAXTER
FOYLE	LIZ	SRO
APED	PILE	OIL
NANA	TELL	NEE

Solution to: September 6, 1958

SHOW	PATS	TNT
IOWA	ALOE	HEM
DELLA	BEA	ERE
	TIC	SHARON
CAMERA	USE	
OVER	DOWNS	DO
DIN	TENET	TOP
ED	HOTEL	AIDE
	KIN	LENNON
GLADYS	SAG	
RIM	DON	TENOR
EVE	ODOR	LIDO
SEN	WADE	ALEE

Solution to: November 1, 1958

SANE	LEGS	HI
EDEN	ARUT	ERA
EDWARDRMURROW		
	MA	BOONE
CASEY	ABC	
ORAL	DALY	BY
DID	IDA	LEO
ED	ANON	LILY
	ANT	ROLLO
GLASS	AM	
MICHAELTHOMAS		
CAR	ROSE	NANA
RE	ANTE	DRIP

Solution to: December 6, 1958

BET	BAA	SHIP
ALI	LOUD	TAKE
RICHARD	RAVEN	
EWER	ORE	
ASTA	ELMS	
REAR	YEA	ALE
MARTINMANULIS		
SRO	MAE	PEAT
BABA	SERE	
ERG	DELE	
ERNIE	ORATORS	
BOOT	SWAY	LIE
BEST	OSS	DOW

Solution to: December 20, 1958

TAG	TRUMPET	
SODA	HAMILTON	
AMES	ALP	YORE
LON	DIE	NOW
OR	AS	HAL
ORION	TULIPS	
NORA	BAT	DREG
WARNER	MOORE	
SON	YE	GO
ASP	POT	PER
WELD	IOU	BRAG
LEEAAKER	BONE	
KAYDETS	CAT	

Solution to: March 7, 1959

NIECE	KIM	
DILLON	ORAL	
LIV	LED	VIDEO
OVER	GAS	AP
RANCH	ARC	PSI
AISLE	TEN	
WEB	DIVER	ADE
ALE	MINOR	
GIN	JON	NADER
ON	DAN	TRAY
NOLAN	EWE	ERE
RAVE	TALMAN	
WET	ASKED	

Solution to: April 4, 1959

WAS	BROD	FIVE
ABE	IOWA	AWAY
NBC	TWENTYONE	
ERLE	ROE	
ESS	WER	HAD
MATT	YEN	EVA
ALA	BAD	NIL
MAR	BAT	EDDY
ANY	ORT	ORE
FOR	LARK	
JOSEMELIS	SAP	
EDIE	TINE	ONE
TEXT	TENN	NEW

Solution to: April 25, 1959

BIB	SMEAR	SEA
ODE	HORSE	ANN
BARBARA	BUDDY	
TENT	PET	
SPAN	PALADIN	
AHA	OPEN	HARE
LOR	NITER	NIT
ARKS	KELO	ESS
NESTLER	BACH	
OUR	TELL	
KNOWS	GARLAND	
IAN	TRUST	RYE
DYE	YANKS	KEN

Solution to: May 2, 1959

MARY	PEP	ASK
ALOE	LEA	DIAL
MARSHALL	ANNE	
ANY	ON	ARM	GO
WOE	DES	AN
ACRID	SID	IRA
LION	VAN	ODOR
AMY	BAT	FLOOD
DA	JAN	ROD
DR	ARE	OR	LIE
IRON	SCOTLAND	
NONE	SOT	ONCE
NET	ASS	BEAR

Solution to: June 3, 1959

FAME	WADE	SAG
ALAS	ALIT	IDA
ROTS	RICHARDS	
METAL	KEG	
WYATT	LOPEZ	
USA	MORT	ARE
RAY	BLAIR	NIL
GIN	DIME	EEL
ELECT	NEILL	
ORE	NOISE	
TOMTULLY	USED	
AWE	SLOE	STAG
DEL	TART	ESTE

Solution to: June 27, 1959

SOFA	CAB	ODES
ADAM	OWE	TOTE
NORA	LEE	TUNE
RONALDREAGAN		
DRY	YEW	
THEATER	LAUGH	
OIL	REL	SIA
DELLA	BOSWELL	
OSS	NEE	
FRANKMCGRATH		
LIND	ILL	VIAL
UNTO	TEE	ELLA
EDEN	HOY	REED

Solution to: July 4, 1959

MATT	ADS	RAG
ARIA	BIT	ALIT
RENT	CAR	YULE
YATES	LIEBMAN	
ED	PAL	
DURWARD	ROADS	
ETUI	YAM	CLEO
BETSY	NOBHILL	
HOP	MU	
RAYBURN	DRAKE	
OLEO	EON	ERIN
DEAN	SRO	TITO
ERE	SAD	ADES

Solution to: July 18, 1959

```
T A G [] S H E B [] O T I S
H U E [] T A R A [] P O R K
I N N [] E L A I N E M A Y []
S T E V E [] S T A R [] []
[] [] B I L L [] [] M A B E L
A L A N [] I S L E [] I D A
B A R T [] N E O [] F L I T
E R R [] B E A R [] A L E E
L A Y N E [] [] I N C H [] []
[] [] O R A L [] Y E A R S
C R A I G H I L L [] Y O U
O U R S [] O L E O [] E V E
P E T E [] Y A W N [] S E T
```

Solution to: August 1, 1959

```
R I P [] S T A T E [] G E E
E V A [] H O N O R [] A R M
B E N N E T T [] L A Y N E
[] [] Z E D [] M E R L I N
O M I T [] B E A [] E Y E D
R I N [] C U L L E N [] []
E L I N O R D O N A H U E
[] A R L E N E [] A S E []
A D A M [] A R E [] O R A L
L I N E U P [] E I R [] []
L A N D S [] M I L L I O N
E R I [] E D E N S [] E W E
N Y E [] D O N N A [] T E D
```

Solution to: September 26, 1959

```
J A N [] D A U B [] W R A P
I D O [] E D G E [] H O N E
M O R T S A H L [] A S T A
[] [] R I M [] S T E E L []
P E R U [] S I T E S [] []
I R A T E [] N O T [] T H E
K A T H R Y N M U R R A Y
E S E [] R O E [] P O O L E
[] C O U R T [] D Y E D []
S H A L L [] U S E [] []
L O L A [] C O R C O R A N
A P E R [] A N N A [] I V E
P E C K [] B E S T [] P A T
```

Solution to: October 3, 1959

```
V I A [] C O M O [] B U R R
E D D [] A B E L [] A S E A
T E A [] M O L E [] D A L Y
S A M M E E T O N G [] []
[] [] S I R [] Y E A R S
E D [] L A S S I E [] N I P
K A T E [] A I R [] U N T O
E V A [] A N D E R S [] A T
D E C O Y [] [] O E R [] []
[] [] P E T E R B R E C K
J A N E [] A L E E [] D U E
O D O R [] T S A R [] D R Y
N O R A [] S A L T [] Y E S
```

Solution to: October 10, 1959

```
[] S A N D S [] A I D A
S T U A R T [] A N D E R S
C U L P [] E B B [] O N C E
A D D [] V I E [] T A T
R I [] W E L L S [] R U
O N I O N S [] T R O O P
[] E R R S [] B E A D []
W E E K S [] B R A N D S
Y D [] E F R E M [] H E
A W E [] L O N [] L A W
T A R A [] O W N [] C O R E
T R I X I E [] E L I N O R
[] D E E D [] R A V E N
```

Solution to: November 21, 1959

```
P E P [] C L A Y [] G E R M
O A R [] L O N E [] E R I E
P R O V O S T [] S O L V E
[] [] I C E [] S T R E E T
F L A C K [] D O U G [] []
L A S T [] B E N N E T T
U N T O [] I N A [] B A I L
[] G A R D N E R [] U L N A
[] B U N S [] P R E S S
A C R O S S [] J A N [] []
C L A R K [] M A R S H A L
H A N G [] M A C K [] O R E
E D G E [] I N K S [] W E E
```

Solution to: December 5, 1959

```
B I L L [] M I T C H E L L
E R I E [] A N N D A V I S
T E E S [] C T [] L I S T
[] [] C O R A [] L A [] []
C A R O L E [] B O A [] []
A L O U D [] H A R D I E
T A L L [] A I R [] V A R Y
[] S L I E S T [] D E N S E
[] E L K [] S U N S E T
A S [] [] B O O T [] []
W I T H [] P A [] U S E D
E D I E H A R T [] R I L E
B E R N A R D I [] E R L E
```

Solution to: January 30, 1960

```
E V I L [] G R A M [] L S T
L I C E [] A C R E [] A T E
M A Y O R L A T R I V I A
[] [] N O [] C L A R K
T O D A Y [] S E E K [] []
O V E R [] T A R [] S A G
R E A D [] R O T [] D O L E
E N D [] S I R [] E D E N
[] A T O M [] S P A C E
J A I M E [] H A [] []
E D D I E A N D E R S O N
T I E [] L I E D [] E E R Y
S T A [] E L B E [] E T T E
```

Solution to: February 27, 1960

```
[] L A R A M I E [] A I D
H O M I C I D E [] F R E D
I L E D [] L O R [] T A M E
P A S [] M E L I S [] N A P
[] G A S [] E O N [] R A
S H O R E [] [] D O V E R
H A R I [] [] R I S E
E W E L L [] [] S T A T E
L A [] L I T [] B A H
D I E [] D E B U T [] T E D
O I L S [] R A T [] T H E E
N A I L [] M I T C H E L L
N A Y [] S T E V E N S []
```

Solution to: March 5, 1960

```
A M O S [] G A S [] B E E
R E B U S [] A R T [] L A W
C L I N T [] R I O [] A V E
[] [] D A N B L O C K E R
A N S A R A [] G E E [] []
D A L Y [] D O S E S [] B E
A M Y [] T E S T S [] R O D
M E [] W O R S E [] S A L E
[] B A N [] N E L S O N
G A R R Y M O O R E [] []
U S A [] D A W [] R E B E L
N E D [] O D E [] S P A C E
N A Y [] W E D [] S T U D
```

Solution to: March 26, 1960

```
A N N A L [] S T U S []
L A I N E [] S H A R P E
S P L I T [] P E R N E L L
[] [] S E A [] S A L E
S E E N [] W R E N [] R A G
A R L E N E [] D E W [] []
L A S S O [] R E B E L
[] T A D [] L O P A K A
H I T [] H O P E [] T R E Y
E L I A [] L E S [] []
P E R R E A U [] T O N T O
D E N N I S [] A L O H A
[] D O D D [] G E N E T
```

Solution to: May 21, 1960

```
[] D O E S [] S C A R
[] D E R M A [] N O L A N
F A [] B U D C O L L Y E R
I V E [] B O [] C R Y
L I M B [] A S P [] O V A
E D M O N D [] A L L E N
[] Y O Y O [] E V I L
S H A M E [] A E R I A L
H A W [] M E T [] A N N A
E R A [] C L [] S I D
S T R I C K L A N D [] T Y
[] E D D I E [] L A U R A
[] S A V E [] A B B E
```

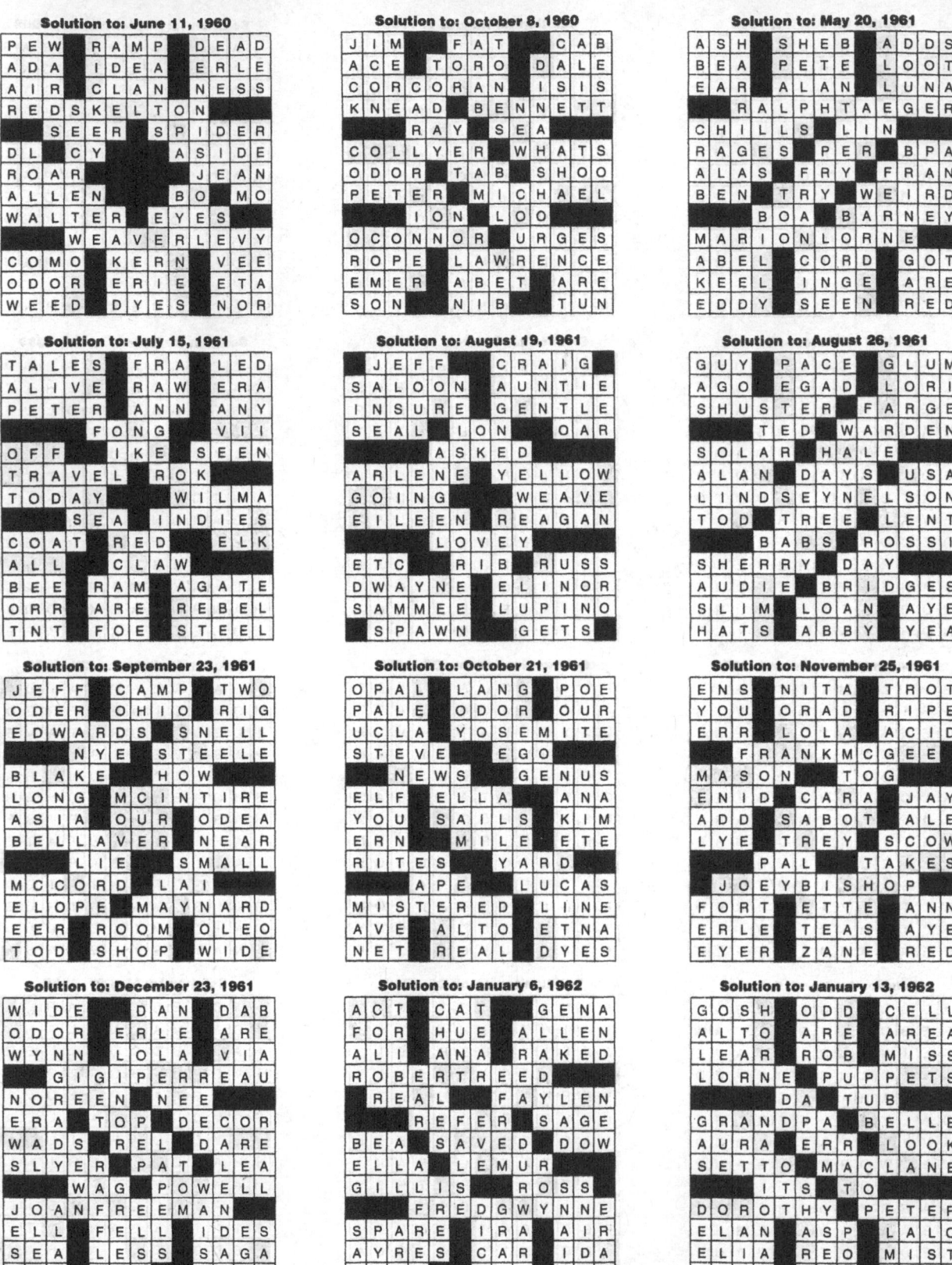

Solution to: February 17, 1962

```
A F T . M E L . . S E T .
A L O E . E Y E . T A I L
W A R D . L E O N A R D O
E N D . S I R . A L L E N
. A L A S . G I L . . . .
M A D A M . Y U L . S E A
A N D Y . R O Y . B I L L
D A Y . L O U . P I X I E
. . N A N . M A T T . . .
E L I O T . C A T . Y E S
R I F L E M A N . A S I A
A N N A . A R E . D I R T
. T I N . N A T . A X E .
```

Solution to: April 14, 1962

```
C A T . D E E P . . I R K
A D O . E L L A . I N C A
R A . A M S T E R D A M .
A M A N D A . R O I . . .
. F R Y . S P I N A C H .
A L E E . T A L C . N E E
M I . . I V O . . R R
E N D . S N O W . D A T E
S T A N L E Y . A N A .
. P O I . D E N N I S
J O H N D E R E K . N O .
A N N E . F I L E . A L L
B E E . T O L D . L Y E .
```

Solution to: May 5, 1962

```
J A Y . C A T . . M O R T
O N E . A N I . S A R A H
E D W A R D S . T R A C E
. . . L O Y . B A I L E Y
C H I L L . A R G O . . .
L O D E . E Y E . N I B S
U P O N . A R E . L O R I
B E L L . T E D . O W E D
. . U T E S . C R A T E
H A R D I N . M A N . . .
E L I D E . R O B E R T S
R E F E R . A D O . E W E
O X E N . Y E T . D O W .
```

Solution to: December 1, 1962

```
R I B . F A T A L . J A B
A D O . A L I B I . O M E
H O R A C E M C M A H O N
. G L E E . B I N S . . .
J O N E S . C L O D . . .
E R I C . B A A . A B B A
S A N . U R N . R U N
S L E W . R O D . B I R D
. E A R L . B E N N Y
H A L L . S O A K . . .
J A C K L E S C O U L I E
A L E . E L I O T . E V A
Y E S . N I N T H . Y E T
```

Solution to: December 22, 1962

```
A S P . A D A M S . E L M
S E E . B E R E T . B E A
H A R R I E T N E L S O N
. N E D . . V I E . . .
S C E N E . . D E N N I S
W A L T . S T O N E . R E
O I L . W H A T S . D O N
O R . S O U L S . D I N S
P O S T O N . E R A S E
. H A S . . S A M . . .
C L I N T E A S T W O O D
O A R . E R N I E . N R A
O W L . R E N D S . D E N
```

Solution to: January 12, 1963

```
E L M . A R C . . G L E E
Y O U . L O O M . R O D E
E L L . L O B E . A N I L
. L L O Y D B R I D G E S
. A N N . . R O Y . . .
L I N E . R A I N . F R A
A R E . D E L L A . L I N
W A Y . R A I L . B I N D
. . W A D . . T O P . .
A N D Y W I L L I A M S .
R O O M . N E A R . A L E
A N N A . G E N E . R U G
B E E N . . R E D . K E G
```

Solution to: March 23, 1963

```
L A M P . T E D . . T I M
A R A R . R A R E . O R E
W A K E . A S I A . M A N
. B E S S M Y E R S O N .
. . . S A P . S T A R .
C A B . M A T . H U R O N
A L E C . S I R . L O N E
T E N O R . N I L . W E D
. C R E W . C E E . . .
. D A N N Y T H O M A S .
H I S . T A R A . B I L L
A C E . S T I R . E D I E
S K Y . . T O D . R A M S
```

Solution to: July 20, 1963

```
S N O W . F E E . . T H E
A B B E . L A Y . G R E W
M C I N T I R E . L A N E
. . D U N S . H E I R S
T A L E N T . B E N N Y .
A D E L E . G O W N . . .
R E A L . S O B . C H I P
. . C H E T . M O O R E
. S T O A T . L A R D E R
S H I R L . C U R B . . .
H O M E . J A C K E L A M
A R M Y . A V A . T A L E
D E Y . Y E S . T W I N .
```

Solution to: August 17, 1963

```
L A D D . B U S . B O W L
O L E O . U S E . E D I E
O D E R . T A R . R I L E
M O R S E L . I N G E L S
. . . A G E . A Y E . . .
T A Y L O R . L E N N O N
E V E . . . . O R O
D E N V E R . W A R N E R
. . I D O . A D O . . .
A W A R D S . R A N G E R
G I N G . C A R . A L S O
A N T I . O L E . L E T O
R E E L . E I N . D E E M
```

Solution to: October 5, 1963

```
E B B . . A D . . G A D
E A R . E R R S . W I D E
L E E . S C A Y . A L A N
. R A L P H B E L L A M Y
. K E Y . V A T . . . .
T H I S . R E E D . B U B
H U N . L O R N E . O N E
E G G . A B A S . B R A N
. . A V E . D O G . . .
R I C H A R D B O O N E .
I D L E . T U R N . I V E
D E E M . S K A T . N E D
S A M . . E D . . E N D
```

Solution to: October 12, 1963

```
P A A R . A H A . J I B
A G I O . B U B . D A N A
M E L B L A N C . A M E N
. . E A S T . E V E R S
S W E R V E . G R I S T
A O R T A . L O R D . .
M E E T . F I T . J A C K
. A T O P . C A N O E
. M A Y O R . L A N D O N
S A L L Y . J A R S . .
O S L O . L U C Y S H O W
D O E R . O N E . E I R E
A N N . T E D . N E E D
```

Solution to: January 18, 1964

```
. L A N E . H O W E .
. B E N E T . A D A M S
D O N N A A N D E R S O N
R E N E L L A . . A R
S R O . G A Z Z A R A .
. N A N S . L O I S .
. N A T . A N N .
. M E S A . N E A R .
D U R W A R D . A I M
O N . R A W H I D E .
E D G A R B U C H A N A N
. O U T E R . H I N E S
. M E T S . E G G S .
```

273

Solution to: February 22, 1964

```
O F F · S H E B · S P A R
N O R · L A T E · C A R A
E R A · A L A N · O T I C
· N O N E · C A T T L E
· S K A T · P A R T Y ·
J E F F · D E S I · P A T
E G O · B R E E D · E V A
D O N · E S P Y · S T I R
· T I N T S · R E E D ·
A M A N D A · P A A R
D A I S · R Y A N · S I D
A N N E · K I N G · E V E
M E E T · E P E E · N E W
```

Solution to: October 10, 1964

```
A V O W · L A S · D O G
D E S I · E L I · C O A L
S E L L · A I L · L U T E
· R O B E R T V A U G H N
· · U R N · E B B ·
A W A R E · P R E S T O N
R O D · B U S · O W E
K E E S H A N · D A N N Y
· T A R · T O M ·
C A R O L B U R N E T T
A L A N · A P E · C H I P
R O V E · R O E · H A L E
L E E · A N N · E T T A
```

Solution to: November 21, 1964

```
· O C T · O P S · P I N
A D A R · A B E T · A V E
P O R E · M E N U · T E D
E R L E G A R D N E R ·
· N O T · T R I A L
M A B · D E A N · S O L O
A L E S · U S A · E T O N
R E N O · R A T E · S E E
C E C I L · A N I ·
· A L E C F L E M I N G
L E S · A L A I · A R E A
A R E · S A M E · G O E S
D A Y · E Y E · E N D
```

Solution to: February 13, 1965

```
· J O H N · P E G G Y
S E R I A L · C A M E R A
A T · E T E · L A U · E T
U S A · O S C A R · B E E
L O D E · T O M · P U N S
· N O R D E N · B A S E
· N O R · E A R ·
C A I N · I N D I A N
S A L E · E D S · S P E D
T S P · C L A I R · E W E
I P · W E S · G E T · M A
F E L I N E · N E W M A N
F R O N T · D O O R
```

Solution to: February 20, 1965

```
W A C · D A N · E D N A
I R A N · E L I · N E E D
S E R A · N B C · S A R A
H A L P I N · E L I N O R
· O R I · R A G ·
G A R L A N D · O N E A L
O P I E · G I G · P A L E
T E N O R · D E C A R L O
· N O T · T A R ·
C R O S B Y · A N K L E S
H O M O · L A W · E A R L
E R A L · E V A · R I L E
T Y R O · R A Y · R E D
```

Solution to: March 27, 1965

```
M S G · P I P E · B A T
L O L A · A L A R · E L I
A D A R · A L A N H A L E
B E T T Y · R I O ·
· T H A T · E B S E N
A B E · W E L K · E R A
H E R · L A I N E · R I M
E L Y · K E E P · G E E
M A S O N · W I P E ·
· P E R · C H A O S
B A S E H A R T · A N T I
O N E · R H E A · S T I R
B Y E · U S E D · E S S
```

Solution to: April 10, 1965

```
D I V A · T A B · F E S S
A C I D · O U R · L A K E
R E E D · A R A · O V E N
E D W A R D A N D R E W S
· M A Y · D O E ·
C R E S T · D E N N I N G
B O B · F A D · N E A
S I B B A L D · T H A W S
· A D E · S E A ·
D A V I D M C C A L L U M
A B E L · I L E · P O S E
L E N E · N U N · I N E E
E D D Y · G E E · N E S T
```

Solution to: May 1, 1965

```
A L A · T O P · J E T
A M I D · A L I · E T O N
B O O M · L E E · A U R A
E R N I E B O R G N I N E
· R I O · R E V ·
T E N A N T · E L A T E D
O R A L · · N I N A
T E N N I S · S I D N E Y
· E V E · A C E ·
M I L L Y A N D E R S O N
I R I S · T E D · P L A Y
A M M O · E E L · Y O R E
A N N · D D E · L E S
```

Solution to: September 18, 1965

```
A G A R · M F R · E C H O
D E L E · A R E · D O O B
D R E E · G A D · S O U R
A M · L I O N · T R I
M A N · R O C S · T E L E
S N O R E · E T U I · O N
· F R A N K S U T T O N
G I · H E R B · T O N G S
E G G S · C A J E · E S T
R H O · V E R A · H A
A T O P · S I R · C H O L
R E S E · E E R · H O W E
D R E G · T R Y · E A S Y
```

Solution to: December 11, 1965

```
C L I O · O F T H E S E A
O A R Y · D O N A D A M S
S N E E · O R T S · B I T
T A N S · R R · E U L A
E W E · E L L Y
L O · L A S S I E · A D E
L O N G H O T S U M M E R
O D E · A R T I S T · A S
· E S A U · I R K
S P O T · C E · G O B I
O A K · P I K A · A N O N
B U R L I V E S · S I R E
S L A T T E R Y · H A N S
```

Solution to: April 9, 1966

```
· E D I E · M U R P H Y
O V A T E · N A T A L I E
H A V E N · E L · Y E L L
· G E M · A T T U · A L P
P A R · S D · E S S
A B O A R D · D A T E D
L O S S · · O D O R
· R E E S E · G L A N C E
· A I D · A T · E A T
T A B · S M O G · L L D
A L U M · O N · S U S A N
L A R A I N E · A T O M S
L E G E N D · D E N S
```

Solution to: June 18, 1966

```
· E N D · A V I V · L A C
P L E A · L A L O · O D A
A L A I · L I L Y · L A S
M A R S H A L · A D A M S
· I O N · A G A · W I
V I E W · T I E · T E D
S I T S · F O R · N O S Y
A C T · T I M · B A R T
M T · E A T · C A T
B O B B Y · M A H A L I A
O R E · L O A N · L I L T
L I E · O D I E · I N E E
T A T · R E D S · E D D
```

Solution to: June 25, 1966

```
HALL  . LAC . RAH
AVOID . IDA . OBI
MORSE . MAR . BUG
. WILLIAMSMITH .
. ELM . SOON .
BEA . APT . NOSES
ULLA . SAY . DOVE
DIANA . BOB . NAT
. NODS . GAP .
JOHNDAVIDSON .
AGA . ARA . GAPES
ILL . MAN . ELITE
LEE . SHE . MESA
```

Solution to: July 9, 1966

```
PETER . CARUSO
UNITED . LIPTON
RD . AIR . ADM . LE
SOL . DAVIS . BAA
ERAL . PAM . CARL
. AWAKEN . SARI .
. RED . DAB .
. OLGA . MALONE
SNEE . SIN . TEDS
HEW . SWAIN . TAP
AI . TOE . EER . MA
PLEASE . LEADER
ELLIOT . REESE
```

Solution to: August 6, 1966

```
KAYE . JUD . FALK
ALAN . ERE . EDEN
OIL . ADAM . WANE
STEPS . LAG . MAW
. RH . RUSS .
SOLO . CHEST . AL
PHEW . LES . JANE
AM . SMART . OPIE
. AEON . AH .
ABC . ANA . INGER
BARE . IDOL . ALE
LEEK . SET . ELSE
ERSE . HST . BEAD
```

Solution to: November 26, 1966

```
. CHARLES . EVER
DIETRICH . VILE
ETA . PHI . ACME
WELLS . ORT . TOD
. EAR . TORO .
PELICAN . THREE
ALE . TUB . IRA
NIECE . TARRANT
. CLEW . DII .
BAR . RIB . MARTA
ALAN . LEA . IAN
TINA . LANDLORD
STEP . STARETT
```

Solution to: April 1, 1967

```
MAPS . ELMS . MID
ALAN . TILT . IDO
METE . AMOR . CLU
ACRES . BROTHER
. IRON . PEA .
NBC . LINT . DEFY
OAK . ONEAL . LIE
DAME . EDGE . CBS
. ALB . SARA .
MCCLURE . KELLY
URN . FADE . ELIA
LEE . FRED . SANK
EWE . YENS . ENDS
```

Solution to: May 20, 1967

```
PAPA . LEAP . EDD
ALAN . ETNA . DIE
REID . SENTINEL
TERRY . ROOTS
. EON . HOUR .
ABC . MOTEL . TOM
LEO . MOA . ONA
BAR . EARTH . NED
. BOLD . HUB .
STEEL . GRETA
PATRICIA . ADAM
ART . OARS . NIKE
SOS . TREK . DEES
```

Solution to: July 1, 1967

```
WADE . ALL . TSAR
ARID . MAE . AMIE
RIO . CATS . MADE
DARBY . EBB . RED
. AD . REST .
HOST . SCOTT . KO
ADAM . TOW . EDEN
LE . AGARN . LANE
. ONER . DL .
ANN . ETA . RANDY
PIES . RUBY . ARE
SCAT . ERA . EMIL
EELY . KAY . REPP
```

Solution to: July 8, 1967

```
LAHR . DAD . DONG
ALAI . RIO . ALEE
MARC . ARR . VEIN
ANTHEM . ORIOLE
. AVA . TAD .
OHARA . THEMAID
CORD . BOY . CLAY
TACKLED . SCENE
. ION . MIA .
LEMMON . ATLAST
ARAB . END . LEAH
MILL . TEA . URGE
PETE . TOM . MOAN
```

Solution to: September 2, 1967

```
CUD . PAUL . ADAM
AGA . ALSO . LENA
PHYLLISDILLER
ESSE . EEN .
. EARN . CHIMP
ESP . MATS . ISLE
THESILENTSPOT
NORA . AREA . YRS
ATENT . PEPE .
. BAR . AMES
BENJAMINPRIDE
OTOE . OSAR . KEN
WARD . SEGO . END
```

Solution to: April 20, 1968

```
CLEM . ABC . SAM
LAVA . COO . LADE
AMIR . OAR . IRIS
WALTER . SONATA
. INN . AID .
EMEND . GULAGER
GIRL . CUT . COLE
GLEASON . GRADY
. NUN . SAI .
WARDEN . ASSERT
AREA . OBI . TROY
LIEU . RON . ALAR
TAD . SOT . LENO
```

Solution to: August 3, 1968

```
PAL . JED . NBC
ARID . IRA . POUR
DESI . MAYBERRY
SATAN . SAT .
. NEAR . LEGAL
. LIABLE . ERNIE
SUCH . AGE . GALE
OBEYS . AVERTS
BERLE . LAVA .
. AWL . EVANS
IRONSIDE . EDEN
LORD . FAR . SARA
EYE . ENE . MOP
```

Solution to: September 28, 1968

```
WRIT . LAMP . POD
HIGH . OLIO . RAY
OTOE . GUNSMOKE
MARGE . MESA
. ODD . EYES
ALTO . IDA . BRAY
CORD . CON . ELLA
TRIG . KEN . REEK
. DOUG . ERR .
. YOGI . AYRES
GETSMART . RUDE
EVE . ELIA . FLEA
MAD . REST . DENT
```

Solution to: October 5, 1968

```
BED ADAMS  CAW
AMA CINCH  ODE
HUNDRED RALES
  CUES  SOLO
TEENS  SQUARES
RARE FEUDS  DC
ERS TEXAS  EGO
AT BREED  SPAT
THREADS SHIRT
  ELMS BOAT
SCALP  BOBHOPE
HAD AWARE  MAY
EDS SEDER  ENE
```

Solution to: November 9, 1968

```
HOG  BIG   SAD
OMAR ERR  ALLE
SILO SKI  LISA
STABLE  FELDON
   EAT FOE
AWARD  DINNERS
RANT BEN  LOOK
TRAMPAS  DUSTY
   OIL SOD
BARREL  ENDORA
USES APE  EPIC
RILE RED  NAME
RAY  DAY   LES
```

Solution to: May 24, 1969

```
ACME  BIL  MAST
MUIR  ADA  ABLE
ELK  CREW  EBON
SPEAR ART  OWN
   MY  EAST
CORA DONNA  PI
ALAN ARC  NORM
RE DANTE  DROP
  BAER   JR
TAR  COP  EAGER
OTIS WARD  ADE
UTAH AGE  ALEE
TUNE NED  LEND
```

Solution to: June 21, 1969

```
 TAD JUDD   EKE
SOLO EDIE  VAS
AMOR DONADAMS
LEWIS   NAGS
   SIT  ANNA
ELK AUDRA  BAA
VEE  LED  OWN
EEN ALLEN  REY
  BENE  NEB
 SEMI   DUFFY
CERUSICO FIRE
BAR SOUL  FLIP
SLY ANTE  YET
```

Solution to: June 28, 1969

```
BAT HEAR  GALA
ODE ANNE  EDAM
BONANZA  STAMP
  NEO CHIMPS
STAGY  THAT
HARE SAID  SPA
ARTLINKLETTER
DAY REED  HALL
  SOAR MARLO
PODUNK  HOT
AMASS  GORSHIN
TINA MOWS  ACE
STAN COLE  LET
```

Solution to: August 9, 1969

```
FATE  ASP   SAG
EMIL ACHE  ARA
ZIMMERMAN  INN
   REED  SNAG
TERESA   BETZ
STARK ALAN
PAT INTER  TOR
  KNEE  BOONE
FREE  BARNEY
SION SOAR
PER ZIMBALIST
ELK ODAY  ECHO
DDE EER  SEEM
```

Solution to: August 16, 1969

```
ALICE  AND  ADA
LEROY REE  DOG
IRENE ELY  ADO
  SANS  SMOG
ABET NAOMI
JEREMY NA  AFT
ALINE  MARLO
RAN EG CARTER
  STRAY MEAN
GOWN EDDS
ALE MEL  TAMER
REB ANI  UNCLE
BOB DEB  DAVID
```

Solution to: November 1, 1969

```
 SHADOWS  DIET
THATGIRL IRMA
ION  LEA  POMP
PEDAL NBC  NYE
  DEE SONS
MEADOWS  BAIRD
INN EAT  DAD
ADDER  DEADEYE
  EGAD ANI
FOR PES  DECRY
ELSA LOU  LIE
LION LUMPLUMP
TONY APPLEBY
```

Solution to: November 22, 1969

```
LANA  LID   SAM
ICER TORE  ILE
LEEMARVIN  GOA
   RUES  THEN
DEBBIE   POTS
ARIES NORM
NAG IRENE  ATE
  ANEW SAXON
KING  ALTERS
HARD TONE
ETA SHADYREST
LIT PITY  ELIE
DEE ASS  DINA
```

Solution to: January 24, 1970

```
 ELEANOR  ERIN
IRONSIDE RENO
RIB  BEG  RYAN
SCOTT RIM  NEE
  ERE SOLO
ASTAIRE MILLY
NEO ABA  DOE
TAMMY  BRONSON
  JOEY IDA
FRO TAR  EBSEN
RONA LEE  NEB
EDEN TINACOLE
DESI ANDREWS
```

Solution to: February 21, 1970

```
WEBB CBS  CLEM
AREA HOT  ROME
SEER ALA  IRIS
 BRIANKEITH
AFFAIR  LID
BOARD DEN  FED
LENA GAY  GORE
ESS DON  BERLE
  SOL CENTER
MARCCOPAGE
ERIE NOR  ROSE
LION KEN  ADAM
DATE ATE  LETS
```

Solution to: March 21, 1970

```
IDEA  COLE  SEA
BOLD AMERICAN
ERLE RED  DARN
XI  ANN  LORNE
 SLADE SOL
ADAMS PAT  DRY
RANI JIM  LIED
AYE SEN  TONYS
  AID JASON
REGIS JAM  OR
ITEM EON  LYLE
FORSYTHE LODE
TNT BENT  DUSK
```

Solution to: April 18, 1970

S	E	R	B		M	A	N	O	L	I	T	O
E	R	I	E		A	M	E	R	I	C	A	N
B	I	N	G		L	E	T		L	I	N	E
A	C		O	N	E	S		P	I	E		
S	C	E	N	E	S		P	I	E	R	R	E
T	H	R	E	E		B	O	A	S		O	S
I	A	N		D	E	E	D	S		D	O	M
A	S		G	L	A	D		T	E	A	S	E
N	E	A	R	E	R		L	E	N	D	E	R
	L	E	S		B	E	R	G		V	A	
A	R	T	E		L	E	A		A	B	E	L
R	E	E	N	T	E	R	S		G	I	L	D
M	E	R	E	D	I	T	H		E	T	T	A

Solution to: May 2, 1970

D	O	G		B	R	A	G		A	D	A	M
I	R	A		E	A	R	L		G	A	L	E
P	A	L		R	I	C	E		E	L	A	N
	L	L	O	Y	D	H	A	Y	N	E	S	
		O	W	L	S		S	A	T			
H	A	W	N		S	O	L		P	A	T	
E	V	A		S	C	E	N	E		A	G	A
P	A	Y		A	R	T		S	T	E	P	
	E	L	I		C	H	A	R				
	J	A	M	E	S	B	R	O	L	I	N	
C	U	R	B		T	E	A	M		C	A	R
A	N	T	E		A	N	N	E		I	V	Y
P	E	E	R		L	E	E	R		A	Y	E

Solution to: August 8, 1970

E	D	A	M		S	P	T		B	A	E	R
D	O	T	E		L	O	O		L	U	L	U
I	D	O	L		A	N	N		A	K	I	N
T	O	M	A	N	D	D	I	C	K			
			N	A	E		G	R	E	E	N	E
C	R	A	I	G		T	H	Y		M	O	D
R	O	L	E		A	R	T		B	I	O	G
A	N	A		A	M	Y		L	O	R	N	E
B	A	N	A	N	A		S	O	B			
			D	I	N	A	H	S	H	O	R	E
M	A	M	A		D	I	E		O	R	A	L
A	D	A	M		A	D	E		P	A	I	L
C	A	S	S		S	E	N		E	N	D	S

Solution to: October 17, 1970

T	I	N	A		C	A	R	D		I	L	K
A	R	I	D		A	G	I	O		V	A	N
B	A	C	H		B	O	B	C	R	A	N	E
U	S	H	E	R	S			A	N	E	W	
		O	R	E		F	O	R	M			
V	A	L	E	T	N	I	N	E		E	D	S
I	N	A		T	A	L	E	S		M	I	A
A	D	S		A	R	M	S	T	R	O	N	G
		A	L	A	S		E	A	T			
S	T	A	R			E	D	D	I	E	S	
H	A	W	A	I	I	A	N		I	O	T	A
U	T	A		A	C	I	D		A	N	D	Y
N	A	Y		N	E	T	S		L	S	S	S

Solution to: January 16, 1971

G	I	N		A	B	C		F	O	P
L	O	O	M		S	E	E		H	O	U	R
E	T	U	I		K	E	N	B	E	R	R	Y
N	A	N	C	Y		T	A	N				
		H	E	I	R		G	R	A	D	Y	
C	A	N	A	S	T	A		S	Y	R	I	A
O	T	O	E		S	I	N		G	I	L	L
W	O	R	L	D		L	U	C	I	L	L	E
S	P	A	C	E		S	N	O	B			
		O	S	E			O	S	C	A	R	
W	I	L	L	I	A	M	S		O	L	E	O
E	D	I	E		R	A	H		N	E	R	O
B	A	T		L	Y	E		M	O	D		

Solution to: March 6, 1971

D	A	M		G	I	R	L		C	L	U
L	A	N	A		A	R	I	A		H	I	S
E	N	D	S		L	E	T	S	M	A	K	E
M	A	Y	O	R			S	E	R	E		
		N	E	W		S	I	L	L			
L	E	S		V	A	N	C	E		T	I	S
A	V	A		L	E	O		O	D	E	
S	A	M		E	L	T	O	N		N	A	N
		A	N	D	Y		P	E	T			
	S	N	A	G			D	O	N	N	A	
B	A	T	T	E	R	E	D		T	O	O	N
A	S	H		O	I	L	Y		I	R	O	N
A	H	A		F	A	K	E		E	A	N	

Solution to: March 13, 1971

P	O	W		S	N	I	P		C	H	E	R
E	V	E		P	A	A	R		H	O	L	E
D	E	S		A	N	N	E		E	L	I	A
I	N	T	E	R	N	S		R	E	B	E	L
		S	K	Y		B	U	R	R			
H	O	L	M	S		F	A	N		O	D	D
A	L	E	E		D	E	Y		J	O	I	N
L	E	E		J	O	E		K	U	K	L	A
		J	O	A	N		A	N	D			
P	E	C	A	N		C	L	O	Y	I	N	G
A	M	O	S		A	H	I	T		V	A	N
G	I	B	E		P	A	C	T		E	V	A
O	R	B	S		O	N	E	S		S	E	T

Solution to: July 17, 1971

P	A	T	T	E		A	C	R	E	S
R	E	R	U	N	S		M	A	G	G	I	E
O	D	E	R		E	G	E	R		O	D	D
D	E	A	N	S		A	N	N	A		S	O
			S	T	I	R		E	V	A		
A	V	E		A	R	A	M		A	N	N	E
D	A	D		R	O	G	E	R		D	E	S
E	L	I	E		N	I	L	E		Y	E	S
		E	A	T		O	S	S	A			
M	P		R	O	L	L		T	A	L	E	S
A	R	U		R	E	A	P		R	O	D	E
S	E	S	A	M	E		G	E	O	R	G	E
P	E	T	E	R		A	R	N	I	E		

Solution to: August 7, 1971

S	K	I		S	H	E	D		W	I	L	D
H	E	R		H	O	L	E		A	R	E	A
O	R	E		R	U	S	E		N	O	E	L
E	R	S	K	I	N	E		H	E	N	R	Y
			E	N	D		C	A	D	S		
F	R	A	N	K		L	A	W		I	A	N
R	E	N	T		D	E	L		E	D	G	E
O	D	D		J	O	E		T	R	E	E	D
		J	O	A	N		M	O	I			
B	L	O	W	N		J	U	K	E	B	O	X
L	I	N	E		G	A	L	E		E	A	R
A	D	E	N		E	V	E	N		E	T	A
B	O	S	S		T	A	S	S		S	H	Y

Solution to: November 6, 1971

A	C	T		A	M	E	S		F	O	R	D
D	A	R		L	A	N	E		A	L	O	E
A	T	E		A	R	I	D		N	E	A	L
	S	A	N	D	Y	D	U	N	C	A	N	
		S	A	Y	S		C	O	Y			
D	O	U	G		L	E	S		B	O	B	
E	A	R		S	M	A	S	H		A	V	A
S	T	Y		H	I	M		A	D	A	M	
		S	O	S		S	A	N	D			
	J	A	M	E	S	G	A	R	N	E	R	
D	A	L	I		I	O	N	S		L	A	D
A	K	A	L		O	N	T	O		E	V	A
G	E	N	E		N	E	O	N		Y	E	N

Solution to: November 13, 1971

O	D	D		C	L	O	T		J	I	G	S
L	E	O		A	L	A	R		I	D	L	E
D	A	N		D	O	T	E		M	E	E	T
	L	A	R	R	Y	H	A	G	M	A	N	
		D	E	E	D		S	A	Y			
C	H	A	D		T	O	M		C	B	S	
A	I	M		S	C	E	N	E		L	E	E
W	E	S		H	A	D		M	A	N	E	
		S	O	S		S	T	A	R			
	J	A	M	E	S	G	A	R	N	E	R	
T	A	L	I		I	O	T	A		N	Y	E
U	N	I	T		D	R	I	P		C	A	R
B	E	T	H		Y	E	N	S		E	N	E

Solution to: December 18, 1971

H	O	P	E		D	A	Y		K	E	N
A	R	T	E		T	I	M	E		A	D	A
D	E	A	N	J	O	N	E	S		R	I	O
			A	N	O	N		B	E	E	S	
J	O	H	N	N	Y		S	O	N	S		
A	D	A	M	S		S	O	H	O			
B	E	N		S	H	O	R	E		R	O	B
		R	E	E	D		R	H	O	D	A	
	O	D	I	N		A	M	A	N	D	A	
S	H	O	P		A	N	N	A				
T	A	R		G	L	E	N	N	F	O	R	D
A	R	I		A	B	C	S		A	L	O	E
G	A	S		D	A	K		T	E	D	S	

Solution to: January 1, 1972

```
TAJ  SERF  GIG
GILA AMIE  ORE
ADAM GUNSMOKE
TENET    TEDS
    SAM FULL
DOM BONUS  ICE
EVA  RUN   FAN
WAR DANNY  ERA
   SOUL  YES
  SHUN   PARIS
BEARCATS  RENT
ELL  AREA GENE
ALL  NEAT  EDS
```

Solution to: January 8, 1972

```
ARM    ELF   PIE
LEAD   LEO  TELL
ANTI  MARSHALL
NOTCH    DOE
    KISS  UPSET
  CAVETT  SALVE
TINA  YUL  RUED
ETONS  CENTER
LYNDE  KEEN
   YAM   BEARS
JACKLORD  RYAN
ABBE  SEA  SAGA
WES   SPY   HEP
```

Solution to: January 15, 1972

```
HER  OARS  DADS
ADE  SWAP  ALOU
SID  CANE  NEON
  EDWARDASNER
    FORD  KAY
ALOE   MEL   PEN
REX  SPARE  RAT
COX  ERR   RUTH
   TWO   APED
  JOHNMCGIVER
NOPE  IRAN  NET
FEAR  SATE  CAR
LYLE  EWES  ELI
```

Solution to: February 26, 1972

```
STATES    SAD
AMERICAN  ADES
HOST  LIE  MAMA
AGT SALLY  YAK
    HIT  LAD RA
BEAT     MANET
EERY      VISA
DARED     PITT
DR  SOT   TED
ICE SHIRT  BSA
EASE  ASE ROAN
STAR TINACOLE
SUE    STUART
```

Solution to: May 27, 1972

```
ANNE  ACTS  ADD
HEEL  BLOT  MIA
HIVE  AUTO  ELL
ALANS BEVERLY
  PAUL   ELI
SEA  DOOR  SCAR
ART  SCRUB  ANE
MATT OTTO  NIX
  EEL   HOSS
VERDUGO  MOTTO
EDS  CODA  RYAN
RIO  IRON  ELSE
YEN  EERY  LESS
```

Solution to: July 8, 1972

```
BAG  ABCS  ABLE
ONA  MAIM  DEAN
BERNARDI   HAND
   ONE   THERE
AGONY   CHER
LIME  CLARENCE
ERN  ARENA  ORD
CLIFFORD  ARUG
  RANK   BLAZE
  CLARK   LEE
LCAN  IRONSIDE
ERIC  TERN  CAR
GENE  EDDY  EYE
```

Solution to: August 26, 1972

```
WEAVER     RID
KINGSTON  IDAS
ERIE  HOE  PENT
NED PETER  ARE
   TAR DEB  OR
BERT      BROWN
LURE       ALAS
ACRES      EDEN
RH  SID  ANY
SAM REELS  GAY
ONES AMI  DALE
NATO  NICHOLAS
NEW    REINER
```

Solution to: December 2, 1972

```
BANACEK   OGLE
COMEDIAN  DEAL
ONE  ARE  DONS
DORIS SET  REE
  ICED   SING
MICHAEL  PIETY
EVA  YON   POE
LYNDA  STREETS
  SARK   HARP
AMT  AHA  TAPED
DAYS  ALA   AGO
ISLE  KANGAROO
THEN  INNARDS
```

Solution to: December 9, 1972

```
ADAM  COG  TERM
DESI  ODE  IDEA
DEAL  SIN  GNAT
   BOBNEWHART
UNRULY    RAT
MOORE  BAR  ERA
BEAN  BEL  BAUR
OLD  RAN  BURST
   SIR  BARNEY
HUGHOBRIAN
ANNO  AER  ERIE
STAR  RED  TONY
HOWE  ADS  TYKE
```

Solution to: February 10, 1973

```
MADIGAN   OMAR
LAURENCE  DONE
EST  URE   DUNE
SHOWS EDS   NED
   AIL  SALT
FORSTER   MEARA
ARI  TOM    ITE
DICKS  BRYNNER
  HOPE   SUE
SPA  YDS  LEDGE
EARL  GIG   OAR
RIDE  ALANALDA
ELSE  ROBERTS
```

Solution to: March 10, 1973

```
CHARLES   TMAN
ALANALDA  ECRU
PAL  BIL   EMIT
TYLER ELF   IDS
   LON  YELL
HAWKEYE   DELTA
UGH  ELM    AIL
MAIDS  SUZANNE
  TREE   DID
DAM  ALS  PETER
AMOS  LAW   OWE
LIRA  ALANSUES
EDEN  STREETS
```

Solution to: April 14, 1973

```
SAM  ELS   LIFT
ORE  LOOP  UTAH
WAR  OVAL  PERI
 TEMPERATURES
   DOES  YES
FLIP   BEA   HEC
ROT  PEARL  ERR
ASH  ANT   DRAY
   OAR   APES
SANFRANCISCO
KNOT  PAUL  HIT
INRE  TITO  ELI
SEAN  LET   LYE
```

278

Solution to: May 12, 1973

```
F L I P ■ A F T ■ E R I C
R O O T ■ G E O ■ D O R A
E D W ■ S E E M ■ S W A P
D E A L S ■ S P Y ■ A N T
■ ■ I E ■ K E A N ■ ■ ■
D E B T ■ A L I S T A I R
A L I T ■ L A N ■ E N D O
W I L L I A M S ■ A D A Y
■ L E A N ■ ■ A S ■ ■
F E M ■ N A P ■ P E T E R
A L A N ■ L A C E ■ O P E
L I C E ■ D U B ■ M O E S
K A Y E ■ A L S ■ S T E T
```

Solution to: August 18, 1973

```
T A T ■ A D A M ■ O T T O
O B I ■ L O L A ■ T A R N
M C M I L L A N ■ O B O E
■ ■ V I E ■ T R O U P ■
E L L E N ■ P O O L ■ ■
L O I S ■ C L O S E U P S
A V A ■ E L A T E ■ N E T
M E R E D I T H ■ R I T A
■ ■ L I F E ■ D A T E R
■ C H I E F ■ L E T ■ ■
A L E X ■ O N A M A T C H
B I B I ■ R E N O ■ E R E
A P E R ■ D E A N ■ D O C
```

Solution to: October 13, 1973

```
D A N E ■ D O M ■ S H E
A G E E ■ T I N A ■ N A Y
R O B R E I N E R ■ O Y E
■ ■ L E E S ■ J O E S ■
M E L E E S ■ R I P S ■ ■
E L E N A ■ A D A M ■ ■
L I T ■ N A N C Y ■ O L D
■ L O R D ■ M A R I A ■
■ G E E R ■ D O N A L D
P E D I ■ G A I N ■ ■ ■
U N I ■ B I L L D A I L Y
N E T ■ O V A L ■ G L E E
I S H ■ B E N ■ A L D A
```

Solution to: November 3, 1973

```
P A P A ■ D E C ■ M E A D
I D O L ■ E R E ■ I D L E
P A U L ■ M I A ■ L I E N
■ M R I R O N S I D E S ■
■ ■ N O N ■ E R R ■ ■
R I P ■ D D T ■ K E N N Y
A R A B ■ S I G ■ D I N O
P E T E R ■ M R S ■ B E N
■ ■ N A G ■ A I M ■ ■
■ T O N Y R A N D A L L ■
R U D E ■ I N D ■ R E E L
A B E T ■ F A M ■ L O N E
T E S T ■ F L A ■ O N T O
```

Solution to: February 23, 1974

```
B O S S ■ L S D ■ G A L E
A L A N ■ O E R ■ E V I L
R E N O ■ R E A ■ O I L S
■ G E O P E P P A R D S ■
■ ■ P A T ■ E R G ■ ■
P A M ■ S T E ■ T E L L Y
E R I C ■ A L P ■ S E E R
R A D A R ■ I R E ■ W E S
■ ■ N E E ■ E V E ■ ■
■ T O N Y M U S A N T E ■
B O N O ■ I S T ■ T O N Y
O M E N ■ L E O ■ E R I E
B A S S ■ Y E N ■ R E D S
```

Solution to: July 13, 1974

```
A L D A ■ T E A M ■ J A M
S O A R ■ H A L E ■ A B E
H U S T L E R ■ D A N E S
■ ■ H E N ■ L I M I T S
D E B U T ■ L A C E S ■ ■
O M A R ■ T U B A S ■ L A
S I R ■ C A R O L ■ D O R
E T ■ C A P E R ■ R O O M
■ B O R E S ■ T I M M Y
S M E A R S ■ L A P ■ ■
T O N T O ■ A I R P O R T
A N N ■ L I V E ■ E R I E
R A Y ■ L E A N ■ R E E D
```

Solution to: August 10, 1974

```
A D S ■ J E A N ■ F R E D
L I T ■ D U N E ■ L E N A
A C E ■ B A S ■ O D D S
N E W S C A S T E R ■ ■
■ ■ T O N ■ S K I ■ O C
B A R ■ O K S ■ E D I T H
E R I C ■ S E W ■ A L O E
A L O H A ■ T I M ■ L E W
N O ■ O H M ■ T I A ■ ■
■ P S Y C H O L O G Y
F L I P ■ R O E ■ G O O
A I D E ■ O U R S ■ R A G
T E A R ■ N E S S ■ E L I
```

Solution to: September 21, 1974

```
R O B ■ B O B ■ J E F F
I D A ■ D O L E ■ A B L E
M E D ■ A L D A ■ M E A N
■ D E M O S T H E N E S
G R E E N ■ R E S ■ ■
W I L L ■ E V I E ■ L A B
E T E S ■ V A C ■ G A L E
N A Y ■ P E T E ■ A W E S
■ F E R ■ S I R E S ■
G E O R G E A P P L E ■
A L M A ■ T E R I ■ N E A
S I A N ■ T R O T ■ C O X
H A N K ■ S O N ■ E N E
```

Solution to: September 28, 1974

```
R O C K ■ J O E ■ B O B
A R I A ■ E I R E ■ A N E
M A R Y T Y L E R ■ G E E
■ ■ H E L L ■ J E A N
T A N N E R ■ B I L L
R H O D A ■ E L A M
E A T ■ P A P E R ■ B E A
■ P E L T ■ B R O W N
■ T E A S ■ D A R R E N
P E S T ■ D O O R ■ ■
A R T ■ V A N P A T T E N
U R E ■ A L E E ■ O B E Y
L Y S ■ L E S ■ M A L E
```

Solution to: October 26, 1974

```
P E T E ■ R T S ■ A D A
T E A R ■ S O R E ■ L A G
A L B E R T S O N ■ L V E
■ ■ O A S T ■ M A I D
L A N D O N ■ S A N D
D E R E K ■ K A T E
S R A ■ I R E N E ■ C O P
■ J E A N ■ W A Y N E
■ G E O S ■ M A L D E N
C E N E ■ L E A R
H O G ■ G O O D T I M E S
A R E ■ E R N E ■ M O R E
S G L ■ T D S ■ P E R A
```

Solution to: December 14, 1974

```
M A M A ■ D A D ■ E B E N
I L E S ■ E G O ■ B R I E
L E A ■ A L E C ■ B A R D
T E L L Y ■ S A M ■ C E S
■ ■ I E ■ D I C K ■ ■
M A R T ■ C H A R L E Y S
O M I T ■ R I M ■ O T E S
M A C L E O D S ■ S T O W
■ ■ H E R N ■ D E ■ ■
A B A ■ E K E ■ A R N E R
C A R L ■ I R O N ■ E R I
R I D E ■ T I N ■ O V I S
E N S E ■ E N E ■ Z A C K
```

Solution to: January 11, 1975

```
M O P ■ S E W ■ S P E D
E N A ■ B L A H ■ P E R A
L O U ■ E I R E ■ O R A L
■ L I T T L E H O U S E
P O S S E ■ L O N ■ ■
O P A L ■ P O E T ■ B A S
G E N E ■ R U R ■ T E N T
O D D ■ H E R S ■ R A T A
■ D A N ■ O U T E R
L U C A S T A N N E R
I R O N ■ I R A E ■ I D A
M A I N ■ S O N S ■ C O X
A L L Y ■ S E A ■ E N E
```

279

Solution to: February 22, 1975

```
R I G █ P A S █ █ █ O N █
E N E █ A W A Y █ █ G A L S
A M E █ L A N D █ █ E M M A
P Y R A M I D █ █ S E E I T
█ █ █ M E T █ C O S T █ █ █
M A J O R █ J O N █ █ H E █
A R E S █ █ A I D █ M A Y O
█ T O █ A L M █ P E T E R █
█ █ █ P A U L █ M I A █ █ █
C L A R K █ W I N N I N G █
B E R T █ L Y N N █ N E A █
S A D I █ O N C E █ T O M █
█ █ Y E █ N E D █ O N E █ █
```

Solution to: March 29, 1975

```
C H A D █ B A T █ S C A B █
L U R E █ R I O █ T O M E █
U S E R █ E D W █ R O B T █
█ K A R E N A N G E L O █ █
█ █ █ Y O D █ S U E █ █ █ █
A M P █ S A L █ S T E V E █
N O R M █ S E A █ S W A T █
G R O O M █ E R N █ E N E █
█ █ V E R █ C E T █ █ █ █ █
█ K H I G H D H I E G H █ █
B A I N █ O R E █ M E O W █
O T R O █ D A R █ P A T E █
B E E N █ A M S █ O L L A █
```

Solution to: April 12, 1975

```
J A N █ A S K █ █ █ C A M █
A L A N █ P O I █ J U N E █
M A M A █ P U N █ A R T E █
B R E N D A █ █ G A M B I T
█ █ █ C O L █ D I E █ █ █ █
S A T Y R █ F O R S T E R █
A N E W █ D A M █ G A G E █
P Y R A M I D █ C A R O L █
█ █ L A G █ B A R █ █ █ █ █
B A R K E R █ A R N E S S █
A L O E █ E R R █ E R I C █
S T A R █ S I R █ R I T A █
S O N █ S P Y █ █ █ N E T █
```

Solution to: May 24, 1975

```
█ L A W A N D A P A G E █ █
V A L E R I E H A R P E R █
A V A L O N █ █ █ I S L E █
N A █ L E A █ D A S █ S T █
█ A E R █ R E S E T █ █ █ █
B I D S █ J A C K N A R Z █
A C E █ A U T O S █ H O E █
R E P O R T E R █ D O W N █
█ █ T R I E S █ D Y E █ █ █
A S █ W A S █ P A N █ M A █
S H O E █ █ A V A T A R █ █
H O T L B A L T I M O R E █
█ P O L I C E S T O R Y █ █
```

Solution to: June 28, 1975

```
H O A G █ █ B O B █ A S H █
A R I A █ P A V E █ A C E █
M A R Y E L L E N █ M O M █
█ █ █ V A I N █ L E T S █ █
E N D M A N █ █ C A S T █ █
M A S O N █ G O O D █ █ █ █
U N O █ S T O R M █ G A R █
█ █ R E E D █ P I E T A █ █
█ P R O S █ C A R T E R █ █
M O A N █ M E A N █ █ █ █ █
U R N █ H A P P Y D A Y S █
F T C █ E R I N █ O P I E █
F O E █ N Y C █ N O P E █ █
```

Solution to: July 12, 1975

```
G R O H █ J O B █ █ R A J A
B E L A █ O P E █ O V E N █
S E E R █ S E A █ B E A N █
█ M O R G E N S T E R N █ █
█ █ █ Y E P █ T E R █ █ █ █
A G E █ T H E █ S T A C Y █
R U T H █ S O F █ S T A R █
O S C A R █ S O G █ E D S █
█ █ R A P █ R E E █ █ █ █ █
█ E S T H E R R O L L E █ █
E D A M █ T O E █ C O L A █
D E N A █ E S S █ A V I D █
W R E N █ R E T █ R E A D █
```

Solution to: August 16, 1975

```
A N T █ B A T █ █ █ P L A T █
B O O █ E L I A █ R O N A █
C A M █ G E E R █ E V I L █
█ H O W A R D C O S E L L █
█ █ R A N T █ H A S █ █ █ █
M A R Y █ F I R █ █ M A T █
A D O █ S A L E S █ E N E █
N E W █ P R Y █ █ A L D A █
█ █ S A L █ M E R V █ █ █ █
E R I C S E V A R E I D █ █
L E N O █ N E R O █ L E O █
M A T T █ E N I D █ L A W █
S L O T █ T E E █ E L L █ █
```

Solution to: October 18, 1975

```
█ B R I D G E S █ A M E S █
L E E G R A N T █ L I S A █
I L I █ R I O █ S T A N █
L A N C E █ F R A █ C U E █
█ █ A R T █ Y E A H █ █ █ █
P E P P A R D █ S T E V E █
O L A █ Y I P █ L I V █ █ █
P A L I K █ P H Y L L I S █
█ █ A L A N █ D A E █ █ █ █
M A N █ M O R █ R O B I N █
O N C E █ R I A █ A D O █ █
A N E S █ M C M I L L A N █
B E S S █ S H A T N E R █ █
```

Solution to: May 1, 1976

```
A M E N █ B O B █ S A R A █
R I C E █ A B E █ C L I P █
A C R E █ R E T █ A I D S █
█ A U D R E Y T O T T E R █
█ █ █ S I T █ Y A M █ █ █ █
P E T █ O T T █ R A D A R █
A R A B █ A I M █ N O V A █
T R O U P █ M O D █ N A Y █
█ █ R A W █ V I A █ █ █ █ █
J O H N D A V I D S O N █ █
A L E E █ Y E N █ N O A H █
B E R T █ N E O █ E Z R A █
S O O T █ E R N █ R E D S █
```

Solution to: May 15, 1976

```
O F F █ M E W █ █ █ S H E D █
W A R █ C O R E █ T O N Y █
N Y E █ I R I S █ E P E E █
█ █ D E T E C T I V E S █ █
R E D D Y █ E V E █ █ █ █ █
A R I D █ G A R Y █ G A S █
J O E Y █ A N N █ V A L E █
A S S █ L L D S █ E M I T █
█ █ H A L █ F R E S H █ █ █
█ S O A P O P E R A S █ █ █
B A R R █ W A V E █ H E R █
A G A R █ A G E D █ O R E █
D A L Y █ Y E N █ W A X █ █
```

Solution to: July 8, 1976

```
W A L T █ N O T E █ █ C B █
A R I A █ E B O N █ T H E █
F L O N █ W O N T █ W A S █
T O N Y T H E T I G E R █ █
█ █ S A R A █ O R N E █ █ █
A S █ I R S █ E A T O N █
C H A D █ T O W █ W Y N N █
H A R E M █ W A R █ E E █ █
█ N E A L █ L A B S █ █ █ █
█ M O R R I S T H E C A T █
S A L █ I N T O █ N O N E █
S I D █ A D E N █ J U N E █
E D █ N A P S █ I T E M █ █
```

Solution to: September 4, 1976

```
M A C K █ F I L M █ S T Y █
T R I O █ L A I R █ T O M █
█ C A R M E N Z A P A T A █
█ █ █ B O W █ N A T O █ █ █
T R O U P █ A N G I E █ █ █
H U N T █ G R E E R █ N B █
U S E █ P A N E L █ S U E █
G H █ S A L A D █ H A L L █
█ V E L E Z █ D E L L A █ █
█ G I G I █ T U G █ █ █ █ █
R O D O L F O H O Y O S █ █
I R A █ L A N E █ E R I C █
M E L █ O T T O █ S A D A █
```

Solution to: September 11, 1976

```
BANK  BOB  CHAP
AREA  ALA  HERO
TEAM  RAT  ARTE
 STEVEFORREST
   NIT  NIL
KEV  ETC  PETER
EVEL  ALF  SAVE
VEGAS  URI  BAD
  ULE  ALP
HENRYWINKLER
ALEE  ETA  ALEC
KARL  LON  CLAY
ENOS  LLD  EARL
```

Solution to: November 27, 1976

```
JAMB  ROB  SALK
ERIE  ILL  ALOE
TART  CIO  VARY
 BETHHOWLAND
  YEA  SAL
PEA  WRY  DAVID
ERIC  DER  SARA
GARRY  TUT  NAY
  OUT  SOD
 JACLYNSMITH
FALK  LIE  NOUN
EDGE  ELL  ANNE
DEAR  REL  HIKE
```

Solution to: December 18, 1976

```
CAAN  JOSE  TAB
OGLE  ORAL  OLE
POLLYHOLLIDAY
   SON  IVAN
BARON  GOOEY
EDEN  BEATS  KC
LAX  BRETT  TEA
AM  PAARS  DORS
 LORDS  SHORE
 POOR  ROI
RACHELROBERTS
AVA  TOOL  GAIL
MEL  TUBE  HEDY
```

Solution to: February 26, 1977

```
ASKS  SOB  SADA
NOAH  ABE  AMID
INTO  NON  VIED
 GEOFFEDWARDS
  TOO  SOL
ALE  ERR  WAITE
GONG  DON  SNOW
AUDIT  BEN  NYE
  LED  WET
BARBARAHOWAR
ALEE  ALA  IRON
STAR  MAR  RICE
SORT  ANT  LAKE
```

Solution to: March 5, 1977

```
SING  SOAP  ACE
PAAR  KNEE  NHL
ANTONIOFARGAS
  VIP  NOLTE
ENGEL  MOUSE
REAR  PARTS  FD
MAP  CORES  BOA
AL  HALTS  MERV
 SALLY  RANDY
STORY  OUR
CHAMPAGNELADY
AIR  SPOT  IGOR
RNS  OTTO  NEWS
```

Solution to: April 9, 1977

```
ALES  LOS  GABE
WALT  IVE  URAL
ERLE  NAG  ITEM
 DAVIDLANDER
  EOS  LEI
TOP  NAB  ENGEL
OLEG  YAK  GIVE
MEARA  ALL  GEE
  ARS  IER
 PINKPANTHER
FORD  ENG  ORAL
CLIP  ENE  DIVA
CASA  DER  ANEW
```

Solution to: June 4, 1977

```
 MTS  GEM  AS
MAHA  REAP  NUB
STEVEANDEYDIE
 JARS  AORTA
GREGS  ERGO
LIFE  CARLISLE
ELF  SARIS  TOM
ELECTRIC  WARM
 ROAR  HARDY
COSBY  GONG
GLOBETROTTERS
SAN  DANA  ETAL
 FS  GAL  DSM
```

Solution to: June 11, 1977

```
 ORA  ALAN  CPO
WHOS  NONE  HUN
HICK  DYNAMITE
YOKEL  ARC
 FRED  SLAVE
WHO  NONO  NEA
OUR  DIODE  DES
OLD  THEN  HST
LASER  SIVA
 LOU  DIRGE
STEFANIE  NOEL
AHA  RING  CLEM
MET  STAG  EDS
```

Solution to: July 23, 1977

```
RPM  MARC  WALT
OAR  AGAR  OLEO
YAK  IAGO  MAAM
 RONNIECLAIRE
  TEEN  KIN
KITT  BEN  FLO
UKE  SPARE  LIL
PER  ARA  MOVE
 MME  BRER
THREESTOOGES
HYER  TARS  NEE
EDEL  OPIE  CAD
MEDE  NESS  END
```

Solution to: October 22, 1977

```
BOOK  CBS  SPUN
ANNA  HAL  ZERO
NEAL  AMY  YOGI
 BAR  ASNER
OBL  BONERZ
REESE  AVENGED
CANT  ADA  YEAR
SUZANNE  UKASE
 BEARDS  RED
WORLD  IAN
AGEE  SEX  ERIN
LEER  AGO  WIDE
TEDS  DON  SPAT
```

Solution to: July 15, 1978

```
SOAR  BAR  CASH
ELLA  EYE  ARIA
EGAN  TAB  BALL
 ANDYTHEROBOT
  ARE  CAT
SEALS  ACT  LEW
HALL  MIA  VERA
ATE  ARA  AIDES
 ARM  ANN
TRICIAANDCYB
HULK  GIG  EVES
ELKE  ODE  NETS
NEAR  OAR  TSAR
```

Solution to: August 19, 1978

```
HEAP  MOP  PAST
ERLE  ILE  AMOR
MIEN  CEE  LIFE
 KENEHOLLIDAY
  YEA  SOL
OLD  LEE  GLASS
DEAL  LAB  ORAL
DAMON  ROD  AMY
 ROE  BUS
ERNESTTHOMAS
MEAT  NEO  IGOR
MART  ALP  TRUE
ALDA  SEE  HALT
```

Solution to: September 16, 1978

```
ARAB LAD  GAIL
BOLE OWE  RICE
COTE RAN  IDEA
 MORLEYSAFER
   YET  ELF
BOB  ETA  LINDA
ERIC ASH  NEAT
TODAY PEN  EYE
   SAM  MOA
 CASKEYSWAIM
BALI MEL  MOOT
EGAD OLE  ETCH
DENY SLY  SAKE
```

Solution to: October 21, 1978

```
ANGELS  CASTOR
CARROT  ARLENE
OMARS    TYLER
RAY  DIE  ODA
NT GRANDPA AN
  HELEN SALLY
   MIA  PIE
  BUNCH SEVEN
PA THEMORE EL
OLE  WOO  AWE
ELVIS   FANTA
TEETER SANTOS
STREET GREENE
```

Solution to: December 2, 1978

```
ESP  ABC  RATE
PAID WAR  ICED
IDEA ANY  CRAG
CARVER  SPHERE
   ILE  TEA
HARDY CARROLL
ERIC GAL  DRAY
MCMAHON  SHORE
   SOO  SHA
ERASED  TETHER
TAXI ERA  COMO
TIED VAN  HUMS
ANDY END  RYE
```

Solution to: April 7, 1979

```
SEW  HEM  THAN
ELI  BOAR ROLE
ALL  ROSS AGAR
 LOUFERRIGNO
STINT   OUT
ORAL TAPE JOB
LIMY EWE  PAGE
OPS  ODER ACRE
  HAL  DUKES
 MIKEFARRELL
OVEN NOON OLE
VEER GODS RON
ESPY EMS  DUD
```

Solution to: April 14, 1979

```
RAMP MAB  ROLE
EPEE ORE  ALAN
PICT RIN  MIME
 CHUCKANDBOB
STANIS  ESO
PUNIC ITO  LAB
ERIA CAT  BAIO
DEC  PAN  RAWLS
  SAM  SABRES
 NIEDERMEYER
MERV ROI  SNOW
CAME OWL  ACNE
STAN NEE  TEST
```

Solution to: July 7, 1979

```
 SIMAS  ASNER
APOLLO  TERROR
DIN  OMAHA SAO
AD  WEEKEND RS
MESH RUN  ELKE
ARNESS  ARMIES
 EER   NEL
AMAZON  DALLAS
TAKE ETE  ZINA
TR  ROSANNA IG
ITO  ABOVE AMA
CHICHI  EVIGAN
ALEUT  RAVEL
```

Solution to: November 17, 1979

```
ABNER   SPORT
BRODIE  BIRNEY
HAT  BYNER OIL
OZ   DEL   NE
RIM  VIOLA HER
 LOUIE  ACTOR
  SAN   TEL
 HERES  SEALS
PAS  STAND YES
RR   ADE   XI
IRA  STORM PTL
MINNIE  DANIEL
ASTIN   POTTS
```

Solution to: December 8, 1979

```
HOGG BAIN  SEL
AUTO AROUETTE
ITSA TIS  BATH
RO   AID  ROGER
 FRANK  NON
STEIN RAY  LST
SHEL TAN  JAYE
TED  LEE  TANNA
  HAL  DAVID
LAMAS KIT  RS
ODOR PAS  STOP
MANTOOTH  KIMO
AMT  PREY IMET
```

Solution to: May 10, 1980

```
ALAI BRA  MASH
JOHN EER  IRIS
 WAGONMASTER
  BANJO  ATA
CE  EI  SLY TF
OLGA AIL  OWL
STEVEANDEYDIE
MOE  NED  DYKE
ON  PIT JE  IT
  SEA  JULIA
 SHACKELFORD
CROC HAI  WAIT
ROWE ANE  ANNA
```

Solution to: July 12, 1980

```
KEPT LAB   PA
ANTA ERA  MADE
FOAL MGR  ALAN
 WHITMORES MD
  ARO  YES
VAN  AND  DESIS
ELOD SAM  YALE
EFREM DID  TEX
  NOS  LEA
AC  NICOLETTE
LONI AWS  ORCA
EBBS LEE  MARY
 BC  EDS  SPUN
```

Solution to: July 26, 1980

```
TATTOO   ASTHE
GRAHAM  ESTHER
 PETE TIE  AA
 HELENSHAVER
MO  AN  TE  ER
IWAS ALI  IAL
CAPTAINSTICKY
ARP  LSD   TAIL
 LM  AE IA  NE
 BEAUBRIDGES
ME  SSE  TEAR
RAQUEL  SAILOR
SNERD   ASNERS
```

Solution to: August 2, 1980

```
LAB  PER  ALAN
AMOK ORO  LINE
DIME LIB  IDEA
DEBRALEESCOTT
   WRY  RAE
ANGIE BTU  ROE
BAIN GAS  DOLL
EGG  ART  CINDY
  ELI  SOL
ONELIFETOLIVE
MOLL FLO  EYED
ALAI ILL  RARE
NAME NAE  RAN
```

Solution to: August 9, 1980

```
A H A   E T H A N   A F L
B A R B A R A B A R R I E
E R I E   E R A   I O N S
  P A L M E R S T O W N
    L A   Y E A
P H I   O R   R E B E L
S U Z A N N E S O M E R S
I R E N E   A S   L E D
    S A S   A V
  F A C T S O F L I F E
R A G U   O N O   E L I S
S U E E L L E N E W I N G
O N E   B O R G E   P E T
```

Solution to: October 4, 1980

```
R A G G E D Y A N N A N D
T H E M A G I C M O V I E
E A R     P T   W E
  A N E W   I A     S A
S A L A M I   O L D M A N
U R D   P L A N   R A N G
R E I D   D I N   U R G E
E T N A   E D E N   I E R
T H E W A R   W A T E R S
Y A   S N   S T A N
  H A   E E     B T Y
T H E L A S T R E M A K E
O F F L A S H G O R D O N
```

Solution to: December 20, 1980

```
  J A F F E   A A M E S
K E L L I N   U R I C H
E N   O R I   R O N   O R
A N N W E D G E W O R T H
T I N E S   A V   S O I E
S E E R   F R O M   O N E
    S O L D I E R
G A M   B A E R   A N S A
A L A N   P N   K N I T S
L E W I S J S T A D L E N
E X   C H A   I T A   V E
  I N H O C   M I L L E R
  S L E E K   S E L L S
```

Solution to: January 17, 1981

```
A L B     K I T   M A T T
L E I F   E L I   A V E S
I N T O   E L M   R I T A
T A S S E L   O L I V E R
    T O Y   T E L
H E L E N   S H O U T E D
E V E R   R A Y   H E R O
R A M B L E D   L E A R N
    R I P   B E N
P A R O L E   R E N N I E
O L E O   N E O   E E L Y
S A N K   T R I   R A K E
E N D S   S A L   L A D
```

Solution to: February 14, 1981

```
  T H E H U M A N F A C E
S H O O K T H E W O R L D
T O W N     R T   E E
A M T   A M M O   A F A R
L A O   L E I   F U R R Y
K S   B I E N   O D E S
    M A C K E N Z I E
  B R I E   R A Z E   V E
C A S T S   V I I   M E L
R A M S   M A L E   A R C
  B U   M O     A R E A
T A I L O R S O L D I E R
M A R R I E D W O M A N
```

Solution to: March 21, 1981

```
F A N T A S Y I S L A N D
O N E L I F E T O L I V E
E N D     A S   D R
    R I O T   A T   C C
S H O T J R   M U R M U R
P A M   S A D A   Y A L U
O R E S   G A D   E R L E
N O R A   E R M A   Y E T
G L O W E D   A L L E N S
E D   X I   D A H L
  P A   A M     L E A
N O R M A N M A I L E R S
I K E E I S E N M A N N S
```

Solution to: May 16, 1981

```
  A N O T H E R W O R L D
O N E D A Y A T A T I M E
B O W   M A T   S I D
I N S   I T S   S E M I
  M I N T   I M   R A D
  F A N G   W I D E   M O
C E N T   H A I   T A I L
A V   O M A R   A N N E
R E L   A T   B R A N
D R A T   B R O   E V A
  C H I   L O U   T O P
F R E E B I E A N D T H E
B O S O M B U D D I E S
```

Solution to: May 23, 1981

```
B A I N S     R A T H E R
E R R O L   I D O I D O
G R O W I N G P A Y N E S
L O N   M O N T Y   T R I
E Y E D   D U O   M E L E
Y O D E L   R H O D E S
  L O G   N U T
A R M O U R   B E B O P
R O A N   A M A   L A H R
T O N   S N E R D   R I O
I M A B I G G I R L N O W
S E N A T E   A R E A S
T R A D E R   W A Y N E
```

Solution to: May 30, 1981

```
L A U R E N   W A L T E R
A R T U R O   A N G E L A
R A E   A L I C E   D A N
R B     A R K     I C
Y I P E   N A Y   B O N O
S A L L Y     R O P E R
  A L E     O L E
M A T E S     D O R I S
I C O N   S A P   S A S H
L T     H E R     R E
L I P   T A C I T   A A R
E V I G A N   S W A N E E
R E G G I E   M A N T L E
```

Solution to: October 10, 1981

```
  J O H N W A L T O N
D O N T B E A F R A I D
O D E   E M   A R T I E
L I O N   K E N     N Y
L E N A   S I A N   A D
    N G   C H A C H I
S L Y   R A   E E   U S E
W A R H O L   M R
E T   C H A D   A S P S
L H     S E T   D A L E
L A T H E   R O   L A W
  M A R Y B E N J A M I N
  C H E C K I N G I N
```

Solution to: October 17, 1981

```
T H E F I S H T H A T
W E R E F I G H T I N G
O R A   B O W   S R   E D
O O   C Y B     D E E
F I L E   H O   S H O R E
U N A   M A N   T I M
S E R M O N   M A T I N S
  O A R   P A N   N E A
O S S I E   A L   D O W D
R E A     C A T   M C
E L   H A   L O B   L O A
F O R T H E L O V E O F
T H A T S M Y L I N E
```

Solution to: November 21, 1981

```
P O L A   F I R   C O M B
E V A S   R A H   A R E A
R E D P L A N E T M A R S
U N S E E N   T W E L V E
    N A T A T O R
O R K   S I D   O A T H
W H I T E C O M A N C H E
L O D E   R A N   T E X
    N I G E R I A
A P P A L L   I T U R B I
T H E B L U E L A G O O N
T I L L   C R Y   I C A N
A L E E   K E N   E A T S
```

Solution to: December 26, 1981

```
PRELIM   ITSA
PATRICIAKLOUS
IM AA CRY MET
GEL RAH    EA
SLIM MAE PAL
 ANAT EL ERLE
THEJOLLYGREEN
NERO AL CONN
 NOR WAR NOEL
SS   SAY TWO
ALF ELK US IV
MEANJOEGREENE
EYRE   RETTIG
```

Solution to: January 30, 1982

```
ESTHER   ERIK
POORMAN  TERI
SMU MEATHEAD
TERRY MAES
AERIE GABLE
MISS   ITO
ON MCMAHON CU
   RAN EROS
 GRANT CLONE
 LUST TYSON
GRASSLES ONE
NEST EDASNER
PASS  DRESSY
```

Solution to: February 13, 1982

```
THEBESTLITTLE
AMERICANDREAM
RS AND   ROSS
   DE PLAYS
ALG FEET   CG
MULDAUR HONOR
ONEAL ENOLA
RANDI MARONEY
ER SIAN   OSS
  BETTE PS
RULA    OLE DO
MILLIONDOLLAR
ROBERTREDFORD
```

Solution to: March 27, 1982

```
ISAAC   AFTER
NURSE GRAINS
TREK NAILED
HES SILLS
OER KEGS TAD
RN ARCH BAIO
KERMITTHEFROG
WOES LEAF LO
SIR HIRT SID
 IRENE RUT
SECURE HOST
ISLAND CANAL
STING  PLANE
```

Solution to: July 10, 1982

```
STALE   FAITH
ARIES REIGNED
LYDIACORNELL
  URBAN ALS
FRED YE CYST
TIARA RHEA
 GRANTTINKER
 KNOB DEGAS
BRAE LO SODA
CUR INANE
 LINDAKELSEYS
RESOLVE LEVEE
IRENE   ANENT
```

Solution to: October 2, 1982

```
 ELKE   DAN
GREENE ENID
BRIDGETHANLEY
IAN HON   LA
ON JARED FALK
TRACER SADA
 AMID LANI
LIED JAUNTS
WINS SADLY HO
IN RIM   SEA
LEEMERIWETHER
ROAD ESTHER
NED   WOOD
```

Solution to: November 27, 1982

```
JEFF TIM GORE
ILIE RNA ABIE
LISA EDD LEAR
LATRAVIATA
 ROAMS RBI
REDFERN ETHAN
ARIA    AURA
RANDI CARMENS
ETA NARDO
 LAGIOCONDA
MIME GER ROOM
ALAN IRE ANNE
RONA ESE LETS
```

Solution to: December 11, 1982

```
BALM CARS IMP
OLEO ACAT RUE
BESTOFTHEWEST
 HUE   WINKS
SAFER PHASE
ODOR FLARE GA
FAR GRANT PEN
AM FRANK REED
 DIANE HARRY
ALANS LOT
JAMESSTEPHENS
ATE LION EVER
RES ERMA REDO
```

Solution to: January 8, 1983

```
SHAKESPEARE
TORNBETWEEN
NEWS ERA   DO
UP INA PEASE
SHINE ERR
 ANDZEE ENTS
LAW EEL EAT
OMAR REESES
III   PUSSY
AKINS THE AJ
LA FHA MARR
THEYOUNGAND
THERESTLESS
```

Solution to: February 19, 1983

```
COLLINS SPAT
GREENER PLOW
SERVI IRE
ST IE NEAR
HER RT MESA
ERIK EVA EYE
DI BARETTA BO
ALE NET ETTU
ALDA HR EUR
SAUL OA RN
IVY AMMAN
KANE REIVERS
STET CODERED
```

Solution to: March 12, 1983

```
CLARAS TASS
HARTMAN OLIO
OUT ELEANORS
PRIES LUKE
SPASM ALDAS
BEST VII
AR STREETS PA
 HER HALL
CLASS CANAL
LONI DANDY
FLORENCE ARE
DOWN SHRINER
RUNE INLAWS
```

Solution to: May 7, 1983

```
GOODMORNING
GREATESTLOVER
HERR RAE SMEE
AE ET ST SA
TN JAZZ GABOR
EDIT OF LENS
EL ARA LA
ABEL TR MARJ
LAPSE OPEN OR
LL ED ON HO
ALDA APR OWNS
YOUCANTGOHOME
TOHOLLYWOOD
```

Solution to: June 11, 1983

```
R I B . . T G . . P A .
C O L D . E R R . I N T O
. O E . R E A L . Y E W .
. R O B E R T M A N D A N
N O M A D I C . . B O . .
I M . T I . H E R . O L D
N A N E T T E F A B R A Y
A N A . H U N . D O . C E
. T O . . K L I N G E R .
M I C K E Y R O O N E Y .
A C H . L E A R . I N . .
N E E D . N U N . E T O N
. Z M . . S E . . S R O .
```

Solution to: September 24, 1983

```
. M A R I O . . B A D .
L O R E N Z O . R I T A .
A R E N A . P L U M . R R
G E N E . S P A N . . N A
. S T . J O E C O N L E Y
. . E A R N . . E A S E .
. J U L I E H A R R I S .
Y O L K . E N I D . . . .
V A L E N T I N O . A H .
E N . E R M A . A B E S .
S I . E D I E . E B O N Y
E V E R . R A Y B U R N .
. S E A . M E A T Y . . .
```

Solution to: October 1, 1983

```
A M B E R . . C A S S I E
L I N D A S . A R M A N D
O R . N E W . R E E . D G
N I N A . O N O . E L I A
G A R . S O I L . O A R .
. M A J E S T Y K . A N S
. . . A R I . N E E . . .
E A R . B E N J A M I N .
W R Y . K A O S . M E L .
I C E R . U R N . P A L O
N T . A R R . E T A . S R
G I D G E T . S E A S O N
S C H U L Z . A R E N A .
```

Solution to: December 10, 1983

```
M O B . A R T . . F I T .
A M A . S E A S . E R M A
C A S H . A L P . L E A R
. R E A L P E O P L E . .
. B S A . O U I . J A . .
A M A S S . A N G E L O U
S A L E . W D S . E A S E
T I L L T H E . O W N E R
A N . H E E . P I G . . .
. B O X L E I T N E R . .
R O O F . A P T . G L E N
O L A F . N I T A . L E O
B E T . C O X . A D D . .
```

Solution to: January 7, 1984

```
A B B Y . R I B . S W A B
B A I O . A D O . T A X I
O I N K . M A R G A R E T
U N G E R . I A N . . . .
. . L O V E S I D N E Y .
B I O . B A D . L E A S E
E R M A . L I V . R I T A
T R A C E . T I N . L E S
H A R T T O H A R T . . .
. R A G . . A R N A Z . .
S U E E L L E N . A I D E
A T E S . E V E . S C A R
M E L S . D A D . H E R O
```

Solution to: January 14, 1984

```
R E I D . S R I . S A L S
K A N E . H O D . A L U M
O R A . B A D E . D O L E
. P H I L D O N A H U E .
. B E A T T Y . A T A . .
O R A L . M D S . . H E .
V E R O N I C A H A M E L
A T . E N D . . L O R I .
. P A T . O S C A R S . .
S T E L S E W H E R E . .
T O T O . R A I N . T W O
A M E N . I L L . C H O U
R A R E . E L L . B E N T
```

Solution to: March 10, 1984

```
M A S S . F M . A R E A .
E R I C . M O I . T O L L
L I L A . A N Y . E A S E
. L O R E N Z O L A M A S
. . L E X . S I M . . . .
O L D E R . S H E . M R S
B O A T . H A I . J O E L
I A N . S O W . P U P P Y
. . A S P . I T S . . . .
C L Y D E K U S A T S U .
H O O D . I N N . M A L E
A G U E . N I T . E L L A
N E R D . S T . N E A R .
```

Solution to: April 14, 1984

```
. S M I T H . E B S E N .
B A R T B R A V E R M A N
A T H O S . M A R S . T O
. . . . F I N N . H A L .
. G R I T S . C O S T .
. D I A R Y . T I G H E
. D I A N E . C O N G A .
G R A N D . L A D D S . .
R A N T . M I N D Y . . .
A G E . M O M S . . . . .
I N . G O O P . S A D I E
L E N N O N S I S T E R S
. T O U R S . D E A N S .
```

Solution to: April 21, 1984

```
A N T S . L B S . T E S S
N O A M . O A R . A T T A
A R T . R R . . T R A P .
. M A R T I N S H E E N .
. . I S . E T E S . . . .
E R I C . T Y R E . E C O
F A T H E R M U L C A H Y
T W O . D U I M . O R E L
. . . F E L L . T R . . .
. C H E R Y L L A D D S .
G O Y A . E A . . E A T .
O V E R . E R N . C A D E
P E R S . A S A . B R A D
```

Solution to: September 1, 1984

```
I F Y O U C O U L D S E E
S O N S A N D L O V E R S
I O . S R O . L O A N S .
S L Y . T E A . N E . . .
. S O . H E R S . D C L .
. . A S A . A V A S T . .
E D . P T . V A . D O . .
B R A E S . I T O . . . .
. U S E . J O H N . A P .
. L L . A N E . T E N . .
. N A M I B . M I O . A A
S E V E N B R O T H E R S
G R E A T A N D S M A L L
```

Solution to: September 29, 1984

```
N E W O D D C O U P L E .
I N A M E R I C A N A R T
. R E N O . T R E B L E .
C O R N . N E O . U S E .
O D E . S E R B . . . . .
H O N A H . N E A R . S G
A R . L O R . R U E . N E
N S . F O U L . E A S E S
. . . B E A R . E A T . .
. P S T . Y O N . B A K E
A R E O L D . G L O B . .
M O M M I E D E A R E S T
. M I S T E R R O G E R S
```

Solution to: November 17, 1984

```
S W A T . B E A . D I A L
E R N E . I S M . E L L A
T I N A . D E B A C L E S
S T A C Y . E L I . . . .
. . . H O W A R D D U F F
R C A . N E W . A E R I E
E A V E . B A H . S A V E
D R I V E . R A E . L E T
D A V I D S E L B Y . . .
. D E E . . B E T T E . .
D E P E N D E D . A R I L
E R I N . A G O . S E L A
W E N T . N O N . T E E N
```

Solution to: January 12, 1985

P	A	M		H	E	R	D		G	R	E	G
E	V	A		E	M	I	R		R	O	L	L
T	I	N		R	I	C	A		E	A	S	E
	D	O	R	O	T	H	Y	L	Y	M	A	N
		R	O	N	S		M	I	S			
W	A	I	T			D	A	N		F	O	B
I	R	A		S	H	O	N	E		L	I	E
G	I	L		K	E	N			L	O	L	A
			P	I	A		A	S	E	A		
L	O	R	E	T	T	A	S	W	I	T	S	
A	B	U	T		E	R	S	E		I	A	N
D	O	T	E		R	E	E	D		N	N	E
D	E	A	R		S	A	T	E		G	E	T

Solution to: February 2, 1985

K	I	T		S	E	E	R		F	A	M	E
I	R	E		I	L	L	S		A	R	I	A
M	A	N	I	M	A	L		S	M	E	L	T
			D	O	N		B	A	I	N		
B	R	I	A	N		W	I	L	L	A	R	D
R	U	M	S		W	I	L	L	Y		E	A
U	M	P		T	E	L	L	Y		T	A	N
C	O		M	I	L	E	S		P	A	I	N
E	R	R	A	N	D	S		T	O	M	M	Y
		O	R	E	S		G	R	O			
E	T	U	I	S		E	M	E	R	A	L	D
B	O	N	N		A	L	E	E		R	E	A
B	O	D	E		D	I	N	S		K	E	Y

Solution to: February 9, 1985

A	J	A	R		C	H	A	O		B	I	O
N	A	T	O		H	A	R	T	M	A	N	S
S	C	A	N		A	C	E		I	N	G	A
A	K		A	R	K		U	N	G	E	R	
	S	M	A	R	T		O	R	K			
C	O	U	N	T		L	A	I		R	B	I
A	N	T	E		M	A	T		B	A	R	N
T	S	E		K	I	D		V	E	G	A	S
			L	E	N		H	A	L	E	N	
A	N	T	O	N		W	O	N		D	D	
L	E	I	A		E	A	R		D	I	O	R
S	A	N	F	O	R	D	S		O	O	N	A
O	L	E		K	N	E	E		M	U	S	T

Solution to: April 6, 1985

B	E	A	V	E	R		H	A	M	L	E	T
A	R	L	E	N	E		G	R	E	E	N	E
R	E	A	R		B	O		T	R	O	D	
		A	L	E	T	T	E	R				
A	T	S		A	C	T	S		I	S		
C	H	E		C	O		S	T	A	T	E	
M	A	R	S	H	A		P	A	T	R	O	L
E	I	G	H	T		P	A		A	R	K	
	E	E		R	I	T	A		H	O	E	
	L	A	V	E	R	N	E					
M	U	L	L		R	I		D	R	U	B	
L	A	R	E	D	O		C	L	E	E	S	E
R	U	N	Y	O	N		K	I	N	S	E	Y

Solution to: June 29, 1985

	C	A	S	A	B	L	A	N	C	A	
	C	E	L	E	S	T	E	H	O	L	M
B	U	L	L	E	T		E	U			
O	T	I	S		A	L	L	A	N	P	O	E
B	E	A		Y	I	E	L	D		A	M	Y
		S	U	R	E		T	Y	N	E		
S	A	M	P	L	E		T	H	E	S	I	S
A	D	A	Y		T	H	I	N			
L	A	T		M	A	N	E	T		C	W	S
T	R	A	V	O	L	T	A		F	L	A	T
		O	T		T	R	E	A	T	Y		
O	N	T	H	E	O	R	I	E	N	T		
P	R	E	S	I	D	E	N	T	S			

Solution to: July 13, 1985

S	E	A	R	C	H		W	O	N	D	E	R
E	N	D	U	R	E		A	L	M	O	S	T
S	T		I	M	A	G	E		W	T		
A	R	I	E	S		I	N	A		A	H	A
M	A	R	Y	T	Y	L	E	R		G	E	M
E	P		D	O	E		R	Y	D	E	R	
		P	I						A	R		
	P	L	E	A	D		A	L	I		P	A
I	R	A		L	A	N	C	A	S	T	E	R
S	A	C		B	I	O		N	Y	L	O	N
	T	A		E	N	D	E	D		P	E	
R	E	T	O	R	T		M	O	R	A	L	S
P	R	E	T	T	Y		U	N	I	T	E	S

Solution to: August 10, 1985

	H	O	T	P	U	R	S	U	I	T		
	O	F	L	O	S	T	L	O	V	E	S	
A	F	T		S	E	A		E	D	E	N	
I	F		F	C		M	A		D	E	Y	
M	A	R	T	H	A	S		S	K	Y		
	O	R	E	G	O	N		O	B	O	E	
E	N	C	O	R	E		A	T	T	E	N	D
M	O	K	O		S	O	N	A	T	A		
		E	P	H		C	A	M	E	R	O	N
I	T	T		O	K		E	R		N	E	
L	O	T	S		I	D	A			U	S	E
	P	E	O	P	L	E	D	O	T	H	E	
	S	W	I	N	G	S	H	I	F	T		

Solution to: September 28, 1985

S	A	M	E		G	E	T		L	A	D	D
S	L	A	V		E	M	U		A	L	O	E
T	A	T	E		N	I	B		M	E	E	T
	S	T	R	E	E	T	B	L	U	E	S	
		T	A	R		S	I	R				
T	A	T		R	A	T		L	A	R	R	Y
A	L	E	C		L	E	S		S	H	O	E
C	A	R	O	B		A	N	N		O	N	S
			L	E	A		O	T	S			
	S	T	E	L	S	E	W	H	E	R	E	
B	E	A	M		T	R	M		V	E	R	A
S	A	R	A		I	D	A		E	R	I	N
A	L	A	N		N	A	N		N	E	E	D

Solution to: March 8, 1986

B	L	A	H		H	E	F		C	O	L	E
A	U	T	O		A	D	A		O	D	E	R
S	L	O	T		L	O	C	K	L	E	A	R
S	U	P	E	R		T	A	B				
	L	I	F	E	S	T	Y	L	E	S		
I	T	S		D	O	N		E	C	O	L	E
D	R	E	W		E	D	S		O	G	L	E
L	O	L	A	S		E	T	A		S	A	M
E	D	F	L	A	N	D	E	R	S			
		T	R	I		T	I	M	E	S		
T	O	H	E	A	V	E	N		M	A	R	E
O	D	O	R		E	V	A		O	D	I	E
M	A	E	S		N	E	T		N	E	E	D

Solution to: May 24, 1986

S	H	E		S	W	A	T		S	T	A	R
C	O	Y		T	H	I	S		T	I	R	E
A	P	E		O	I	L		T	I	M	I	D
R	E	R	E	N	T		L	I	N	E		
			N	E	E	D	I	N	G		H	I
A	D	I	O	S		A	R	T		B	A	D
B	O	S	S		A	V	A		P	U	R	E
E	L	M		A	R	E		P	A	S	T	A
S	E		W	H	I	S	K	E	R			
	W	O	O	D		N	E	E	D	L	E	
L	A	R	R	Y		B	O	W		R	I	D
E	V	E	L		M	A	T	E		I	K	E
T	E	N	D		E	R	S	E		P	E	N

Solution to: May 31, 1986

	D	A	N	E		G	R	A	N	T		
	D	A	V	I	D	B	I	R	N	E	Y	
R	O	N		N	A	N		T	I	N	A	
I	N		C	A	R	O	L		L	E	N	
	L	E	O	S		A	M		D	I		
C	E	L	L		S	U	E		A	T		
T	H	E		B	S		M	R		A	L	A
R	A		E	Y	E		E	M	M	Y		
E	D		T	C		G	N	A	T			
A	L	S		O	P	S	I	S		A	S	
T	O	A	D		E	B	B		A	D	O	
	W	H	O	S	T	H	E	B	O	S	S	
	E	L	L	I	E		D	O	N	A		

Solution to: August 23, 1986

B	E	L	L		R	E	M	O		M	O	E
O	L	E	O		I	R	A	N		A	N	D
Z	I	M	B	A	L	I	S	T		R	I	G
			D	E	N	T		S	L	O	E	
C	O	M	E	D	Y		D	E	A	N		
M	I	A	M	I		P	N	Y	X			
D	L	X		S	I	M	O	N		A	P	E
			P	O	S	T		A	L	L	E	N
	A	L	A	N		I	S	L	A	N	D	
E	L	A	M		C	A	S	T				
E	L	M		H	O	L	L	Y	W	O	O	D
R	I	A		A	L	E	E		E	D	N	A
Y	E	S		T	E	X	T		E	D	E	N

Solution to: November 8, 1986

E	P	E	E		S	T	A	R		W	H	O
A	R	I	D		K	A	T	H	L	E	E	N
S	I	N	S		A	L	A		O	R	A	L
T	N		A	T	E		E	V	E	R	Y	
	C	A	B	L	E		S	S	E			
M	E	R	Y	L		T	H	E		M	A	L
O	S	T	E		D	E	E		B	A	T	E
E	S	S		B	A	D		B	O	I	L	S
			K	E	N		D	R	A	M	A	
T	E	P	I	D		R	I	O		N	C	
A	N	O	N		S	E	A		H	A	T	E
K	I	N	G	L	E	A	R		A	M	I	D
E	D	D		A	L	L	Y		L	A	C	E

Solution to: November 15, 1986

E	R	A	S		O	F		P	A	T	S
L	O	N	I		A	M	I		E	D	I	E
M	A	T	T		D	A	D		R	A	T	E
R	I	C	H	A	R	D	P	R	Y	O	R
	O	U	R		L	O	Y				
C	R	I	M	E		R	E	X		B	O	Y
B	E	N	S		W	A	R		W	I	N	E
S	O	N		F	A	T		G	E	N	E	S
	A	L	G		B	O	B				
S	A	M	D	O	N	A	L	D	S	O	N
P	L	E	A		E	M	U		T	I	A	S
A	D	A	M		R	O	E		E	L	S	A
T	A	N	S		S	S		R	Y	A	N

Solution to: April 11, 1987

R	U	T	H		T	I	M		C	H	E	R
O	P	I	E		O	R	Y		H	E	R	O
B	O	N	D		M	A	R	G	A	R	E	T
S	N	A	G	S		N	O	R			
			E	L	I	W	A	L	L	A	C	H
C	E	A		Y	O	U		D	E	L	A	Y
H	A	R	E		N	R	C		S	A	N	D
I	C	I	N	G		S	A	M		N	E	E
C	H	A	R	L	O	T	T	E	S		
			O	E	R		N	U	R	S	E
C	O	L	L	E	G	E	S		S	E	A	N
A	B	E	L		A	N	A		A	N	T	I
P	I	E	S		N	E	D		N	E	E	D

Solution to: June 13, 1987

L	A	M	A	S		S	A	M	A	R
B	E	W	A	R	E		I	M	A	G	E	S
E	N	A	M	E	L		M	E	N	A	C	E
A	N	K	A		L	I	O	N		I	L	L
N	Y	E		P	E	N	N		S	N	U	B
		R	A	C	K		M	I	S	S	Y	
	B	R	E	A	K		D	A	N	T	E	
C	L	A	I	R		R	O	S	S		
L	E	N	D		R	O	U	T		A	S	H
A	D	D		L	O	N	G		T	A	M	E
U	S	A	G	E	S		L	A	U	R	E	L
S	O	L	U	T	E		A	R	N	O	L	D
	E	L	T	O	N		S	C	E	N	T	

Solution to: August 29, 1987

B	E	D		S	T	O	P		B	A	N	K
A	D	O		H	O	L	E		O	B	O	E
S	I	R		E	N	D		D	O	N	N	Y
S	T	O	N	E	Y		G	A	M	E		
	T	A	N		C	A	M	E	R	O	N	
J	O	H	N		C	A	T	E	R		M	E
A	N	Y		D	A	N	E	S		H	A	W
N	E		H	E	R	O	D		B	E	R	T
E	S	T	E	L	L	E		T	E	A		
	I	S	I	S		R	I	T	T	E	R	
K	I	T	T	S		B	U	M		H	I	E
A	R	L	O		D	O	T	E		E	R	E
T	E	E	N		R	A	H	S		R	E	D

Solution to: September 26, 1987

A	M	O	S		S	H	O	P		G	D	G
L	A	N	A		T	Y	N	E		O	U	R
I	R	O	N	S	I	D	E		M	O	N	A
			T	A	L	E		D	A	N	N	Y
S	E	S	A	M	E		A	L	S		
L	I	E			S	C	R	O	O	G	E
E	R	A	S		C	U	E		N	O	R	M
W	E	S	T	E	R	N		P	O	M	
	A	N	Y		M	A	R	S	H	A	
A	L	I	C	E		L	U	L	U		
D	I	R	K		J	O	N	A	T	H	A	N
A	M	A		M	A	U	D		H	A	L	E
M	E	N		A	N	D	Y		S	L	E	D

Solution to: November 14, 1987

	M	A	R	C		C	O	S	M	O	S
	T	I	G	E	R		A	N	T	O	N	S
T	O	L	E	D	O		P	E	E	W	E	E
A	M	A	N	D	A		I	M	P		
C	A	N	T		K	A	T	O		O	L	A
			M	O	R	A	N	I	S		
C	R	A	B	A	P	P	L	E	C	O	V	E
C	I	T	A	D	E	L					
C	O	P		D	R	E	W		A	C	T	S
	S	I	R		E	N	D	O	R	A	
A	S	S	I	S	I		N	O	O	S	E	D
P	O	I	S	O	N		D	A	R	B	Y	
B	O	D	I	N	E		T	H	E	Y	

Solution to: November 21, 1987

S	I	D		B	E	L	A		S	T	A	R
A	D	O		O	R	E	M		M	O	N	A
M	A	C	C	H	I	O		C	A	R	N	E
	O	A	K		B	A	R	N	E	S	
G	R	A	D	Y		G	R	I	T		
A	I	D	E		D	E	E	R		H	B	S
S	C	A	R	L	E	T	T	O	H	A	R	A
H	E	M		A	B	E	T		A	L	A	N
			B	U	R	R		K	N	O	T	S
Z	A	D	O	R	A		E	L	K		
O	H	A	R	A		P	R	E	S	T	O	N
L	O	N	I		T	O	N	I		O	N	E
A	Y	E	S		O	P	E	N		M	J	W

Solution to: February 20, 1988

B	A	S	S		R	A	T		E	V	A
O	R	T	H		I	V	E		O	V	A	L
P	L	E	A		C	O	P		F	E	L	L
	O	P	R	A	H	W	I	N	F	R	E	Y
			O	N	A		D	E	E		
C	O	N	N	O	R	S		D	R	E	S	S
A	W	E		D	O	C		A	R	A	
P	E	T	E	R		N	A	T	U	R	A	L
			R	E	B		R	O	N		
J	O	H	N	F	O	R	S	Y	T	H	E	
A	L	A	I		W	H	O		R	E	V	A
K	E	N	E		E	E	N		U	R	I	S
E	S	S		D	A	S		E	E	L	S

Solution to: June 18, 1988

	I	L	O	V	E		D	I	N	O
S	T	E	L	L	A	S	T	E	V	E	N	S
E	T	A		T	I	L	E		E	L	
U	A		D	A	N	I	E	L		E	D	O
S	K	E	L	T	O	N	S		F	I	A	T
S	E	D		L	D	G		D	A	L	Y	S
	S	A	R	A			U	R	E	A	
D	A	M	E	S		L	V	C		E	T	S
R	T	E	S		B	U	C	H	A	N	A	N
E	H	S		D	A	R	R	Y	L		T	O
A	I		N	A	R	C			B	I	O	
M	E	A	N	D	T	H	E	C	H	I	M	P
	F	O	E	S			W	R	O	T	E	

Solution to: July 2, 1988

A	C	T		W	K	R	P		S	L	O	T
R	O	I		E	R	O	S		N	O	T	E
K	E	N	O	L	I	N		H	A	U	T	E
			P	B	S		G	O	R	D	O	N
H	E	N	R	Y		B	I	L	L		
A	R	I	A		B	U	L	L		W	O	E
R	I	C	H	A	R	D	D	Y	S	A	R	T
I	N	K		S	A	D	A		T	H	A	T
			A	N	D	Y		R	O	L	L	E
S	I	D	N	E	Y		D	O	C		
C	R	Y	E	R		J	A	C	K	S	O	N
O	M	A	N		H	A	N	K		U	N	A
W	A	N	T		G	R	A	Y		N	O	T

Solution to: August 20, 1988

E	V	E		D	A	L	E		F	A	T	E
A	I	L		A	M	I	D		R	A	I	N
R	E	V		R	O	Z		H	I	R	E	D
S	W	I	T	E	K		L	I	D	O	
			R	O	D		M	E	L	A	N	I	E
S	I	A	M		T	A	N	D	Y		T	D
E	N	S		C	H	I	N	A		V	A	N
L	T		S	H	I	N	Y		L	I	L	A
F	O	R	T	U	N	E		D	O	N	
	E	A	T	S		D	A	N	C	E	S	
W	H	E	R	E		B	E	N		E	L	L
E	A	V	E		D	E	A	N		N	I	A
S	P	E	D		M	A	R	Y		T	A	P

287